W9-BID-172

SOURCES

Notable Selections in *Psychology*

SOURCES

About the Editor

TERRY F. PETTIJOHN is a professor of psychology at the Ohio State University at Marion, where he has been teaching introductory psychology for two decades. As an undergraduate, he attended Alma College and Michigan State University, where he earned his B.S. in 1970. He obtained his M.A. in 1972 and his Ph.D. in experimental psychology in 1974 from Bowling Green State University. He is the author of a number of teaching publications for the introductory psychology course, including *Psychology: A Concise Introduction*, 3rd ed. (The Dushkin Publishing Group, 1992), as well as the accompanying teaching and testing materials. He has served as editor of the *MicroPsych Computer Network Newsletter*, and he currently serves on the Advisory Board for the Dushkin Publishing Group's *Annual Editions: Psychology*. In addition to introductory psychology, he teaches social, experimental, and physiological psychology, learning and memory, motivation, and adjustment. Dr. Pettijohn has been recognized for his teaching efforts, including twice being a recipient of the University Distinguished Teaching Award. His current research interests include animal social behavior, human memory, and computer-assisted learning. He is a member of the American Psychological Society, the Psychonomic Society, the Animal Behavior Society, the Society for Computers in Psychology, and the American Psychological Association, where he is affiliated with the Division of the Teaching of Psychology.

SOURCES
Notable Selections
in *Psychology*

Edited by

TERRY F. PETTIJOHN
Ohio State University

The Dushkin Publishing Group, Inc.

© 1994 by The Dushkin Publishing Group, Inc., Guilford, Connecticut 06437

Copyright law prohibits the reproduction, storage, or transmission in any form by any means of any portion of this publication without the express written permission of The Dushkin Publishing Group, Inc., and of the copyright holder (if different) of the part of the publication to be reproduced. The Guidelines for Classroom Copying endorsed by Congress explicitly state that unauthorized copying may not be used to create, to replace, or to subsitute for anthologies, compilations, or collective works.

Manufactured in the United States of America

First Edition, First Printing

Library of Congress Cataloging-in-Publication Data
  Main entry under title:
    Sources: notable selections in psychology/edited by Terry F. Pettijohn.
    Includes bibliographical references and index.
      1. Psychology—History—Sources. I. Pettijohn, Terry F., *comp.*
      BF81.S5887   150—dc20
      ISBN: 1–56134–263–7   93–34527

 Printed on Recycled Paper

ACKNOWLEDGMENTS

1.1 From *The Principles of Psychology* (Vol. 1, pp. 1, 4–8) by W. James, 1950. New York: Dover Publications. (Original work published 1890.) Notes omitted.

1.2 From "Psychology as the Behaviorist Views It" by J. B. Watson, 1913, *Psychological Review, 20*, pp. 158–177.

1.3 From "Some Issues Concerning the Control of Human Behavior: A Symposium" by C. R. Rogers and B. F. Skinner, 1956, *Science, 124*, pp. 1057–1064. Copyright © 1956 by The American Association for the Advancement of Science. Reprinted by permission. Notes omitted.

1.4 From "Experiments in Group Conflict" by M. Sherif, 1956, *Scientific American, 195*, pp. 54–58. Copyright © 1956 by Scientific American, Inc. All rights reserved. Reprinted by permission.

Acknowledgments and copyrights are continued at the back of the book on pages 351–353, which constitute an extension of the copyright page.

Preface

*A*lthough barely a century old as a formal discipline, the study of psychology has revolutionized how we look at ourselves and others. Psychology is the science of behavior and cognition; it is a rigorous brain science and, at the same time, it seeks to help people. Psychologists study behaviors, such as eating, talking, writing, running, or fighting, precisely because they can be observed and recorded. But psychologists also study mental processes, such as dreaming, thinking, remembering, and problem solving, which are not directly observable and are often studied through reports provided by human research subjects. Psychologists are also interested in the physiological processes that often accompany both overt behavior and cognition. Finally, some psychologists are concerned with applying psychological principles to help people.

As a discipline, psychology has evolved its own history of ideas and thinkers, research methods, and theories. In this volume I have put into your hands directly those researchers and writers whose works are essential to the study of psychology. *Sources: Notable Selections in Psychology* brings together 46 selections of enduring intellectual value—classic articles, book excerpts, and research studies—that have shaped the study of psychology and our contemporary understanding of it. The book includes carefully edited selections from the works of the most distinguished psychological researchers and practitioners, past and present, from Sigmund Freud and B. F. Skinner to Robert J. Sternberg and Elizabeth F. Loftus. These selections allow you to obtain a behind-the-scenes look, so to speak, at psychology in the making.

Sources: Notable Selections in Psychology represents over 100 years of psychological thought and application. The actual dates of publication range from 1890 to 1992. I have made every effort to portray psychology as a dynamic and changing discipline. Obviously, new research has modified our understanding of some of the ideas covered in some of the selections; nonetheless, using these original sources will enrich your understanding of psychology and its elemental concepts.

Selection procedure I paid great attention to finding those classic works that could best communicate the excitement of psychology. Readability was the top priority, and each selection was carefully edited so that the essence of the original work could be readily understood.

I started with over 300 possible sources for inclusion. After organizing them by area and author, I eliminated works that overlapped. Next, I asked my own students to help me select the most readable articles and to make suggestions. Some of the selections provide theories that have shaped our discipline. Some discuss crucial issues that have confronted psychologists during the past century. And many present the results of original research studies. Together, they comprise a snapshot of psychology as it currently exists, including the important landmarks in its development.

Organization of the book The selections are organized topically around the major areas of study within psychology: Part 1 includes selections on the Foundations of Psychology; Part 2, Perceptual Processes; Part 3, Learning and Cognitive Processes; Part 4, Motivation and Emotion; Part 5, Personality and Adjustment; Part 6, Psychological Disorders; and Part 7, Social Processes. The selections are organized so as to parallel most introduction to psychology textbooks. This means that these original sources, these classic works that underlie the key psychological concepts covered in the textbooks, can be easily read along with any textbook. But each selection is independent and can be read in any order and used in any way.

Suggestions for reading each selection As you read these original writings, it is important to keep in mind that ideas and standards have changed over the last century. In particular, changes in ethical concerns and in how language is used need to be mentioned here. Currently there are very strict ethical guidelines for conducting human and animal research. Today, researchers must submit proposals to committees that ensure that ethical standards are met. Some of the studies carried out in the past would not be approved now. As you read these selections, consider how the research contributed to psychology and whether or not the benefits outweighed the potential harm to the subjects.

Each selection is representative of the time in which it was written. Just as psychologists have become more sensitive to ethical considerations over the years, so too have they become more aware of the issue of gender, particularly as regards language. Many of the older articles use the masculine pronoun "he" when referring to both men and women, and many of the early studies had only male subjects. I recommend that you view each selection in the context of when it was written and focus on the psychological issues it reveals. These classic studies have had a major impact on the development of psychology as a discipline and should be read from that perspective.

Each selection is preceded by an introductory headnote, which establishes the relevance of the selection, provides biographical information about the author, and includes a brief background discussion of the topic. I have also provided suggestions for understanding statistical tests and thought questions designed to guide critical thinking.

Let me make a couple of suggestions to help you get the most out of each selection. First, be sure to read the headnote to gain background information on the topic and on the author. Recognize that some of these selections are easy to read and understand, whereas others may have more challenging language, theories, or statistical concepts. Try to focus on the main ideas and important concepts in each selection. Remember that journal research articles include an introduction to the problem, a description of the research methods, a presentation of the results, and a discussion of the significance of the results. When you finish reading a selection, reread the headnote to make sure that you focused on the important concepts. Finally, take notes on the selection and reflect upon the importance of the writing to psychology.

Supplements An *Instructor's Manual With Test Questions* (including multiple-choice and essay questions) is available for instructors using *Sources: Notable Selections in Psychology* in the classroom.

Acknowledgments I was extremely excited when Rick Connelly, president of The Dushkin Publishing Group, first approached me with the idea for *Sources: Notable Selections in Psychology*. For a long time I have wanted to be able to introduce my students to original writings in psychology. I am thrilled to be able to share with students the excitement of learning directly from some of the most influential figures in psychology.

This project is very much a joint effort. Although my name as editor is the only one on the cover, I had lots of help from many people. Whenever I had a question about the readability or relevance of an article, my psychology students provided comments and suggestions. Mimi Egan, program manager for the Sources series at the DPG, kept everything functioning smoothly, as did David Dean, administrative editor, and David Brackley, copy editor. My wife, Bernie, typed the reference lists and headnotes and provided much emotional support. And my children, Terry, Karen, and Tommy, were patient as I worked on this project and missed some family activities.

Sources: Notable Selections in Psychology is designed particularly to meet the needs of those instructors who want to convey to students the richness of the psychological perspective through original writings. I have worked hard to produce a valuable resource, and I would very much appreciate any comments or suggestions you might have on the book. Although I feel that these selections represent some of the most significant studies in psychology, not everyone will agree with all of the particular selections. I promise to carefully consider all of your suggestions as the book goes through the revision process.

Terry F. Pettijohn
Ohio State University

Contents

the goose dream of?' and answers: 'Of maize.' The whole theory that the dream is the fulfilment of a wish is contained in these two sentences."

"Learned helplessness is caused by learning that responding is independent
of reinforcement; so the model suggests that the cause of depression is the
belief that action is futile."

"What follows is a demonstration of behaviour techniques for the intensive
individual treatment of psychotic behaviour. Specific pathological behaviour patterns of a single patient were treated by manipulating the patient's
environment."

"Individuals have within themselves vast resources for self-understanding
and for altering their self-concepts, basic attitudes, and self-directed behavior; these resources can be tapped if a definable climate of facilitative psychological attitudes can be provided."

"Psychological skills (integrating, labeling, and interpreting experience) can
be applied to correcting the psychological aberrations. Since the central
psychological *problem* and the psychological *remedy* are both concerned with
the patient's thinking (or cognitions), we call this form of help cognitive
therapy."

"Life in society requires consensus. . . . When consensus comes under the
dominance of conformity, the social process is polluted and the individual
at the same time surrenders the powers on which his functioning as a
feeling and thinking being depends."

PART ONE

Foundations of Psychology

CHAPTER 1

Introducing Psychology

1.1 WILLIAM JAMES

The Scope of Psychology

The American psychologist William James's *Principles of Psychology,* published in 1890, marked a major milestone in the history of psychology. In it, James asserts that psychology should focus on the functions of consciousness, an idea that helped establish the school of functionalism and that continues to be important to the study of psychology today.

James (1842–1910) obtained his M.D. from Harvard University in 1869 and accepted a teaching position in psychology there three years later. During his lifetime, he wrote on a variety of topics, including consciousness, emotion, personality, learning, and religion.

This selection is taken from James's most famous work, the two-volume *Principles of Psychology.* In it, James argues that psychology is the "science of mental life." Although he includes feelings and cognitions in his definition of psychology, he emphasizes the role of the brain in behaviors that serve the function of survival. His book formed the cornerstone of many early psychology courses, and it encouraged psychologists to take a broad view of their discipline. This book is still very much read and studied today.

Key Concept: an early definition of psychology

*P*sychology is the Science of Mental Life, both of its phenomena and their conditions. The phenomena are such things as we call feelings, desires, cognitions, reasonings, decisions, and the like; and, superficially considered, their variety and complexity is such as to leave a chaotic impression on the observer. . . .

[R]eflection shows that phenomena [experience in the outer world] have absolutely no power to influence our ideas until they have first impressed our senses and our brain. The bare existence of a past fact is no ground for our remembering it. Unless we have seen it, or somehow *undergone* it, we shall never know of its having been. The experiences of the body are thus one of the conditions of the faculty of memory being what it is. And a very small amount of reflection on facts shows that one part of the body, namely, the brain, is the part whose experiences are directly concerned. If the nervous communication be cut off between the brain and other parts, the experiences of those other parts are non-existent for the mind. The eye is blind, the ear deaf, the hand insensible and motionless. And conversely, if the brain be injured, conscious-ness is abolished or altered, even although every other organ in the body be ready to play its normal part. A blow on the head, a sudden subtraction of blood, the pressure of an apoplectic hemorrhage, may have the first effect; whilst a very few ounces of alcohol or gains of opium or hasheesh, or a whiff of chloroform or nitrous oxide gas, are sure to have the second. The delirium of fever, the altered self of insanity, are all due to foreign matters circulating through the brain, or to pathological changes in that organ's substance. The fact that the brain is the one immediate bodily condition of the mental opera-tions is indeed so universally admitted nowadays that I need spend no more time in illustrating it, but will simply postulate it and pass on. . . .

Bodily experiences, therefore, and more particularly brain-experiences, must take a place amongst those conditions of the mental life of which Psy-chology need take account. . . .

Our first conclusion, then, is that a certain amount of brain-physiology must be presupposed or included in Psychology.

In still another way the psychologist is forced to be something of a nerve-physiologist. Mental phenomena are not only conditioned . . . by bodily pro-cesses; but they lead to them. . . . That they lead to *acts* is of course the most familiar of truths, but I do not merely mean acts in the sense of voluntary and deliberate muscular performances. Mental states occasion also changes in the calibre of blood-vessels, or alteration in the heart-beats, or processes more sub-tle still, in glands and viscera. If these are taken into account, as well as acts which follow at some *remote period* because the mental state was once there, it will be safe to lay down the general law that *no mental modification ever occurs which is not accompanied or followed by a bodily change.* The ideas and feelings, *e.g.,* which these present printed characters excite in the reader's mind not only occasion movements of his eyes and nascent movements of articulation in him, but will some day make him speak, or take sides in a discussion, or give advice, or choose a book to read, differently from what would have been the case had they never impressed his retina. Our psychology must therefore take account not only of the conditions antecedent to mental states, but of their resultant consequences as well.

But actions originally prompted by conscious intelligence may grow so automatic by dint of habit as to be apparently unconsciously performed. Standing, walking, buttoning and unbuttoning, piano-playing, talking, even saying one's prayers, may be done when the mind is absorbed in other things. The performances of animal *instinct* seem semi-automatic, and the *reflex acts* of self-preservation certainly are so. Yet they resemble intelligent acts in bringing about the *same ends* at which the animals' consciousness, on other occasions, deliberately aims. Shall the study of such machine-like yet purposive acts as these be included in Psychology?

The boundary line of the mental is certainly vague. It is better not to be pedantic, but to let the science be as vague as its subject, and include such phenomena as these if by so doing we can throw any light on the main business in hand. It will ere long be seen, I trust, that we can; and that we gain much more by a broad than by a narrow conception of our subject. At a certain stage in the development of every science a degree of vagueness is what best consists with fertility. On the whole, few recent formulas have done more real service of a rough sort in psychology than the . . . one that the essence of mental life and of bodily life are one, namely, 'the adjustment of inner to outer relations.' Such a formula is vagueness incarnate; but because it takes into account the fact that minds inhabit environments which act on them and on which they in turn react; because, in short, it takes mind in the midst of all its concrete relations, it is immensely more fertile than the old-fashioned 'rational psychology,' which treated the soul as a detached existent, sufficient unto itself, and assumed to consider only its nature and properties. I shall therefore feel free to make any sallies into zoology or into pure nerve-physiology which may seem instructive for our purposes, but otherwise shall leave those sciences to the physiologists.

Can we state more distinctly still the manner in which the mental life seems to intervene between impressions made from without upon the body, and reactions of the body upon the outer world again? Let us look at a few facts.

If some iron filings be sprinkled on a table and a magnet brought near them, they will fly through the air for a certain distance and stick to its surface. A savage seeing the phenomenon explains it as the result of an attraction or love between the magnet and the filings. But let a card cover the poles of the magnet, and the filings will press forever against its surface without its ever occurring to them to pass around its sides and thus come into more direct contact with the object of their love. . . .

If now we pass from such actions as these to those of living things, we notice a striking difference. Romeo wants Juliet as the filings want the magnet; and if no obstacles intervene he moves towards her by as straight a line as they.

But Romeo and Juliet, if a wall be built between them, do not remain idiotically pressing their faces against its opposite sides like the magnet and the filings with the card. Romeo soon finds a circuitous way, be scaling the wall or otherwise, of touching Juliet's lips directly. With the filings the path is fixed; whether it reaches the end depends on accidents. With the lover it is the end which is fixed, the path may be modified indefinitely.

Such contrasts between living and inanimate performances end by leading men to deny that in the physical world final purposes exist at all. Loves and desires are today no longer imputed to particles of iron or of air. No one supposes now that the end of any activity which they may display is an ideal purpose presiding over the activity from its outset. . . . The end, on the contrary, is deemed a mere passive result, . . . having had, so to speak, no voice in its own production. Alter the pre-existing conditions, and with inorganic materials you bring forth each time a different apparent end. But with intelligent agents, altering the conditions changes the activity displayed, but not the end reached; for here the idea of the yet unrealized end co-operates with the conditions to determine what the activities shall be.

The pursuance of future ends and the choice of means for their attainment are thus the mark and criterion of the presence of mentality in a phenomenon. We all use this test to discriminate between an intelligent and a mechanical performance. We impute no mentality to sticks and stones, because they never seem to move for *the sake of* anything, but always when pushed, and then indifferently and with no sign of choice. So we unhesitatingly call them senseless.

Just so we form our decision upon the deepest of all philosophic problems: Is the [C]osmos [the universe] an expression of intelligence rational in its inward nature, or a brute external fact pure and simple? If we find ourselves, in contemplating it, unable to banish the impression that it is a realm of final purposes, that it exists for the sake of something, we place intelligence at the heart of it and have a religion. If, on the contrary, in surveying its irremediable flux, we can think of the present only as so much mere mechanical sprouting from the past, occurring with no reference to the future, we are atheists and materialists.

1.2 JOHN B. WATSON

Psychology as the Behaviorist Views It

From the 1920s through the 1960s the field of psychology was largely dominated by behaviorists, who focus on the objective measurement of behavior. The founder of the school of behaviorism was John B. Watson, whose view of psychology as a "purely objective experimental branch of natural science" had a major influence on early psychologists. Watson's belief that psychology should be the science of overt behavior, modeled after the natural sciences, is expressed in this selection.

Watson (1878–1958) earned his Ph.D. in experimental psychology from the University of Chicago in 1903. He began teaching at the Johns Hopkins University in 1908 and stayed there until he resigned in 1920. Although he left academic psychology after only 12 years of teaching, his influence is still felt in the discipline today.

This selection, "Psychology as the Behaviorist Views It," published in the *Psychological Review* in 1913, marks the introduction of the school of behaviorism. In it, Watson discards the subject of consciousness and the method of introspection from psychology and argues for an objective study of the behavior of both people and animals. His goal is to help psychology become more applicable in other areas (such as education, law, and business) as it develops into an experimental natural science.

Key Concept: school of behaviorism

*P*sychology as the behaviorist views it is a purely objective experimental branch of natural science. Its theoretical goal is the prediction and control of behavior. Introspection forms no essential part of its methods, nor is the scientific value of its data dependent upon the readiness with which they lend themselves to interpretation in terms of consciousness. The behaviorist, in his efforts to get a unitary scheme of animal response, recognizes no dividing line between man and brute. The behavior of man, with all of its refinement and complexity, forms only a part of the behaviorist's total scheme of investigation. . . .

The time seems to have come when psychology must discard all reference to consciousness; when it need no longer delude itself into thinking that it is making mental states the object of observation. We have become so enmeshed in speculative questions concerning the elements of mind, the nature of conscious content (for example, imageless thought, attitudes, . . . etc.) that I, as an experimental student, feel that something is wrong with our premises and the types of problems which develop from them. There is not longer any guarantee that we all mean the same thing when we use the terms now current in psychology. Take the case of sensation. A sensation is defined in terms of its attributes. One psychologist will state with readiness that the attributes of a visual sensation are *quality, extension, duration,* and *intensity.* Another will add *clearness.* Still another that of *order.* I doubt if any one psychologist can draw up a set of statements describing what he means by sensation which will be agreed to by three other psychologists of different training. Turn for a moment to the question of the number of isolable sensations. Is there an extremely large number of color sensations—or only four, red, green, yellow and blue? Again, yellow, while psychologically simple, can be obtained by superimposing red and green spectral rays upon the same diffusing surface! If, on the other hand, we say that every just noticeable difference in the spectrum is a simple sensation, and that every just noticeable increase in the white value of a given color gives simple sensations, we are forced to admit that the number is so large and the conditions for obtaining them so complex that the concept of sensation is unusable, either for the purpose of analysis or that of synthesis. Titchener, who has fought the most valiant fight in this country for a psychology based upon introspection, feels that these differences of opinion as to the number of sensations and their attributes; as to whether there are relations (in the sense of elements) and on the many others which seem to be fundamental in every attempt at analysis, are perfectly natural in the present undeveloped state of psychology. While it is admitted that every growing science is full of unanswered questions, surely only those who are wedded to the system as we now have it, who have fought and suffered for it, can confidently believe that there will ever be any greater uniformity than there is now in the answers we have to such questions. I firmly believe that two hundred years from now, unless the introspective method is discarded, psychology will still be divided on the question as to whether auditory sensations have the quality of 'extension,' whether intensity is an attribute which can be applied to color, whether there is a difference in 'texture' between image· and sensation and upon many hundreds of others of like character. . . .

I was greatly surprised some time ago when I opened Pillsbury's book and say psychology defined as the 'science of behavior.' A still more recent text states that psychology is the 'science of mental behavior.' When I saw these promising statements I thought, now surely we will have texts based upon different lines. After a few pages the science of behavior is dropped and one finds the conventional treatment of sensation, perception, imagery, etc., along with certain shifts in emphasis and additional facts which serve to give the author's personal imprint. . . .

This leads me to the point where I should like to make the argument constructive. I believe we can write a psychology, define it as Pillsbury, and never go back upon our definition: never use the terms consciousness, mental states, mind, content, introspectively verifiable, imagery, and the like. . . . It can be done in terms of stimulus and response, in terms of habit formation, habit integrations and the like. Furthermore, I believe that it is really worth while to make this attempt now.

The psychology which I should attempt to build up would take as a starting point, first, the observable fact that organisms, man and animal alike, do adjust themselves to their environment by means of hereditary and habit equipments. These adjustments may be very adequate or they may be so inadequate that the organism barely maintains its existence; secondly, that certain stimuli lead the organisms to make the responses. In a system of psychology completely worked out, given the response the stimuli can be predicted; given the stimuli the response can be predicted. Such a set of statements is crass and raw in the extreme, as all such generalizations must be. Yet they are hardly more raw and less realizable than the ones which appear in the psychology texts of the day. I possibly might illustrate my point better by choosing an everyday problem which anyone is likely to meet in the course of his work. Some time ago I was called upon to make a study of certain species of birds. Until I went to Tortugas I had never seen these birds alive. When I reached there I found the animals doing certain things: some of the acts seemed to work peculiarly well in such an environment, while others seemed to be unsuited to their type of life. I first studied the responses of the group as a whole and later those of individuals. In order to understand more thoroughly the relation between what was habit and what was hereditary in these responses, I took the young birds and reared them. In this way I was able to study the order of appearance of hereditary adjustments and their complexity, and later the beginnings of habit formation. My efforts in determining the stimuli which called forth such adjustments were crude indeed. Consequently my attempts to control behavior and to produce responses at will did not meet with much success. Their food and water, sex and other social relations, light and temperature conditions were all beyond control in a field study. I did find it possible to control their reactions in a measure by using the nest and egg (or young) as stimuli. It is not necessary in this paper to develop further how such a study should be carried out and how work of this kind must be supplemented by carefully controlled laboratory experiments. . . . In the main, my desire in all such work is to gain an accurate knowledge of adjustments and the stimuli calling them forth. My final reason for this is to learn general and particular methods by which I may control behavior. . . . If psychology would follow the plan I suggest, the educator, the physician, the jurist and the business man could utilize our data in a practical way, as soon as we are able, experimentally, to obtain them. Those who have occasion to apply psychological principles practically would find no need to complain as they do at the present time. Ask any physician or jurist today whether scientific psychology plays a practical part in his daily routine and you will hear him deny that the psychology of the laboratories finds a place in his scheme of work. I think the criticism is extremely just. One of the earliest conditions which made me dissatisfied with psychology was the feeling that there was no realm of application for the principles which were being worked out in content terms.

What gives me hope that the behaviorist's position is a defensible one is the fact that those branches of psychology which have already partially withdrawn from the parent, experimental psychology, and which are consequently less dependent upon introspection are today in a most flourishing condition. Experimental pedagogy, the psychology of drugs, the psychology of advertising, legal psychology, the psychology of tests, and psychopathology are all vigorous growths. These are sometimes wrongly called "practical" or "applied" psychology. Surely there was never a worse misnomer. In the future there may grow up vocational bureaus which really apply psychology. At present these fields are truly scientific and are in search of broad generalizations which will lead to the control of human behavior. For example, we find out by experimentation whether a series of stanzas may be acquired more readily if the whole is learned at once, or whether it is more advantageous to learn each stanza separately and then pass to the succeeding. We do not attempt to apply our findings. The application of this principle is purely voluntary on the part of the teachers. In the psychology of drugs we may show the effect upon behavior of certain doses of caffeine. We may reach the conclusion that caffeine has a good effect upon the speed and accuracy of work. But these are general principles. We leave it to the individual as to whether the results of our tests shall be applied or not. Again, in legal testimony, we test the effects of recency upon the reliability of a witness's report. We test the accuracy of the report with respect to moving objects, stationary objects, color, etc. It depends upon the judicial machinery of the country to decide whether these facts are ever to be applied. For a 'pure' psychologist to say that he is not interested in the questions raised in these divisions of the science because they relate indirectly to the application of psychology shows, in the first place, that he fails to understand the scientific aim in such problems, and secondly, that he is not interested in a psychology which concerns itself with human life. The only fault I have to find with these disciplines is that much of their material is stated in terms of introspection, whereas a statement of terms of objective results would be far more valuable. There is no reason why appeal should ever be made to consciousness in any of them. Or why introspective data should ever be sought during the experimentation, or published in the results. In experimental pedagogy especially one can see the desirability of keeping all of the results on a purely objective plane. . . .

In concluding, I suppose I must confess to a deep bias on these questions. I have devoted nearly twelve years to experimentation on animals. It is natural that such a one should drift into a theoretical position which is in harmony with his experimental work. Possibly I have put up a straw man and have been fighting that. . . . Certainly the position I advocate is weak enough at present and can be attacked from many standpoints. Yet when all this is admitted I still feel that the considerations which I have urged should have a wide influence upon the type of psychology which is to be developed in the future. What we need to do is to start work upon psychology, making *behavior,* not *consciousness,* the objective point of our attack. Certainly there are enough problems in the control of behavior to keep us all working many lifetimes without ever allowing us time to think of consciousness. . . . Once launched in the undertaking, we will find ourselves in a short time as far divorced from an introspective psychology as the psychology of the present time is divorced from faculty psychology.

John B. Watson

Some Issues Concerning the Control of Human Behavior: A Symposium

From the 1950s through most of the 1980s, psychologists witnessed an ongoing debate between two intellectual giants. One represented the behavioristic approach to the study and application of psychology, the other, the humanistic approach. B. F. Skinner represented behaviorism, as he worked to extend the experimental analysis of behavior to a variety of practical applications. Carl R. Rogers argued for the humanistic approach, emphasizing the worth and dignity of the human being. One focal point of the debate was the issue of control.

Rogers (1902–1987), originally a student of theology, became interested in helping disturbed children, so he studied clinical psychology and earned his Ph.D. from Columbia University in 1931. Skinner (1904–1990) is one of the most famous and influential figures in contemporary psychology, particularly for his studies in behavior and learning. He earned his Ph.D. in psychology in 1931 from Harvard University, where he also taught for most of his career.

This selection, "Some Issues Concerning the Control of Human Behavior: A Symposium," was published in *Science* in 1956. It contains the views on behavior control presented by Rogers and Skinner at the 1956 annual meeting of the American Psychological Association in Chicago. Skinner's view is that we need to understand how a behavioral technology for predicting and controlling behavior can be applied to our lives. Rogers questions the purposes of such control and asserts that we must agree on the values we are willing to accept before we explore behavioral technologies. Although the details of this selection may be challenging, if you try to focus on the larger issues being discussed, your efforts will be rewarded.

Key Concept: behaviorism vs. humanistic psychology

Carl R. Rogers and B. F. Skinner

I [SKINNER]

Science is steadily increasing our power to influence, change, mold—in a word, control—human behavior. It has extended our "understanding" (whatever that may be) so that we deal more successfully with people in nonscientific ways, but it has also identified conditions or variables which can be used to predict and control behavior in a new, and increasingly rigorous, technology. . . . It is the experimental study of behavior which carries us beyond awkward or inaccessible "principles," "factors," and so on, to variables which can be directly manipulated.

It is also, and for more or less the same reasons, the conception of human behavior emerging from an experimental analysis which most directly challenges traditional views. Psychologists themselves often do not seem to be aware of how far they have moved in this direction. But the change is not passing unnoticed by others. Until only recently it was customary to deny the possibility of a rigorous science of human behavior by arguing, either that a lawful science was impossible because man was a free agent, or that merely statistical predictions would always leave room for personal freedom. But those who used to take this line have become most vociferous in expressing their alarm at the way these obstacles are being surmounted.

Now, the control of human behavior has always been unpopular. Any undisguised effort to control usually arouses emotional reactions. We hesitate to admit, even to ourselves, that we are engaged in control, and we may refuse to control, even when this would be helpful, for fear of criticism. . . .

Man's natural inclination to revolt against selfish control has been exploited to good purpose in what we call the philosophy and literature of democracy. The doctrine of the rights of man has been effective in arousing individuals to concerted action against governmental and religious tyranny. The literature which has had this effect has greatly extended the number of terms in our language which express reactions to the control of men. But the ubiquity and ease of expression of this attitude spells trouble for any science which may give birth to a powerful technology of behavior. . . . I am not so much concerned here with the political or economic consequences for psychology, although research following certain channels may well suffer harmful effects. We ourselves, as intelligent men and women, and as exponents of Western thought, share these attitudes. They have already interfered with the free exercise of a scientific analysis, and their influence threatens to assume more serious proportions.

Three broad areas of human behavior supply good examples. The first of these—*personal control*—may be taken to include person-to-person relationships in the family, among friends, in social and work groups, and in counseling and psychotherapy. Other fields are *education* and *government*. A few examples from each will show how nonscientific preconceptions are affecting our current thinking about human behavior.

Personal Control

People living together in groups come to control one another with a technique which is not inappropriately called "ethical." When an individual behaves in a fashion acceptable to the group, he receives admiration, approval, affection, and many other reinforcements which increase the likelihood that he will continue to behave in that fashion. When his behavior is not acceptable, he is criticized, censured, blamed, or otherwise punished. In the first case the group calls him "good"; in the second, "bad." This practice is so thoroughly ingrained in our culture that we often fail to see that it is a technique of control. Yet we are almost always engaged in such control, even though the reinforcements and punishments are often subtle.

The practice of admiration is an important part of a culture, because behavior which is otherwise inclined to be weak can be set up and maintained with its help. The individual is especially likely to be praised, admired, or loved when he acts for the group in the face of great danger, for example, or sacrifices himself or his possessions, or submits to prolonged hardship, or suffers martyrdom. These actions are not admirable in any absolute sense, but they require admiration if they are to be strong. Similarly, we admire people who behave in original or exceptional ways, not because such behavior is itself admirable, but because we do not know how to encourage original or exceptional behavior in any other way. The group acclaims independent, unaided behavior in part because it is easier to reinforce than to help.

As long as this technique of control is misunderstood, we cannot judge correctly an environment in which there is less need for heroism, hardship, or independent action. We are likely to argue that such an environment is itself less admirable or produces less admirable people. In the old days, for example, young scholars often lived in undesirable quarters, ate unappetizing or inadequate food, performed unprofitable tasks for a living or to pay for necessary books and materials or publication. Older scholars and other members of the group offered compensating reinforcement in the form of approval and admiration for these sacrifices. When the modern graduate student receives a generous scholarship, enjoys good living conditions, and has his research and publication subsidized, the grounds for evaluation seem to be pulled from under us. Such a student no longer *needs* admiration to carry him over a series of obstacles (no matter how much he may need it for other reasons), and, in missing certain familiar objects of admiration, we are likely to conclude that such *conditions* are less admirable. Obstacles to scholarly work may serve as a useful measure of motivation—and we may go wrong unless some substitute is found—but we can scarcely defend a deliberate harassment of the student for this purpose. The productivity of any set of conditions can be evaluated only when we have freed ourselves of the attitudes which have been generated in us as members of an ethical group. . . .

Education

The techniques of education were once frankly aversive. The teacher was usually older and stronger than his pupils and was able to "make them learn." This meant that they were not actually taught but were surrounded by a threatening world from which they could escape only by learning. Usually they were left to their own resources in discovering how to do so. . . .

Progressive education was a humanitarian effort to substitute positive reinforcement for such aversive measures, but in the search for useful human values in the classroom it has never fully replaced the variables it abandoned. Viewed as a branch of behavioral technology, education remains relatively inefficient. We supplement it, and rationalize it, by admiring the pupil who learns *for himself;* and we often attribute the learning process, or knowledge itself, to something *inside* the individual. We admire behavior which seems to have inner sources. Thus we admire one who *recites* a poem more than one who simply *reads* it. We admire one who *knows* the answer more than one who *knows where to look it up.* We admire the *writer* rather than the *reader.* We admire the arithmetician who can do a problem in his head rather than with a slide rule or calculating machine, or in "original" ways rather than by a strict application of rules. In general we feel that any aid or "crutch"—except those aids to which we are now thoroughly accustomed—reduces the credit due. . . .

By admiring the student for knowledge and blaming him for ignorance, we escape some of the responsibility of teaching him. We resist any analysis of the educational process which threatens the notion of inner wisdom or questions the contention that the fault of ignorance lies with the student. More powerful techniques which bring about the same changes in behavior by manipulating *external* variables are decried as brainwashing or thought control. We are quite unprepared to judge *effective* educational measures. As long as only a few pupils learn much of what is taught, we do not worry about uniformity or regimentation. . . .

Government

Government has always been the special field of aversive control. The state is frequently defined in terms of the power to punish, and jurisprudence leans heavily upon the associated notion of personal responsibility. Yet it is becoming increasingly difficult to reconcile current practice and theory with these earlier views. In criminology, for example, there is a strong tendency to drop the notion of responsibility in favor of some such alternative as capacity or controllability. But no matter how strongly the facts, or even practical expedience, support such a change, it is difficult to make the change in a legal system designed on a different plan. When governments resort to other techniques (for example, positive reinforcement), the concept of responsibility is no longer relevant and the theory of government is no longer applicable. . . .

The dangers inherent in the control of human behavior are very real. The possibility of the misuse of scientific knowledge must always be faced. We cannot escape by denying the power of a science of behavior or arresting its development. It is no help to cling to familiar philosophies of human behavior simply because they are more reassuring. As I have pointed out elsewhere; the new techniques emerging from a science of behavior must be subject to the explicit countercontrol which has already been applied to earlier and cruder forms. Brute force and deception, for example, are now fairly generally suppressed by ethical practices and by explicit governmental and religious agencies. A similar countercontrol of scientific knowledge in the interests of the group is a feasible and promising possibility. Although we cannot say how devious the course of its evolution may be, a cultural pattern of control and countercontrol will presumably emerge which will be most widely supported because it is most widely reinforcing. . . .

If the advent of a powerful science of behavior causes trouble, it will not be because science itself is inimical to human welfare but because older conceptions have not yielded easily or gracefully. We expect resistance to new techniques of control from those who have heavy investments in the old, but we have no reason to help them preserve a series of principles that are not ends in themselves but rather outmoded means to an end. What is needed is a new conception of human behavior which is compatible with the implications of a scientific analysis. All men control and are controlled. The question of government in the broadest possible sense is not how freedom is to be preserved but what kinds of control are to be used and to what ends. Control must be analyzed and considered in its proper proportions. No one, I am sure, wishes to develop new master-slave relationships or bend the will of the people to despotic rulers in new ways. These are patterns of control appropriate to a world without science. They may well be the first to go when the experimental analysis of behavior comes into its own in the design of cultural practices.

II [ROGERS]

There are, I believe, a number of matters in connection with this important topic on which the authors of this article, and probably a large majority of psychologists, are in agreement. These matters then are not issues as far as we are concerned, and I should like to mention them briefly in order to put them to one side.

Points of Agreement

I am sure we agree that men—as individuals and as societies—have always endeavored to understand, predict, influence, and control human behavior—their own behavior and that of others.

I believe we agree that the behavioral sciences are making and will continue to make increasingly rapid progress in the understanding of behavior, and that as a consequence the capacity to predict and to control behavior is developing with equal rapidity. . . .

I believe we are in agreement that the tremendous potential power of a science which permits the prediction and control of behavior may be misused, and that the possibility of such misuse constitutes a serious threat. . . .

Points at Issue

With these several points of basic and important agreement, are there then any issues that remain on which there are differences? I believe there are. They can be stated very briefly: Who will be controlled? Who will exercise control? What type of control will be exercised? Most important of all, toward what end or what purpose, or in the pursuit of what value, will control be exercised?

It is on questions of this sort that there exist ambiguities, misunderstandings, and probably deep differences. These differences exist among psychologists, among members of the general public in this country, and among various world cultures. Without any hope of achieving a final resolution of these questions, we can, I believe, put these issues in clearer form. . . .

Ends and Values in Relation to Science

In sharp contradiction to some views that have been advanced, I would like to propose a two-pronged thesis: (i) In any scientific endeavor—whether "pure" or applied science—there is a prior subjective choice of the purpose or value which that scientific work is perceived as serving. (ii) This subjective value choice which brings the scientific endeavor into being must always lie outside of that endeavor and can never become a part of the science involved in that endeavor.

Let me illustrate the first point from Skinner himself. It is clear that in his earlier writing it is recognized that a prior value choice is necessary, and it is specified as the goal that men are to become happy, well-behaved, productive, and so on. I am pleased that Skinner has retreated from the goals he then chose, because to me they seem to be stultifying values. I can only feel that he was choosing these goals for others, not for himself. I would hate to see Skinner become "well-behaved," as that term would be defined for him by behavioral scientists. His recent article in the *American Psychologist* shows that he certainly does not want to be "productive" as that value is defined by most psychologists. And the most awful fate I can imagine for him would be to have him constantly "happy." It is the fact that he is very unhappy about many things which makes me prize him.

In the first draft of his part of this article, he also included such prior value choices, saying for example, "We must decide how we are to use the knowledge which a science of human behavior is now making available." Now he has dropped all mention of such choices, and if I understand him correctly, he believes that science can proceed without them. He has suggested this view in another recent paper, stating that "We must continue to experiment in cultural design . . . testing the consequences as we go. Eventually the practices which make for the greatest biological and psychological strength of the group will presumably survive."

I would point out, however, that to choose to experiment is a value choice. Even to move in the direction of perfectly random experimentation is a value choice. To test the consequences of an experiment is possible only if we have first made a subjective choice of a criterion value. And implicit in his statement is a valuing of biological and psychological strength. So even when trying to avoid such choice, it seems inescapable that a prior subjective value choice is necessary for any scientific endeavor, or for any application of scientific knowledge.

I wish to make it clear that I am not saying that values cannot be included as a subject of science. It is not true that science deals only with certain classes of "facts" and that these classes do not include values. It is a bit more complex than that, as a simple illustration or two may make clear.

If I value knowledge of the "three R's" as a goal of education, the methods of science can give me increasingly accurate information on how this goal may be achieved. If I value problem-solving ability as a goal of education, the scientific method can give me the same kind of help. . . .

Thus I return to the proposition with which I began this section of my remarks—and which I now repeat in different words. Science has its meaning as the objective pursuit of a purpose which has been subjectively chosen by a person or persons. This purpose or value can never be investigated by the particular scientific experiment or investigation to which it has given birth and meaning. Consequently, any discussion of the control of human beings by the behavioral sciences must first and most deeply concern itself with the subjectively chosen purposes which such an application of science is intended to implement. . . .

Possible Concept of the Control of Human Behavior

It is quite clear that the point of view I am expressing is in sharp contrast to the usual conception of the relationship of the behavioral sciences to the control of human behavior. . . . I will state this possibility [thusly:]

1) It is possible for us to choose to value man as a self-actualizing process of becoming; to value creativity, and the process by which knowledge becomes self-transcending.

2) We can proceed, by the methods of science, to discover the conditions which necessarily precede these processes and, through continuing experimentation, to discover better means of achieving these purposes.

3) It is possible for individuals or groups to set these conditions, with a minimum of power or control. According to present knowledge, the only authority necessary is the authority to establish certain qualities of interpersonal relationship.

4) Exposed to these conditions, present knowledge suggests that individuals become more self-responsible, make progress in self-actualization, become more flexible, and become more creatively adaptive.

5) Thus such an initial choice would inaugurate the beginnings of a social system or subsystem in which values, knowledge, adaptive skills, and even the concept of science would be continually changing and self-transcending. The emphasis would be upon man as a process of becoming.

I believe it is clear that such a view as I have been describing does not lead to any definable utopia. It would be impossible to predict its final outcome. It involves a step-by-step development, based on a continuing subjective choice of purposes, which are implemented by the behavioral sciences. . . .

I trust it is also evident that the whole emphasis is on process, not on end-states of being. I am suggesting that it is by choosing to value certain qualitative elements of the process of becoming that we can find a pathway toward the open society.

Carl R. Rogers and B. F. Skinner

Experiments in Group Conflict

Prejudice is a major problem in our society. Psychologists have studied prejudice and its causes to learn how it might be reduced. Social psychologist Muzafer Sherif studied prejudice by introducing conflict between groups of adolescents. His findings indicate that conflict increases hostility between groups but also that hostility is reduced when groups are forced to work together to solve a common problem. The contact theory of prejudice reduction, which is evident in Sherif's work, suggests that cooperation to reach goals is important.

Sherif (1906–1988) was born in Turkey and moved to the United States in 1929. After receiving his Ph.D. from Columbia University in 1935, he became interested in attitudes and intergroup conflict. He was a professor at the University of Oklahoma when he conducted the research published in *The Robber's Cave Experiment: Intergroup Conflict and Cooperation* (University Press of New England, 1954).

This selection, "Experiments in Group Conflict," was published in *Scientific American* in 1956. In it, Sherif summarizes a series of studies of conflict and cooperation among boys at a summer camp. This research has served as a model for studying the development and consequent reduction of prejudice in groups. As you read this selection, notice the techniques used to promote intergroup harmony and decide if they would work with groups with which you are familiar.

Key Concept: reduction of group prejudice

Conflict between groups—whether between boys' gangs, social classes, "races" or nations—has no simple cause, nor is mankind yet in sight of a cure. It is often rooted deep in personal, social, economic, religious and historical forces. Nevertheless it is possible to identify certain general factors which have a crucial influence on the attitude of any group toward others. Social scientists have long sought to bring these factors to light by studying what might be called the "natural history" of groups and group relations. Intergroup conflict and harmony is not a subject that lends itself easily to laboratory experiments. But in recent years there has been a beginning of attempts to investigate the problem under controlled yet lifelike conditions, and I shall report here the results of a program of experimental studies of groups which I started in 1948. Among the persons working with me were Marvin B. Sussman, Robert Huntington, O. J. Harvey, B. Jack White, William R. Hood and Carolyn W. Sherif.

We wanted to conduct our study with groups of the informal type, where group organization and attitudes would evolve naturally and spontaneously, without formal direction or external pressures. For this purpose we conceived that an isolated summer camp would make a good experimental setting, and that decision led us to choose as subjects boys about 11 or 12 years old, who would find camping natural and fascinating. Since our aim was to study the development of group relations among these boys under carefully controlled conditions, with as little interference as possible from personal neuroses, background influences or prior experiences, we selected normal boys of homogeneous background who did not know one another before they came to the camp.

They were picked by a long and thorough procedure. We interviewed each boy's family, teachers and school officials, studied his school and medical records, obtained his scores on personality tests and observed him in his classes and at play with his schoolmates. With all this information we were able to assure ourselves that the boys chosen were of like kind and background: all were healthy, socially well-adjusted, somewhat above average in intelligence and from stable, white, Protestant, middle-class homes.

None of the boys was aware that he was part of an experiment on group relations. The investigators appeared as a regular camp staff—camp directors, counselors and so on. The boys met one another for the first time in buses that took them to the camp, and so far as they knew it was a normal summer of camping. To keep the situation as lifelike as possible, we conducted all our experiments within the framework of regular camp activities and games. We set up projects which were so interesting and attractive that the boys plunged into them enthusiastically without suspecting that they might be test situations. Unobtrusively we made records of their behavior, even using "candid" cameras and microphones when feasible.

We began by observing how the boys became a coherent group. The first of our camps was conducted in the hills of northern Connecticut in the summer of 1949. When the boys arrived, they were all housed at first in one large bunkhouse. As was to be expected, they quickly formed particular friendships and chose buddies. We had deliberately put all the boys together in this expectation, because we wanted to see what would happen later after the boys were separated into different groups. Our object was to reduce the factor of personal attraction in the formation of groups. In a few days we divided the boys into two groups and put them in different cabins. Before doing so, we asked each boy informally who his best friends were, and then took pains to place the "best friends" in different groups so far as possible. (The pain of separation was assuaged by allowing each group to go at once on a hike and camp-out.)

As everyone knows, a group of strangers brought together in some common activity soon acquires an informal and spontaneous kind of organization. It comes to look upon some members as leaders, divides up duties, adopts unwritten norms of behavior, develops an *esprit de corps.* Our boys followed this pattern as they shared a series of experiences. In each group the boys pooled their efforts, organized duties and divided up tasks in work and play. Different individuals assumed different responsibilities. One boy excelled in cooking. Another led in athletics. Others, though not outstanding in any one skill, could be counted on to pitch in and do their level best in anything the group attempted. One or two seemed to disrupt activities, to start teasing at the wrong moment or offer useless suggestions. A few boys consistently had good suggestions and showed ability to coordinate the efforts of others in carrying them through. Within a few days one person had proved himself more resourceful and skillful than the rest. Thus, rather quickly, a leader and lieutenants emerged. Some boys sifted toward the bottom of the heap, while others jockeyed for higher positions.

We watched these developments closely and rated the boys' relative positions in the group, not only on the basis of our own observations but also by informal sounding of the boys' opinions as to who got things started, who got things done, who could be counted on to support group activities.

As the group became an organization, the boys coined nicknames. The big, blond, hardy leader of one group was dubbed "Baby Face" by his admiring followers. A boy with a rather long head became "Lemon Head." Each group developed its own jargon, special jokes, secrets and special ways of performing tasks. One group, after killing a snake near a place where it had gone to swim, named the place "Moccasin Creek" and thereafter preferred this swimming hole to any other, though there were better ones nearby.

Wayward members who failed to do things "right" or who did not contribute their bit to the common effort found themselves receiving the "silent treatment," ridicule or even threats. Each group selected symbols and a name, and they had these put on their caps and T-shirts. The 1954 camp was conducted in Oklahoma, near a famous hideaway of Jesse James called Robber's Cave. The two groups of boys at this camp named themselves the Rattlers and the Eagles.

Our conclusions on every phase of the study were based on a variety of observations, rather than on any single method. For example, we devised a game to test the boys' evaluations of one another. Before an important baseball game, we set up a target board for the boys to throw at, on the pretense of making practice for the game more interesting. There were no marks on the front of the board for the boys to judge objectively how close the ball came to a bull's-eye, but, unknown to them, the board was wired to flashing lights behind so that an observer could see exactly where the ball hit. We found that the boys consistently overestimated the performances by the most highly regarded members of their group and underestimated the scores of those of low social standing.

The attitudes of group members were even more dramatically illustrated during a cook-out in the woods. The staff supplied the boys with unprepared food and let them cook it themselves. One boy promptly started to build a fire, asking for help in getting wood. Another attacked the raw hamburger to make patties. Others prepared a place to put buns, relishes and the like. Two mixed soft drinks from flavoring and sugar. One boy who stood around without helping was told by the others to "get to it." Shortly the fire was blazing and the cook had hamburgers sizzling. Two boys distributed them as rapidly as they became edible. Soon it was time for the watermelon. A low-ranking member of the group took a knife and started toward the melon. Some of the boys protested. The most highly regarded boy in the group took over the knife, saying, "You guys who yell the loudest get yours last."

When the two groups in the camp had developed group organization and spirit, we proceeded to the experimental studies of intergroup relations. The groups had had no previous encounters; indeed, in the 1954 camp at Robber's Cave the two groups came in separate buses and were kept apart while each acquired a group feeling.

Our working hypothesis was that when two groups have conflicting aims—*i.e.*, when one can achieve its ends only at the expense of the other—their members will become hostile to each other even though the groups are composed of normal well-adjusted individuals. There is a corollary to this assumption which we shall consider later. To produce friction between the groups of boys we arranged a tournament of games: baseball, touch football, a tug-of-war, a treasure hunt and so on. The tournament started in a spirit of good sportsmanship. But as it progressed good feeling soon evaporated. The members of each group began to call their rivals "stinkers," "sneaks" and "cheaters." They refused to have anything more to do with individuals in the opposing group. The boys in the 1949 camp turned against buddies whom they had chosen as "best friends" when they first arrived at the camp. A large proportion of the boys in each group gave negative ratings to all the boys in the other. The rival groups made threatening posters and planned raids, collecting secret hoards of green apples for ammunition. In the Robber's Cave camp the Eagles, after a defeat in a tournament game, burned a banner left behind by the Rattlers; the next morning the Rattlers seized the Eagles' flag when they arrived on the athletic field. From that time on name-calling, scuffles and raids were the rule of the day.

Within each group, of course, solidarity increased. There were changes: one group deposed its leader because he could not "take it" in the contests with the adversary; another group overnight made something of a hero of a big boy who had previously been regarded as a bully. But morale and cooperativeness within the group became stronger. It is noteworthy that this heightening of cooperativeness and generally democratic behavior did not carry over to the group's relations with other groups.

We now turned to the other side of the problem: How can two groups in conflict be brought into harmony? We first undertook to test the theory that pleasant social contacts between members of conflicting groups will reduce friction between them. In the 1954 camp we brought the hostile Rattlers and

Eagles together for social events: going to the movies, eating in the same dining room and so on. But far from reducing conflict, these situations only served as opportunities for the rival groups to berate and attack each other. In the dining-hall line they shoved each other aside, and the group that lost the contest for the head of the line shouted "Ladies first!" at the winner. They threw paper, food and vile names at each other at the tables. An Eagle bumped by a Rattler was admonished by his fellow Eagles to brush "the dirt" off his clothes.

We then returned to the corollary of our assumption about the creation of conflict. Just as competition generates friction, working in a common endeavor should promote harmony. It seemed to us, considering group relations in the everyday world, that where harmony between groups is established, the most decisive factor is the existence of "superordinate" goals which have a compelling appeal for both but which neither could achieve without the other. To test this hypothesis experimentally, we created a series of urgent, and natural, situations which challenged our boys.

One was a breakdown in the water supply. Water came to our camp in pipes from a tank about a mile away. We arranged to interrupt it and then called the boys together to inform them of the crisis. Both groups promptly volunteered to search the water line for the trouble. They worked together harmoniously, and before the end of the afternoon they had located and corrected the difficulty.

A similar opportunity offered itself when the boys requested a movie. We told them that the camp could not afford to rent one. The two groups then got together, figured out how much each group would have to contribute, chose the film by a vote and enjoyed the showing together.

One day the two groups went on an outing at a lake some distance away. A large truck was to go to town for food. But when everyone was hungry and ready to eat, it developed that the truck would not start (we had taken care of that). The boys got a rope—the same rope they had used in their acrimonious tug-of-war—and all pulled together to start the truck.

These joint efforts did not immediately dispel hostility. At first the groups returned to the old bickering and name-calling as soon as the job in hand was finished. But gradually the series of cooperative acts reduced friction and conflict. The members of the two groups began to feel more friendly to each other. For example, a Rattler whom the Eagles disliked for his sharp tongue and skill in defeating them became a "good egg." The boys stopped shoving in the meal line. They no longer called each other names, and sat together at the table. New friendships developed between individuals in the two groups.

In the end the groups were actively seeking opportunities to mingle, to entertain and "treat" each other. They decided to hold a joint campfire. They took turns presenting skits and songs. Members of both groups requested that they go home together on the same bus, rather than on the separate buses in which they had come. On the way the bus stopped for refreshments. One group still had five dollars which they had won as a prize in a contest. They decided to spend this sum on refreshments. On their own initiative they invited their former rivals to be their guests for malted milks.

Our interviews with the boys confirmed this change. From choosing their "best friends" almost exclusively in their own group, many of them shifted to listing boys in the other group as best friends. They were glad to have a second chance to rate boys in the other group, some of them remarking that they had changed their minds since the first rating made after the tournament. Indeed they had. The new ratings were largely favorable.

Efforts to reduce friction and prejudice between groups in our society have usually followed rather different methods. Much attention has been given to bringing members of hostile groups together socially, to communicating accurate and favorable information about one group to the other, and to bringing the leaders of groups together to enlist their influence. But as everyone knows, such measures sometimes reduce intergroup tensions and sometimes do not. Social contacts, as our experiments demonstrated, may only serve as occasions for intensifying conflict. Favorable information about a disliked group may be ignored or reinterpreted to fit stereotyped notions about the group. Leaders cannot act without regard for the prevailing temper in their own groups.

What our limited experiments have shown is that the possibilities for achieving harmony are greatly enhanced when groups are brought together to work toward common ends. Then favorable information about a disliked group is seen in a new light, and leaders are in a position to take bolder steps toward cooperation. In short, hostility gives way when groups pull together to achieve overriding goals which are real and compelling to all concerned.

CHAPTER **2** Psychobiology

Hemisphere Deconnection and Unity in Conscious Awareness

The fact that the human brain is divided into two cerebral hemispheres has always intrigued scientists. In the 1950s, neurosurgeon Philip Vogel developed the technique of cutting the corpus callosum (the neural bundle connecting the two cerebral hemispheres) to reduce the severity of seizures in epileptic patients. This allowed researchers, particularly Roger W. Sperry, to study the conscious behavior of so-called split-brain patients.

Sperry (b. 1913) received his Ph.D. from the University of Chicago in 1941. He has been a professor of psychobiology at the California Institute of Technology since 1954. Sperry initially studied cerebral hemisphere disconnection in cats, then he moved on to study humans who underwent split-brain surgery. In 1981, Sperry received a Nobel Prize in physiology and medicine for his research on the brain.

This selection, "Hemisphere Deconnection and Unity in Conscious Awareness," published in 1968 in the *American Psychologist*, describes some of the research conducted by Sperry and his colleagues. Through his research, Sperry discovered that the two cerebral hemispheres have distinct functions—the left side is involved in reasoning, language, and writing, whereas the right side is involved in nonverbal processes, such as art, music, and creativity. This selection conveys the excitement of discovering how human consciousness functions and the intricacies of the human brain.

Key Concept: split-brain research

Roger W.
Sperry

*T*he following article is a result of studies my colleagues and I have been conducting with some neurosurgical patients of Philip J. Vogel of Los Angeles. These patients were all advanced epileptics in whom an extensive midline section of the cerebral commissures had been carried out in an effort to contain severe epileptic convulsions not controlled by medication. In all these people the surgical sections included division of the corpus callosum in its entirety, plus division also of the smaller anterior and hippocampal commissures, plus in some instances the massa intermedia. So far as I know, this is the most radical disconnection of the cerebral hemispheres attempted thus far in human surgery. The full array of sections was carried out in a single operation.

No major collapse of mentality or personality was anticipated as a result of this extreme surgery: earlier clinical observations on surgical section of the corpus callosum in man, as well as the results from dozens of monkeys on which I had carried out this exact same surgery, suggested that the functional deficits might very likely be less damaging than some of the more common forms of cerebral surgery, such as frontal lobotomy, or even some of the unilateral lobotomies performed more routinely for epilepsy.

The first patient on whom this surgery was tried had been having seizures for more than 10 years with generalized convulsions that continued to worsen despite treatment that had included a sojourn in Bethesda at the National Institutes of Health. At the time of the surgery, he had been averaging two major attacks per week, each of which left him debilitated for another day or so. Episodes of *status epilepticus* (recurring seizures that fail to stop and represent a medical emergency with a fairly high mortality risk) had also begun to occur at 2- to 3-month intervals. Since leaving the hospital following his surgery over 5½ years ago, this man has not had, according to last reports, a single generalized convulsion. It has further been possible to reduce the level of medication and to obtain an overall improvement in his behavior and well being (see Bogen & Vogel, 1962).

The second patient, a housewife and mother in her 30s, also has been seizure-free since recovering from her surgery, which was more than 4 years ago (Bogen, Fisher, & Vogel, 1965). Bogen related that even the EEG has regained a normal pattern in this patient. The excellent outcome in the initial, apparently hopeless, last-resort cases led to further application of the surgery to some nine more individuals to date, the majority of whom are too recent for therapeutic evaluation. Although the alleviation of the epilepsy has not held up 100% throughout the series (two patients are still having seizures, although their convulsions are much reduced in severity and frequency and tend to be confined to one side), the results on the whole continue to be predominantly beneficial, and the overall outlook at this time remains promising for selected severe cases.

The therapeutic success, however, and all other medical aspects are matters for our medical colleagues, Philip J. Vogel and Joseph E. Bogen. Our own work has been confined entirely to an examination of the functional outcome, that is, the behavioral, neurological, and psychological effects of this surgical disruption of all direct cross-talk between the hemispheres. Initially we were concerned as to whether we would be able to find in these patients any of the numerous symptoms of hemisphere deconnection that had been demonstrated in the so-called "split-brain" animal studies of the 1950s (Myers, 1961; Sperry, 1967a, 1967b). The outcome in man remained an open question in view of the historic Akelaitis (1944) studies that had set the prevailing doctrine of the 1940s and 1950s. This doctrine maintained that no important functional symptoms are found in man following even complete surgical section of the corpus callosum and anterior commissure, provided that other brain damage is excluded.

These earlier observations on the absence of behavioral symptoms in man have been confirmed in a general way to the extent that it remains fair to say today that the most remarkable effect of sectioning the neocortical commissures is the apparent lack of effect so far as ordinary behavior is concerned. This has been true in our animal studies throughout, and it seems now to be true for man also, with certain qualifications that we will come to later. At the same time, however—and this is in contradiction to the earlier doctrine set by the Akelaitis studies—we know today that with appropriate tests one can indeed demonstrate a large number of behavioral symptoms that correlate directly with the loss of the neocortical commissures in man as well as in animals (Gazzaniga, 1967; Sperry, 1967a, 1967b; Sperry, Gazzaniga, & Bogen, 1968). Taken collectively, these symptoms may be referred to as the syndrome of the neocortical commissures or the syndrome of the forebrain commissures or, less specifically, as the syndrome of hemisphere deconnection.

One of the more general and also more interesting and striking features of this syndrome may be summarized as an apparent doubling in most of the realms of conscious awareness. Instead of the normally unified single stream of consciousness, these patients behave in many ways as if they have two independent streams of conscious awareness, one in each hemisphere, each of which is cut off from and out of contact with the mental experiences of the other. In other words, each hemisphere seems to have its own separate and private sensations; its own perceptions; its own concepts; and its own impulses to act, with related volitional, cognitive, and learning experiences. Following the surgery, each hemisphere also has thereafter its own separate chain of memories that are rendered inaccessible to the recall processes of the other.

This presence of two minds in one body, as it were, is manifested in a large number and variety of test responses which, for the present purposes, I will try to review very briefly and in a somewhat streamlined and simplified form. First, however, let me take time to emphasize that the work reported here has been very much a team project. The surgery was performed by Vogel at the White Memorial Medical Center in Los Angeles. He has been assisted in the surgery and in the medical treatment throughout by Joseph Bogen. Bogen has also been collaborating in our behavioral testing program, along with a num-

FIGURE 1 *Apparatus for Studying Lateralization of Visual, Tactual, Lingual, and Associated Functions in the Surgically Separated Hemispheres*

29

Roger W. Sperry

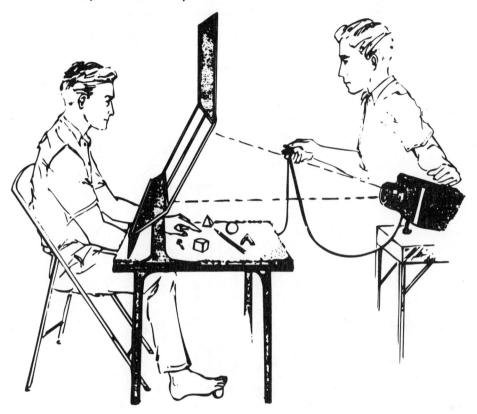

ber of graduate students and postdoctoral fellows, among whom M. S. Gazzaniga, in particular, worked closely with us during the first several years and managed much of the testing during that period. The patients and their families have been most cooperative, and the whole project gets its primary funding from the National Institute of Mental Health.

Most of the main symptoms seen after hemisphere deconnection can be described for convenience with reference to a single testing setup—shown in Figure 1. Principally, it allows for the lateralized testing of the right and left halves of the visual field, separately or together, and the right and left hands and legs with vision excluded. The tests can be arranged in different combinations and in association with visual, auditory, and other input, with provisions for eliminating unwanted stimuli. In testing vision, the subject with one eye covered centers his gaze on a designated fixation point on the upright translucent screen. The visual stimuli on 35-millimeter transparencies are arranged in a standard projector equipped with a shutter and are then back-projected at $\frac{1}{10}$ of a second or less—too fast for eye movements to get the material into the wrong half of the visual field. Figure 2 is merely a reminder that everything

FIGURE 2 *Things Seen to the Left of a Central Fixation Point With Either Eye Are Projected to the Right Hemisphere and Vice-versa*

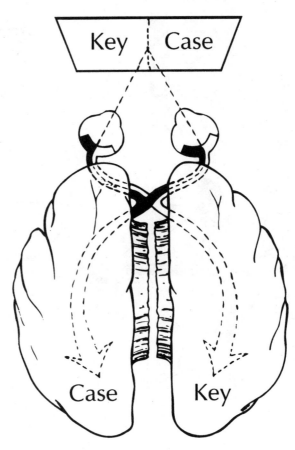

seen to the left of the vertical meridian through either eye is projected to the right hemisphere and vice versa. The midline division along the vertical meridian is found to be quite precise without significant gap or overlap (Sperry, 1968).

When the visual perception of these patients is tested under these conditions the results indicate that these people have not one inner visual world any longer, but rather two separate visual inner worlds, one serving the right half of the field of vision and the other the left half—each, of course, in its respective hemisphere. This doubling in the visual sphere shows up in many ways: For example, after a projected picture of an object has been identified and responded to in one half field, we find that it is recognized again only if it reappears in the same half of the field of vision. If the given visual stimulus reappears in the opposite half of the visual field, the subject responds as if he had no recollection of the previous exposure. In other words, things seen through the right half of the visual field (i.e., through the left hemisphere) are registered in mental experience and remembered quite separately from things seen in the other half of the field. Each half of the field of vision in the commissurotomized patient has its own train of visual images and memories.

This separate existence of two visual inner worlds is further illustrated in reference to speech and writing, the cortical mechanisms for which are centered in the dominant hemisphere. Visual material projected to the right half of the field—left-hemisphere system of the typical right-handed patient—can be described in speech and writing in an essentially normal manner. However, when the same visual material is projected into the left half of the field, and hence to the right hemisphere, the subject consistently insists that he did not see anything or that there was only a flash of light on the left side. The subject acts as if he were blind or agnostic for the left half of the visual field. If, however, instead of asking the subject to tell you what he saw, you instruct him to use his left hand to point to a matching picture or object presented among a collection of other pictures or objects, the subject has no trouble as a rule in pointing out consistently the very item that he has just insisted he did not see.

We do not think the subjects are trying to be difficult or to dupe the examiner in such tests. Everything indicates that the hemisphere that is talking to the examiner did in fact not see the left-field stimulus and truly had no experience with, nor recollection of, the given stimulus. The other, the right or nonlingual hemisphere, however, did see the projected stimulus in this situation and is able to remember and recognize the object and can demonstrate this by pointing out selectively the corresponding or matching item. This other hemisphere, like a deaf mute or like some aphasics, cannot talk about the perceived object and, worse still, cannot write about it either.

If two different figures are flashed simultaneously to the right and left visual fields, as for example a "dollar sign" on the left and a "question mark" on the right and the subject is asked to draw what he saw using the left hand out of sight, he regularly reproduces the figure seen on the left half of the field, that is, the dollar sign. If we now ask him what he has just drawn, he tells us without hesitation that the figure he drew was the question mark, or whatever appeared in the right half of the field. In other words, the one hemisphere does not know what the other hemisphere has been doing. The left and the right halves of the visual field seem to be perceived quite separately in each hemisphere with little or no cross-influence.

When words are flashed partly in the left field and partly in the right, the letters on each side of the midline are perceived and responded to separately. In the "key case" example shown in Figure 2 the subject might first reach for and select with the left hand a key from among a collection of objects indicating perception through the minor hemisphere. With the right hand he might then spell out the word "case" or he might speak the word if verbal response is in order. When asked what kind of "case" he was thinking of here, the answer coming from the left hemisphere might be something like "in *case* of fire" or "the *case* of the missing corpse" or "a *case* of beer," etc., depending upon the particular mental set of the left hemisphere at the moment. Any reference to "key case" under these conditions would be purely fortuitous, assuming that visual, auditory, and other cues have been properly controlled.

A similar separation in mental awareness is evident in tests that deal with stereognostic [involving tactile recognition] or other somesthetic [related to bodily sensations] discriminations made by the right and left hands, which are projected separately to the left and right hemispheres, respectively. Objects put in the right hand for identification by touch are readily described or named in speech or writing, whereas, if the same objects are placed in the left hand, the subject can only make wild guesses and may often seem unaware that anything at all is present. As with vision in the left field, however, good perception, comprehension, and memory can be demonstrated for these objects in the left hand when the tests are so designed that the subject can express himself through nonverbal responses. For example, if one of these objects which the subject tells you he cannot feel or does not recognize is taken from the left hand and placed in a grab bag or scrambled among a dozen other test items, the subject is then able to search out and retrieve the initial object even after a delay of several minutes is deliberately interposed. Unlike the normal subject, however, these people are obliged to retrieve such an object with the same hand with which it was initially identified. They fail at cross-retrieval. That is, they cannot recognize with one hand something identified only moments before with the other hand. Again, the second hemisphere does not know what the first hemisphere has been doing.

When the subjects are first asked to use the left hand for these stereognostic tests they commonly complain that they cannot "work with that hand," that the hand "is numb," they they "just can't feel anything or can't do anything with it," or that they "don't get the message from that hand." If the subjects perform a series of successful trials and correctly retrieve a group of objects which they previously stated they could not feel, and if this contradiction is then pointed out to them, we get comments like "Well, I was just guessing," or "Well, I must have done it unconsciously." . . .

Much of the foregoing is summarized schematically in Figure 3. The left hemisphere in the right-handed patients is equipped with the expressive mechanisms for speech and writing and with the main centers for the comprehension and organization of language. This "major" hemisphere can communicate its experiences verbally and in an essentially normal manner. It can communicate, that is, about the visual experiences of the right half of the optic field and about the somesthetic and volitional experiences of the right hand and leg and right half of the body generally. In addition, and not indicated in the figure, the major hemisphere also communicates, of course, about all of the more general, less lateralized cerebral activity that is bilaterally represented and common to both hemispheres. On the other side we have the mute aphasic and agraphic right hemisphere, which cannot express itself verbally, but which through the use of nonverbal responses can show that it is not agnostic; that mental processes are indeed present centered around the left visual field, left hand, left leg, and left half of the body; along with the auditory, vestibular, axial somatic, and all other cerebral activities that are less lateralized and for which the mental experiences of the right and left hemispheres may be characterized as being similar but separate.

It may be noted that nearly all of the symptoms of cross-integrational impairment that I have been describing are easily hidden or compensated un-

FIGURE 3 *Schematic Outline of the Functional Lateralization Evident in Behavioral Tests of Patients With Forebrain Commissurotomy*

33

Roger W. Sperry

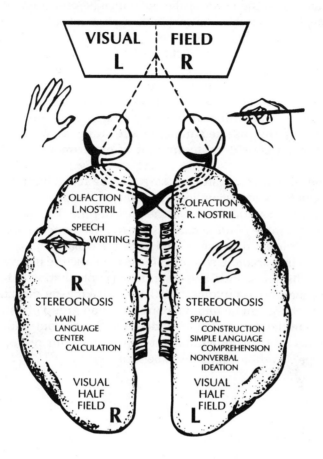

der the conditions of ordinary behavior. For example, the visual material has to be flashed at $\frac{1}{10}$ of a second or less to one half of the field in order to prevent compensation by eye movements. The defects in manual stereognosis are not apparent unless vision is excluded; nor is doubling in olfactory perception evident without sequential occlusion of right and left nostril and elimination of visual cues. In many tests the major hemisphere must be prevented from talking to the minor hemisphere and thus giving away the answer through auditory channels. And, similarly, the minor hemisphere must be prevented from giving nonverbal signals of various sorts to the major hemisphere. There is a great diversity of indirect strategies and response signals, implicit as well as overt, by which the informed hemisphere can be used to cue-in the uninformed hemisphere (Levy-Agresti, 1968).

Normal behavior under ordinary conditions is favored also by many other unifying factors. Some of these are very obvious, like the fact that these two separate mental spheres have only one body, so they always get dragged to the same places, meet the same people, and see and do the same things all the time and thus are bound to have a great overlap of common, almost identical, experience. Just the unity of the optic image—and even after chiasm section in animal experiments, the conjugate movements of the eyes—means that both hemispheres automatically center on, focus on, and hence probably attend to, the same items in the visual field all the time. Through sensory feedback a unifying body schema is imposed in each hemisphere with common components that similarly condition in parallel many processes of perception and motor action onto a common base. To get different activities going and different experiences and different memory chains built up in the separated hemispheres of the bisected mammalian brain, as we do in the animal work, requires a considerable amount of experimental planning and effort. . . .

Let me emphasize again in closing that the foregoing represents a somewhat abbreviated and streamlined account of the syndrome of hemisphere deconnection as we understand it at the present time. The more we see of these patients and the more of these patients we see, the more we become impressed with their individual differences, and with the consequent qualifications that must be taken into account. Although the general picture has continued to hold up in the main as described, it is important to note that, with respect to many of the deconnection symptoms mentioned, striking modifications and even outright exceptions can be found among the small group of patients examined to date. Where the accumulating evidence will settle out with respect to the extreme limits of such individual variations and with respect to a possible average "type" syndrome remains to be seen.

REFERENCES

Akelaitis, A. J. A study of gnosis, praxis, and language following section of the corpus callosum and anterior commissure. *Journal of Neurosurgery,* 1944, 1, 94–102.

Bogen, J. E., Fisher, E. D., & Vogel, P. J. Cerebral commissurotomy: A second case report. *Journal of the American Medical Association,* 1965, 194, 1328–1329.

Bogen, J. E., & Vogel, P. J. Cerebral commissurotomy: A case report. *Bulletin of the Los Angeles Neurological Society,* 1962, 27, 169.

Gazzaniga, M. S. The split brain in man. *Scientific American,* 1967, 217, 24–29.

Levy-Agresti, J. Ipsilateral projection systems and minor hemisphere function in man after neocommissurotomy. *Anatomical Record,* 1968, 160, 384.

Myers, R. E. Corpus callosum and visual gnosis. In J. F. Delafresnaye (Ed.), *Brain mechanisms and learning.* Oxford: Blackwell, 1961.

Sperry, R. W. Mental unity following surgical disconnection of the hemispheres. *The Harvey lectures.* Series 62. New York: Academic Press, 1967. (a)

Sperry, R. W. Split-brain approach to learning problems. In G. C. Quarton, T. Melnechuk, & F. O. Schmitt (Eds.), *The neurosciences: A study program.* New York: Rockefeller University Press, 1967. (b)

Sperry, R. W. Apposition of visual half-fields after section of neocortical commissures. *Anatomical Record*, 1968, 160, 498–499.

Sperry, R. W., Gazzaniga, M. S., & Bogen, J. E. Function of neocortical commissures: Syndrome of hemisphere deconnection. In P. J. Vinken & G. W. Bruyn (Eds.), *Handbook of neurology*. Amsterdam: North Holland, 1968, in press.

The Central Nervous System and the Reinforcement of Behavior

James Olds's discovery of pleasure centers in the brain in the early 1950s demonstrated that reinforcement of behavior has a physiological basis. The early work in electrical brain stimulation performed by Olds and his colleagues has been followed by increasingly sophisticated techniques designed to unravel the mysteries of the brain.

Olds (1922–1976) received his Ph.D. from Harvard University in 1952. He taught at the University of Michigan and then at the California Institute of Technology. Through his research, he discovered much about the regions of the brain that are responsible for the effects of reinforcement and punishment.

This selection, "The Central Nervous System and the Reinforcement of Behavior," published in the *American Psychologist* in 1969, summarizes much of the brain research conducted by Olds and his colleagues and shows how the brain is involved in our daily experiences. The detailed description of the function of the hypothalamus and its various pathways illustrates how reinforcement is related to motivation. Notice how the entire research program developed from a fortuitous chance event to a systematic program involving the investigation of various brain sites.

Key Concept: reinforcement through brain stimulation

*R*eward and drive processes are intricately related to those of learning. Therefore brain studies of reward can be expected to provide a basis or at least an introduction to the study of physiological mechanisms underlying learning. Rewards and drives have been studied with lesions and electric stimulations which usually affected many hundreds of neurons at a time. While the grossness of these methods was not a clearly insuperable obstacle in the study of motivational processes, the methods have not yet proved fruitful in the study of the more detailed aspects of learning. It is possible to suppose that the root of the difficulty lies in our inability, with these methods, to study neurons one at a time or in very small families. Newer single unit studies are therefore currently pursued with the hope of finding by their use a key to the mnemonic aspects of brain function. However, in view of the large number of neurons and areas that might be sampled, it has seemed that certain guidelines might be provided if we organized the newer pursuits on the basis of the more solid generalizations distilled from the data obtained with the older methods.

A long and reasonably happy research program was launched in 1953 when a rat fortuitously evidenced a neuronal rewarding effect by returning to the place on a table top where it had been when an electrical stimulus was applied to the brain via chronically implanted electrodes (Olds, 1955). The ensuing studies provided not only a neural substrate as a focal point for further study of a key psychological concept, namely the law of effect, but also a stable method for studying many brain behavior relationships. On the basis of accomplishments to date, the method bodes well in its own way to prove as fruitful as other well-known landmarks in the behavioral sciences such as Skinner's method for studying operant behavior or Lashley's method for studying discrimination and choice on a jumping stand.

The initial observation led to studies which showed that electrical excitation in a restricted region of the central nervous system caused rats to work steadily at arbitrarily assigned tasks (see Figure 1) in order to obtain the electric stimulus (Olds & Milner, 1954). The behavior was easily reproducible from animal to animal, it was sustained during extended periods of testing, and it was not accompanied by any other obvious pathological signs. It seemed, therefore, possible to view this self-stimulation behavior as evidence of an artificial activation of the brain's normal positive reinforcement mechanism. This discovery has led to much research in our laboratory and has instigated parallel investigations in many other laboratories. At first much of this work was related to the question of whether we were being fooled by the data. Was this a psychologically valid reward or merely a sham having the appearance but not the substance of a positive emotional effect? Experiments showed that animals would improve performance in a maze, running faster and eliminating errors from trial to trial, in order to arrive at the goal point where stimulation was administered (Olds, 1956). Twenty-three hours after a previous brain stimulation they would run purposefully through the maze without errors and without dalliance. In an obstruction box animals repeatedly crossed an electrified grid which applied aversive shock to the feet in order to obtain brain rewards (Olds, 1961). In performance tests when a choice between food and brain stimulation rewards was presented to hungry rats, they often chose brain rewards and underwent the danger of starvation (Routtenberg & Lindy, 1965). In a Skinner box animals would press one bar 50 or even 100 times in order to gain access to a second bar with which they could stimulate their brains (Pliskoff, Wright, & Hawkins, 1965). In extinction experiments animals which had learned to press one of two pedals for brain rewards continued to press that pedal in preference to the other for days after the brain rewards were discon-

FIGURE 1 *The Self-Stimulation Experiment
(By depressing a lever the animal delivers a brief electric
shock to the appropriate point in the brain)*

tinued (Koenig, 1967). All of these tests fostered a positive answer to the question of whether this was a psychologically valid reward.

The anatomical study of brain rewards showed a relatively unified system to be involved (see Figure 2), consisting of the "old" olfactory cortex, nearby nuclear masses, and the hypothalamus which is a descending extension of this system connecting it to parts of the midbrain (Olds & Olds, 1963). The upper or cortical parts of this system had previously been correlated by neurological evidence and speculation with "emotional experience" (Papez, 1937). The lower part, that is, the hypothalamus, had been connected by experimental work with the control of consummatory responses and basic drives related to food, water, sex, temperature, and so forth (Miller, 1958; Stellar, 1954).

The main two pathways connecting this relatively unified system together are the medial forebrain bundle (Kappers, Huber, & Crosby, 1936) and the fornix (Nauta, 1956). In the hypothalamus the medial forebrain bundle, which is the main one of the two, forms a relatively compact lateral hypothalamic bundle but in anterior parts it fans out to the various olfactory cortical centers. In it, messages from the paleocortex seem to converge upon hypothalamus and messages from hypothalamus diverge to cortex. After rewarding effects were obtained by stimulating in the paleocortical emotional system and in the hypothalamic drive system which were connected by the medial forebrain bundle, it was not surprising to obtain the same effects by stimulating some parts of the anatomically related reticular system which had been previously shown to be involved in awakening and arousing the animal (Moruzzi & Magoun, 1949). But it was paradoxical to obtain these positive effects by stimu-

FIGURE 2 *Brain Map With Arrows Indicating the Parts of the Brain Involved in Reward and Titles Indicating Other Functions Ascribed to These Areas.*

39

James Olds

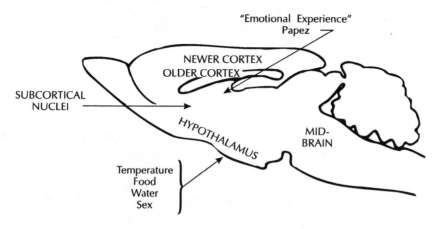

lating some of the same areas which had previously been shown to be involved in neurally stimulated aversive behavior (Delgado, Roberts, & Miller, 1954). The rewarding effects were not very stable or intense when evoked from the mixed positive and negative areas, and they were often similarly mild or variable when evoked in paleocortex. They were stable and intense when evoked from the lateral hypothalamic bundle, that is, the compact part of the medial forebrain bundle. These are some of the same arenas which have been called drive centers on the basis of other investigations. Therefore, we have thought that the hypothalamic drive centers are the main focus of the brain-stimulated reward effect.

The relations between brain-stimulated positive reinforcement and similarly stimulated negative reinforcement or pain behavior were clarified to some degree in a series of experiments.

In one hypothalamic center with three connecting pathways, stimulation of the first yielded positive reinforcement, stimulation of the second yielded negative reinforcement, and stimulation of the third yielded positive reinforcement again (Olds & Olds, 1963; Roberts, 1958). Stimulation of the center itself yielded mixed positive-negative effects. It was appealing to suppose that such a center receiving both plus and minus emotional inputs might give rise to a set of output messages which would reflect the integrated sum of the organism's emotional state at a given time and which would be effective in determining later behavior.

In keeping with the theory that interaction occurred, we found that stimulation of reward pathway number one inhibited behavior driven by escape pathway number two (Routtenberg & Olds, 1963). Stimulation of escape pathway number two inhibited behavior induced by stimulating reward pathway three (Olds & Olds, 1962). Stimulation at number three did not inhibit anything, but lesions here impaired both self-stimulation and escape behavior so we supposed that this might be the common pathway between reward and punishment (Olds & Olds, 1964). Because stimulation in this pathway itself yielded self-stimulation, we concluded that reward was an active excitatory or incremental process in these neurons, and negative reinforcement might be a negative inhibitory process in the same group.

Because of time limitations, I will bypass details and go on to a discussion of the second important series of interaction studies, namely, those relating neural rewards to the basic drives. In midline hypothalamic centers, lesions have been found by previous investigators to cause overeating and obesity (Brobeck, 1946). Here also, electric stimulation caused cessation of eating (Wyrwicka & Dobrzecka, 1960). Because this stimulus terminated feeding it seemed that it might be drive reducing and rewarding. In fact, there were only aversive effects of stimulating this part of the hypothalamus (Krasne, 1962). In a more lateral area, lesions caused starvation (Anand & Brobeck, 1951) and electric stimulation caused animals to work for food and to eat even when satiated (Miller, 1960). Because this seemed to be a drive-inducing stimulus it was expected to have aversive properties. The finding again was quite the opposite. Stimulating at these feeding center points was often rewarding (Margules & Olds, 1962). Our first interpretation of this was to guess that the stimulation induced not a drive but a consummatory response and therefore might well be rewarding. However, stimulation here caused not only eating of food when food was available but also working for food when food was absent (Miller, 1960). This belied the supposition that these were mere consummatory centers and suggested that there was the induction by stimulation at these points of something very much like the hunger drive itself. The association of neural reward in its strongest form with brain points where basic drives were also induced was later confirmed by other experiments which found drinking and self-stimulation to be induced by stimulation in some nearby brain areas (Mogenson & Stevenson, 1966) and sexual responding and self-stimulation in others (Caggiula & Hoebel, 1966; Herberg, 1963). Thus, the common denominator between many drive-inducing points was the fact that their stimulation was quite often rewarding to the animal.

In trying to make sense out of the feeding data, it was easy to imagine that medial hypothalamic satiety caused an aversive condition of the organism which brought eating to a halt. While this reversed a priori notions about relations between satiety and reward, it was not out of harmony with everyday experience which indicates that eating ceases to be rewarding and even becomes aversive when the animal eats too much. Second, during a meal or between meals there might be a middle condition in which eating would induce rewarding effects and these might induce further eating. This also might be out of harmony with the a priori notions about connections between hunger and negative factors, but it was in harmony with experience which shows that food often is positively reinforcing and simultaneously induces further hunger. What was missing was a center representing the other extreme from satiety, namely starvation. It seemed that we should find somewhere in the hypothalamus an area where stimulation would be aversive but would also induce eating. In recent research we believe we have found this center in the dorsal part of the medial hypothalamic area. Here, not too far from the lateral hypothalamic feeding center, instrumental and consummatory feeding responses were induced by electric stimulation together with aversive behavior. In another dorsal area, not too far from this, stimulation induced eating with no reinforcing side effects at all. We have thought that both satiety and starvation centers might inhibit a lateral hypothalamic food-reward center. And both the lateral hypothalamic food-reward center and the starvation center might excite a dorsal drive center.

Hypothalamic reward centers related to other drives such as sex or temperature regulation might have equally complex relations but they would not need to be parallel to these. Each drive must have its own problems.

REFERENCES

Anand, B., & Brobeck, J. R. Hypothalamic control of food intake in rats and cats. *Yale Journal of Biology and Medicine*, 1951, **24,** 123–140.

Broceck J. R. Mechanisms of the development of obesity in animals with hypothalamic lesions. *Physiological Review,* 1946, **26,** 541–559.

Caggiula, A. R., & Hoebel, B. G. "Copulation-reward site" in the posterior hypothalamus. *Science*, 1966, **153,** 1284–1285.

Delgado, J. M. R., Roberts, W. W., & Miller, N. E. Learning motivated by electrical stimulation of the brain. *American Journal of Physiology,* 1954, **179,** 587–593.

Herberg, L. J. Seminal ejaculation following positively reinforcing electrical stimulation of the rat hypothalamus. *Journal of Comparative and Physiological Psychology,* 1963, **56,** 679–685.

Kappers, C. U. A., Huber, G. C., & Crosby, E. C. *The comparative anatomy of the nervous system of vertebrates.* New York: Macmillan, 1936.

Koenig, I. D. V. The reinforcement value of intracranial stimulation and its interaction with arousal level. Cited in D. E. Berlyne, Arousal and reinforcement, *Nebraska Symposium of Motivation,* 1967, **15,** 1–110.

Krasne, F. B. General disruption resulting from electrical stimulus of ventro-medial hypothalamus. *Science*, 1962, **138,** 822–823.

Margules, D. L., & Olds, J. Identical "feeding" and "rewarding" systems in the lateral hypothalamus of rats. *Science*, 1962, **135,** 374–375.

Miller, N. E. Central stimulation and other new approaches to motivation and reward. *American Psychologist,* 1958, **13,** 100–108.

Miller, N. E. Motivational effects of brain stimulation and drugs. *Federation Proceedings,* 1960, **19,** 846–854.

Mogenson, G. J., & Stevenson, J. A. F. Drinking and self-stimulation with electrical stimulation of the lateral hypothalamus. *Physiology and Behavior,* 1966, **1,** 251–254.

Moruzzi, G., & Magoun, H. W. Brain stem reticular formation and activation of the EEG. *Electroencephalography and Clinical Neurophysiology,* 1949, **1,** 455–473.

Nauta, W. J. H. An experimental study of the fornix system in the rat. *Journal of Comparative Neurology,* 1956, **104,** 247–271.

Olds, J. Physiological mechanisms of reward. *Nebraska Symposium on Motivation,* 1955, **3,** 73–138.

Olds J. Runway and maze behavior controlled by basomedial forebrain stimulation in the rat. *Journal of Comparative and Physiological Psychology,* 1956, **49,** 507–512.

Olds, J. Differential effects of drives and drugs on self-stimulation at different brain sites. In D. E. Sheer (Ed.), *Electrical stimulation of the brain.* Austin: University of Texas Press, 1961.

Olds, J., & Milner, P. Positive reinforcement produced by electrical stimulation of septal area and other regions of rat brain. *Journal of Comparative and Physiological Psychology,* 1954, **47,** 419–427.

Olds, J., & Olds, M. E. The mechanisms of voluntary behavior. In R. G. Heath (Ed.), *The role of pleasure in behavior.* New York: Hoeber Medical Division, Harper & Row, 1964.

Olds, M. E., & Olds, J. Approach-escape interactions in rat brain. *American Journal of Physiology,* 1962, **203,** 803–810.

Olds, M. E., & Olds, J. Approach-avoidance analysis of rat diencephalon. *Journal of Comparative Neurology,* 1963, **120,** 259–295.

Papez, J. W. A proposed mechanism of emotion. *Archives of Neurology and Psychiatry,* 1937, **38,** 725–743.

Persson, N. Self-stimulation in the goat. *Acta Physiologica Scandinavica,* 1962, **55,** 276–285.

Pliskoff, S. S., Wright, J. E., & Hawkins, D. T. Brain stimulation as a reinforcer: Intermittent schedules. *Journal of the Experimental Analyses of Behavior,* 1965, **8,** 75–88.

Roberts, W. W. Both rewarding and punishing effects from stimulation of posterior hypothalamus of cat with same electrode at same intensity. *Journal of Comparative and Physiological Psychology,* 1958, **51,** 400–407.

Routtenberg, A., & Lindy, J. Effects of the availability of rewarding septal and hypothalamic stimulation on bar-pressing for food under conditoins of deprivation. *Journal of Comparative and Physiological Psychology,* 1965, **60,** 158–161.

Routtenberg, A., & Olds, J. The attenuation of response to an aversive brain stimulus by concurrent rewarding septal stimulation. *Federation Proceedings,* 1963, **22** (No. 2, Part I), 515. (Abstract)

Stellar, E. The physiology of motivation. *Psychological Review,* 1954, **61,** 5–22.

Wyrwicka, W., & Dobrzecka, C. Relationship between feeding and satiation centers of the hypothalamus. *Science,* 1960, **132,** 805–806.

2.3 LARRY R. SQUIRE

Mechanisms of Memory

For many years, psychologists have been trying to pinpoint where memory is stored in the brain. After experiencing numerous false starts, psychologists have recently made much progress in identifying the specific brain structures involved in memory storage and retrieval. Researchers have also found that various kinds of memory are processed and stored in different places in the brain. One researcher at the forefront of memory research is Larry R. Squire.

Squire earned his Ph.D. in cognitive psychology in 1968 from the Massachusetts Institute of Technology. He is currently a research career scientist at the San Diego Veterans Administration Medical Center and a professor of psychiatry at the University of California School of Medicine in La Jolla. For his studies of memory, Squire has used imaging techniques that allow him to view the activity of the brain while a subject is processing information. Among his numerous publications is *Memory and the Brain* (Oxford University Press, 1987).

This selection, "Mechanisms of Memory," published in 1986 in *Science*, provides an exciting look at current research in the biology of memory. In reviewing some of the findings of current memory research, Squire notes that memory appears to be tied to the same area of the brain that originally processed the specific learning. Also, the finding that the brain is organized to store different kinds of memories helps to explain forgetting. In reading this selection, be prepared to focus on the larger issues of memory and brain functions, and on the physical bases of memory, rather than on Squire's references to specific brain structures.

Key Concept: location of memory storage in the brain

*M*ost species are able to adapt in the face of events that occur during an individual lifetime. Experiences modify the nervous system, and as a result animals can learn and remember. One powerful strategy for understanding memory has been to study the molecular and cellular biology of plasticity in individual neurons and their synapses, where the changes that represent stored memory must ultimately be recorded (1). Indeed, behavioral experience directly modifies neuronal and synaptic morphology [form and structure] (2). Of course, the problem of memory involves not only the important issue of how synapses change, but also questions about the organization of memory in the brain. Where is memory stored? Is there one kind of memory or are there many? What brain processes or systems are involved in memory and what jobs do they do? In recent years, studies of complex vertebrate nervous systems, including studies in humans and other primates, have begun to answer these questions.

MEMORY STORAGE: DISTRIBUTED OR LOCALIZED?

The collection of neural changes representing memory is commonly known as the engram (3), and a major focus of contemporary work has been to identify and locate engrams in the brain. The brain is organized so that separate regions of neocortex simultaneously carry out computations on specific features or dimensions of the external world (for example, visual patterns, location, and movement). The view of memory that has emerged recently, although it still must be regarded as hypothesis, is that information storage is tied to the specific processing areas that are engaged during learning (4, 5). Memory is stored as changes in the same neural systems that ordinarily participate in perception, analysis, and processing of the information to be learned. For example, in the visual system, the inferotemporal cortex (area TE) is the last in a sequence of visual pattern-analyzing mechanisms that begins in the striate cortex (6). Cortical area TE has been proposed to be not only a higher order visual processing region, but also a repository of the visual memories that result from this processing (4).

The idea that information storage is localized in specific areas of the cortex differs from the well-known conclusion of Lashley's classic work (7) that memory is widely and equivalently distributed throughout large brain regions. In his most famous study, Lashley showed that, when rats relearned a maze problem after a cortical lesion, the number of trials required for relearning was proportional to the extent of the lesion and was unrelated to its location. Yet Lashley's results are consistent with the modern view if one supposes that the maze habit depends on many kinds of information (for example, visual, spatial, and olfactory) and that each kind of information is separately processed and localized. Indeed, the brain regions, or functional units, within which information is equivalently distributed may be very small (5, 8). Thus, memory is localized in the sense that particular brain systems represent specific aspects of each event (9), and it is distributed in the sense that many neural systems participate in representing a whole event.

THE NEUROPSYCHOLOGICAL-NEURAL SYSTEMS APPROACH

One useful strategy for learning about the neural organization of memory has been to study human memory pathology. In some patients with brain injury or disease, memory impairment occurs as a circumscribed disorder in the absence of other cognitive deficits. Careful study of these cases has led to a number of insights into how the brain accomplishes learning and memory (10–12). Moreover, animal models of human amnesia have recently been developed in the monkey (4,13) and rat (14). Animal models make it possible to identify the specific neural structures that when damaged produce the syndrome, and they set the stage for more detailed biological studies.

It has been known for nearly 100 years that memory is impaired by bilateral damage to either of two brain regions—the medial aspect of the temporal lobe and the midline of the diencephalon. Damage to these areas makes it difficult to establish new memories (anterograde amnesia) as well as to retrieve some memories formed before the onset of amnesia (retrograde amnesia). General intellectual capacity is intact, as is immediate memory (for example, the ability to repeat correctly six or seven digits), language and social skills, personality, and memory for the remote past, especially childhood. Because amnesia can occur against a background of normal cognition, the severity of the condition is often underappreciated. For example, patient N.A. (an example of diencephalic amnesia) became amnesic in 1960 after an accident with a miniature fencing foil (15). Radiographic (CT) evidence identified damage in the left mediodorsal thalamic nucleus (16). More recent evidence from magnetic resonance imaging identified a larger diencephalic lesion involving thalamus and hypothalamus (19). This patient is a pleasant man with an agreeable sense of humor, who could join in any social activity without special notice. However, he would be unable to learn the names of his colleagues, or keep up with a developing conversation, or speak accurately about public events that have occurred since his injury. He has an intelligence quotient (IQ) of 124, can make accurate predictions of his own memory abilities (17), and has no noticeable impairment of higher cognitive functions except a severe verbal memory problem.

Medial temporal amnesia is best illustrated by the noted amnesic patient H.M. (18), who sustained a bilateral resection of the medial temporal lobes in 1953 in an effort to relieve severe epileptic seizures. Since that time, H.M. has exhibited profound anterograde amnesia, forgetting the events of daily life almost as fast as they occur. His defect in memory extends to both verbal and nonverbal material, and it involves information acquired through all sensory modalities. . . .

SHORT-TERM AND LONG-TERM MEMORY

The study of amnesia has provided strong evidence for distinguishing between a capacity-limited immediate (sometimes called short-term) memory, which is intact in amnesia, and more long-lasting (long-term) memory, which is impaired (10, 23). Amnesic patients can keep a short list of numbers in mind for several minutes if they rehearse them and hold their attention to the task. The difficulty comes when the amount of material to be remembered exceeds what can be held in immediate memory or when recovery of even a small amount of material is attempted after an intervening period of distraction. Immediate memory is independent of the medial temporal and diencephalic regions damaged in amnesia. One possibility is that immediate memory is an intrinsic capacity of each cortical processing system (24). Thus, temporary information storage may occur within each brain area where stable changes in synaptic efficacy (long-term memory) can eventually develop. The capacity for long-term memory requires the integrity of the medial temporal and diencephalic regions, which must operate in conjunction with the assemblies of neurons that represent stored information.

DECLARATIVE AND NONDECLARATIVE KNOWLEDGE

In addition to a distinction between short-term and long-term memory functions, recent findings suggest a further distinction within the domain of long-term memory. The memory deficit in amnesia is narrower than previously thought in that not all kinds of learning and memory are affected. Amnesic patients (i) demonstrate intact learning and retention of certain motor, perceptual, and cognitive skills and (ii) exhibit intact priming effects: that is, their performance, like that of normal subjects, can be influenced by recent exposure to stimulus material. Both skill learning and priming effects can occur in amnesic patients without their conscious awareness of prior study sessions and without recognition, as measured by formal tests, of the previously presented stimulus material. . . .

These results [of studies with amnesic patients] suggest a distinction between at least two kinds of memory (12, 35, 39), a distinction that is reminiscent of earlier accounts in psychology and philosophy about how knowledge is represented (33, 34). The kind of memory that is impaired in amnesia has been termed declarative memory. It is accessible to conscious awareness and includes the facts, episodes, lists, and routes of everyday life. It can be declared, that is, it can be brought to mind verbally as a proposition or nonverbally as an image. It includes both episodic memory (specific time-and-place events) and semantic memory (facts and general information gathered in the course of specific experiences) (36, 37). Declarative memory depends on the integrity of the neural systems damaged in amnesia as well as on the particular neural systems that store the information being learned.

In contrast, examples of intact learning in amnesia are implicit and accessible only through performance. The term "procedural" has been used to describe these intact abilities (12, 35). This term aptly applies to skill learning, but the similarities and differences between the various examples of preserved abilities are still poorly understood (e.g., skill learning and priming), so that it may be better to refer to them specifically (40). Indeed, the preserved abilities are collectively better described by a negative feature (they lack the characteristics of declarative knowledge, i.e., they are nondeclarative) than by any positive feature that can be identified at this time.

FIGURE 1 *A Tentative Taxonomy of Memory* **47**

Larry R. Squire

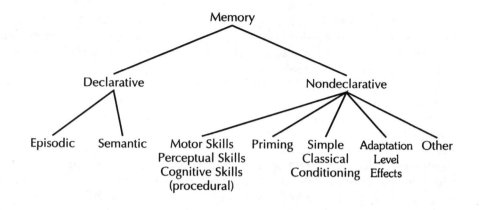

Nondeclarative memory seems to be embedded in specific procedures or stored as tunings, biases, or activations. In these cases, experience culminates in behavioral change without requiring conscious recollection of the learning episodes. Skill learning may depend on the participation of the extrapyramidal motor system (*41*).

A number of considerations suggest that procedural learning is phylogenetically old [developed over the course of evolution] (*5*). It may have developed as a collection of encapsulated, special-purpose learning abilities (*44*). Memory was then realized as cumulative changes stored within the particular neural systems engaged during learning. By this view, some simple forms of associative learning, which occur in invertebrates (*45*) and are prominently developed in mammals (*46*), are examples of nondeclarative learning. These would be expected to be fully available to amnesic patients (*47*). In contrast, the capacity for declarative knowledge is phylogenetically recent, reaching its greatest development in mammals with the full elaboration and medial temporal structures, especially the hippocampal formation and associated cortical areas. This capacity allows an animal to record and access the particular encounters that led to behavioral change. The stored memory is flexible and accessible to all modalities.

The evidence thus supports the idea that the brain has organized its memory functions around fundamentally different information storage systems (Fig. 1). This notion necessarily accepts the concepts of conscious and unconscious memory as serious topics for experimental work. In most cases the same experience would engage both memory systems. For example, perception of a word transiently activates the preexisting assembly of neural elements whose conjoint activity corresponds to that perception. This activation subserves the priming effect, an unconscious process that temporarily facilitates processing of the same word and associated words. The same stimulus also establishes a longer lasting declarative, and conscious, memory that the word was seen, and seen at a particular time and place, through participation of the neural systems within the medial temporal and diencephalic regions. . . .

CONCLUSION

In neuroscience, questions about memory have often been focused at the cellular and molecular level—for example, how do synapses change when memory is formed? In psychology, memory has often been studied as whole behavior, without reference to the brain, and as a problem of what computations learning and memory require. This article describes what can be learned from an intermediate, neuropsychological level of analysis, which focuses on the brain processes and brain systems involved in learning and memory. Study of animals with complex nervous systems, including humans and other primates, has led to a view of memory and the brain that should have considerable generality across vertebrate species, and certainly across all mammals. The ultimate goal is to be able to move across levels of analysis, from formal descriptions of cognition to underlying brain systems and finally to the neurons and cellular events within these systems. The problem of memory needs to be studied at all these levels, and should draw jointly on the disciplines of cognitive psychology, neuropsychology, and neurobiology.

REFERENCES AND NOTES

1. E. R. Kandel and J. H. Schwartz, *Science* **218**, 433 (1982); G. Lynch and M. Baudry, *ibid.* **224**, 1057 (1984); J. P. Changeux and M. Konishi, Eds., *Neural and Molecular Mechanisms of Learning* (Springer-Verlag, Berlin, 1987).

2. M. R. Rosenzweig, in *Development and Evolution of Brain Size: Behavioral Implications*, M. E. Hahn, C. Jensen, B. Dudek, Eds. (Academic Press, New York, 1979), pp. 263–294; W. T. Greenough, in *Neurobiology of Learning and Memory*, G. Lynch, J. L. McGaugh, N. M. Weinberger, Eds. (Guilford, New York, 1984), pp. 470–478.

3. R. Semon, *die Mneme als erhaltendes Prinzip im Wechsel des organishcen Geschehens* (Wilhelm Engelmann, Leipzig, 1904); D. L. Schacter, *Stranger Behind the Engram* (Erlbaum, Hillsdale, NJ, 1982).

4. M. Mishkin, *Philos. Trans. R. Soc. London Ser. B* **298**, 85 (1982).

5. L. R. Squire, in *Handbook of Physiology: The Nervous System*, J. M. Brookhart and V. B. Mountcastle, Eds. (American Physiological Society, Bethesda, MD, 1987); *Memory and Brain* (Oxford Univ. Press, New York, 1987).

6. C. G. Gross, in *Handbook of Sensory Physiology*, R. Jung, Ed. (Springer-Verlag, Berlin, 1973), pp. 451–452; A. Cowey, in *The Organization of the Cerebral Cortex*, F. O. Schmitt, F. G. Worden, G. Adelman, S. G. Dennis, Eds. (MIT Press, Cambridge, MA, 1981), pp. 395–413; W. Ungerleider and M. Mishkin, in *The Analysis of Visual Behavior*, D. J. Ingle, R. J. W. Mansfield, M. A. Goodale, Eds. (MIT Press, Cambridge, MA, 1982), pp. 549–586.

7. K. S. Lashley, *Brain Mechanisms and Intelligence: A Quantitative Study of Injuries to the Brain* (Univ. of Chicago Press, Chicago, 1929).

8. V. B. Mountcastle, in *The Neurosciences*, F. O. Schmitt and F. G. Worden, Eds. (MIT Press, Cambridge, MA, 1979), pp. 21–42.

9. M. Davis, D. S. Gendelman, M. D. Tischler, P. M. Gendelman, *J. Neurosci.* **2,** 791 (1982); R. F. Thompson, T. W. Berger, J. Madden, *Annu. Rev. Neurosci.* **6**, 447 (1983); D. H. Cohen, in *Memory Systems of the Brain*, N. M. Weinberger, J. L. McGaugh, G. Lynch, Eds. (Guilford, New York, 1985), pp. 27–48.

10. B. Milner, *Clin. Neurosurg.* **19,** 421 (1972); L. Weiskrantz, in *Philos. Trans. R. Soc. London* **298,** 97 (1982); L. S. Cermak, Ed., *Human Memory and Amnesia* (Erlbaum, Hillsdale, NJ, 1982); A. Mayes and P. Meudell, in *Memory in Animals and Humans,* A. Mayes, Ed. (Van Nostrand Reinhold, Berkshire, England, 1983), pp. 203–252.

11. W. Hirst, *Psychol. Bull.* **91,** 435 (1982); D. Schacter, in *Memory Systems of the Brain,* N. M. Weinberger, J. L. McGaugh, G. Lynch, Eds. (Guilford, New York, 1985), pp. 351–379.

12. L. R. Squire and N. J. Cohen, in *Neurobiology of Learning and Memory,* G. Lynch, J. L. McGaugh, N. M. Weinberger, Eds. (Guilford, New York, 1984), pp. 3–64.

13. L. R. Squire and S. Zola-Morgan, in *The Physiological Basis of Memory,* J. A. Deutsch, Ed. (Academic Press, New York, ed. 2, 1983); H. Mahut and M. Moss, in *Neuropsychology of Memory,* L. R. Squire and N. Butters, Eds. (Guilford, New York, 1984), pp. 297–315.

14. D. S. Olton, in *Neuropsychology of Memory,* L. R. Squire and N. Butters, Eds. (Guilford, New York, 1984), pp. 367–373; B. T. Volpe, W. A. Pulsinelli, J. Tribuna, H. P. Davis, *Stroke* **15,** 558 (1984); R. P. Kesner and B. V. DiMattia, in *Neuropsychology of Memory,* L. R. Squire and N. Butters, Eds. (Guilford, New York, 1984), pp. 385–398.

15. H. L. Teuber, B. Milner, H. G. Vaughan, *Neuropsychology* **6,** 267 (1968); P. I. Kaushall, M. Zetin, L. R. Squire, *J. Nerv. Ment. Dis.* **169,** 383 (1981).

16. L. R. Squire and R. Y. Moore, *Ann. Neurol.* **6,** 503 (1979).

17. A. P. Shimamura and L. R. Squire, *J. Exp. Psychol. Learn. Mem. Cognit.* **12,** 452 (1986).

18. W. B. Scoville and B. Milner, *J. Neurol. Psychiatry* **20,** 11 (1957); S. Corkin, *Semin. Neurol.* **4,** 249 (1984).

19. L. R. Squire, D. G. Amaral, S. Zola-Morgan, M. Kritchevsky, G. Press, *Exp. Neurol.,* in press.

23. A. D. Baddeley and E. K. Warrington, *J. Verb. Learn. Verb. Behav.* **9,** 176 (1970); R. C. Atkinson and R. M. Schiffrin, in *The Psychology of Learning and Motivation: Advances in Research and Theory,* K. W. Spence and J. T. Spence, Eds. (Academic Press, New York, 1968), vol. 2, pp. 89–195. This division between short-term and long-term memory expresses an idea at the level of neural systems, not at the level of neurons and synapses. Memory is first in a short-term store for a period of seconds to minutes, depending on rehearsal. The normal operation of the neural systems damaged in amnesia enables storage in and retrieval from long-term memory. The same terms have also been used in a different sense, at the level of single neurons, to describe the temporal sequence of synaptic change that leads to permanent memory.

24. S. Monsell, in *International Symposium on Attention and Performance,* H. Bouma and D. Bouwhuis, Eds. (Erlbaum, Hillsdale, NJ, 1984), vol. 10, pp. 327–350.

33. H. Bergson, *Matter and Memory* (Allen & Unwin, London, 1911); G. Ryle, *The Concept of Mind* (Hutchinson, San Francisco, 1949); J. S. Bruner, in *The Pathology of Memory,* G. A. Talland and N. C. Waugh, Eds. (Academic Press, New York, 1969), pp. 253–259.

34. T. Winograd, in *Representation and Understanding: Studies in Cognitive Science,* D. Bobrow and A. Collins, Eds. (Academic Press, New York, 1975), pp. 185–210; J. R. Anderson, *Language, Memory, and Thought* (Erlbaum, Hillsdale, NJ, 1976).

35. N. J. Cohen, thesis. University of California, San Diego (1981).

36. E. Tulving, *Elements of Episodic Memory* (Clarendon, Oxford, 1983).

37. A. P. Shimamura and L. R. Squire, *J. Exp. Psychol. Learn. Mem. Cognit.* **13,** 464 (1987).

38. M. Mishkin, B. Malamut, J. Bachevalier, in *Neurobiology of Learning and Memory,* G. Lynch, J. L. McGaugh, N. M. Weinberger, Eds. (Guilford, New York, 1984), pp. 65–77.

39. L. R. Squire and S. Zola-Morgan, *Trends in Neurosi,* **11,** 125 (1988).

40. D. L. Schacter, *J. Exp. Psychol. Learn. Mem. Cognit.* **13,** 501 (1987).

44. P. Rozin, *Prog. Psychobiol. Physiol. Psyhol.* **6,** 245 (1976).

45. G. J. Mpistos and W. J. Davis, *Science* **180,** 317 (1973); T. J. Chang and A. Gelperin, *Proc. Natl. Acad. Sci. U.S.A.* **77,** 6204 (1980); C. Sahley, A. Gelperin, J. W. Rudy, *ibid.* **78,** 640 (1981); R. D. Hawkins, T. W. Abrams, T. J. Carew, E. R. Kandel, *Science* **219,** 400 (1983); D. L. Alkon, *ibid.* **226,** 1037 (1984).

46. N. J. Mackintosh, *Conditioning and Associative Learning* (Oxford Univ. Press, New York, 1983); R. A. Rescorla and A. R. Wagner, in *Classical Conditioning II: Current Research and Theory,* A. Black and W. Prokasy, Eds. (Appleton-Century-Crofts, New York, 1972), pp. 64–99.

47. L. Weiskrantz and E. K. Warrington, *Neuropsychologia* **17,** 187 (1979); I. Daum, S. Channon, A. Canavan, *J. Neurol., Neurosurg., Psychiatry,* **52,** 47 (1989); see N. J. Mackintosh [in *Memory Systems of the Brain,* N. M. Weinberger, J. L. McGaugh, G. Lynch, Eds. (Guilford, New York, 1985), pp. 335–350] for a discussion of how some classical conditioning paradigms can produce both declarative and procedural knowledge: see R. T. Ross, W. B. Orr, P. C. Holland, T. W. Berger [*Behav. Neurosci.* **98,** 211 (1984)] for examples of classical conditioning that are affected by hippocampal lesions.

2.4   ROBERT PLOMIN

Environment and Genes: Determinants of Behavior

The importance of nature (genetics) and nurture (environment) on behavioral development has been debated for centuries. Only in the past few decades, however, have psychologists begun to discover the specific mechanisms by which heredity influences cognition and behavior. At the same time, psychologists have found that behavior is also influenced by one's environment and that, in fact, all behavior is the result of the interaction of heredity and the environment. Behavior geneticist Robert Plomin has been studying this interaction.

Plomin (b. 1948) earned his Ph.D. in biological psychology from the University of Texas at Austin in 1974. Currently working at Pennsylvania State University, he has been actively involved in behavioral genetic research, and he is a coauthor of the textbook *Behavioral Genetics: A Primer,* 2d ed. (W. H. Freeman, 1989).

This article, "Environment and Genes: Determinants of Behavior," was published in the *American Psychologist* in 1989. In it, Plomin reviews some of the research findings in the field of behavior genetics that came to light during the 1980s. The field of behavior genetics is important because it helps us understand ourselves and those around us. Today, reports are being made regularly on how specific genes influence intelligence, personality, and psychopathology, as well as other bodily processes. As you read this article, notice Plomin's emphasis on how heredity and environment both influence human behavior.

Key Concept: behavior genetics

*A*BSTRACT: *Recent behavioral genetic research has demonstrated that genetic influence on individual differences in behavioral development is usually significant and often substantial and, paradoxically, also supports the important role of the environment. This article reviews research on the heritability of intellectual factors, personality factors, and psychopathology It discusses the importance of investigating*

51

within-family environmental differences in order to understand the environmental origins of individual differences in development.

Increasing acceptance of hereditary influence on individual differences in development represents one of the most remarkable changes in the field of psychology that has occurred during the decade since the 1979 special issue of the *American Psychologist* on children. Even for IQ scores, traditionally one of the most controversial areas, a recent survey of over 1,000 scientists and educators indicates that most now believe that individual differences in IQ scores are at least partially inherited (Snyderman & Rothman, 1987). Recent behavioral genetic research providing the empirical basis for this trend is reviewed in the first half of this article.

The wave of acceptance of genetic influence on behavior is growing into a tidal wave that threatens to engulf the second message of this research: These same data provide the best available evidence for the importance of environmental influence. Variability in complex behaviors of interest to psychologists and to society is due at least as much to environmental influences as it is to genetic influences. Because its methods recognize both environmental and genetic influences on behavior, behavioral genetic research has made some novel advances in understanding the environment. . . .

Although the brevity of this article precludes a discussion of the theory and methods of behavioral genetics, the two major methods are the twin design, in which identical twin resemblance is compared with fraternal twin resemblance, and the adoption design, in which genetically related individuals reared apart and genetically unrelated individuals reared together are studied. These methods are used to assess heritability, a statistic that describes the proportion of observed variance for a behavior that can be ascribed to genetic differences among individuals in a particular population. . . .

Two conceptual issues about the field of behavioral genetics need to be mentioned. First, behavioral genetic theory and methods address the genetic and environmental sources of differences among individuals. Behavioral genetics has little to say about universals of development (e.g., why the human species uses language) or about average differences between groups (e.g., why girls perform better than boys on verbal tests). This critical issue, the cause of much misunderstanding, is discussed at length elsewhere (Plomin, DeFries, & Fulker, 1988). Second, when genetic differences among children are found to relate to differences in their behavior, this is a probabilistic relationship in much the same way as finding associations between environmental factors and children's development. . . . [G]enetic influences on behavior are multifactorial—that is, they involve many genes, each with small effects—as well as environmental influences. In other words, genetic influences on the complex behaviors of interest to psychologists do not fit the deterministic model of a single-gene effect—like Mendel's pea-plant characteristics or like some genetic diseases such as sickle-cell anemia—which operates independently of other genes or of environmental influences. . . .

HIGHLIGHTS OF RECENT BEHAVIORAL GENETIC RESEARCH

This section provides a brief overview of recent human behavioral genetic research indicating that behavior can no longer be considered innocent of genetic influence until proven guilty. The litany includes intellectual factors, including IQ, specific cognitive abilities, academic achievement, reading disability . . . ; personality factors, including extraversion and neuroticism, temperament in childhood, and attitudes and beliefs; and psychopathology, including schizophrenia, affective disorders, delinquent and criminal behavior, and alcoholism.

Intellectual Factors

IQ. More behavioral genetic data have been obtained for IQ than for any other trait. A summary of dozens of studies prior to 1980 includes nearly 100,000 twins and biological and adoptive relatives and makes it difficult to escape the conclusion that heredity importantly influences individual differences in IQ scores (Bouchard & McGue, 1981). For example, genetically related individuals adopted apart show significant resemblance, and identical twins are substantially more similar than fraternal twins. An interesting twist is that, for reasons as yet unknown, studies in the 1970s yielded lower estimates of heritability (about 50%) than older studies (about 70%; Plomin & DeFries, 1980; cf. Loehlin, Willerman, & Horn, 1988).

Recent studies include two ongoing studies of twins reared apart that will triple the number of identical twins reared apart who have been studied for IQ and will also, for the first time, add hundreds of pairs of the equally important group of fraternal twins reared apart. Preliminary reports from these two studies indicate that their results are in line with the rest of the behavioral genetics literature in implicating substantial genetic influence on IQ scores (Bouchard, 1984; Pedersen, McClearn, Plomin, & Friberg, 1985). . . .

Specific cognitive abilities. Although there is some evidence that verbal and spatial abilities show greater genetic influence than do perceptual speed tests and memory tests, the general message is that diverse cognitive tests show significant and often substantial (almost as much as for IQ) genetic influence throughout the life span (Plomin, 1988). In 10 twin studies, tests of creativity show less genetic influence than any other dimension within the cognitive domain, especially when IQ is controlled (R. C. Nichols, 1978).

Research on specific cognitive abilities during the past decade includes a study of over 6,000 individuals in nearly 2,000 families, three twin studies in childhood and one in adulthood, and several parent–offspring adoption studies in addition to the two studies of twins reared apart mentioned in relation to IQ (Plomin, 1986).

Academic achievement. Although no new behavioral genetic research on school-relevant behavior has been reported during the past decade, genetic influence is pervasive here as well. Twin studies of academic-achievement test scores show substantial genetic influence, about the same as for specific cognitive abilities. Even report-card grades and years of schooling show substantial genetic influence. Vocational interests are also substantially influenced by genetic factors, as shown in twin and adoption studies. (For references, see Plomin, 1986.)

Reading disability. Reading disability shows considerable familial resemblance (DeFries, Vogler, & LaBuda, 1985). One recent twin study found evidence for a genetic basis for this familial resemblance (DeFries, Fulker, & LaBuda, 1987); another twin study found genetic influence on spelling disability but not on other aspects of reading disability (Stevenson, Graham, Fredman, & McLoughlin, 1987). A single-gene effect has been proposed for spelling disability (Smith, Kimberling, Pennington, & Lubs, 1983), although subsequent analyses have not confirmed the linkage (Kimberling, Fain, Ing, Smith, & Pennington, 1985; McGuffin, 1987). . . .

Personality Factors

Extraversion and neuroticism. One focus of recent research on personality involves two "super factors" of personality: extraversion and neuroticism. A review of research involving over 25,000 pairs of twins yielded heritability estimates of about 50% for these two traits (Henderson, 1982). This review also pointed out that extraversion and other personality traits often show evidence for nonadditive genetic variance. Nonadditive effects of genes involve unique combinations of genes that contribute to the similarity of identical twins but not to the resemblance of first-degree relatives. These conclusions are supported by a recent large-scale twin study in Australia (N. G. Martin & Jardine, 1986) and by two studies of twins reared apart (Pedersen, Plomin, McClearn, & Friberg, 1988; Tellegen et al., 1988). The presence of nonadditive genetic variance may be responsible for the lower estimates of heritability from adoption studies of first-degree relatives (Loehlin, Willerman, & Horn, 1982, 1985; Scarr, Webber, Weinberg, & Wittig, 1981).

Emotionality, activity, and sociability (EAS). Extraversion and neuroticism are global traits that encompass many dimensions of personality. The core of extraversion, however, is sociability, and the key component of neuroticism is emotionality. From infancy to adulthood, these two traits and activity level have been proposed as the most heritable components of personality, a theory referred to with the acronym EAS (Buss & Plomin, 1984). A review of behavioral genetic data for these three traits in infancy, childhood, adolescence, and adulthood lends support to the EAS theory (Plomin, 1986). However, note that many personality traits display genetic influence, and it is difficult to prove that some traits are more heritable than others, perhaps because of the pervasive genetic influence of extraversion and neuroticism (Loehlin, 1982). . . .

Attitudes and beliefs. Surprisingly, some attitudes and beliefs show almost as much genetic influence as do other behavioral traits. One focus of recent interest is traditionalism, the tendency to follow rules and authority and to endorse high moral standards and strict discipline. For example, a large twin study estimated that half of the variance on this measure is due to genetic influence (N. G. Martin et al., 1986), and a report of twins reared apart has also found substantial genetic influence for traditionalism (Tellegen et al., 1988). Religiosity and certain political beliefs, however, show no genetic influence.

Psychopathology

Behavioral genetic research on psychopathology in children and adults is especially active (Loehlin et al., 1988; Vandenberg, Singer, & Pauls, 1986). This section provides a brief overview of recent research in schizophrenia, affective disorders, delinquent and criminal behavior, alcoholism, and other psychopathology.

Schizophrenia. In 14 older studies involving over 18,000 first-degree relatives of schizophrenics, the risk for first-degree relatives was about 8%, eight times greater than the risk for individuals chosen randomly from the population (Gottesman & Shields, 1982). Recent family studies continue to yield similar results.

Twin studies suggest that this familial resemblance is due to heredity. The most recent twin study involved all male twins who were veterans of World War II (Kendler & Robinette, 1983). Twin concordances were 30.9% for 164 pairs of identical twins and 6.5% for 268 pairs of fraternal twins. Adoption studies of schizophrenia support the twin findings of genetic influence on schizophrenia. . . .

Affective disorders. Although twin results for affective disorders suggest even greater genetic influence than for schizophrenia, adoption studies indicate less genetic influence (Loehlin et al., 1988). In one recent adoption study, affective disorders were diagnosed in only 5.2% of biological relatives of affectively-ill adoptees, although this risk is greater than the risk of 2.3% found in the biological relatives of control adoptees (Wender et al., 1986). The biological relatives of affected adoptees also showed greater rates of alcoholism (5.4% vs. 2.0%) and attempted or actual suicide (7.3% vs. 1.5%). . . .

Delinquent and criminal behavior. The spotlight on controversies concerning genetic influence on IQ has switched to criminal behavior with the publication of a recent book (Wilson & Herrnstein, 1985) claiming that biology affects such behaviors. Six twin studies of juvenile delinquency yielded 87% concordance for identical twins and 72% concordance for fraternal twins, suggesting slight genetic influence and substantial environmental sources of resemblance (Gottesman, Carey, & Hanson, 1983). A recent quantitative study of delinquent acts indicated greater genetic influence than did earlier studies that attempted to diagnose delinquency (Rowe, 1983b).

It has been suggested that juvenile delinquents who go on to become adult criminals may have a genetic liability (Wilson & Herrnstein, 1985). Eight older twin studies of adult criminality yielded identical and fraternal twin concordances of 69% and 33%, respectively. Adoption studies are consistent with the hypothesis of some genetic influence on adult criminality, although the evidence is not as striking as in the twin studies (Mednick, Gabrielli, & Hutchings, 1984).

Alcoholism. Alcoholism runs in families. Alcoholism in a first-degree relative is by far the single best predictor of alcoholism (Mednick, Moffitt, & Stack,

1987). About 25% of the male relatives of alcoholics are themselves alcoholics, as compared with fewer than 5% of the males in the general population. Although twin studies of normal drinkers show substantial genetic influence (for example, Pedersen, Friberg, Floderus-Myrhed, McClearn, & Plomin, 1984), no twin studies have focused on alcoholism per se. A Swedish adoption study provides the best evidence for genetic influence on alcoholism, at least in males (Bohman, Cloninger, Sigvardsson, & von Knorring, 1987; cf. Peele, 1986). Twenty-two percent of the adopted-away sons of biological fathers who abused alcohol were alcoholic, suggesting substantial genetic influence.

Other psychopathology. Although most research on psychopathology has focused on psychoses, criminality, and alcoholism, attention has begun to turn to other disorders. Areas of recent research include a family study of anxiety neurosis sometimes known as panic disorder, twin and family studies of anorexia nervosa, and family and adoption studies of somatization disorder that involves multiple and chronic physical complaints of unknown origin (Loehlin et al., 1988).

Summary

The first message of behavioral genetic research is that genetic influence on individual differences in behavioral development is usually significant and often substantial. Genetic influence is so ubiquitous and pervasive in behavior that a shift in emphasis is warranted: Ask not what is heritable, ask what is not heritable.

The second message is just as important: These same data provide the best available evidence of the importance of the environment. The data reviewed in this section suggest pandemic genetic influence, but they also indicate that nongenetic factors are responsible for more than half of the variance for most complex behaviors. For example, identical twins show concordance of less than 40% for schizophrenia. Because identical twins are genetically identical, most of the reason one person is diagnosed as schizophrenic and another is not has to do with environmental rather than genetic reasons. The phrase "behavioral genetics" is in a sense a misnomer because it is as much the study of nurture as nature. In addition to documenting the importance of environmental variation, it provides a novel perspective for viewing environmental influences, especially the family environment, in the context of heredity. . . .

The move away from a rigid adherence to environmental explanations of behavioral development to a more balanced perspective that recognizes genetic as well as environmental sources of individual differences must be viewed as healthy for the social and behavioral sciences. The danger now, however, is that the swing from environmentalism will go too far. During the 1970s, I found I had to speak gingerly about genetic influence, gently suggesting heredity might be important in behavior. Now, however, I more often have to say, "Yes, genetic influences are significant and substantial, but environmental influences are just as important." This seems to be happening most clearly in the field of psychopathology, where evidence of significant genetic influence has led to a search for single genes and simple neurochemical triggers at the expense of research on its psychosocial origins. It would be wonderful if some simple, and presumably inexpensive, biochemical cure could be found for schizophrenia. However, this happy outcome seems highly unlikely given that schizophrenia is as much influenced by environmental factors as it is by heredity.

Furthermore, as mentioned earlier, genetic effects on behavior are polygenic and probabilistic, not single gene and deterministic. The characteristics in the pea plant that Mendel studied and a few diseases such as Huntington's disease and sickle-cell anemia are due to single genes that have their effects regardless of the environment or the genetic background of the individual. The complexity of behaviors studied by psychologists makes it unlikely that such a deterministic model and the reductionistic approach that it suggests will pay off. There is as yet no firm evidence for a single-gene effect that accounts for a detectable amount of variation for any complex behavior. . . .

As the pendulum swings from environmentalism, it is important that the pendulum be caught midswing before its momentum carries it to biological determinism. Behavioral genetic research clearly demonstrates that both nature and nurture are important in human development.

REFERENCES

Bohman, M., Cloninger, R., Sigvardsson, S., & von Knorring, A. L. (1987). The genetics of alcoholisms and related disorders. *Journal of Psychiatric Research, 21,* 447–452.

Bouchard, T. J. (1984). Twins reared together and apart: What they tell us about human diversity. In S. W. Fox (Ed.), *Individuality and determinism* (pp. 147–178). New York: Plenum Press.

Bouchard, T. J., Jr., & McGue, M. (1981). Familial studies of intelligence: A review. *Science, 212,* 1055–1059.

Buss, A. H., & Plomin, R. (1984). *Temperament: Early developing personality traits.* Hillsdale, NJ: Erlbaum.

DeFries, J. C., Fulker, D. W., & LaBuda, M. C. (1987). Evidence for a genetic etiology in reading disability in twins. *Nature, 329,* 537–539.

DeFries, J. C., Vogler, G. P., & LaBuda, M. C. (1985). Colorado Family Reading Study: An overview. In J. L. Fuller & E. C. Simmel (Eds.), *Behavior genetics: Principles and applications II.* (pp.357–368). Hillsdale, NJ: Erlbaum.

Donis-Keller, H., Green, P., Helms, C., Cartinhour, S., & Weiffenbach, B. (1987). A human gene map. *Cell, 51,* 319–337.

Egeland, J. A., Gerhard, D. S., Pauls, D. L., Sussex, J. N., & Kidd, K. K. (1987). Bipolar affective disorders linked to DNA markers on chromosome 11. *Nature, 325,* 783–787.

Gottesman, I. I., Carey, G., & Hanson, D. R. (1983). Pearls and perils in epigenetic psychopathology. In S. B. Guze, E. J. Earls, & J. E. Barrett (Eds.), *Childhood psychopathology and development* (pp. 287–300). New York: Raven Press.

Gottesman, I. I., & Shield, J. (1982). *Schizophrenia: The epigenetic puzzle.* Cambridge, England: Cambridge University Press.

Gusella, J. F., Wexler, N. S., Conneally, P. M., Naylor, S. L., Anderson, M. A., Tanzi, R. E., Watkins, P. C., & Ottina, K. (1983). A polymorphic DNA marker genetically linked to Huntington's disease. *Nature, 306,* 234–238.

Henderson, N. D. (1982). Human behavior genetics. *Annual Review of Psychology, 33,* 403–440.

Kendler, K. S., & Robinette, C. D. (1983). Schizophrenia in the National Academy of Sciences–National Research Council twin registry: A 16-year update. *American Journal of Psychiatry, 140,* 1551–1563.

Kimberling, W. J., Fain, P. R., Ing, P. S., Smith, S. D., & Pennington, B. F. (1985). Linkage analysis of reading disability with chromosome 15. *Behavior Genetics, 15,* 597–598.

Loehlin, J. C. (1982). Are personality traits differentially heritable? *Behavior Genetics, 12,* 417–428.

Loehlin, J. C., Willerman, L., & Horn, J. M. (1982). Personality resemblances between unwed mothers and their adopted-away offspring. *Journal of Personality and Social Psychology, 42,* 1089–1099.

Loehlin, J. C., Willerman, L., & Horn, J. M. (1985). Personality resemblance in adoptive families when the children are late adolescents and adults. *Journal of Personality and Social Psychology, 48,* 376–392.

Loehlin, J. C., Willerman, L., & Horn, J. M. (1988). Human behavior genetics, *Annual Review of Psychology, 38,* 101–133.

Martin, J. B. (1987). Molecular genetics: Applications to the clinical neurosciences. *Science, 238,* 765–772.

Martin, N. G., Eaves, L. J., Heath, A. C., Jardine, R., Feingold, L. M., & Eysenck, H. J. (1986). Transmission of social attitudes. *Proceedings of the National Academy of Sciences, USA, 83,* 4364–4368.

Martin, N. G., & Jardine, R. (1986). Eysenck's contributions to behaviour genetics. In S. Modgil & C. Modgil (Eds.), *Hans Eysenck: Consensus and controversy* (pp. 13–27). Philadelphia: Falmer.

McGuffin, P. (1987). The new genetics and childhood psychiatric disorder. *Journal of Child Psychology and Psychiatry, 28,* 215–222.

Mednick, S. A., Gabrielli, W. F., Jr., & Hutchings, B. (1984). Genetic influences in criminal convictions: Evidence from an adoption cohort. *Science, 224,* 891–894.

Mednick, S. A., Moffitt, T. E., & Stack, S. (1987). *The causes of crime: New biological approaches.* New York: Cambridge University Press.

Nichols, R. C. (1978). Twin studies of ability, personality, and interests. *Homo, 29,* 158–173.

Pedersen, N. L., Friberg, L., Floderus-Myrhed, B., McClearn, G. E., & Plomin, R. (1984). Swedish early separated twins: Identification and characterization. *Acta Geneticae Medicae et Gemellologiae, 33,* 243–250.

Pedersen, N. L., McClearn, G. E., Plomin, R., & Friberg, L. (1985). Separated fraternal twins: Resemblance for cognitive abilities. *Behavior Genetics, 15,* 407–419.

Pedersen, N. L., Plomin, R., McClearn, G. E., & Friberg, L. (1988). Neuroticism, extraversion, and related traits in adult twins reared apart and reared together. *Journal of Personality and Social Psychology, 55,* 950–957.

Peele, S. (1986). The implications and limitations of genetic models of alcoholism and other addictions. *Journal of Studies on Alcohol, 47,* 63–73.

Plomin, R. (1986). *Development, genetics, and psychology.* Hillsdale, NJ: Erlbaum.

Plomin, R. (1988). The nature and nurture of cognitive abilities. In R. J. Sternberg (Ed.), *Advances in the psychology of human intelligence* (Vol. 4, pp. 1–33). Hillsdale, NJ: Erlbaum.

Plomin, R., & DeFries, J. C. (1980). Genetics and intelligence: Recent data. *Intelligence, 4,* 15–24.

Plomin, R., DeFries, J. C., & Fulker D. W. (1988). *Nature and nurture during infancy and early childhood.* New York: Cambridge University Press.

Robert Plomin

Roew, D. C. (1983b). Biometrical genetic models of self-reported delinquent behavior: Twin study. *Behavior Genetics, 13,* 473–489.

Scarr, S., Webber, P. I., Weinberg, R. A., & Wittig, M. A. (1981). Personality resemblance among adolescents and their parents in biologically related and adoptive families. *Journal of Personality and Social Psychology, 40,* 885–898.

Smith, S. D., Kimberling, W. J., Pennington, B. F., & Lubs, H. A. (1983). Specific reading disability: Identification of an inherited form through linkage analysis. *Science, 219,* 1345–1347.

Snyderman, M., & Rothman, S. (1987). Survey of expert opinion on intelligence and aptitude testing. *American Psychologist, 42,* 137–144.

Stevenson, J., Graham, P., Fredman, G., & McLoughlin, V. (1987). A twin study of genetic influences on reading and spelling ability and disability. *Journal of Child Psychology and Psychiatry, 28,* 229–247.

Tellegen, A., Lykken, D. T., Bouchard, T. J., Wilcox, K., Segal, N., & Rich, S. (1988). Personality similarity in twins reared apart and together. *Journal of Social and Personality Psychology, 54,* 1031–1039.

Vandenberg, S. G., Singer, S. M., & Pauls, D. L. (1986). *The heredity of behavior disorders in adults and children.* New York: Plenum.

Wender, P. H., Kety, S. S., Rosenthal, D., Schulsinger, F., Ortmann, J., & Lunde, I. (1986). Psychiatric disorders in the biological and adoptive families of adopted individuals with affective disorders. *Archives of General Psychiatry, 43,* 923–929.

Wilson, J. Q., & Herrnstein, R. J. (1985). *Crime and human nature.* New York: Simon & Schuster.

Wyman, A. R., & White, R. L. (1980). A highly polymorphic locus in human DNA. *Proceedings of the National Academy of Sciences, 77,* 6754–6758.

Preparation of this article was supported in part by grants from the National Science Foundation (BNS-8643938) and the National Institute of Aging (AG-04563).

3.1 JEAN PIAGET AND
BÄRBEL INHELDER

The Sensori-motor Level

Psychologists have traditionally had difficulty studying cognitive development in children because young children cannot effectively communicate their thoughts to others. Swiss psychologist Jean Piaget, however, became interested in cognitive development in infants and children, and he spent nearly 60 years investigating the differences between the thought processes of children and those of adults. Piaget was greatly assisted during 48 of those years by his student and chief collaborator, Bärbel Inhelder.

Piaget (1896–1980) earned his Ph.D. in zoology from the University of Neuchâtel in 1918. His training helped him in his studies on children's cognitive development because he learned how to make careful observations of noncommunicative organisms solving problems. He theorized that when children are unsuccessful at solving particular problems, they develop more complex mental structures to help them in the future. Piaget was the founder and director of the International Center of Genetic Epistemology in Geneva and a professor of psychology at the University of Geneva. Inhelder (b. 1913), the coauthor with Piaget of *The Psychology of the Child* (Basic Books, 1969), from which this selection is taken, was a professor of child and adolescent psychology and the chairperson of genetic and experimental psychology at the University of Geneva before she retired in 1983. She also pioneered the application of genetic epistemology to the study of mental deficiency, to cross-cultural research, and to learning.

This selection is from chapter 1, "The Sensori-motor Level," of *The Psychology of the Child.* The book summarizes Piaget's theory of cognitive development. Because cognition is central to psychology today, it is critical to understand how we develop our ability to think and reason. As you read this selection, try to understand development from the perspective of a child.

61

Jean Piaget and Bärbel Inhelder

Key Concept: cognitive development

*I*f the child partly explains the adult, it can also be said that each period of his development partly explains the periods that follow. This is particularly clear in the case of the period where language is still absent. We call it the "sensori-motor" period because the infant lacks the symbolic function; that is, he does not have representations by which he can evoke persons or objects in their absence. In spite of this lack, mental development during the first eighteen months[1] of life is particularly important, for it is during this time that the child constructs all the cognitive substructures that will serve as a point of departure for his later perceptive and intellectual development, as well as a certain number of elementary affective reactions that will partly determine his subsequent affectivity.

SENSORI-MOTOR INTELLIGENCE

Whatever criteria for intelligence one adopts—purposeful groping (E. Claparède), sudden comprehension or insight (W. Köhler or K. Bühler), coordination of means and ends, etc.—everyone agrees in recognizing the existence of an intelligence before language. Essentially practical—that is, aimed at getting results rather than at stating truths—this intelligence nevertheless succeeds in eventually solving numerous problems of action (such as reaching distant or hidden objects) by constructing a complex system of action-schemes[2] and organizing reality in terms of spatio-temporal and causal structures. In the absence of language or symbolic function, however, these constructions are made with the sole support of perceptions and movements and thus by means of a sensori-motor coordination of actions, without the intervention of representation or thought.

Stimulus-Response and Assimilation

There certainly is such a thing as a sensori-motor intelligence, but it is very difficult to specify the exact moment when it appears. Actually, the question makes no sense, for the answer always depends upon an arbitrary choice of criterion. What one actually finds is a remarkably smooth succession of stages, each marking a new advance, until the moment when the acquired behavior presents characteristics that one or another psychologist recognizes as those of "intelligence." (All writers are in agreement in attributing this quality to at least the last of these stages, from twelve to eighteen months.) There is a continuous progression from spontaneous movements and reflexes to acquired habits and from the latter to intelligence. The real problem is not to locate the first appearance of intelligence but rather to understand the mechanism of this progression.

For many psychologists this mechanism is one of association, a cumulative process by which conditionings are added to reflexes and many other acquisitions to the conditionings themselves. According to this view, every acquisition, from the simplest to the most complex, is regarded as a response to external stimuli, a response whose associative character expresses a complete control of development by external connections. One of us,[3] on the other hand, has argued that this mechanism consists in *assimilation* (comparable to biological assimilation in the broad sense): meaning that reality data are treated or modified in such a way as to become incorporated into the structure of the subject. In other words, every newly established connection is integrated into an existing schematism. According to this view, the organizing activity of the subject must be considered just as important as the connections inherent in the external stimuli, for the subject becomes aware of these connections only to the degree that he can assimilate them by means of his existing structures. In other words, associationism conceives the relationship between stimulus and response in a unilateral manner: $S \rightarrow R$; whereas the point of view of assimilation presupposes a reciprocity $S \rightleftarrows R$; that is to say, the input, the stimulus, is filtered through a structure that consists of the action-schemes (or, at a higher level, the operations of thought), which in turn are modified and enriched when the subject's behavioral repertoire is accommodated to the demands of reality. The filtering or modification of the input is called *assimilation*; the modification of internal schemes to fit reality is called *accommodation*.

Stage 1

The point of departure of development should not be sought in the reflexes conceived as simple isolated responses, but in the spontaneous and total activities of the organism (studied by E. von Holst and others). There are relatively fixed and predictable reflexes embedded in this total activity, but they can be viewed as a differentiation of this global activity, as we shall see. Some of these reflexes are developed by exercise instead of remaining unchanged or atrophying and are the points of departure for the development of schemes of assimilation.

On the one hand, it has been shown by the study of animal behavior as well as by the study of the electrical activity of the nervous system that the organism is never passive, but presents spontaneous and global activities whose form is rhythmic. On the other hand, embryological analysis of the reflexes (G. E. Coghill and others) has enabled us to establish the fact that reflexes are formed by differentiation upon a groundwork of more global activities. In the case of the locomotive reflexes of the batrachians [frogs and toads], for example, it is an overall rhythm which culminates in a succession of differentiated and coordinated reflexes, and not the reflexes which lead to that rhythm.

As far as the reflexes of the newborn child are concerned, those among them that are of particular importance for the future (the sucking reflex and the palmar reflex, which will be integrated into later intentional grasping) give rise to what has been called a "reflex exercise"; that is, a consolidation by means of functional exercise. This explains why after a few days the newborn child nurses with more assurance and finds the nipple more easily when it has slipped out of his mouth than at the time of his first attempts.[4] The reproductive or functional assimilation that accounts for this exercise also gives rise to a generalizing assimilation (sucking on nothing between meals or sucking new objects) and a recognitive assimilation (distinguishing the nipple from other objects).

We cannot label these modifications of sucking acquisitions in a strict sense, since the assimilating exercise does not yet go beyond the preestablished boundaries of the hereditary apparatus. Nevertheless, the assimilation fulfills a fundamental role in developing this activity. This makes it impossible to regard the reflex as a pure automatism and also accounts for later extensions of the reflex scheme and for the formation of the first habits. In the case of sucking we observe, sometimes as early as the second month, the commonplace but nonetheless instructive phenomenon of a baby sucking his thumb. Fortuitous or accidental thumbsucking may occur as early as the first day. The more advanced sucking is systematic and dependent upon a coordination of the movements of arm, hand, and mouth. Associationists see here only an effect of repetition (but what is the source of this repetition, since it is not imposed by external connections?), and psychoanalysts already see a symbolic behavior by representative identification of the thumb and the breast (but what is the source of this symbolic or evocative power, well before the formation of the first mental images?). We suggest that this acquisition be interpreted as a simple extension of the sensori-motor assimilation at work as early as the reflex. It is quite clear that this is a genuine case of acquisition in a broad sense, since there exists no reflex or instinct for sucking one's thumb (indeed, the appearance of this activity and its frequency are subject to variation). But this acquisition is not a random affair: it is introduced into a reflex scheme that is already formed, extending it through the integration of sensori-motor elements hitherto independent of this scheme. Such integration already characterizes Stage 2. Although the child's actions seem to reflect a sort of magical belief in causality without any material contact, his use of the same means to try to achieve different ends indicates that he is on the threshold of intelligence.

Stage 2

Some such pattern characterizes the formation of the first habits, whether they depend directly upon an activity of the subject, as in the foregoing case, or seem to be imposed from the outside, as in the case of "conditionings." A conditioned reflex is never stabilized by the force of its associations alone, but only by the formation of a scheme of assimilation: that is, when the result attained satisfies the need inherent in the assimilation in question (as with Pavlov's dog, which salivates at the sound of the bell as long as this sound is identified with a signal for food, but which ceases to salivate if food no longer follows the signal).

But even if we use "habits"—for lack of a better word—to refer to acquired behavior while it is being formed as well as after it has become automatized, habit is still not the same as intelligence. An elementary "habit" is based on a general sensori-motor scheme within which there is not yet, from the subject's point of view, any differentiation between means and ends. The end in question is attained only by a necessary succession of movements which lead to it, without one's being able to distinguish either an end pursued from the start or means chosen from among various possible schemes. In an act of intelligence, on the other hand, the end is established from the outset and pursued after a search for the appropriate means. These means are furnished by the schemes known to the subject (or "habit" schemes), but they are used to achieve an aim that had its source in a different scheme.

Stage 3

The most interesting aspect of the development of sensori-motor actions during the first year of the child's life is that it not only leads to elementary learning experiences which are the source of simple habits on a level where intelligence, strictly speaking, is not yet observed, but it also provides a continuous series of intermediaries between habitual and intelligent reactions. Thus after the reflex stage (Stage l) and the stage of the first habits (Stage 2), a third stage (Stage 3) introduces the next transitions after the beginning of coordination between vision and prehension—around four and a half months on the average. The baby starts grasping and manipulating everything he sees in his immediate vicinity. For example, a subject of this age catches hold of a cord hanging from the top of his cradle, which has the effect of shaking all the rattles suspended above him. He immediately repeats the gesture a number of times. Each time the interesting result motivates the repetition. This constitutes a "circular reaction" in the sense of J. M. Baldwin, or a new habit in the nascent state, where the result to be obtained is not differentiated from the means employed. Later you need only hang a new toy from the top of the cradle for the child to look for the cord, which constitutes the beginning of a differentiation between means and end. In the days that follow, when you swing an object from a pole two yards from the crib, and even when you produce unexpected and mechanical sounds behind a screen, after these sights or sounds have ceased the child will again look for and pull the magic cord. Although the child's actions seem to reflect a sort of magical belief in causality without any material connection, his use of the same means to try to achieve different ends indicates that he is on the threshold of intelligence.

Stages 4 and 5

In a fourth stage (Stage 4), we observe more complete acts of practical intelligence. The subject sets out to obtain a certain result, independent of the means he is going to employ: for example, obtaining an object that is out of reach or has just disappeared under a piece of cloth or a cushion. The instrumental acts appear only later and they are obviously seen from the outset as means: for example, seizing the hand of an adult and moving it in the direction of the unreachable object, or lifting the screen that masks the hidden object. In the course of this fourth stage, the coordination of means and ends is new and is invented differently in each unforeseen situation (otherwise we would not speak of intelligence), but the means employed are derived only from known schemes of assimilation. (In the case of the object that is hidden and found again, the combination is also new, as we shall see in the next section. But the fact of seizing and moving a cushion corresponds to a habitual scheme.)

In the course of a fifth stage (Stage 5), which makes its appearance around eleven or twelve months, a new ingredient is added to the foregoing behavior: the search for new means by differentiation from schemes already known. An example of this is what we call the "behavior pattern of the support." An object has been placed on a rug out of the child's reach. The child, after trying in vain to reach the object directly, may eventually grasp one corner of the rug (by chance or as a substitute), and then, observing a relationship between the movements of the rug and those of the object, gradually comes to pull the rug in order to reach the object. An analogous discovery characterizes the behavior pattern of the string, studied first by Bühler and then by many others: bringing the objective to oneself by pulling the string to which it is attached.

Stage 6

Finally, a sixth stage marks the end of the sensori-motor period and the transition to the following period. In this stage the child becomes capable of finding new means not only by external or physical groping but also by internalized combinations that culminate in sudden comprehension or *insight*. For example, a child confronted by a slightly open matchbox containing a thimble first tries to open the box by physical groping (reaction of the fifth stage), but upon failing, he presents an altogether new reaction: he stops the action and attentively examines the situation (in the course of this he slowly opens and closes his mouth, or, as another subject did, his hand, as if in imitation of the result to be attained, that is, the enlargement of the opening), after which he suddenly slips his finger into the crack and thus succeeds in opening the box.

It is at this same stage that one generally finds the well-known behavior pattern of the stick, first studied by Köhler in chimpanzees and later by others in the human infant. But Köhler, like Bühler, considers that there is an act of intelligence involved only in cases where there is sudden comprehension. He banishes groping from the domain of intelligence and classifies it with the behavior of substitution, etc. Claparède, on the other hand, saw groping as the criterion of intelligence, attributing the onset of hypotheses to an externalized groping. This criterion is surely too broad, since groping exists as early as the reflex and the formation of habits. But the criterion of *insight* is certainly too narrow, for it is by means of an uninterrupted succession of assimilations on various levels (Stages 1 through 5) that the sensori-motor schemes lead to those new combinations and internalizations that finally make immediate comprehension possible in certain situations. This last level (Stage 6) cannot therefore be separated from the others; it merely marks their completion.

NOTES

1. Ages indicated in this book are always average and approximate.
2. A scheme is the structure or organization of actions as they are transferred or generalized by repetition in similar or analogous circumstances.
3. Jean Piaget, *The Origins of Intelligence in Children* (New York: International Universities Press, 1951; London: Routledge and Kegan Paul, 1953).
4. Similar reflex exercises are observed in animals too, as in the groping that characterizes the first efforts at copulation in Lymnaeae.

3.2 LAWRENCE KOHLBERG

The Child as a Moral Philosopher

The development of the awareness of ethical behavior, or moral development, is an important part of a child's socialization. Psychologists are therefore interested in how an individual acquires moral reasoning. One important theory, based on three levels of moral thinking, was proposed by Lawrence Kohlberg.

Kohlberg (1927–1987) spent a considerable part of his career studying moral development. He is particularly well known for his 1969 book *Stages in the Development of Moral Thought and Action*.

This article, "The Child as a Moral Philosopher," published in 1968 in *Psychology Today*, gives a very readable account of Kohlberg's theory of moral development. In addition to outlining his theory, Kohlberg describes the results of some cross-cultural research that confirm the generality of his data. Note that the original data were collected only on boys. As you read this selection, consider whether the results are applicable to both sexes or only to males.

Key Concept: moral development

*H*ow can one study morality? Current trends in the fields of ethics, linguistics, anthropology and cognitive psychology have suggested a new approach which seems to avoid the morass of semantical confusions, value-bias and cultural relativity in which the psychoanalytic and semantic approaches to morality have foundered. New scholarship in all these fields is now focusing upon structures, forms and relationships that seem to be common to all societies and all languages rather than upon the features that make particular languages or cultures different.

For 12 years, my colleagues and I studied the same group of 75 boys, following their development at three-year intervals from early adolescence through young manhood. At the start of the study, the boys were aged 10 to 16.

We have now followed them through to ages 22 to 28. In addition, I have explored moral development in other cultures—Great Britain, Canada, Taiwan, Mexico and Turkey.

Inspired by Jean Piaget's pioneering effort to apply a structural approach to moral development, I have gradually elaborated over the years of my study a typological scheme describing general structures and forms of moral thought which can be defined independently of the specific content of particular moral decisions or actions.

The typology contains three distinct levels of moral thinking, and within each of these levels distinguishes two related stages. These levels and stages may be considered separate moral philosophies, distinct views of the socio-moral world.

We can speak of the child as having his own morality or series of moralities. Adults seldom listen to children's moralizing. If a child throws back a few adult cliches and behaves himself, most parents—and many anthropologists and psychologists as well—think that the child has adopted or internalized the appropriate parental standards.

Actually, as soon as we talk with children about morality, we find that they have many ways of making judgments which are not "internalized" from the outside, and which do not come in any direct and obvious way from parents, teachers or even peers.

MORAL LEVELS

The *preconventional* level is the first of three levels of moral thinking; the second level is *conventional*, and the third *postconventional* or autonomous. While the preconventional child is often "well-behaved" and is responsive to cultural labels of good and bad, he interprets these labels in terms of their physical consequences (punishment, reward, exchange of favors) or in terms of the physical power of those who enunciate the rules and labels of good and bad.

This level is usually occupied by children aged four to 10, a fact long known to sensitive observers of children. The capacity of "properly behaved" children of this age to engage in cruel behavior when there are holes in the power structure is sometimes noted as tragic (*Lord of the Flies, High Wind in Jamaica*), sometimes as comic (Lucy in *Peanuts*).

The second or *conventional* level also can be described as conformist, but that is perhaps too smug a term. Maintaining the expectations and rules of the individual's family, group or nation is perceived as valuable in its own right. There is a concern not only with *conforming* to the individual's social order but in *maintaining*, supporting and justifying this order.

The *postconventional* level is characterized by a major thrust toward autonomous moral principles which have validity and application apart from authority of the groups or persons who hold them and apart from the individual's identification with those persons or groups.

Within each of these three levels there are two discernible stages. At the preconventional level we have:

Stage 1: Orientation toward punishment and unquestioning deference to superior power. The physical consequences of action regardless of their human meaning or value determine its goodness or badness.

Stage 2: Right action consists of that which instrumentally satisfies one's own needs and occasionally the needs of others. Human relations are viewed in terms like those of the marketplace. Elements of fairness, of reciprocity and equal sharing are present, but they are always interpreted in a physical, pragmatic way. Reciprocity is a matter of "you scratch my back and I'll scratch yours" not of loyalty, gratitude or justice.

And at the conventional level we have:

Stage 3: Good-boy–good-girl orientation. Good behavior is that which pleases or helps others and is approved by them. There is much conformity to stereotypical images of what is majority or "natural" behavior. Behavior is often judged by intention—"he means well" becomes important for the first time, and is overused, as by Charlie Brown in *Peanuts*. One seeks approval by being "nice."

Stage 4: Orientation toward authority, fixed rules and the maintenance of the social order. Right behavior consists of doing one's duty, showing respect for authority and maintaining the given social order for its own sake. One earns respect by performing dutifully.

At the postconventional level, we have:

Stage 5: A social-contract orientation, generally with legalistic and utilitarian overtones. Right action tends to be defined in terms of general rights and in terms of standards which have been critically examined and agreed upon by the whole society. There is a clear awareness of the relativism of personal values and opinions and a corresponding emphasis upon procedural rules for reaching consensus. Aside from what is constitutionally and democratically agreed upon, right or wrong is a matter of personal "values" and "opinion." The result is an emphasis upon the "legal point of view," but with an emphasis upon the possibility of *changing* law in terms of rational considerations of social utility, rather than freezing it in the terms of Stage 4 "law and order." Outside the legal realm, free agreement and contract are the binding elements of obligation. This is the "official" morality of American government, and finds its ground in the thought of the writers of the Constitution.

Stage 6: Orientation toward the decisions of conscience and toward self-chosen *ethical principles* appealing to logical comprehensiveness, universality and consistency. These principles are abstract and ethical (the Golden Rule, the categorical imperative); they are not concrete moral rules like the Ten Commandments. Instead, they are universal principles of *justice*, of the *reciprocity* and *equality* of human rights, and of respect for the dignity of human beings as *individual persons.* . . .

MORAL REASONS

In our research, we have found definite and universal levels of development in moral thought. In our study of 75 American boys from early adolescence on, these youths were presented hypothetical moral dilemmas, all deliberately philosophical, some of them found in medieval works of casuistry.

On the basis of their reasoning about these dilemmas at a given age, each boy's stage of thought could be determined for each of 25 basic moral concepts or aspects. One such aspect, for instance, is "Motive Given for Rule Obedience or Moral Action." In this instance, the six stages look like this:

1. Obey rules to avoid punishment.
2. Conform to obtain rewards, have favors returned, and so on.
3. Conform to avoid disapproval, dislike by others.
4. Conform to avoid censure by legitimate authorities and resultant guilt.
5. Conform to maintain the respect of the impartial spectator judging in terms of community welfare.
6. Conform to avoid self-condemnation.

In another of these 25 moral aspects, the value of human life, the six stages can be defined thus:

1. The value of a human life is confused with the value of physical objects and is based on the social status or physical attributes of its possessor.
2. The value of a human life is seen as instrumental to the satisfaction of the needs of its possessor or of other persons.
3. The value of a human life is based on the empathy and affection of family members and others toward its possessor.
4. Life is conceived as sacred in terms of its place in a categorical moral or religious order of rights and duties.
5. Life is valued both in terms of its relation to community welfare and in terms of life being a universal human right.
6. Belief in the sacredness of human life as representing a universal human value of respect for the individual.

I have called this scheme a typology. This is because about 50 per cent of most people's thinking will be at a single stage, regardless of the moral dilemma involved. We call our types *stages* because they seem to represent an *invariant developmental sequence.* "True" stages come one at a time and always in the same order.

All movement is forward in sequence, and does not skip steps. Children may move through these stages at varying speeds, of course, and may be found half in and half out of a particular stage. An individual may stop at any give stage and at any age, but if he continues to move, he must move in accord with these steps. Moral reasoning of the conventional or Stage 3–4 kind never occurs before the preconventional Stage-1 and Stage-2 thought has taken place. No adult in Stage 4 has gone through Stage 6, but all Stage-6 adults have gone at least through 4.

While the evidence is not complete, my study strongly suggests that moral change fits the stage pattern just described. (The major uncertainty is whether all Stage 6s go through Stage 5 or whether these are two alternate mature orientations.) . . .

ACROSS CULTURES

When I first decided to explore moral development in other cultures, I was told by anthropologist friends that I would have to throw away my culture-bound moral concepts and stories and start from scratch learning a whole new set of values for each new culture. My first try consisted of a brace of villages, one Atayal (Malaysian aboriginal) and the other Taiwanese.

My guide was a young Chinese ethnographer who had written an account of the moral and religious patterns of the Atayal and Taiwanese villages. Taiwanese boys in the 10–13 age group were asked about a story involving theft of food. A man's wife is starving to death but the store owner won't give the man any food unless he can pay, which he can't. Should he break in and steal some food? Why? Many of the boys said, "He should steal the food for his wife because if she dies he'll have to pay for her funeral and that costs a lot."

My guide was amused by these responses, but I was relieved: they were of course "classic" Stage-2 responses. In the Atayal village, funerals weren't such a big thing, so the Stage-2 boys would say, "He should steal the food because he needs his wife to cook for him."

This means that we need to consult our anthropologists to know what content a Stage-2 child will include in his instrumental exchange calculations, or what a Stage-4 adult will identify as the proper social order. But one certainly doesn't have to start from scratch. What made my guide laugh was the difference in form between the children's Stage-2 thought and his own, a difference definable independently of particular cultures. . . .

TRADING UP

In summary, the nature of our sequence is not significantly affected by widely varying social, cultural or religious conditions. The only thing that is affected is the *rate* at which individuals progress through this sequence.

Why should there be such a universal invariant sequence of development? In answering this question, we need first to analyze these developing social concepts in terms of their internal logical structure. At each stage, the same basic moral concept or aspect is defined, but at each higher stage this definition is more differentiated, more integrated and more general or universal. When one's concept of human life moves from Stage 1 to Stage 2 the value of life becomes more differentiated from the value of property, more integrated (the value of life enters an organizational hierarchy where it is "higher" than property so that one steals property in order to save life) and more universalized (the life of any sentient being is valuable regardless of status or property). The same advance is true at each stage in the hierarchy. Each step of development then is a better cognitive organization than the one before it, one which takes account of everything present in the previous stage, but making new distinctions and organizing them into a more comprehensive or more equilibrated structure. The fact that this is the case has been demonstrated by a series of studies indicating that children and adolescents comprehend all stages up to their own, but not more than one stage beyond their own. And importantly, *they prefer this next stage.*

We have conducted experimental moral discussion classes which show that the child at an earlier stage of development tends to move forward when confronted by the views of a child one stage further along. In an argument between a Stage-3 and Stage-4 child, the child in the third stage tends to move toward or into Stage 4, while the Stage-4 child understands but does not accept the arguments of the Stage-3 child.

Moral thought, then, seems to behave like all other kinds of thought. Progress through the moral levels and stages is characterized by increasing differentiation and increasing integration, and hence is the same kind of progress that scientific theory represents. Like acceptable scientific theory—or like *any* theory or structure of knowledge—moral thought may be considered partially to generate its own data as it goes along, or at least to expand so as to contain in a balanced, self-consistent way a wider and wider experiential field. The raw data in the case of our ethical philosophies may be considered as conflicts between roles, or values, or as the social order in which men live.

3.3 HARRY F. HARLOW, MARGARET K. HARLOW, AND STEPHEN J. SUOMI

From Thought to Therapy: Lessons from a Primate Laboratory

Social attachment helps individuals maintain an emotional bond with one another. We now know that the development of attachment during the first year of infancy is important to a person's self-concept and ability to interact successfully with others. However, due to the difficulty in using human infants for research, psychologists had to develop animal models of attachment to study the attachment process. One successful research program was conducted at the University of Wisconsin and is discussed in this selection.

Harry F. Harlow (1905–1981) received his Ph.D. in experimental psychology in 1930 from Stanford University. He began teaching psychology that same year at the University of Wisconsin, where he remained until he retired in 1974. Margaret K. Harlow (d. 1971) received her Ph.D. from the University of Iowa in 1944 and was a professor of educational psychology at the University of Wisconsin. Stephen J. Suomi earned his Ph.D. in developmental psychology from the University of Wisconsin in 1971, where he now teaches. He is also currently with the National Institutes of Health.

This selection, "From Thought to Therapy: Lessons from a Primate Laboratory," published in the *American Scientist* in 1971, gives a glimpse of how one major research program developed—specifically, Harlow et al.'s studies on the learning abilities of rhesus monkeys at the Primate Laboratory in Wisconsin. Note how the various studies tie in to one another, providing a significant overall picture of the research area. Harlow's surrogate mother model for studying attachment in primates has helped psychologists to better understand the role of contact comfort in human attachment formation.

Key Concept: development of attachment

73

A basic maxim of scientific investigation is that significant research directed toward providing an answer for a particular question will inevitably generate a host of new problems awaiting resolution. Rarely is a scientific inquiry germinated and subsequently resolved in a vacuum. The endless effort required to solve any major problem frequently leads to other channels of thought and the creation of new areas of interest—often by chance or almost chance associations.

Multiple illustrative cases substantiating this point have evolved from research carried out over the years at the University of Wisconsin Primate Laboratory. We have never completely forsaken any major research goal once we pursued it, and we are still searching for the end of each and every rainbow—even though we have already found our fair share of research gold.

During the Primate Laboratory's 40 years of existence we have maintained an ongoing research program investigating the learning capability of rhesus monkeys. Learning has been the key directing the creation, not the culmination, of many of our major research efforts. The first of a series of studies stemming from the earlier learning researches determined the effects of lesions in specific cortical regions, including unilateral and bilateral occipital (1), frontal (2), and temporal (3) lobes, on learning task performance. Just as the early lesion research developed from learning, later learning research stemmed from the lesion research. To assess lesion effects we were forced to create more reliable and lucid learning tasks and to develop and standardize them into a battery of tests that covered varied abilities and cortical locations. A natural problem raised then concerned the ontogenetic development (4) of ability to perform these various tests, for we already knew that some tests were so difficult that they could not be solved by monkeys younger than three years, and some were so simple they could be solved by monkeys in the first weeks of life.

To study developing learning abilities in monkeys required a large number of subjects spanning the age range from birth through adolescence, and so we instituted a breeding program and devised means for rearing monkey subjects in the laboratory from birth onward. In order to reduce the incidence of both confounding variables and contagious disease, we separated the babies from their mothers a few hours after birth and raised them in individual cages where they were hand-fed and received human care (5). The infants were provided with cheesecloth diapers to serve as baby blankets, and we noticed that many of the neonates developed such strong attachments to the cheesecloth blanket that it was hard to tell where the diaper ended and the baby began. Furthermore, the monkeys became greatly disturbed when the diapers were removed from their cages for essential sanitary services.

THE SURROGATE MOTHERS

Dirty diapers and distressed infants were produced for some years—an adequate time for insightful learning to occur—before the true significance of the diaper was duly recognized. It is a long way from brains to blankets, but this is the strange, mysterious way in which research programs develop. Many creative ideas have suddenly appeared in a flight of fancy, but the surrogate mother concept appeared during the course of a fancy flight. The cloth surrogate mother was literally born, or perhaps we should say baptized, in 1957 in the belly of a Boeing stratocruiser high over Detroit during a Northwest Airlines champagne flight. . . . The senior author turned to look out the window and saw the cloth surrogate mother sitting in the seat beside him with all her bold and barren charms. The author quickly outlined the researches and drafted part of the text and verses which would form the basis of his American Psychological Association presidential address (6) a year later. The research implications and possibilities seemed to be immediately obvious, and they were subsequently brought to full fruition by three wise men—one of whom was a woman.

The original theoretical problem to be solved by the surrogate mother researches was to measure the relative strength of bodily contact comfort as opposed to satisfaction of nutritional needs, or activities associated with the breast, as motivational forces eliciting love for mother in rhesus neonates. Actually the primary purpose was to continue to dismantle derived drive theory (7). The results of the now famous cloth-mother and wire-mother experiments provided total support for contact comfort as the superordinate variable or motive binding infant to mother. As pictures of baby monkeys clinging contentedly to soft surrogates unfolded across tabloid pages throughout the world, the downfall of primary drive reduction as the predominant theory to account for the development of social attachment was assured. The cloth mother became the first female to attain fame so quickly while still retaining her virginal virtues. There is more than merely milk to human kindness.

On the basis of the diaper data it came as no great surprise to find that monkey infants overwhelmingly preferred nonlactating cloth mothers to lactating wire surrogates. However, during the course of testing infants in novel environments we discovered an unexpected trait possessed by our cloth surrogates: the capacity to instill a sense of basic security and trust in their infants (8). This is the way creative research often arises—sometimes by insight and sometimes by accident. Baby monkeys placed in an unfamiliar playroom devoid of a cloth surrogate, or with a wire surrogate present, typically rolled into tight furry balls, screeching in terror.

When the same infants were placed in the same environment in the presence of cloth surrogate mothers, they initially scurried to the surrogates and clung for dear life. After their first fears abated, the monkeys would then venture away from the surrogates and explore the environment, but often returned to their inanimate mothers for a reassuring clasp or a deep embrace to desensitize fear or alleviate insecurity. This response was predicated upon a psychiatric principle discovered by baby monkeys long before the advent of Watson (9), Wolpe (10), or any of the Skinnerians. Basic trust was the achievement of the first of Erikson's (11) eight human developmental crises, and although basic trust may not be fashioned out of whole cloth, for baby monkeys it apparently can be fashioned from cloth alone.

Subsequently we recognized the obvious truth that no major act of animal behavior is determined by a single variable. To illustrate this axiom we created surrogates of varying form and function, and they disclosed that many variables other than contact comfort possessed more than measurable effects on infant monkey maternal attachment (*12*). These findings led naturally to a series of studies designed to measure all possible variables, regardless of importance, relating to the maternal efficiency of our man-made mothers. The researches disclosed a number of variables secondary in importance to contact comfort. With contact comfort held constant by constructing lactating and non-lactating terry-cloth surrogates, it was possible to demonstrate that nursing, or activities associated with the breast, was a significant variable during the first 90 days of life. Thus, by this ingenious research we learned what had been totally obvious to everyone else, except psychologists, for centuries. Furthermore, rocking surrogates and rocking cribs were preferred to nonrocking surrogates and cribs for about 160 days. Body surfaces other than wire or cloth were also investigated, with predictable results. Satins and silks might be adult symbols of prestige, but they do not warm the infant heart as does terry cloth.

Infant rhesus monkeys preferred a warm wire surrogate to a cool cloth surrogate for the first 15 days of life, illustrating the limited temporal span of some variables and confirming the well-known "hot mama" or "warm woman" hypothesis. Warmth was the only variable to lend even transient preference to the wire surrogate. However, the most striking maternal temperature data were recently obtained by Suomi (*13*), who constructed a cold cloth surrogate with ice water in her veins. Neonatal monkeys tentatively attached to this cold cloth figure, but then retreated to a far corner of the cage, and remained aloof from mother forever. There is only one social affliction worse than an ice-cold wife, and that is an ice-cold mother.

Finally, we compared the efficiency of our man-made mothers with their natural counterparts, and we are convinced that real motherhood is superior and that it is here to stay. The cloth mother may serve milk, but not in the cozy continuous containers provided by the real mother. The real mother eliminates nonnutritional sucking by her infant, whereas no surrogate mother . . . can inhibit nonnutritional sucking. The real monkey mother trains her infant to be a placer, rather than a spreader, of feces (*14*). The real mother trains her infant to comprehend the gestural and vocal communications of other monkeys (*15*), while language learning is beyond surrogate love. The real mother is dynamic and responds to the infant's needs and behavior, but the surrogate can only passively accept. Subsequently the mother plays an active role in separating the infant from her body, which results, probably inadvertently, in the exploration of the surrounding animate and inanimate environment. Finally, and of most importance for future peer adjustment, the real mother is far more efficient than the cloth surrogate in the regulation of early infant play, the primary activity leading to effective age-mate love.

We might have remained imprinted on surrogate mothers forever had it not been for a comment made to the senior author independently by an eminent psychologist and an eminent psychiatrist within a single month. Both said, "You, know, Harry, you are going to go down in the history of psychology

as the father of the cloth mother!" This was too much! In a desperate effort to
escape this fate we branched out into new areas of research . . . : the nature of
normal and natural love of rhesus monkeys. . . .

77

*Harry F.
Harlow et al.*

THE NATURAL NATURE OF LOVE

I enlisted the aid of my wife, and we fell in love, or at least in love with love, in
all its multifaceted forms. Normal and natural love in rhesus monkeys develops through the sequencing and interaction of five major love systems: maternal love; infant love, or love of the infant for the mother; peer love, which other
psychologists and psychoanalysts will someday discover; heterosexual love;
and paternal love.

Maternal love has always been obvious, and even Freud was fully aware
of it. We have already described its social functions. An extremely important
basic function is the management of infant play so that infant monkeys play
together effectively instead of in a disorganized manner. Maternal love serves
as an important antecedent to the development of peer or age-mate love.

The variables underlying the love of the infant for the mother have already been described in the surrogate researches. It is our opinion that a more
important love system, in fact, the most important from the view of the whole
life span, is age-mate love, which develops first through curiosity and exploration and later through multiple forms of play. Peer interactions enhance the
formation of affection for associates, the development of basic social roles, the
inhibition of aggression, and maturation of basic sexuality. We believe heterosexual behavior in primates is another love system, evolving from peer love
very much as peer love evolves from maternal love.

Heterosexual love was not discovered by Freud. Freud became lost in the
libido even before he experienced it, and he never fully learned about love.
Heterosexual love differs in form and function in various animal families.
Beach (16) eventually discovered love in beagles, but so had the beagles. . . .
Heterosexual love in rats and people is planned in different fashions. If you are
a rat, your sex life may be endocrinologically determined, and you will do very
well. However, if you are a primate—monkey, ape, or man—and your heterosexual life is primarily gonadally determined, you face a grim and grave future, and the sooner the grave, the better. Sex without antecedent and
concurrent love is disturbed and disordered (17).

After resolving the nurture and nature of maternal, infant, peer, and heterosexual love, the only thing that remained was paternal love. Having analyzed monkey love as far as we could with our existing facilities, I realized that
we had no love with father, and I dejectedly proclaimed to my wife that,
although paternal love in feral baboons and monkeys had been described, this
love system could not be analyzed and resolved under laboratory restraints. A
month later Margaret Harlow brought me the experimental design for paternal
laboratory love and a plan for the necessary housing facilities. After the rela-

FIGURE 1 *Nuclear Family Living Apparatus*

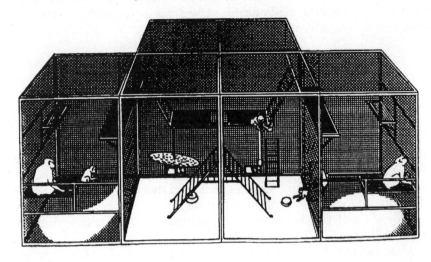

 = 1 Foot

tively simple task of rebuilding the attic over our laboratory had been achieved, the analysis of paternal love was on its way.

THE NUCLEAR FAMILY

The nuclear family apparatus, shown in Figure 1, is a redesigned, redefined, replanned, and magnified playpen apparatus where four pairs of male and female macaques live with their offspring in a condition of blissful monogamy. In the nuclear family apparatus each and every male has physical access to his own female and communicative access to all others. It is obvious from time to time that some males and females would like to have physical access to their neighbors' mates, but their courting must be limited to calls and lip-smacking and visual fixation. Fortunately, they accept their frustration with minimal effects on their mates.

Most important of all, each and every infant has access to every male, and, perhaps because of the cunning and curiosity of all the infants, most nuclear fathers responded socially to most infants. Finally, the apparatus provides unrivaled opportunities to study sibling interactions and friendship formation in infants of similar and disparate ages.

Creation of the nuclear family has provided us with a body of basic information concerning paternal love. The nuclear fathers do not allow mothers, their mates, and neighbors, to abuse or abandon infants, and the fathers serve as a cohesive force guarding the group against predators—primarily experimenters. In addition, the fathers, through some developmental mechanism which we do not yet understand, show affection in varying degrees to all infants. Many fathers engage in reciprocal play with the infants at a level far surpassing that of the mothers, and the fathers ignore aggression from the infants and juveniles, including pinching, biting, and tail- and ear-pulling—behaviors the fathers would never accept from adolescents and adults of either sex.

Preadolescent monkey males, unlike females, exhibit limited interest in all new infants except their siblings until the babies can play. The males largely ignore them, while the female preadolescents continually struggle to make contact with the new babies. The precursors of paternal behavior are present, however, for the older male infants and juveniles cradle, carry, and protect young infants that venture in their path. The watchful eyes of the adults and their ready threats may abet the gentle behavior of the older infants and possibly begin the inculcation of protection of all young. We have still much more to learn about the variables in the development of paternal behavior.

The advent of the second and third infants in the families has disclosed interesting aspects of maternal love and sibling interaction. We had long presumed that the appearance of a second monkey gift from Heaven would exaggerate the mother-infant separative mechanisms long in progress, and that neonatal fairy fingers playing upon the maternal heartstrings would rapidly dissipate the love for the older infant. True to prediction, the immediate reaction of the newly delivered mother to her older infant was negative. She threatened body contact, prevented nipple contact, and cradled the new infant continuously. But every mother eventually reversed this policy toward the older infant. The only individual difference was the interval between the new birth and contact with the older infant, which ranged from 8 hours to a matter of days. Most displaced infants or juveniles spent a night or two without maternal contact, often with their fathers, but one managed to achieve contact with mother the very first night and every night thereafter by persistent approach, cooing and squealing until her mother made room for her too. Although she had a good relationship with her father, she made no attempt to substitute him.

Much to our surprise, the displaced infants did not overtly exhibit punitive signs of jealousy toward the newcomers, probably because of fear of the mother, although one male juvenile did engage in teasing his little sister at every opportunity when mother was not looking. All displaced infants showed disturbance in this situation of denial and despair, of suspicion and separation, and the older infants would spend hours trying to achieve contact comfort, real or symbolic, from the body of the mother—both awake and asleep. Indeed, initial contact was usually made when the mother was sleepy and had reduced her vigilance. In desperation, when this failed, some would enter adjacent living chambers and make overtures to other mothers, who generally accepted their presence but denied them bodily contact. Alternatively, proximity and contact with their fathers were sought when mothers were not available.

In spite of the fact that the nuclear families provided a wealth of new data on the affectional systems, the most striking psychological contribution of the nuclear family has not been to love but to learning.

LONELY LEARNING

For a number of years we had assiduously studied the effects of early environment upon later learning capability, and to achieve this we had always used groups of normal monkeys and groups of socially isolated monkeys. We knew that total social isolation damaged or destroyed the social-sexual capabilities of monkeys, . . . but it did not depress learning ability. Our socially deprived monkeys were reared under conditions of 6, 9, or 12 months of total social isolation, a condition of deprivation or privation so severe that no one will ever impose it upon human children.

Our "normal" monkeys had been reared in partial social isolation. We had recognized the fact that partial social isolation would hardly qualify as a haven or Heaven, but because of limited facilities this is the manner in which we had always reared our normal monkeys. For decades our normal monkeys have achieved learning performances better than those achieved in any other laboratory, owing no doubt to the unusual care we took in adapting them to the test situation.

Finally, S. D. Singh (18), who had had extensive test experience on the Wisconsin General Test Apparatus (WGTA) in the United States and in India, reported that feral animals (reared in forests or in temples) were not intellectually different from each other and were not superior to our monkeys reared in partial social isolation. Furthermore, Singh's test battery was adapted from our own, utilizing discrimination problems which rhesus monkeys are able to solve at 6 months of age, delayed-response tests at 10 months of age, learning-set tasks mastered at 12 months of age, and, later, complex oddity-learning-set tasks which are not efficiently solved by monkeys until 36 months of age. Singh's data gave every indication that partial isolation cages were just as stimulating to intellectual development as were temples and forests.

We had assumed that "enriched" environments were in no way superior to the deprived environments in stimulation and development of the intellectual processes. To demonstrate this, we compared the performance of monkeys reared from birth in the nuclear family apparatus with that of totally socially isolated monkeys and our normal monkeys. Just as predicted, the enormously socially enriched monkeys reared in interacting family groups did no better than deprived monkeys or control monkeys on discrimination tasks, delayed-response tasks, and complex learning-set tasks. My world of happy intellectual isolation was jolted, however, when the socially enriched preadolescents and adolescents, as contrasted with the socially isolated adolescents and controls, proved to be superior at the .001 significance level on our most complex problem-oddity-learning set. Had there been a progressive separation in performance between enriched and deprived monkeys as they traversed through tests of increasing complexity, we would gladly have conceded a difference, but the difference appeared only when the most complicated learning test was administered.

One can only conclude that this enriched early environment, at least, enables monkeys adequately adapted and trained to reach more lofty intellectual performance levels than those attained by deprived monkeys. The basis for the performance difference, however, is by no means established. Superiority could stem from nonintellectual factors as readily as from intellectual differences. The nuclear family animals give every evidence of being the most self-confident, self-assured, fearless animals we have ever tested. They are more relaxed in the test situation than other subjects and could well be more persistent, thus persevering after "normal" subjects give up. This difference would not be apparent on unchallenging tasks, but when the problems become very difficult, the personality factors could operate to produce performance differences. Unfortunately, it is as difficult to test as is the hypothesis that middle-class children excel intellectually over lower-class children because of their environmental advantages. . . .

CONCLUSION

Thus we have traveled from thought to therapy by a route neither straight nor narrow. There have been obstacles and detours, but we have found throughout the years that these are to be cherished, not chastised, as blessings in disguise. . . . Tomorrow there will be new problems, new hopes, and new horizons. Since knowledge is itself forever changing, the search for knowledge never ends.

REFERENCES

1. Harlow, H. F. 1939. Recovery of pattern discrimination in monkeys following unilateral occipital lobectomy. *J. Comp. Psychology* 27:467–89.
2. Harlow, H. F., and T. Spaet. 1943. Problem solution by monkeys following bilateral removal of the prefrontal areas. *J. Experimental Psychology* 33:500–07.
3. Harlow, H. F., R. T. Davis, P. H. Settlage, and D. R. Meyer. 1952. Analysis of frontal and posterior association syndromes in brain-damaged monkeys. *J. Comp. and Physiol. Psychology* 45:419–429.
4. Harlow, H. F. 1959. The development of learning in the rhesus monkey. *Amer. Sci.* 47:459–79.
5. Blomquist, A. J., and H. F. Harlow. 1961. The infant rhesus monkey program at the University of Wisconsin Primate Laboratory. *Proc. Animal Care Panel* 11:57–64.
6. Harlow, H. F. 1958. The nature of love. *Amer. Psychologist* 13:673–85.
7. Harlow, H. F. 1953. Mice, monkeys, men, and motives. *Psychol. Rev.* 60:23–32.
8. Harlow, H. F., and R. R. Zimmermann. 1959. Affectional responses in the infant monkey. *Science* 130:421–32.
9. Watson, J. B. 1924. *Behaviorism.* New York: Norton.
10. Wolpe, J. 1958. *Psychotherapy by Reciprocal Inhibition.* Stanford: Stanford University Press.
11. Erikson, E. H. 1950. *Childhood and Society.* New York: Norton.
12. Furchner, C. S., and H. F. Harlow. 1969. Preference for various surrogate surfaces among infant rhesus monkeys. *Psychonomic Sci.* 17:279–80.
13. Harlow, H. F., and S. J. Suomi. 1970. The nature of love—simplified. *Amer. Psychologist* 25:161–68.
14. Hediger, H. 1955. *Studies of the Psychology and Behaviour of Captive Animals in Zoos and Circuses.* New York: Criterion Books.

15. Miller, R. E., J. V. Murphy, and I. A. Mirsky. 1959. Relevance of facial expression and posture as cues in communication of affection between monkeys. *AMA Arch. General Psychiatry* 1:480–88.

16. Beach, F. A. 1969. Locks and beagles. *Amer. Psychologist* 24:921–49.

17. Harlow, H. F. 1965. Sexual behavior in the rhesus monkey. In F. A. Beach (Ed.), *Sex and Behaviour*. New York: Wiley, pp. 234–65.

18. Singh, S. D. 1969. Urban monkeys. *Scientific American* 24:108–15.

3.4 JANET SHIBLEY HYDE

Children's Understanding of Sexist Language

Sexism in the English language (for example, the use of the pronoun *he* to refer to both sexes) has important implications for our daily lives. However, empirical research on the consequences of this bias has occurred slowly. In examining this problem, psychologists have become interested in how children learn to interpret gender-neutral pronouns, as shown in this selection by Janet Shibley Hyde.

Hyde (b. 1948) received her Ph.D. from the University of California at Berkeley in 1972. She taught at Bowling Green State University and Denison University before going to the University of Wisconsin, where she is currently a professor of psychology. She is interested in gender issues, and she has written several books, including *Half the Human Experience: The Psychology of Women,* 3rd ed. (D.C. Heath, 1985).

This article, "Children's Understanding of Sexist Language," was published in 1984 in the American Psychological Association's journal *Developmental Psychology.* In addition to providing the results of research on how children interpret sexist language, it is a good example of the research article format. Note that in Hyde's experiment, significantly more students wrote a story about females when they were cued beforehand with "he or she" rather than with "he" alone. In a second experiment not included in this selection, Hyde found that when a fictitious, gender-neutral occupation was described, children rated the ability of women to do the job significantly higher when "she" was used than when "he" was used.

Do not worry about Hyde's specific statistical analyses, but remember that a *p* (probability) value that is .05 or smaller is significant (which means that there is a real difference between groups). Psychologists use such statistical techniques to help them generalize from their subjects to a larger population.

Key Concept: children's understanding of sexist language

83

*B*eginning a little more than a decade ago, the feminist movement raised a number of issues, including equal pay for equal work and availability of day care. One of those issues was sexism in language—the notion that the English language contains sex bias, particularly in usages such as "he" and "man" to refer to everyone (e.g., Martyna, 1980).

Concern over sexism in language raises a number of interesting questions for which the psychologist can provide empirical answers. How do people process gender-neutral uses of "he?" How do they interpret that pronoun when they hear or read it? And how does that processing affect other factors such as memory, stereotyping, or attitudes?

Moulton, Robinson, and Elias (1978) conducted an important first empirical study on sex bias in language use. College students were asked to make up a story about a fictional character who fit the following theme: "In a large coeducational institution the average student will feel isolated in ___ introductory courses." One third of the students received the pronoun "his" in the blank, one third received "his or her," and one third received "their." (Some students instead received a sentence concerning personal appearance, but the coeducational-institution cue is most relevant to the present study because it is explicitly gender neutral.) There was a strong tendency for male subjects to write stories about male characters and for female subjects to write about female characters. But strikingly, over all conditions, when the pronoun "his" was used, 35% of the stories were about females, compared with 46% for "their" and 56% female stories for "his or her." Thus, this study demonstrated that, although "his" may be gender-neutral in a grammatical sense, it is not gender neutral in a psychological sense. Even when the rest of the sentence explicitly provides a gender-neutral context, subjects more often think of a male when the pronoun is "his." . . .

In theoretical accounts and empirical investigations of gender-role development, the roles of imitation and reinforcements (Bandura & Walters, 1963; Mischel, 1966) and level of cognitive development (Kohlberg, 1966) have received great attention. In contrast, the role of language in gender-role development has been virtually ignored. The foregoing studies of adults raise some important questions for the developmental psychologist. How do children process sexist language, specifically gender-neutral "he?" Does their processing change with age, and does it differ from adults' processing? Is language a contributor to gender-role development, and can it be integrated into theories of gender-role development? . . .

A more complete statement of the cognitive approach is Bem's Gender Schema Theory (1981; see also Martin & Halverson, 1981). Bem argued that children learn a gender schema, a set of associations linked with maleness and femaleness in our society. This schema in turn organizes perception and affects the processing of information. Sex typing occurs because the self-concept becomes assimilated to the gender schema. Her studies with college students provided evidence consistent with the processing of information according to a gender schema, based on measures of clustering in free-recall and reaction times. Although she provided no data for children, she cited two studies, the results of which are consistent with the existence of gender-schematic processing in children as early as 6 years of age (Kail & Levine, 1976; Liben & Signorella, 1980). Martin and Halverson (1983) have also demonstrated, with 5- and 6-year-olds, that children distort information in sex-inconsistent pictures to make them sex consistent, a result that is congruent with the Gender Schema Theory. According to Bem, there are numerous inputs into the formation of the gender schema, and one of these is language, although she did not pursue this point empirically.

Two lines of thought, then—concern over sexist language as a social issue and a concern for a theoretical understanding of inputs into gender-role development—combine to raise a number of questions. How do children, compared with adults, process sexist language, specifically gender-neutral "he?" What is the effect on children of the use of gender-neutral "he"—does it contribute to the sex-typing process? Does it contribute to stereotyping, for example, stereotyping of occupations? Does it affect the formation of the gender schema? If so, what specific aspects of the gender schema might be affected—stereotyping of occupations, or perhaps more diffuse aspects, such as the relative status attached to the male and female roles, or the relative status of the self as a male or female?

The purpose of Experiment 1 was to replicate the Moulton et al. study with college students, and to extend it to first, third, and fifth graders, to assess age differences in responses to gender-neutral "he." Several other tasks were included in order to gain a more complete understanding of the nature of the responses. A fill-in task was used, and subjects were questioned for their understanding of the grammatical rule underlying the use of gender-neutral "he."

EXPERIMENT 1

Method

Subjects   A total of 310 subjects participated: 60 first graders (23 boys, 37 girls, 5–8* to 7–8, M = 6–7), 67 third graders (34 boys, 33 girls, 7–8 to 10–2, M = 8–11), 59 fifth graders (26 boys, 33 girls, 9–8 to 12–0, M = 10–10), and 124 college students (57 men, 67 women, 17–11 to 21–9, M = 19–3). College students participated in order to fulfill the requirements for introductory psychology. The parents of all elementary subjects had returned signed consent forms for their children to participate. The elementary school children were drawn from three elementary schools, two middle-class, the other working-class to lower class.

Procedure   All elementary school children were interviewed individually, half by a male interviewer, half by a female.

*[Age 5–8 means 5 years, 8 months.—Ed.]

Stories. After a brief warm up, the interviewer said "I'm going to tell you a little bit about a kid, and then I want you to make up a story about that child and tell it to me, and I'll write it down. When a kid goes to school, ___ often feels excited on the first day." One third of the subjects received "he" for the blank, one third "they" and one third "he or she." The cue sentence was designed as an age-appropriate parallel to the neutral sentence used by Moulton et al. The interviewers recorded the basic content of the story, including the character's name. Later in the interview (at the end of the correct-sentences task), subjects were explicitly asked "Is (name of their character) a boy or a girl? Why did you make up your story about a ___?"

Fill-in sentences. Next, children were questioned in several ways to determine their understanding of gender-neutral masculine pronoun use. First they were asked to complete a fill-in-the-blank task. In each case, the interviewer read the following sentences (or allowed the child to read it if he or she wanted to and was able):

1. If a kid likes candy, ___ might eat too much.
2. Most parents want ___ kids to get good grades.
3. When a kid plays football, ___ likes to play with friends.
4. When a kid learns to read, ___ can do more at school.

Correct sentences. Children were then asked to correct sentences with pronouns. They were told, "Now I'm going to read you some sentences and I want you to tell me if they're right or wrong, and if they're wrong, what's wrong with them. For example, if I say 'he goed to the store,' would that be right or wrong? Why?"

1. When a baby starts to walk ___ often falls down. Right or wrong? Why?
2. Usually a kid wants to be just like ___ own parents. Right or wrong? Why?
3. The average kid learns to read before ___ can write. Right or wrong? Why?
4. The average kid likes to play football with ___ friends. Right or wrong? Why?

Each child randomly received one of the following four pronouns replacing the blank: his (or he), they (or their), he or she (or his or her), or her (she).

Rule knowledge. Subjects were asked "When you use 'he' in a sentence, does it always mean it's a boy? For example, when I say 'When a kid goes to school, he often feels excited on the first day,' does that mean the kid is a boy?" If the child answered no, then he or she was asked what it did mean.

College students. College students were tested in groups using a printed form. The form said:

Your task is to make up a story creating a fictional character who fits the following theme. Please do not write about yourself.

In a large coeducational institution the average student will feel isolated in ___ introductory courses.

87

Janet Shibley
Hyde

One third received "his" for the blank, one third "his or her," and one third "their."

When subjects had completed the task, they were told to turn the papers over and answer the following questions briefly:

> When a person uses "he" or "his" in a sentence, does it always mean it's a male? For example, if I say "In a large coeducational institution the average student will feel isolated in his introductory courses," does that mean that the student is a male? If your answer is no, then what does the "he" or "his" mean?

Results

Sex of Character in Story   The results, tabulated as percentage of stories written about female characters, are shown in Figure 1. The data were analyzed using a four-way chi-square* (Sex of Subject × Sex of Character in Story × Pronoun × Grade). Following the recommendation of Everitt (1977) the first test carried out was for the mutual independence of all four variables (or equivalently, whether sex of subject, pronoun, and grade showed a three-way interaction in affecting the dependent variable, sex of character). The results were highly significant, $x^2(40, N = 310) = 95.36$, $p < .001$ [N = number of subjects; p = probability that results were not due to random chance]. Once this test was significant, other specific hypotheses of interest could be tested (Everitt, 1977). In particular, the main effect [that is, examining one variable at a time,] for sex of subject was significant, $x^2(1, N = 310) = 35.54$, $p < .001$, with males overall telling 8% of their stories about females and females telling 38% female stories. The main effect for pronoun was also significant, $x^2(2, N = 310) = 28.81$, $p < .001$. When the pronoun was "he" or "his," overall 12% of the stories were about females; when it was "they" or "their," 18% were female, and when the pronoun was "his" or "her" ("he" or "she"), 42% of the stories were about females. The main effect of grade level was not significant, $x^2(3, N = 310) = 5.34$, although it must be remembered that grade level interacted significantly with sex of subject and pronoun as noted above. The nature of this interaction can be seen in Figure 1. Note that not a single first-grade boy told a story about a female. Third-grade boys produced no female stories when the pronoun was "he" or "they," but nearly 30% of their stories were about females in response to "his" or "her."

Correct Sentences   Overall, children (the correct-sentences task was not given to college students) judged most sentences to be correct (76%). Sentences with "he" inserted were judged wrong 19% of the time, whereas sentences with "she" were judged wrong 28% of the time. The children's judgments

---

*[Chi-square is a statistical test.—Ed.]

FIGURE 1 *Percentage of Stories About Female Characters Written Under the "His," "Their," and "His or Her" Pronoun Conditions, for Male and Female Subjects at the Three Grade Levels*

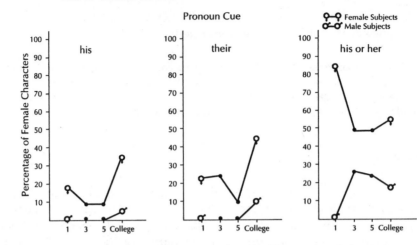

interacted with the sex typing of the sentence. For example, in the sentence about football, "he" was judged wrong 6% of the time, but "she" was judged wrong 39% of the time. This effect in turn showed age trends. "She" in the football sentence was judged wrong by 18% of the first graders and by 67% of the fifth graders. . . .

Fill-In Sentences . . . At all grade levels, the great majority of children supplied "he" or "his" in the sentences, with the exception of Sentence 2, in which "their" was correct, and was correctly supplied. In the remaining three singular sentences, the sex typing of the sentence was varied, "candy" being gender-neutral, "football" masculine, and "read" feminine. In fact, "he" was supplied so uniformly and frequently that the sex typing of the sentence had little impact. The most important sentence is the first, in which the cue is explicitly gender neutral (referring to candy), yet 72% of first graders, 88% of third graders, and 76% of fifth graders provided the pronoun "he" for the blank.

Rule Knowledge Knowledge of the rule that, in gender-neutral contexts, "he" refers to both males and females was tested by asking "When you use 'he' in a sentence, does it always mean it's a boy? For example, when I say 'when a kid goes to school, he often feels excited on the first day,' does that mean the kid is a boy?" If the subject responded "no" and indicated that it could be a boy or girl, the subject was scored as knowing the rule. Knowledge of the rule increased with age: 28% of first graders, 32% of third graders, 42% of fifth graders, and 84% of college students gave responses indicating they knew the rule. An additional 6% of college students gave "feminist" responses indicating that they knew the rule but disagreed with it—for example, "Yes, he refers to males, so one should use 'he or she' to be clear that everyone is included." . . .

Discussion

In general, the results from the college students in Experiment 1 replicate those of Moulton et al. (1978), although with even lower percentages of female stories (39% in Moulton et al.'s study vs. 30% in the present study). As Moulton et al. found, females are more likely to write stories about female characters than males are. The pronoun "his" yielded the lowest percentage of female stories, and "his or her" yielded the highest percentage. If "his" were gender neutral in a psychological sense, then approximately 50% of stories would be about females, yet college students created only 21% of their stories about females in response to "his." Thus the conclusion from the present data is the same as the conclusion of Moulton et al. (1978): "His" is not gender neutral in a psychological sense.

The data for the children are equally striking. The tendency for first, third, and fifth graders to create male characters when the pronoun is "he" is even stronger than it is for college students. Only 7% of elementary school children's stories were about females when the pronoun was "he." . . .

The strong tendency for children to tell stories about male characters in response to the "he" cue becomes more understandable when one looks at the data on the children's knowledge of the grammatical rule. Few know the rule and the majority apparently believe that "he" always means the person is a male.

The data from the fill-in task indicate that elementary school children, and particularly third and fifth graders, have already learned to supply "he" in a singular, gender-neutral context, although the correct-sentences task indicates that they cannot articulate why they do so. The results of the fill-in task are quite similar to those of Martyna (1978) with college students completing sentences. . . .

Therefore, it seems reasonable to conclude that (a) the majority of elementary school children have learned to supply "he" in gender-neutral contexts, and (b) the majority of elementary school children do not know the rule that "he" in gender-neutral contents refers to both males and females, and have a strong tendency to think of males in creating stories from "he" cues. The chain of concepts for them, then, is that (a) the typical person is a "he"; and (b) "he" refers only to males. Logically then, might they not conclude (c) the typical person is a male?

We know that by first grade, girls have less self-confidence and lower expectations for success than do boys (Block, 1976; Crandall, 1969, 1978). A speculation as to one of the causes of that phenomenon arises from the present studies, namely that language may be a contributor. That is, if first graders routinely use "he" to refer to everyone without knowing the grammatical rule behind the use, might they not begin to attach greater status and normativeness to the male, and correspondingly devalue the female? If Bem (1981) is correct that self-concept is assimilated to the gender schema, could low self-confidence in females be related to aspects of the gender schema that have been shaped by sexist language? These are important questions deserving research. . . .

In summary, it is clear that the tendency for subjects to think of males when they hear "he" in a gender-neutral context (story-telling data) is present from first grade through the college years. . . . The contributions of language to sex role development are deserving of considerably more attention, both theoretical and empirically. We must find out how children think about sexist language and other gender-related features of language, and how these features influence the developing gender schema.

REFERENCES

Bandura, A., & Walters, R. H. (1963). *Social learning and personality development.* New York: Holt, Rinehart & Winston.

Bem, S. L. (1981). Gender schema theory: A cognitive account of sex typing. *Psychological Review, 88.* 354–364.

Block, J. H. (1976). Issues, problems, and pitfalls in assessing sex differences: A critical review of *The Psychology of Sex Differences. Merrill-Palmer Quarterly, 22,* 283–308.

Crandall, V. C. (1969). Sex differences in expectancy of intellectual and academic reinforcement. In C. P. Smith (Ed.), *Achievement related motives in children.* New York: Russell Sage.

Crandall, V. C. (1978, August). *Expecting sex differences and sex differences in expectancies: A developmental analysis.* Paper presented at the meeting of the American Psychological Association, Toronto.

Everitt, B. S. (1977). *The analysis of contingency tables.* London: Chapman and Hall.

Kail, R. V., & Levine, L. E. (1976). Encoding processes and sex-role preferences. *Journal of Experimental Child Psychology, 21,* 256–263.

Kohlberg, L. (1966). A cognitive-developmental analysis of children's sex-role concepts and attitudes. In E. E. Maccoby (Ed.), *The development of sex differences* (pp. 82–172). Stanford, CA: Stanford University Press.

Liben, L. S., & Signorella, M. L. (1980). Gender-related schemata and constructive memory in children. *Child Development, 51,* 11–18.

Martin, C. L., & Halverson, C. F. (1981). A schematic processing model of sex-typing and stereotyping in children. *Child Development, 52,* 1119–1134.

Martin, C. L., & Halverson, C. F. (1983). The effects of sex-typing schemas on young children's memory. *Child Development, 54,* 563–574.

Martyna, W. (1978, Winter). What does "he" mean? Use of the generic masculine. *Journal of Communication, 28,* 131–138.

Martyna, W. (1980). Beyond the "he/man" approach: The case for nonsexist language. *Signs, 5,* 482–493.

Mischel, W. (1966). A social-learning view of sex differences in behavior. In E. E. Maccoby (Ed.), *The development of sex differences.* Stanford, CA: Stanford University Press.

Moulton, J., Robinson, G. M., & Elias, C. (1978). Psychology in action: Sex bias in language use: "Neutral" pronouns that aren't. *American Psychologist, 33,* 1032–1036.

PART TWO

Perceptual Processes

CHAPTER 4 Sensation and Perception

4.1 ELEANOR J. GIBSON AND RICHARD D. WALK

The "Visual Cliff"

Vision is an important sense for humans, and psychologists believe that knowledge of how visual perception develops in infants can help us understand its role in a child's adjustment. Psychologists have also shown interest in depth perception (the ability to perceive distance to an object) because it can shed light on the importance of heredity and environment in human development. Experimental psychologists Eleanor J. Gibson and Richard D. Walk developed the "visual cliff" described in this selection to study depth perception in human infants and young animals.

Gibson (b. 1919) earned her Ph.D. in experimental psychology from Yale University in 1938. She spent much of her professional career at Cornell University studying perception. Walk (b. 1920) received his Ph.D. in experimental psychology from Harvard University in 1951. He taught psychology at George Washington University until his retirement in 1991.

This selection, "The 'Visual Cliff,'" was published in *Scientific American* in 1960. The "visual cliff" that Gibson and Walk devised allowed them to test depth perception in infants as soon as they could crawl. As you read this article, consider the degree to which heredity and experience might determine depth perception. Also, why do you think the experimenters tested animals in addition to humans?

Key Concept: the "visual cliff" and depth perception

93

*H*uman infants at the creeping and toddling stage are notoriously prone to falls from more or less high places. They must be kept from going over the brink by side panels on their cribs, gates on stairways and the vigilance of adults. As their muscular coordination matures they begin to avoid such accidents on their own. Common sense might suggest that the child learns to recognize falling-off places by experience—that is, by falling and hurting himself. But is experience really the teacher? Or is the ability to perceive and avoid a brink part of the child's original endowment?

Answers to these questions will throw light on the genesis of space perception in general. Height perception is a special case of distance perception: information in the light reaching the eye provides stimuli that can be utilized for the discrimination both of depth and or receding distance on the level. At what stage of development can an animal respond effectively to these stimuli? Does the onset of such response vary with animals of different species and habitats?

At Cornell University we have been investigating these problems by means of a simple experimental setup that we call a visual cliff. The cliff is a simulated one and hence makes it possible not only to control the optical and other stimuli (auditory and tactual, for instance) but also to protect the experimental subjects. It consists of a board laid across a large sheet of heavy glass which is supported a foot or more above the floor. On one side of the board a sheet of patterned material is placed flush against the undersurface of the glass, giving the glass the appearance as well as the substance of solidity. On the other side a sheet of the same material is laid upon the floor; this side of the board thus becomes the visual cliff.

We tested 36 infants ranging in age from six months to 14 months on the visual cliff. Each child was placed upon the center board, and his mother called him to her from the cliff side and the shallow side successively. All of the 27 infants who moved off the board crawled out on the shallow side at least once; only three of them crept off the brink onto the glass suspended above the pattern on the floor. Many of the infants crawled away from the mother when she called to them from the cliff side; others cried when she stood there, because they could not come to her without crossing an apparent chasm. The experiment thus demonstrated that most human infants can discriminate depth as soon as they can crawl.

The behavior of the children in this situation gave clear evidence of their dependence on vision. Often they would peer down through the glass on the deep side and then back away. Others would pat the glass with their hands, yet despite this tactual assurance of solidity would refuse to cross. It was equally clear that their perception of depth had matured more rapidly than had their locomotor abilities. Many supported themselves on the glass over the deep side as they maneuvered awkwardly on the board; some even backed out onto the glass as they started toward the mother on the shallow side. Were it not for the glass some of the children would have fallen off the board. Evidently infants should not be left close to a brink, no matter how well they may discriminate depth.

*Eleanor J.
Gibson and
Richard D. Walk*

This experiment does not prove that the human infant's perception and avoidance of the cliff are innate. Such an interpretation is supported, however, by the experiments with nonhuman infants. On the visual cliff we have observed the behavior of chicks, turtles, rats, lambs, kids, pigs, kittens and dogs. These animals showed various reactions, each of which proved to be characteristic of their species. In each case the reaction is plainly related to the role of vision in the survival of the species, and the varied patterns of behavior suggest something about the role of vision in evolution.

In the chick, for example, depth perception manifests itself with special rapidity. At an age of less than 24 hours the chick can be tested on the visual cliff. It never makes a "mistake" and always hops off the board on the shallow side. Without doubt this finding is related to the fact that the chick, unlike many other young birds, must scratch for itself a few hours after it is hatched.

Kids and lambs, like chicks, can be tested on the visual cliff as soon as they can stand. The response of these animals is equally predictable. No goat or lamb ever stepped onto the glass of the deep side, even at one day of age. When one of these animals was placed upon the glass on the deep side, it displayed characteristic stereotyped behavior. It would refuse to put its feet down and would back up into a posture of defense, its front legs rigid and its hind legs limp. In this state of immobility it could be pushed forward across the glass until its head and field of vision crossed the edge of the surrounding solid surface, whereupon it would relax and spring forward upon the surface.

At the Cornell Behavior Farm a group of experimenters has carried these experiments with kids and goats a step further. They fixed the patterned material to a sheet of plywood and were thus able to adjust the "depth" of the deep side. With the pattern held immediately beneath the glass, the animal would move about the glass freely. With the optical floor dropped more than a foot below the glass, the animal would immediately freeze into its defense posture. Despite repeated experience of the tactual solidity of the glass, the animals never learned to function without optical support. Their sense of security or danger continued to depend upon the visual cues that give them their perception of depth.

The rat, in contrast, does not depend predominantly upon visual cues. Its nocturnal habits lead it to seek food largely by smell, when moving about in the dark, it responds to tactual cues from the stiff whiskers (vibrissae) on its snout. Hooded rats tested on the visual cliff show little preference for the shallow side so long as they can feel the glass with their vibrissae. Placed upon the glass over the deep side, they move about normally. But when we raise the center board several inches, so that the glass is out of reach of their whiskers, they evince good visual depth-discrimination: 95 to 100 per cent of them descend on the shallow side.

Cats, like rats, are nocturnal animals, sensitive to tactual cues from their vibrissae. But the cat, as a predator, must rely more strongly on its sight. Kittens proved to have excellent depth-discrimination. At four weeks—about the earliest age that a kitten can move about with any facility—they invariably choose the shallow side of the cliff. On the glass over the deep side, they either freeze or circle aimlessly backward until they reach the center board.

The animals that showed the poorest performance in our series were the turtles. The late Robert M. Yerkes of Harvard University found in 1904 that aquatic turtles have somewhat poorer depth-discrimination than land turtles. On the visual cliff one might expect an aquatic turtle to respond to the reflections from the glass as it might to water and so prefer the deep side. They showed no such preference: 76 per cent of the aquatic turtles crawled off the board on the shallow side. The relatively large minority that choose the deep side suggests either that this turtle has poorer depth-discrimination than other animals, or that its natural habitat gives it less occasion to "fear" a fall.

All of these observations square with what is known about the life history and ecological niche of each of the animals tested. The survival of a species requires that its members develop discrimination of depth by the time they take up independent locomotion, whether at one day (the chick and the goat), three to four weeks (the rat and the cat) or six to 10 months (the human infant). That such a vital capacity does not depend on possibly fatal accidents of learning in the lives of individuals is consistent with evolutionary theory.

To make sure that no hidden bias was concealed in the design of the visual cliff we conducted a number of control experiments. In one of them we eliminated reflections from the glass by lighting the patterned surfaces from below the glass (to accomplish this we dropped the pattern below the glass on both sides, but more on one side than on the other). The animals—hooded rats—still consistently chose the shallow side. As a test of the role of the patterned surface we replaced it on either side of the centerboard with a homogeneous gray surface. Confronted with this choice, the rats showed no preference for either the shallow or the deep side. We also eliminated the optical difference between the two sides of the board by placing the patterned surface directly against the undersurface of the glass on each side. The rats then descended without preference to either side. When we lowered the pattern 10 inches below the glass on each side, they stayed on the board.

We set out next to determine which of two visual cues plays the decisive role in depth perception. To an eye above the center board the optical pattern on the two sides differs in at least two important respects. On the deep side distance decreases the size and spacing of the pattern elements projected on the retina. "Motion parallax," on the other hand, causes the pattern elements on the shallow side to move more rapidly across the field of vision when the animal moves its head, just as nearby objects seen from a moving car appear to pass by more quickly than distant ones. To eliminate the potential distance cue provided by pattern density we increased the size and spacing of the pattern elements on the deep side in proportion to its distance from the eye. With only the cue of motion parallax to guide them, adult rats still preferred the shallow side, though not so strongly as in the standard experiment. Infant rats chose the shallow side nearly 100 per cent of the time under both conditions, as did day-old chicks. Evidently both species can discriminate depth by differential motion alone, with no aid from texture density and probably little help from other cues. The perception of distance by binocular parallax, which doubtless plays an important part in human behavior, would not seem to have a significant role, for example, in the depth perception of chicks and rats.

Eleanor J. Gibson and Richard D. Walk

To eliminate the cue of motion parallax we placed the patterned material directly against the glass on either side of the board but used smaller and more densely spaced pattern-elements on the cliff side. Both young and adult hooded rats preferred the side with the larger pattern, which evidently "signified" a nearer surface. Day-old chicks, however, showed no preference for the larger pattern. It may be that learning plays some part in the preference exhibited by the rats, since the young rats were tested at a somewhat older age than the chicks. This supposition is supported by the results of our experiments with animals reared in the dark.

The effects of early experience and of such deprivations as dark-rearing represent important clues to the relative roles of maturation and learning in animal behavior. The first experiments along this line were performed by K. S. Lashley and James T. Russell at the University of Chicago in 1934. They tested light-reared and dark-reared rats on a "jumping stand" from which they induced animals to leap toward a platform placed at varying distances. Upon finding that both groups of animals jumped with a force closely correlated with distance, they concluded that depth perception in rats is innate. Other investigators have pointed out, however, that the dark-reared rats required a certain amount of "pretraining" in the light before they could be made to jump. Since the visual-cliff technique requires no pretraining, we employed it to test groups of light-reared and dark-reared hooded rats. At the age of 90 days both groups showed the same preference for the shallow side of the apparatus, confirming Lashley's and Russell's conclusion.

Recalling our findings in the young rat, we then took up the question of whether the dark-reared rats relied upon motion parallax or upon contrast in texture density to discriminate depth. When the animals were confronted with the visual cliff, cued only by motion parallax, they preferred the shallow side, as had the light-reared animals. When the choice was cued by pattern density, however, they departed from the pattern of the normal animals and showed no significant preference. The behavior of dark-reared rats thus resembles that of the day-old chicks, which also lack visual experience. It seems likely, therefore, that of the two cues only motion parallax is an innate cue for depth discrimination. Responses to differential pattern-density may be learned later.

One cannot automatically extrapolate these results to other species. But experiments with dark-reared kittens indicate that in these animals, too, depth perception matures independently of trial and error learning. In the kitten, however, light is necessary for normal visual maturation. Kittens reared in the dark to the age of 27 days at first crawled or fell off the center board equally often on the deep and shallow sides. Placed upon the glass over the deep side, they did not back in a circle like normal kittens but showed the same behavior that they had exhibited on the shallow side. Other investigators have observed equivalent behavior in dark-reared kittens; they bump into obstacles, lack normal eye movement and appear to "stare" straight ahead. These difficulties pass after a few days in the light. We accordingly tested the kittens every day. By the end of the week they were performing in every respect like normal kittens. They showed the same unanimous preference for the shallow side. Placed upon the glass over the deep side, they balked and circled backward to a visually secure surface. Repeated descents to the deep side, and placement upon the glass during their "blind" period, had not taught them that the deep side was "safe." Instead they avoided it more and more consistently. The initial blindness of dark-reared kittens makes them ideal subjects for studying the maturation of depth perception. With further study it should be possible to determine which cues they respond to first and what kinds of visual experience accelerate or retard the process of maturation.

From our first few years of work with the visual cliff we are ready to venture the rather broad conclusion that a seeing animal will be able to discriminate depth when its locomotion is adequate, even when locomotion begins at birth. But many experiments remain to be done, especially on the role of different cues and on the effects of different kinds of early visual experience.

4.2   ROBERT L. FANTZ

Pattern Vision in Newborn Infants

For many years, psychologists believed that the senses in newborn infants did not function well, partly because they found it impossible to properly test newborns to determine what they could perceive. Over the years, however, new techniques have been developed to measure the sensory capabilities of infants. One pioneer in the field, Robert L. Fantz, developed a technique for studying pattern vision in newborn infants.

Fantz was a psychology professor at Western Reserve University in Cleveland during the 1960s when he studied visual perception in infants. This article, "Pattern Vision in Newborn Infants," was published in *Science* in 1963. The "chamber" (its full name is "looking chamber") Fantz refers to in the article is his own invention. During experimentation with the chamber, visual targets are shown on the ceiling of the chamber, and the eye movements and fixation points of the subject (infant), who is inside the chamber, can be observed through a peephole. Because Fantz had developed a simple design for research, his techniques became useful for other psychologists to learn about visual preference in newborn infants. Since the early studies by Fantz, much more sophisticated procedures have been developed to study infants. As you read this article, consider the implications of providing a stimulating visual environment for newborn infants. Also, why is it important to understand the sensory capabilities of infants?

Key Concept: vision in newborn infants

*A*bstract. *Human infants under 5 days of age consistently looked more at black-and-white patterns than at plain colored surfaces, which indicates the innate ability to perceive form.*

It is usually stated or implied that the infant has little or no pattern vision during the early weeks or even months, because of the need for visual learning or because of the immature state of the eye and brain, or for both reasons (1).

This viewpoint has been challenged by the direct evidence of differential attention given to visual stimuli varying in form or pattern (2). This evidence has shown that during the early months of life, infants: (i) have fairly acute pattern vision (resolving 1/8-inch stripes at a 10-inch distance; (ii) show greater visual interest in patterns than in plain colors; (iii) differentiate among patterns of similar complexity; and (iv) show visual interest in a pattern similar to that of a human face.

The purpose of the present study was to determine whether it was possible to obtain similar data on newborn infants and thus further exclude visual learning or postnatal maturation as requirements for pattern vision. It is a repetition of a study of older infants which compared the visual responsiveness to patterned and to plainly colored surfaces (3). The results of the earlier study were essentially duplicated, giving further support for the above conclusions.

The subjects were 18 infants ranging from 10 hours to 5 days old. They were selected from a much larger number on the basis of their eyes remaining open long enough to be exposed to a series of six targets at least twice. The length of gaze at each target was observed through a tiny hole in the ceiling of the chamber and recorded on a timer. The fixation time started as soon as one or both eyes of the infant were directed towards the target, using as criterion the superposition over the pupil of a tiny corneal reflection of the target; it ended when the eyes turned away or closed. The six targets were presented in random order for each infant, with the sequence repeated up to eight times when possible. Only completed sequences were included in calculating the percentage of total fixation time for each target.

The targets were circular, 6 inches in diameter, and had nonglossy surfaces. Three contained black-and-white patterns—a schematic face, concentric circles, and a section of newspaper containing print 1/16 to 1/4 inch high. The other three were unpatterned—white, fluorescent yellow, and dark red. The relative luminous reflectance was, in decreasing order: yellow, white, newsprint, face and circles, red. Squares containing the patterns or colors were placed in a flat holder which slid horizontally into a slightly recessed portion of the chamber ceiling to expose the pattern or color to the infant through a circular hole in the holder. The chamber and underside of the holder were lined with blue felt to provide a contrasting background for the stimuli, and to diffuse the illumination (between 10 and 15 ft-ca) from lights on either side of the infant's head. The subject was in a small hammock crib with head facing up directly under the targets, 1 foot away.

The results in Table 1 show about twice as much visual attention to patterns as to plainly colored surfaces. Differences in response to the six stimulus objects are significant for the infants both under and over 2 days of age; results from these groups do not differ reliably from each other, and are similar to earlier results from much older infants. The selectivity of the visual responses is brought out still more strikingly by tabulating the longest-fixated target for each newborn infant: 11 for face, 5 for concentric circles, 2 for newsprint, and 0 for white, yellow, and red. For comparison, the first choices of infants 2 to 6 months were distributed as follows: 16, 4, 5, 0, 0, 0.

Three infants under 24 hours could be tested sufficiently to indicate the individual consistency of response. Two of these showed a significant (.005 and

TABLE 1 **101**

Relative Duration of Initial Gaze of Infants at Six Stimulus Objects in Successive and Repeated Presentations

Robert L. Fantz

Age group	N	Mean Percentage of Fixation Time						
		Face	Circles	News	White	Yellow	Red	P*
Under 48 hours	8	29.5	23.5	13.1	12.3	11.5	10.1	.005
2 to 5 days	10	29.5	24.3	17.5	9.9	12.1	6.7	.001
2 to 6 months†	25	34.3	18.4	19.9	8.9	8.2	10.1	.001

*Significance level.
† From an earlier study (2).

.05) difference among the targets in successive sets of exposures, one looking longest at the face pattern in 7 of 8 exposures, the other looking longest at the "bull's-eye" in 3 of 6 exposures. The third infant 10 hours after birth looked longest at the face in 3 of 8 exposures.

It is clear that the selective visual responses were related to pattern rather than hue or reflectance, although the latter two variables are often thought to be primary visual stimuli.... The results do not imply "instinctive recognition" of a face or other unique significance of this pattern; it is likely there are other patterns which would elicit equal or greater attention. Longer fixation of the face suggests only that a pattern with certain similarities to social objects also has stimulus characteristics with considerable intrinsic interest or stimulating value; whatever the mechanism underlying this interest, it should facilitate the development of social responsiveness, since what is responded to must first be attended to.

Substantiation for the visual selection of patterned over unpatterned objects is given in an independent study of newborn infants in which more visual attention was given to a colored card with a simple figure, when held close to the infant, than to a plain card of either color (6).

The results of Table 1 demonstrate that pattern vision can be tested in newborn infants by recording differential visual attention; these and other results call for a revision of traditional views that the visual world of the infant is initially formless or chaotic and that we must learn to see configurations.

REFERENCES AND NOTES

1. See, for example, Evelyn Dewey, *Behavior Development in Infants* (Columbia Univ. Press. New York, 1935).
2. R. L. Fantz, J. M. Ordy, M. S. Udelf, *J. Comp. Physiol. Psychol.* **55,** 907 (1962); R. L. Fantz, *Psychol. Rec.* **8,** 43 (1958).
3. R. L. Fantz, *Sci. Am.* **204,** No. 5, 66 (1961).
4. F. Stirnimann, *Ann. Paediat.* **163,** 1 (1944).

CHAPTER 5 Sleep and Consciousness

5.1 WILLIAM C. DEMENT

Two Kinds of Sleep

Until the early 1950s, researchers did not differentiate between the two major types of sleep: REM (rapid eye movement) and NREM (non–rapid eye movement). Since their discovery, however, these two kinds of sleep have been studied intensely. Because we spend approximately one-third of our lives in this altered state of consciousness, it is important to understand the functions of sleep. William C. Dement, who was the first to use the term *REM,* has been involved in this research effort from the beginning.

Dement (b. 1928) earned his M.D. from the University of Chicago in 1955 and his Ph.D. in physiology in 1957. In 1963, he established the sleep laboratory at Stanford University, where he currently serves as director. Dement founded the publication *Sleep Reviews,* and he has written numerous papers on sleep and dreaming.

This selection is from chapter 2, "Two Kinds of Sleep," of Dement's book *Some Must Watch While Some Must Sleep: Exploring the World of Sleep* (W. W. Norton, 1978). The book presents an inside look at sleep research, and in this chapter, Dement presents the distinctions between REM and NREM sleep and describes what happens during a typical night of sleep. Although tremendous progress in sleep research has been made in recent years and a number of theories have been proposed—in part because of Dement's pioneering work—psychologists still do not know everything about the functions of these two types of sleep. As you read this selection, think about how you might study the functions of sleep.

103

*William C.
Dement*

Key Concept: REM and NREM sleep

*E*arly sleep researchers faced an insurmountable problem: it was almost impossible to study sleep without awakening the sleeper! They tried taking the subject's blood pressure or "gently" prying open his eyelids to see if his pupils were dilated. Obviously it's impossible to study sleep in a subject who has just been rudely awakened. This problem remained unsolved until brain wave techniques became available in the 1930s.

It must have been difficult in those early days to find individuals who were willing to be poked and prodded all night long in the interest of medical science. Many of the early researchers tried to experiment on themselves—but of, course it isn't easy to study sleep while sleeping! . . .

Since contemporary sleep laboratories throughout the world are quite similar to one another, let us use the Stanford University Sleep Laboratory as an example of such facilities. The Stanford lab consists of six bedrooms, all connected to a larger room in which monitoring devices are located. Carpeted and tastefully decorated, the bedrooms are made to seem "like home." In addition, they are soundproof, temperature-controlled, and pitch black when the lights are turned off.

Although the rooms are attractive and the scientific equipment is almost entirely hidden, it is still hard to find volunteers willing to sleep in them. People are reluctant to spend a night or a series of nights away from their homes and their families, to sleep in a strange bed in an unfamiliar setting, and to be observed while they sleep. Consequently, the majority of subjects who volunteer for sleep studies are college students to whom the promise of five or ten dollars a night ("Just to sleep?") is a great incentive.

HOW SLEEP IS MEASURED

In order to identify and classify sleep, it is necessary to record the electrical activity of three systems: the brain, the eyes, and the muscles. These systems are monitored simultaneously by an instrument called the polygraph, which allows measurements to be made continuously throughout the night without disturbing the sleeping subject. Tiny electrodes attached to the scalp and face of the subject convey signals to the polygraph where they are recorded on moving chart paper by pens that move up and down automatically in response to changes in electrical potentials.

The up-and-down movement of the pens and the lateral movement of the paper produces a pattern of waves. These waves are meaningless scribbles to the uninformed observer, but if they are recorded in a standard and conventional manner, a night of sleep can be interpreted accurately by any knowledgeable researcher. In somewhat the manner of the experienced surfer watching ocean waves, the sleep researcher looks for changes in form and frequency of brain waves.

The record of brain activity is called *electroencephalogram* or EEG. The polygraph records the voltage fluctuations between two points on the scalp or, in the case of animals, within the brain itself. The record of eye movements is called an *electrooculogram* or EOG. The eyes are like tiny batteries with a difference of electrical potential between the cornea and the retina. Changes of the electrical field are recorded as transorbital potential differences whenever the eyes move. The record of muscle activity is called an *electromyogram* (EMG). It shows the electrical potentials generated in the muscle fibers.

In routine studies of nocturnal sleep, the subject arrives at the laboratory about an hour before his usual bedtime. He prepares for bed by going through the same bedtime ritual he is accustomed to at home, while the experimenter checks the equipment. When the subject is ready for bed, the experimenter begins the routine application of electrodes. All of this must be completed, and fail-safe, before the subject goes to sleep so it will not be necessary to make adjustments in the middle of the night and therefore disturb the normal sleep pattern. In certain subjects or patients, these recordings are continued around-the-clock for many days, and the subject essentially lives in the laboratory.

The first step in the electrode attachment is a thorough cleansing of the skin or scalp with acetone or alcohol at points where the electrodes are to be placed. Scalp electrodes are attached by means of a cotton or gauze pad soaked in collodion and quick-dried with a flow of compressed air. Surgical tape is used to attach the electrodes to facial regions. When all the electrodes are in place, the wires are brought together into a bundle and anchored to the scalp in a kind of "pony tail," which the subject carries with him when he retires to bed. The experimenter plugs each of the wires into a numbered panel on the headboard, which is connected by cable to a similar panel on the polygraph. By using corresponding numbers, the experimenter can "tune in" the appropriate channels on the polygraph as if it were a television set.

After a final equipment check, the experimenter wishes the subject a good night's sleep, turns off the light, and closes the door as he departs. By the time the subject awakens in the morning—to be greeted by a sleepy-eyed experimenter—nearly one thousand feet of chart paper or magnetic tape will have been traced with a record of brain waves, eye movements, and muscle activity. Although the subject may experience minor discomfort from the electrodes taped to his face, there is no pain involved in sleep recording, and at no time is any current flowing from the polygraph to the subject.

In addition to studying human sleep, we study the sleep effects of various drugs and surgical procedures in cats, rats, hampsters, mice, and monkeys. Although it is often necessary to implant electrodes into the brains of cats, the procedures we use are not painful to the cats. When the study is completed, we are usually able to remove the electrodes and to "rehabilitate" the animals as house pets. Unfortunately, we sometimes experience considerable difficulty finding homes for our "rehabilitated veterans." When this happens, some member of the laboratory staff (occasionally this author) adds one more cat to the household menagerie.

There are people who simply cannot condone any kind of experimentation performed upon animals. I receive a great deal of hate mail, including threats upon my life, from some of these animal lovers. One letter writer warned that he will be stalking me with a high-powered rifle! We believe that some use of animals is necessary to advance our knowledge of normal and pathological states, but I can readily assure the reader that we have never caused an animal to suffer.

THE DISCOVERY OF REM SLEEP

Every day every human being—every mammal, in fact—experiences two kinds of sleep that alternate rhythmically throughout the entire sleep period. These two kinds of sleep are as different from each other as sleep is from wakefulness. If there is a cat or a dog in your household, chances are you have observed the two states of sleep many times. At one moment the sleeping animal seems to be lifeless except for its regular breathing. Then the breathing becomes irregular, paws and whiskers begin to twitch, lips and tongue begin to move—and someone says, "Oh, look at Rover! He's *dreaming*!"

The discovery of the two kinds of sleep occurred almost accidentally at the University of Chicago. In 1952 Dr. [Nathaniel] Kleitman became interested in the slow rolling eye movements that accompany sleep onset and decided to look for these eye movements throughout the night to determine whether they were related to the depth or quality of sleep. Kleitman gave the assignment of watching eye movements to one of his graduate students in the department of physiology, Eugene Aserinsky.

The young student soon noticed an entirely new kind of eye movement. At certain times during the night, the eyes began to dart about furiously beneath the closed lids. These unexpected episodes were startlingly different from the familiar slow, pendular movements that were the original object of the study.

Over the years, many people have asked me, "How can you see the eye moving when the lids are closed?" As a matter of fact, it is very easy to see eye movements when the eyes are closed. Have someone do it and see for yourself. However, Aserinsky was using the polygraph to monitor the subject, and the eye movements were actually discovered on the chart paper. It was not until we directly observed these movements in sleeping subjects that we could believe the spectacular inked-out deviations. It would be difficult today to understand how skeptical we were. These eye movements, which had all the attributes of waking eye movements, had absolutely no business appearing in sleep. In those days, sleep was conceived of as a state of neural depression or inhibition quiescence, rest. It was definitely not a condition in which the brain could be generating highly coordinated eye movements that were, in many instances, faster and sharper than the subject could execute while awake.

This was *the* breakthrough—the discovery that changed the course of sleep research from a relatively pedestrian inquiry into an intensely exciting endeavor pursued with great determination in laboratories and clinics all over the world. And there is nothing more exciting to a researcher than findings that are totally different from what he had expected.

Of course, the change in all our concepts of sleep didn't occur overnight. Having joined the research effort at this point as a sophomore medical student under Kleitman, I began to record the electroencephalograph and other physiological variables, along with eye movement activity. Since I didn't know what to expect, I kept my eyes glued to the moving chart paper all night long. After many nights, certain definite relationships were discernible in the enormous amounts of data. Rapid eye movements were always accompanied by very distinctive brain wave patterns, a change in breathing, and other striking departures from the normal, quiet sleep pattern. In addition, what we now call the basic ninety-minute sleep pattern began to emerge from the night-to-night variability.

As more and more physiological changes were discovered and described, we realized that sleep was not a quiet resting state that continued without variance as long as the subject was fortunate enough to remain asleep. No. For the first time we realized what has probably been true of man's sleep since he crawled out of the primordial slime. Man has two kinds of sleep. His nocturnal solitude contains two entirely different phenomena.

REM AND NREM SLEEP

I coined the term "REM" (for rapid-eye-movement) sleep to define the phenomenon my colleagues and I had observed. The other kind of sleep eventually acquired the name "NREM" (pronounced non-REM) sleep.

Most of the changes typically associated with falling asleep are the consequence of reclining and relaxing. Cardiac and respiratory rates will decrease, body temperature will fall, blood pressure will decline, and metabolic activity will drop. If we continue to lie still and relax, we may fall asleep without the occurrence of any further changes.

The NREM state is often called "quiet sleep" because of the slow, regular breathing, the general absence of body movement, and the slow, regular brain activity shown in the EEG. It is important to remember that the body is not paralyzed during NREM sleep; it *can* move, but it *does not* move because the brain doesn't order it to move. The sleeper has lost contact with his environment. There is a shut-down of perception because the five senses are no longer gathering information and communicating stimuli to the brain. When gross body movements (such as rolling over) occur during NREM, the EEG suggests a transient intrusion of wakefulness—yet the individual may not be responsive at the time, nor recall having moved if subsequently awakened. In one respect the term "quiet sleep" is a misnomer: it is mostly during NREM sleep that snoring occurs.

REM sleep, which has been called "active sleep," is an entirely different state of existence. At the onset of REM sleep, the sleeper's body is still immobile, but we can see small, convulsive twitches of his face and fingertips. His snoring ceases, and his breathing becomes irregular—very fast, then slow—he may even appear to stop breathing for several seconds. Under the eyelids the corneal bulges of his eyes dart around, back and forth. If we gently pull back the eyelids, the subject seems to be actually looking at something. Cerebral blood flow and brain temperature soar to new heights, but the large muscles of the body are completely paralyzed; arms, legs, and trunk cannot move. Throbbing penile erections occur in adult—and newborn—males.

There is some speculation that REM sleep is not really sleep at all, but a state in which the subject is awake, but paralyzed and hallucinating. (Some evidence for this point of view exists in narcolepsy. . . .)

All of the short-lived events or bursts of activity that occur *within* the periods of REM sleep—individual eye movements, muscle twitches, and so forth—are collectively called phasic activity. This includes short-lived contractions of the middle ear muscles that occur in sleep only during the REM state. These contractions are identical with middle ear muscle activity seen in wakefulness as a response to various intensities and pitches of sound. . . .

All of these discoveries are helping to bring the mystery of REM sleep—and maybe even the fantasy of dreams—out of the shadowy dusk of speculation and into the clear bright light of observable phenomena. Sometimes it seems a shame, to anyone who believes that mystery and fantasy enrich our lives. Nonetheless, a researcher is obliged to state the facts—to describe phenomena in terms of what we know. Speaking in such a strict manner with regard to REM sleep, I can only say: "It's there. It looks the way I've described it." We just don't know yet, despite twenty years of intensive research, *why* it's there. In many ways, REM periods resemble epileptic seizures. Perhaps they are equally useful.

COURSE OF EVENTS DURING THE NIGHT

Frequently associated with the reverie of sleep onset is a feeling of floating or falling, which often terminates abruptly in a jerk returning us to wakefulness. Such starts, called myoclonias, generally occur only during the first five minutes of sleep and are a normal occurrence, seemingly more prevalent in "nervous" people. On some occasions the myoclonia may be an arousal response to a very weak, insignificant external stimulus.

Even with an EEG reading it is impossible to pinpoint the exact instant of sleep onset. The essential difference between wakefulness and sleep is the loss of awareness. Sleep onset occurs at the exact instant when a meaningful stimulus fails to elicit its accustomed response. . . .

A dramatic illustration of the nature of sleep onset has been obtained in the laboratory through the use of visual stimuli. A sleepy subject lies in bed with his eyes taped open (which can be achieved, believe it or not, with relatively little discomfort). A very bright strobe light is placed about six inches in front of his face and is flashed into his eyes at the rate of about once every second or two. A microswitch is taped to his finger, which he is instructed to press every time he sees a flash. A simple task. How can he possibly avoid seeing the flash? The subject will press and press. Suddenly he stops. If we immediately ask why, he will be surprised. The light exploded right into his widely open eyes, yet he was totally unaware. In one second, he was awake, seeing, hearing, responding—in the very next second, he was functionally blind and asleep.

At the moment when visual perception ceases, the eyes begin to drift slowly from side to side either synchronously or asynchronously. This slow rolling of the eyes is one of the most reliable signs of the onset of sleep. The first sleep of the night is always NREM sleep, which must progress through its various stages before the first REM period occurs. Along with the slowly rolling eye movements, we see a gradual transition in the pattern of EEG waves from the characteristic rhythm of wakefulness to the NREM Stage I configuration.

What follows is a progressive descent from Stage I into other stages of NREM sleep. The term "descent" is meant to imply a progression along the depth-of-sleep continuum as sleep becomes deeper and deeper, the sleeper becomes more remote from the environment, and increasingly more potent stimuli are necessary to cause arousal.

Each new stage is announced by its own characteristic pattern in the EEG. After only a few minutes of Stage I, the onset of Stage 2 is established by the appearance of spindling and K complexes. Several minutes later the slow delta waves of Stage 3 become apparent. After about ten minutes of this stage, the delta activity becomes more and more predominant and signals the presence of Stage 4. At this point it is extremely difficult to awaken the sleeper. A child in this stage of sleep is virtually unreachable and may take several minutes to return to full awareness if he can be aroused at all. It is during this period that sleeptalking, sleepwalking, night terrors, and bed-wetting are initiated in young children.

In Stage 4, thirty or forty minutes following sleep onset, a series of body movements heralds the start of a re-ascent through the stages of NREM sleep. Approximately seventy or eighty minutes from the onset of sleep the Stage I EEG pattern occurs again. But now there are sawtooth waves in the EEG, rapid eye movements in the EOG, a suppression of activity in the EMG, and a host of other physiological changes. The first REM period has begun. It will last about ten minutes.

Throughout the night this cyclic variation between NREM and REM sleep continues. The NREM-REM cycle varies from seventy to 110 minutes but averages around ninety minutes. In the early part of the night, sleep is dominated by the NREM state, particularly Stages 3 and 4, but as the night wears on, REM sleep periods become progressively longer, sometimes as long as sixty minutes, and the interspersed NREM sleep is almost entirely Stage 2.

An adult who sleeps seven and one-half hours each night generally spends one and one-half to two hours in REM sleep. Since people who are awakened during REM periods usually recall a dream, it can be said that we dream roughly every ninety minutes all night long. After offering us several short episodes early in the night, the brain may produce an hour-long "feature film." . . .

109

*William C.
Dement*

ONTOGENY

One of the most remarkable aspects of REM sleep is the very large amount that is present in most mammals immediately after birth. In the newborn human baby who sleeps an average of sixteen to eighteen hours per day, at least 50 percent of all this sleep (eight to nine hours!) is occupied by REM periods. People invariably ask, "What can they be dreaming about in all that time?" The occurrence of so much REM sleep in newborn infants will raise some difficult questions about the relationship of REM sleep, rapid eye movements, and dreaming. . . .

In premature infants of thirty-two to thirty-six weeks gestation, the percent of REM sleep is even higher, around 75 percent of the total amount of sleep. This finding suggests that there is a phase in the early intrauterine life of the child when REM sleep is the all-encompassing mode of existence.

After birth, the amount of REM sleep declines gradually and reaches the level of about 25 percent of the total sleep time at around five years of age. From age five to adulthood, Stage 4 patterns are at their peak.

In some animals, the predominance of REM sleep in early life is even more spectacular. For example, in the newborn kitten, REM sleep is the *only* sleep. This is also true of the newborn puppy, rat, and hamster. On the other hand, the newborn guinea pig has very little REM sleep.

Because of the extraordinary amount of REM sleep in infants and our difficulty in demonstrating the purpose of REM sleep in adults, we cannot help wondering if the real function of REM sleep is fulfilled early in life. Perhaps REM sleep is necessary for the normal pre- and post-natal maturation of the brain. This fits with the guinea pig data because this animal is "mature" at birth.

The Dream as a Wish-Fulfilment

If you sleep eight hours per night, you spend approximately two of those hours dreaming. People have always been fascinated with dreams, and many have proposed theories to explain the functions and meaning of dreams. The most popular and well known dream theory was proposed by Sigmund Freud in 1900. Freud believed that dreams were the road to the elusive unconscious mind. His theory of dreams as wish fulfillments, which is examined in this selection, has sparked a great deal of controversy over the years.

Freud (1856–1939), a neurologist, received his M.D. in 1881 from Vienna University. He spent most of his life in Vienna, Austria, practicing medicine and studying mental disorders through clinical observation. As the father of psychoanalysis, Freud significantly influenced many areas of psychology, including personality, development, and clinical psychology.

In Freud's book *The Interpretation of Dreams* (1900), he presents his theory of the meaning of dreams. This selection is from chapter 3, "The Dream as a Wish-Fulfilment," of that book, and it illustrates one of the main points of Freud's dream theory. This selection allows you to see how Freud conceptualized dream interpretation as well as psychoanalysis. As you read this chapter, think about how you interpret your own dreams.

Key Concept: Freud's theory of dreaming

When, after passing through a narrow defile, one suddenly reaches a height beyond which the ways part and a rich prospect lies outspread in different directions, it is well to stop for a moment and consider whither one shall turn next. We are in somewhat the same position after we have mastered this first interpretation of a dream. We find ourselves standing in the light of a sudden discovery. The dream is not comparable to the irregular sounds of a musical instrument, which, instead of being played by the hand of a musician, is struck by some external force; the dream is not meaningless, not absurd, does not presuppose that one part of our store of ideas is dormant while another part begins to awake. It is a perfectly valid psychic phenomenon, actually a wish-fulfilment; it may be enrolled in the continuity of the intelligible psychic activities of the waking state; it is built up by a highly complicated intellectual activity. But at the very moment when we are about to rejoice in this discovery a host of problems besets us. If the dream, as this theory defines it, represents a fulfilled wish, what is the cause of the striking and unfamiliar manner in which this fulfilment is expressed? What transformation has occurred in our dream-thoughts before the manifest dream, as we remember it on waking, shapes itself out of them? How has this transformation taken place? Whence comes the material that is worked up into the dream? What causes many of the peculiarities which are to be observed in our dream-thoughts; for example, how is it that they are able to contradict one another? . . . Is the dream capable of teaching us something new concerning our internal psychic processes, and can its content correct opinions which we have held during the day? I suggest that for the present all these problems be laid aside, and that a single path be pursued. We have found that the dream represents a wish as fulfilled. Our next purpose should be to ascertain whether this is a general characteristic of dreams, or whether it is only the accidental content of [a] particular dream . . . ; for even if we conclude that every dream has a meaning and psychic value, we must nevertheless allow for the possibility that this meaning may not be the same in every dream. The first dream . . . [may be] the fulfilment of a wish; another may turn out to be the realization of an apprehension; a third may have a reflection as its content; a fourth may simply reproduce a reminiscence. Are there, then, dreams other than wish-dreams; or are there none but wish-dreams?

It is easy to show that the wish-fulfilment in dreams is often undisguised and easy to recognize, so that one may wonder why the language of dreams has not long since been understood. There is, for example, a dream which I can evoke as often as I please, experimentally, as it were. If, in the evening, I eat anchovies, olives, or other strongly salted foods, I am thirsty at night, and therefore I wake. The waking, however, is preceded by a dream, which has always the same content, namely, that I am drinking. I am drinking long draughts of water; it tastes as delicious as only a cool drink can taste when one's throat is parched; and then I wake, and find that I have an actual desire to drink. The cause of this dream is thirst, which I perceive when I wake. From this sensation arises the wish to drink, and the dream shows me this wish as fulfilled. It hereby serves a function, the nature of which I soon surmise. I sleep well, and am not accustomed to being waked by a bodily need. If I succeed in appeasing my thirst by means of the dream that I am drinking, I need not wake up in order to satisfy that thirst. It is thus a *dream of convenience*. The dream takes the place of action, as elsewhere in life. Unfortunately, the need of water to quench the thirst cannot be satisfied by a dream, as can my thirst for revenge upon [some adversary], but the intention is the same. Not long ago I had the same dream in a somewhat modified form. On this occasion I felt thirsty before going to bed, and emptied the glass of water which stood on the little chest beside my bed. Some hours later, during the night, my thirst returned, with the consequent discomfort. In order to obtain water, I should have had to get up and fetch the glass which stood on my wife's bed-table. I thus quite appropriately dreamt that my wife was giving me a drink from a vase; this vase was an Etruscan cinerary urn, which I had brought home from Italy, and had since given away. But the water in it tasted so salty (apparently on account of the ashes) that I was forced to wake. It may be observed how conveniently the dream is capable of arranging matters. Since the fulfilment of a wish is its only purpose, it may be perfectly egoistic. Love of comfort is really not compatible with consideration for others. The introduction of the cinerary urn is probably once again the fulfilment of a wish; I regret that I no longer possess this vase; it, like the glass of water at my wife's side, is inaccessible to me. The cinerary urn is appropriate also in connection with the sensation of an increasingly salty taste, which I know will compel me to wake.

Such convenience-dreams came very frequently to me in my youth. Accustomed as I had always been to working until late at night, early waking was always a matter of difficulty. I used then to dream that I was out of bed and standing at the washstand. After a while I could no longer shut out the knowledge that I was not yet up; but in the meantime I had continued to sleep. The same sort of lethargy-dream was dreamed by a young colleague of mine, who appears to share my propensity for sleep. With him it assumed a particularly amusing form. The landlady with whom he was lodging in the neighbourhood of the hospital had strict orders to wake him every morning at a given hour, but she found it by no means easy to carry out his orders. One morning sleep was especially sweet to him. The woman called into his room: "Herr Pepi, get up; you've got to go to the hospital." Whereupon the sleeper dreamt of a room in the hospital, of a bed in which he was lying, and of a chart pinned over his head, which read as follows: "Pepi M., medical student, 22 years of age." He told himself in the dream: "If I am already at the hospital, I don't have to go there," turned over, and slept on. He had thus frankly admitted to himself his motive for dreaming.

Here is yet another dream of which the stimulus was active during sleep: One of my women patients, who had been obliged to undergo an unsuccessful operation on the jaw, was instructed by her physicians to wear by day and night a cooling apparatus on the affected cheek; but she was in the habit of throwing it off as soon as she had fallen asleep. One day I was asked to reprove her from doing so; she had again thrown the apparatus on the floor. The patient defended herself as follows: "This time I really couldn't help it; it was the result of a dream which I had during the night. In the dream I was in a box at the opera, and was taking a lively interest in the performance. But Herr Karl Meyer was lying in the sanatorium and complaining pitifully on account of pains in his jaw. I said to myself, 'Since I haven't the pains, I don't need the apparatus either'; that's why I threw it away." The dream of this poor sufferer reminds me of an expression which comes to our lips when we are in a disagreeable situation: "Well, I can imagine more amusing things!" The dream presents these "more amusing things!" Herr Karl Meyer, to whom the dreamer attributed her pains, was the most casual acquaintance of whom she could think.

It is quite as simple a matter to discover the wish-fulfilment in several other dreams which I have collected from healthy persons. A friend who was acquainted with my theory of dreams, and had explained it to his wife, said to me one day: "My wife asked me to tell you that she dreamt yesterday that she was having her menses. You will know what that means." Of course I know: if the young wife dreams that she is having her menses, the menses have stopped. I can well imagine that she would have liked to enjoy her freedom a little longer, before the discomforts of maternity began. It was a clever way of giving notice of her first pregnancy. Another friend writes that his wife had dreamt not long ago that she noticed milk-stains on the front of her blouse. This also is an indication of pregnancy, but not of the first one; the young mother hoped she would have more nourishment for the second child than she had for the first.

A young woman who for weeks had been cut off from all society because she was nursing a child who was suffering from an infectious disease dreamt, after the child had recovered, of a company of people in which Alphonse Daudet, Paul Bourget, Marcel Prévost and others were present; they were all very pleasant to her and amused her enormously. In her dream these different authors had the features which their portraits give them. M. Prévost, with whose portrait she is not familiar, looked like the man who had disinfected the sickroom the day before, the first outsider to enter it for a long time. Obviously the dream is to be translated thus: "It is about time now for something more entertaining than this eternal nursing."

Perhaps this collection will suffice to prove that frequently, and under the most complex conditions, dreams may be noted which can be understood only as wish-fulfilments, and which present their content without concealment. In most cases these are short and simple dreams, and they stand in pleasant contrast to the confused and overloaded dream-compositions which have almost exclusively attracted the attention of the writers on the subject. But it will repay us if we give some time to the examination of these simple dreams. The simplest dreams of all are, I suppose, to be expected in the case of children whose psychic activities are certainly less complicated than those of adults. Child psychology, in my opinion, is destined to render the same services to the psychology of adults as a study of the structure or development of the lower animals renders to the investigation of the structure of the higher orders of animals. Hitherto but few deliberate efforts have been made to make use of the psychology of the child for such a purpose.

The dreams of little children are often simple fulfilments of wishes, and for this reason are, as compared with the dreams of adults, by no means interesting. They present no problem to be solved, but they are invaluable as affording proof that the dream, in its inmost essence, is the fulfilment of a wish. I have been able to collect several examples of such dreams from the material furnished by my own children.

For two dreams, one that of a daughter of mine, at that time eight and a half years of age, and the other that of a boy of five and a quarter, I am indebted to an excursion to Hallstatt, in the summer of 1896. I must first explain that we were living that summer on a hill near Aussee, from which, when the weather was fine, we enjoyed a splendid view of the Dachstein. With a telescope we could easily distinguish the Simony hut. The children often tried to see it through the telescope—I do not know with what success. Before the excursion I had told the children that Hallstatt lay at the foot of the Dachstein. They looked forward to the outing with the greatest delight. From Hallstatt we entered the valley of Eschern, which enchanted the children with its constantly changing scenery. One of them, however, the boy of five, gradually became discontented. As often as a mountain came into view, he would ask: "Is that the Dachstein?" whereupon I had to reply: "No, only a foot-hill." After this question had been repeated several times he fell quite silent, and did not wish to accompany us up the steps leading to the waterfall. I thought he was tired. But the next morning he came to me, perfectly happy, and said: "Last night I dreamt that we went to the Simony hut." I understood him now; he had expected, when I spoke of the Dachstein, that on our excursion to Hallstatt he would climb the mountain, and would see at close quarters the hut which had been so often mentioned when the telescope was used. When he learned that he was expected to content himself with foot-hills and a waterfall he was disappointed, and became discontented. But the dream compensated him for all this. I tried to learn some details of the dream; they were scanty. "You go up steps for six hours," as he had been told.

On this excursion the girl of eight and a half had likewise cherished wishes which had to be satisfied by a dream. We had taken with us to Hallstatt our neighbour's twelve-year-old boy; quite a polished little gentleman, who, it seemed to me, had already won the little woman's sympathies. Next morning she related the following dream: "Just think, I dreamt that Emil was one of the family, that he said 'papa' and 'mamma' to you, and slept at our house, in the big room, like one of the boys. Then mamma came into the room and threw a handful of big bars of chocolate, wrapped in blue and green paper, under our beds." The girl's brothers, who evidently had not inherited an understanding of dream-interpretation, declared . . . : "That dream is nonsense." The girl defended at least one part of the dream, and from the standpoint of the theory of the neuroses it is interesting to learn which part it was that she defended: "That Emil was one of the family was nonsense, but that part about the bars of chocolate wasn't." It was just this latter part that was obscure to me, until my wife furnished the explanation. On the way home from the railway-station the children had stopped in front of a slot-machine, and had wanted exactly such bars of chocolate, wrapped in paper with a metallic lustre, such as the machine, in their experience, provided. But the mother thought, and rightly so, that the day had brought them enough wish-fulfilments, and therefore left this wish to be satisfied in the dream. This little scene had escaped me. That portion of the dream which had been condemned by my daughter I understood without any difficulty. I myself had heard the well-behaved little guest enjoining the children, as they were walking ahead of us, to wait until 'papa' or 'mamma' had come up. For the little girl the dream turned this temporary relationship into a permanent adoption. Her affection could not as yet conceive of any other way of enjoying her friend's company permanently than the adoption pictured in her dream, which was suggested by her brothers. Why the bars of chocolate were thrown under the bed could not, of course, be explained without questioning the child.

From a friend I have learned of a dream very much like that of my little boy. It was dreamed by a little girl of eight. Her father, accompanied by several children, had started on a walk to Dornbach, with the intention of visiting the Rohrer hut, but had turned back, as it was growing late, promising the children to take them some other time. On the way back they passed a signpost which pointed to the Hameau. The children now asked him to take them to the Hameau, but once more, and for the same reason, they had to be content with the promise that they should go there some other day. Next morning the little girl went to her father and told him, with a satisfied air: "Papa, I dreamed last night that you were with us at the Rohrer hut, and on the Hameau." Thus, in the dream her impatience had anticipated the fulfilment of the promise made by her father.

Another dream, with which the picturesque beauty of the Aussee inspired my daughter, at that time three and a quarter years of age, is equally straightforward. The little girl had crossed the lake for the first time, and the trip has passed too quickly for her. She did not want to leave the boat at the landing, and cried bitterly. The next morning she told us: "Last night I was sailing on the lake." Let us hope that the duration of this dream-voyage was more satisfactory to her.

My eldest boy, at that time eight years of age, was already dreaming of the realization of his fancies. He had ridden in a chariot with Achilles, with Diomedes as charioteer. On the previous day he had shown a lively interest in a book on the myths of Greece which had been given to his elder sister.

If it can be admitted that the talking of children in their sleep belongs to the sphere of dreams, I can relate the following as one of the earliest dreams in my collection: My youngest daughter, at that time nineteen months old, vomited one morning, and was therefore kept without food all day. During the night she was heard to call excitedly in her sleep: "Anna F(r)eud, *st'awbewy, wild st'awbewy, om'lette, pap!*" She used her name in this way in order to express the act of appropriation; the menu presumably included everything that would seem to her a desirable meal; the fact that two varieties of strawberry appeared in it was a demonstration against the sanitary regulations of the household, and was based on the circumstance, which she had by no means overlooked, that the nurse had ascribed her indisposition to an over-plentiful consumption of strawberries; so in her dream she avenged herself for this opinion which met with her disapproval.

When we call childhood happy because it does not yet know sexual desire, we must not forget what a fruitful source of disappointment and renunciation, and therefore of dream-stimulation, the other great vital impulse may be for the child. Here is a second example. My nephew, twenty-two months of age, had been instructed to congratulate me on my birthday, and to give me a present of a small basket of cherries, which at that time of the year were scarce, being hardly in season. He seemed to find the task a difficult one, for he repeated again and again: "Cherries in it," and could not be induced to let the little basket go out of his hands. But he knew how to indemnify himself. He had, until then, been in the habit of telling his mother every morning that he had dreamt of the "white soldier," an officer of the guard in a white cloak, whom he had once admired in the street. On the day after the sacrifice on my birthday he woke up joyfully with the announcement, which could have referred only to a dream: *"He[r] man eaten all the cherries!"*

What animals dream of I do not know. A proverb for which I am indebted to one of my pupils professes to tell us, for it asks the question: "What does the goose dream of?" and answers: "Of maize." The whole theory that the dream is the fulfilment of a wish is contained in these two sentences.

We now perceive that we should have reached our theory of the hidden meaning of dreams by the shortest route had we merely consulted the vernacular. Proverbial wisdom, it is true, often speaks contemptuously enough of dreams—it apparently seeks to justify the scientists when it says that "dreams are bubbles"; but in colloquial language the dream is predominantly the gracious fulfiller of wishes. "I should never have imagined that in my wildest dreams," we exclaim in delight if we find that the reality surpasses our expectations.

PART THREE

Learning and Cognitive Processes

CHAPTER 6 Learning

6.1 JOHN B. WATSON AND ROSALIE RAYNER

Conditioned Emotional Reactions

The desire of early researchers to apply the techniques of classical and operant conditioning—two forms of behavioral learning involving stimulus association and reinforcement—to understand practical problems led to John B. Watson's well-known Little Albert experiment, which is discussed in this selection. This classic experiment of how Albert learned to fear a white rat—and other furry or rat-like stimuli—has been a favorite of students and instructors alike.

Watson (1878–1958), the founder of the school of behaviorism, received his Ph.D. from the University of Chicago in 1903, where he taught for five years before moving to the Johns Hopkins University. Rosalie Rayner (d. 1935), the coauthor of this selection, was an assistant in the psychology laboratory during the Little Albert experiment. Eventually, Rayner and Watson were married.

This selection, "Conditioned Emotional Reactions," was published in the *Journal of Experimental Psychology* in 1920. Although the Little Albert experiment was originally intended as a pilot study and had some methodological flaws, it serves as a classic example of how conditioning can modify behavior. Watson and Rayner describe explicitly the procedures they used and the results they obtained. Unfortunately, Albert's mother removed him from the hospital after the experiment was conducted; hence, the experimenters could not develop a technique to remove the conditioned fear reaction from him. As you read this selection, try to remember how you learned to fear certain events as you were growing up.

Key Concept: conditioned emotional reactions in infants

*I*n recent literature various speculations have been entered into concerning the possibility of conditioning various types of emotional response, but direct experimental evidence in support of such a view has been lacking. If the theory advanced by Watson and Morgan to the effect that in infancy the original emotional reaction patterns are few, consisting so far as observed of fear, rage and love, then there must be some simple method by means of which the range of stimuli which can call out these emotions and their compounds is greatly increased. Otherwise, complexity in adult response could not be accounted for. These authors without adequate experimental evidence advanced the view that this range was increased by means of conditioned reflex factors. It was suggested there that the early home life of the child furnishes a laboratory situation for establishing conditioned emotional responses. The present authors have recently put the whole matter to an experimental test.

Experimental work has been done so far on only one child, Albert B. This infant was reared almost from birth in a hospital environment; his mother was a wet nurse in the Harriet Lane Home for Invalid Children. Albert's life was normal: he was healthy from birth and one of the best developed youngsters ever brought to the hospital, weighing twenty-one pounds at nine months of age. He was on the whole stolid and unemotional. His stability was one of the principal reasons for using him as a subject in this test. We felt that we could do him relatively little harm by carrying out such experiments as those outlined below.

At approximately nine months of age we ran him through the emotional tests that have become a part of our regular routine in determining whether fear reactions can be called out by other stimuli than sharp noises and the sudden removal of support. . . . In brief, the infant was confronted suddenly and for the first time successively with a white rat, a rabbit, a dog, a monkey, with masks with and without hair, cotton wool, burning newspapers, etc. A permanent record of Albert's reactions to these objects and situations has been preserved in a motion picture study. Manipulation was the most usual reaction called out. *At no time did this infant ever show fear in any situation.* These experimental records were confirmed by the casual observations of the mother and hospital attendants. No one had ever seen him in a state of fear and rage. The infant practically never cried.

Up to approximately nine months of age we had not tested him with loud sounds. The test to determine whether a fear reaction could be called out by a loud sound was made when he was eight months, twenty-six days of age. The sound was that made by striking a hammer upon a suspended steel bar four feet in length and three-fourths of an inch in diameter. The laboratory notes are as follows:

*John B. Watson
and Rosalie
Rayner*

One of the two experimenters caused the child to turn its head and fixate her moving hand; the other, stationed back of the child, struck the steel bar a sharp blow. The child started violently, his breathing was checked and the arms were raised in a characteristic manner. On the second stimulation the same thing occurred, and in addition the lips began to pucker and tremble. On the third stimulation the child broke into a sudden crying fit. This is the first time an emotional situation in the laboratory has produced any fear or even crying in Albert.

We had expected just these results on account of our work with other infants brought up under similar conditions. It is worth while to call attention to the fact that removal of support (dropping and jerking the blanket upon which the infant was lying) was tried exhaustively upon this infant on the same occasion. It was not effective in producing the fear response. This stimulus is effective in younger children. At what age such stimuli lose their potency in producing fear is not known. Nor is it known whether less placid children ever lose their fear of them. This probably depends upon the training the child gets. It is well known that children eagerly run to be tossed into the air and caught. On the other hand it is equally well known that in the adult fear responses are called out quite clearly by the sudden removal of support, if the individual is walking across a bridge, walking out upon a beam, etc. There is a wide field of study here which is aside from our present point.

The sound stimulus, thus, at nine months of age, gives us the means of testing several important factors. I. Can we condition fear of an animal, *e.g.*, a white rat, by visually presenting it and simultaneously striking a steel bar? II. If such a conditioned emotional response can be established, will there be a transfer to other animals or other objects? . . .

I. The establishment of conditioned emotional responses. At first there was considerable hesitation upon our part in making the attempt to set up fear reactions experimentally. A certain responsibility attaches to such a procedure. We decided finally to make the attempt, comforting ourselves by the reflection that such attachments would arise anyway as soon as the child left the sheltered environment of the nursery for the rough and tumble of the home. We did not begin this work until Albert was eleven months, three days of age. Before attempting to set up a conditioned response we, as before, put him through all of the regular emotional tests. *Not the slightest sign of a fear response was obtained in any situation.*

The steps taken to condition emotional responses are shown in our laboratory notes.

11 Months 3 Days

1. White rat suddenly taken from the basket and presented to Albert. He began to reach for rat with left hand. Just as his hand touched the animal the bar was struck immediately behind his head. The infant

jumped violently and fell forward, burying his face in the mattress. He did not cry, however.

2. Just as the right hand touched the rat the bar was again struck. Again the infant jumped violently, fell forward and began to whimper.

In order not to disturb the child too seriously no further tests were given for one week.

11 Months 10 Days

1. Rat presented suddenly without sound. There was steady fixation but no tendency at first to reach for it. The rat was then placed nearer, whereupon tentative reaching movements began with the right hand. When the rat nosed the infant's left hand, the hand was immediately withdrawn. He started to reach for the head of the animal with the forefinger of the left hand, but withdrew it suddenly before contact. It is thus seen that the two joint stimulations given the previous week were not without effect. He was tested with his blocks immediately afterwards to see if they shared in the process of conditioning. He began immediately to pick them up, dropping them, pounding them, etc. In the remainder of the tests the blocks were given frequently to quiet him and to test his general emotional state. They were always removed from sight when the process of conditioning was under way.

2. Joint stimulation with rat and sound. Started, then fell over immediately to right side. No crying.

3. Joint stimulation. Fell to right side and rested upon hands, with head turned away from rat. No crying.

4. Joint stimulation. Same reaction.

5. Rat suddenly presented alone. Puckered face, whimpered and withdrew body sharply to the left.

6. Joint stimulation. Fell over immediately to right side and began to whimper.

7. Joint stimulation. Started violently and cried, but did not fall over.

8. Rat alone. *The instant the rat was shown the baby began to cry. Almost instantly he turned sharply to the left, fell over on left side, raised himself on all fours and began to crawl away so rapidly that he was caught with difficulty before reaching the edge of the table.*

This was as convincing a case of a completely conditioned fear response as could have been theoretically pictured. In all seven joint stimulations were given to bring about the complete reaction. It is not unlikely had the sound been of greater intensity or of a more complex clang character that the number of joint stimulations might have been materially reduced. Experiments designed to define the nature of the sounds that will serve best as emotional stimuli are under way.

II. When a conditioned emotional response has been established for one object, is there a transfer? Five days later Albert was again brought back into the laboratory and tested as follows:

John B. Watson and Rosalie Rayner

11 Months 15 Days

1. Tested first with blocks. He reached readily for them, playing with them as usual. This shows that there has been no general transfer to the room, table, blocks, etc.
2. Rat alone. Whimpered immediately, withdrew right hand and turned head and trunk away.
3. Blocks again offered. Played readily with them, smiling and gurgling.
4. Rat alone. Leaned over to the left side as far away from the rat as possible, then fell over, getting up on all fours and scurrying away as rapidly as possible.
5. Blocks again offered. Reached immediately for them, smiling and laughing as before.
   The above preliminary test shows that the conditioned response to the rat had carried over completely for the five days in which no tests were given. The question as to whether or not there is a transfer was next taken up.
6. Rabbit alone. The rabbit was suddenly placed on the mattress in front of him. The reaction was pronounced. Negative responses began at once. He leaned as far away from the animal as possible, whimpered, then burst into tears. When the rabbit was placed in contact with him he buried his face in the mattress, then got up on all fours and crawled away, crying as he went. This was a most convincing test.
7. The blocks were next given him, after an interval. He played with them as before. It was observed by four people that he played far more energetically with them than ever before. The blocks were raised high over his head and slammed down with a great deal of force.
8. Dog alone. The dog did not produce as violent a reaction as the rabbit. The moment fixation occurred the child shrank back and as the animal came nearer he attempted to get on all fours but did not cry at first. As soon as the dog passed out of his range of vision he became quiet. The dog was then made to approach the infant's head (he was lying down at the moment). Albert straightened up immediately, fell over to the opposite side and turned his head away. He then began to cry.
9. The blocks were again presented. He began immediately to play with them.
10. Fur coat (seal). Withdrew immediately to the left side and began to fret. Coat put close to him on the left side, he turned immediately, began to cry and tried to crawl away on all fours.
11. Cotton wool. The wool was presented in a paper package. At the end the cotton was not covered by the paper. It was placed first on his feet. He kicked it away but did not touch it with his hands. When his hand was laid on the wool he immediately withdrew it but did not show the

shock that the animals or fur coat produced in him. He then began to play with the paper, avoiding contact with the wool itself. He finally, under the impulse of the manipulative instinct, lost some of his negativism to the wool.

12. Just in play W. put his head down to see if Albert would play with his hair. Albert was completely negative. Two other observers did the same thing. He began immediately to play with their hair. W. then brought the Santa Claus mask and presented it to Albert. He was again pronouncedly negative. . . .

From the above results it would seem that emotional transfers do take place. Furthermore it would seem that the number of transfers resulting from an experimentally produced conditioned emotional reaction may be very large. In our observations we had no means of testing the complete number of transfers which may have resulted. . . .

INCIDENTAL OBSERVATIONS

(a) Thumb sucking as a compensatory device for blocking fear and noxious stimuli. During the course of these experiments, . . . it was noticed that whenever Albert was on the verge of tears or emotionally upset generally he would continually thrust his thumb into his mouth. The moment the hand reached the mouth he became impervious to the stimuli producing fear. Again and again while the motion pictures were being made at the end of the thirty-day rest period, we had to remove the thumb from his mouth before the conditioned response could be obtained. This method of blocking noxious and emotional stimuli (fear and rage) through erogenous stimulation seems to persist from birth onward. . . .

(b) Equal primacy of fear, love and possibly rage. While in general the results of our experiment offer no particular points of conflict with Freudian concepts, one fact out of harmony with them should be emphasized. According to proper Freudians sex (or in our terminology, love) is the principal emotion in which conditioned responses arise which later limit and distort personality. We wish to take sharp issue with this view on the basis of the experimental evidence we have gathered. Fear is as primal a factor as love in influencing personality. Fear does not gather its potency in any derived manner from love. It belongs to the original and inherited nature of man. Probably the same may be true of rage although at present we are not so sure of this. . . .

It is probable that many of the phobias in psychopathology are true conditioned emotional reactions either of the direct or the transferred type. One may possibly have to believe that such persistence of early conditioned responses will be found only in persons who are constitutionally inferior. Our argument is meant to be constructive. Emotional disturbances in adults cannot be traced back to sex alone. They must be retraced along at least three collateral lines—to conditioned and transferred responses set up in infancy and early youth in all three of the fundamental human emotions.

Shaping and Maintaining Operant Behavior

Reinforcement—an event that increases the probability that the behavior preceding it will be repeated—can have a profound effect on behavior, and we typically do things that lead to reinforcement. Much of what scientists originally discovered about the effects of reinforcement on animals has been applied to human behavior. The study of how reinforcement changes behavior is known as operant conditioning.

B. F. Skinner (1904–1990) was a pioneer in the study of operant conditioning. Skinner earned a B.A. in English from Hamilton College in 1926, but he decided he did not have anything important to say, so he went back to school and earned a Ph.D. in psychology from Harvard University in 1931. Indeed, he did have much to say, and he wrote numerous books, including *The Behavior of Organisms* (1938) and the fictional *Walden Two* (1948), in which Skinner describes a utopian society run in accordance with operant principles. In *Beyond Freedom and Dignity* (Alfred A. Knopf, 1971), he explains why it is important to understand how we control behavior in our day-to-day lives.

This selection is from chapter 6, "Shaping and Maintaining Operant Behavior," of Skinner's *Science and Human Behavior* (MacMillan, 1953). Although Skinner's favorite subject for study was the pigeon, as illustrated in this selection, he believed that the laws of behavior apply to all organisms. Note how Skinner neatly applies the results of his animal research to human beings, as well as how clearly he defines the four intermittent schedules of reinforcement.

Key Concept: operant conditioning

THE CONTINUITY OF BEHAVIOR

*O*perant conditioning [a process in which reinforcement changes the frequency of a behavior] shapes behavior as a sculptor shapes a lump of clay.

Although at some point the sculptor seems to have produced an entirely novel object, we can always follow the process back to the original undifferentiated lump, and we can make the successive stages by which we return to this condition as small as we wish. At no point does anything emerge which is very different from what preceded it. The final product seems to have a special unity or integrity of design, but we cannot find a point at which this suddenly appears. In the same sense, an operant [behavior generated by reinforcement consequences] is not something which appears full grown in the behavior of the organism. It is the result of a continuous shaping process.

The pigeon experiment demonstrates this clearly. "Raising the head" is not a discrete unit of behavior. It does not come, so to speak, in a separate package. We reinforce only slightly exceptional values of the behavior observed while the pigeon is standing or moving about. We succeed in shifting the whole range of heights at which the head is held, but there is nothing which can be accurately described as a new "response." A response such as turning the latch in a problem box appears to be a more discrete unit, but only because the continuity with other behavior is more difficult to observe. In the pigeon, the response of pecking at a spot on the wall of the experimental box seems to differ from stretching the neck because no other behavior of the pigeon resembles it. If in reinforcing such a response we simply wait for it to occur—and we may have to wait many hours or days or weeks—the whole unit appears to emerge in its final form and to be strengthened as such. There may be no appreciable behavior which we could describe as "almost pecking the spot."

The continuous connection between such an operant and the general behavior of the bird can nevertheless easily be demonstrated. It is the basis of a practical procedure for setting up a complex response. To get the pigeon to peck the spot as quickly as possible we proceed as follows: We first give the bird food when it turns slightly in the direction of the spot from any part of the cage. This increases the frequency of such behavior. We then withhold reinforcement until a slight movement is made toward the spot. This again alters the general distribution of behavior without producing a new unit. We continue by reinforcing positions successively closer to the spot, then by reinforcing only when the head is moved slightly forward, and finally only when the beak actually makes contact with the spot. We may reach this final response in a remarkably short time. A hungry bird, well adapted to the situation and to the food tray, can usually be brought to respond in this way in two or three minutes.

The original probability of the response in its final form is very low; in some cases it may even be zero. In this way we can build complicated operants which would never appear in the repertoire of the organism otherwise. By reinforcing a series of successive approximations, we bring a rare response to a very high probability in a short time. This is an effective procedure because it recognizes and utilizes the continuous nature of a complex act. The total act of turning toward the spot from any point the box, walking toward it, raising the head, and striking the spot may seem to be a functionally coherent unit of behavior; but it is constructed by a continual process of differential reinforcement from undifferentiated behavior, just as the sculptor shapes his figure from a lump of clay. When we wait for a single complete instance, we reinforce a similar sequence but far less effectively because the earlier steps are not optimally strengthened.

This account is inaccurate in one respect. We may detect a discontinuity between bringing the head close to the spot and pecking. The pecking movement usually emerges as an obviously preformed unit. There are two possible explanations. A mature pigeon will already have developed a well-defined pecking response which may emerge upon the present occasion. The history of this response might show a similar continuity if we could follow it. It is possible, however, that there is a genetic discontinuity, and that in a bird such as the pigeon the pecking response has a special strength and a special coherence as a form of species behavior. Vomiting and sneezing are human responses which probably have a similar genetic unity. Continuity with other behavior must be sought in the evolutionary process. But these genetic units are rare, at least in the vertebrates. The behavior with which we are usually concerned, from either a theoretical or practical point of view, is continuously modified from a basic material which is largely undifferentiated.

Through the reinforcement of slightly exceptional instances of his behavior, a child learns to raise himself, to stand, to walk, to grasp objects, and to move them about. Later on, through the same process, he learns to talk, to sing, to dance, to play games—in short, to exhibit the enormous repertoire characteristic of the normal adult. When we survey behavior in these later stages, we find it convenient to distinguish between various operants which differ from each other in topography and produce different consequences. In this way behavior is broken into parts to facilitate analysis. These parts are the units which we count and whose frequencies play an important role in arriving at laws of behavior. They are the "acts" into which, in the vocabulary of the layman, behavior is divided. But if we are to account for many of its quantitative properties, the ultimately continuous nature of behavior must not be forgotten. . . .

THE MAINTENANCE OF BEHAVIOR

One reason the term "learning" is not equivalent to "operant conditioning" is that traditionally it has been confined to the process of learning *how to do something*. In trial-and-error learning, for example, the organism learns how to get out of a box or how to find its way through a maze. It is easy to see why the acquisition of behavior should be emphasized. Early devices for the study of learning did not reveal the basic process directly. The effect of operant reinforcement is most conspicuous when there is a gross change in behavior. Such a chance occurs when an organism learns how to make a response which it did not or could not make before. A more sensitive measure, however, enables us to deal with cases in which the acquisition of behavior is of minor importance.

Operant conditioning continues to be effective even when there is no further change which can be spoken of as acquisition or even as improvement in skill. Behavior continues to have consequences and these continue to be important. If consequences are not forthcoming, extinction occurs. When we come to consider the behavior of the organism in all the complexity of its everyday life, we need to be constantly alert to the prevailing reinforcements, which maintain its behavior. We may, indeed, have little interest in how that behavior was first acquired. Our concern is only with its present probability of occurrence, which can be understood only through an examination of current contingencies of reinforcement. This is an aspect of reinforcement which is scarcely ever dealt with in classical treatments of learning.

INTERMITTENT REINFORCEMENT

In general, behavior which acts upon the immediate physical environment is consistently reinforced. We orient ourselves toward objects and approach, reach for, and seize them with a stable repertoire of responses which have uniform consequences arising from the optical and mechanical properties of nature. It is possible, of course, to disturb the uniformity. In a "house of mirrors" in an amusement park, or in a room designed to supply misleading cues to the vertical, well-established responses may fail to have their usual effects. But the fact that such conditions are so unusual as to have commercial value testifies to the stability of the everyday world.

A large part of behavior, however, is reinforced only intermittently. A given consequence may depend upon a series of events which are not easily predicted. We do not always win at cards or dice, because the contingencies are so remotely determined that we call them "chance." We do not always find good ice or snow when we go skating or skiing. Contingencies which require the participation of people are especially likely to be uncertain. We do not always get a good meal in a particular restaurant because cooks are not always predictable. We do not always get an answer when we telephone a friend because the friend is not always at home. We do not always get a pen by reaching into our pocket because we have not always put it there. The reinforcements characteristic of industry and education are almost always intermittent because it is not feasible to control behavior by reinforcing every response.

As might be expected, behavior which is reinforced only intermittently often shows an intermediate frequency of occurrence, but laboratory studies of various schedules have revealed some surprising complexities. Usually such behavior is remarkably stable and shows great resistance to extinction.* An experiment has already been mentioned in which more than 10,000 responses appeared in the extinction curve of a pigeon which had been reinforced on a special schedule. Nothing of the sort is ever obtained after continuous reinforcement. Since this is a technique for "getting more responses out of an organism" in return for a given number of reinforcements, it is widely used. Wages are paid in special ways and betting and gambling devices are designed

*[Extinction is a decline in behavior frequency due to the withholding of reinforcement.—Ed.]

to "pay off" on special schedules because of the relatively large return on the reinforcement in such a case. Approval, affection, and other personal favors are frequently intermittent, not only because the person supplying the reinforcement may behave in different ways at different times, but precisely because he may have found that such a schedule yields a more stable, persistent, and profitable return.

It is important to distinguish between schedules which are arranged by a system outside the organism and those which are controlled by the behavior itself. An example of the first is a schedule of reinforcement which is determined by a clock—as when we reinforce a pigeon every five minutes, allowing all intervening responses to go unreinforced. An example of the second is a schedule in which a response is reinforced after a certain number of responses have been emitted—as when we reinforce every fiftieth response the pigeon makes. The cases are similar in the sense that we reinforce intermittently in both, but subtle differences in the contingencies lead to very different results, often of great practical significance.

Interval reinforcement. If we reinforce behavior at regular intervals, an organism such as a rat or pigeon will adjust with a nearly constant rate of responding, determined by the frequency of reinforcement. If we reinforce it every minute, the animal responds rapidly; if every five minutes, much more slowly. A similar effect upon probability of response is characteristic of human behavior. How often we call a given number on the telephone will depend, other things being equal, upon how often we get an answer. If two agencies supply the same service, we are more likely to call the one which answers more often. We are less likely to see friends or acquaintances with whom we only occasionally have a good time, and we are less likely to write to a correspondent who seldom answers. The experimental results are precise enough to suggest that in general the organism gives back a certain number of responses for each response reinforced. We shall see, however, that the results of schedules of reinforcement are not always reducible to a simple equating of input with output.

Since behavior which appears under interval reinforcement is especially stable, it is useful in studying other variables and conditions. The size or amount of each reinforcement affects the rate—more responses appearing in return for a larger reinforcement. Different kinds of reinforcers also yield different rates, and these may be used to rank reinforcers in the order of their effectiveness. The rate varies with the immediacy of the reinforcement: a slight delay between response and the receipt of the reinforcer means a lower over-all rate. Other variables which have been studied under interval reinforcement will be discussed in later chapters. They include the degree of deprivation and the presence or absence of certain emotional circumstances.

Optimal schedules of reinforcement are often of great practical importance. They are often discussed in connection with other variables which affect the rate. Reinforcing a man with fifty dollars at one time may not be so effective as reinforcing him with five dollars at ten different times during the same period. This is especially the case with primitive people where conditioned reinforcers have not been established to bridge the temporal span between a response and its ultimate consequence. There are also many subtle interactions between schedules of reinforcement and levels of motivation, immediacy of reinforcement, and so on.

If behavior continues to be reinforced at fixed intervals, another process intervenes. Since responses are never reinforced just after reinforcement, a change ... eventually takes place in which the rate of responding is low for a short time after each reinforcement. The rate rises again when an interval of time has elapsed which the organism presumably cannot distinguish from the interval at which it is reinforced. These changes in rate are not characteristic of the effect of wages in industry, which would otherwise appear to be an example of a fixed-interval schedule. The discrepancy is explained by the fact that other reinforcing systems are used to maintain a given level of work. . . . Docking a man for time absent guarantees his presence each day by establishing a time-card entry as a conditioned reinforcer. The aversive reinforcement supplied by a supervisor or boss is, however, the principal supplement to a fixed-interval wage.

A low probability of response just after reinforcement is eliminated with what is called *variable-interval* reinforcement. Instead of reinforcing a response every five minutes, for example, we reinforce every five minutes *on the average*, where the intervening interval may be as short as a few seconds or as long as, say, ten minutes. Reinforcement occasionally occurs just after the organism has been reinforced, and the organism therefore continues to respond at that time. Its performance under such a schedule is remarkably stable and uniform. Pigeons reinforced with food with a variable interval averaging five minutes between reinforcements have been observed to respond for as long as fifteen hours at a rate of from two to three responses per second without pausing longer than fifteen or twenty seconds during the whole period. It is usually very difficult to extinguish a response after such a schedule. Many sorts of social or personal reinforcement are supplied on what is essentially a variable-interval basis, and extraordinarily persistent behavior is sometimes set up.

Ratio reinforcement. An entirely different result is obtained when the schedule of reinforcement depends upon the behavior of the organism itself—when, for example, we reinforce every fiftieth response. This is reinforcement at a "fixed ratio"—the ratio of reinforced to unreinforced responses. It is a common schedule in education, where the student is reinforced for completing a project or a paper or some other specific amount of work. It is essentially the basis of professional pay and of selling on commission. In industry it is known as piecework pay. It is a system of reinforcement which naturally recommends itself to employers because the cost of the labor required to produce a given result can be calculated in advance.

Fixed-ratio reinforcement generates a very high rate of response provided the ratio is not too high. This should follow from the input-output relation alone. Any slight increase in rate increases the frequency of reinforcement with the result that the rate should rise still further. If no other factor intervened, the rate should reach the highest possible value. A limiting factor, which makes itself felt in industry, is simple fatigue. The high rate of responding and the long hours of work generated by this schedule can be dangerous to health. This is the main reason why piecework pay is usually strenuously opposed by organized labor.

Another objection to this type of schedule is based upon the possibility that as the rate rises, the reinforcing agency will move to a larger ratio. In the laboratory, after first reinforcing every tenth response and then every fiftieth, we may find it possible to reinforce only every hundredth, although we could not have used this ratio in the beginning. In industry, the employee whose productivity has increased as the result of a piecework schedule may receive so large a weekly wage that the employer feels justified in increasing the number of units of work required for a given unit of pay.

Under ratios of reinforcement which can be sustained, the behavior eventually shows a very low probability just after reinforcement, as it does in the case of fixed-interval reinforcement. The effect is marked under high fixed ratios because the organism always has "a long way to go" before the next reinforcement. Wherever a piecework schedule is used—in industry, education, salesmanship, or the professions—low morale or low interest is most often observed just after a unit of work has been completed. When responding begins, the situation is improved by each response and the more the organism responds, the better the chances of reinforcement become. The result is a smooth gradient of acceleration as the organism responds more and more rapidly. The condition eventually prevailing under high fixed-ratio reinforcement is not an efficient over-all mode of responding. It makes relatively poor use of the available time, and the higher rates of responding may be especially fatiguing.

The laboratory study of ratio reinforcement has shown that for a given organism and a given measure of reinforcement there is a limiting ratio beyond which behavior cannot be sustained. The result of exceeding this ratio is an extreme degree of extinction of the sort which we call abulia. Long periods of inactivity begin to appear between separate ratio runs. This is not physical fatigue, as we may easily show by shifting to another schedule. It is often called "mental" fatigue, but this designation adds nothing to the observed fact that beyond a certain high ratio of reinforcement the organism simply has no behavior available. In both the laboratory study of ratio reinforcement and its practical application in everyday life, the first signs of strain imposed by too high a ratio are seen in these breaks. Before a pigeon stops altogether—in complete "abulia"—it will often not respond for a long time after reinforcement. In the same way, the student who has finished a term paper, perhaps in a burst of speed at the end of the gradient, finds it difficult to start work on a new assignment.

Exhaustion can occur under ratio reinforcement because there is no self-regulating mechanism. In interval reinforcement, on the other hand, any tendency toward extinction is opposed by the fact that when the rate declines, the next reinforcement is received in return for fewer responses. The variable-interval schedule is also self-protecting: an organism will stabilize its behavior at a given rate under any length of interval.

We get rid of the pauses after reinforcement on a fixed-ratio schedule by adopting essentially the same practice as in variable-interval reinforcement: we simply vary the ratios over a considerable range around some mean value. Successive responses may be reinforced or many hundreds of unreinforced responses may intervene. The probability of reinforcement at any moment remains essentially constant and the organism adjusts by holding to a constant rate. This "variable-ratio reinforcement" is much more powerful than a fixed-ratio schedule with the same mean number of responses. A pigeon may respond as rapidly as five times per second and maintain this rate for many hours.

The efficacy of such schedules in generating high rates has long been known to the proprietors of gambling establishments. Slot machines, roulette wheels, dice cages, horse races, and so on pay off on a schedule of variable-ratio reinforcement. Each device has its own auxiliary reinforcements, but the schedule is the important characteristic. Winning depends upon placing a bet and in the long run upon the number of bets placed, but no particular payoff can be predicted. The ratio is varied by any one of several "random" systems. The pathological gambler exemplifies the result. Like the pigeon with its five responses per second for many hours, he is the victim of an unpredictable contingency of reinforcement. The long-term net gain or loss is almost irrelevant in accounting for the effectiveness of this schedule.

6.3 ALBERT BANDURA, DOROTHEA ROSS, AND SHEILA A. ROSS

Imitation of Film-mediated Aggressive Models

Rising levels of crime and destructive aggression have been studied by psychologists for decades. One ongoing debate has focused on whether or not observation and imitation is a problem with regard to aggression that occurs in the media. Do children imitate the aggressive acts they observe in movies and on television? Through a series of studies, Albert Bandura and his colleagues have begun to answer this question.

Bandura (b. 1925), a leading theorist in observational learning, received his Ph.D. from the University of Iowa in 1952. Shortly afterward, he began his academic career at Stanford University, where he has remained. He has written many books, including *Aggression: A Social Learning Analysis* (Prentice Hall, 1973) and *Social Learning Theory* (Prentice Hall, 1977). Dorothea Ross and Sheila A. Ross were collaborators with Bandura on the research project described in this selection.

This selection, "Imitation of Film-mediated Aggressive Models," was published in the *Journal of Abnormal and Social Psychology* in 1963. It details Bandura et al.'s classic study on aggression imitation in standard research article format. Note the care with which the procedure was carried out. An important point for understanding the statistical results is that a probability (p) level less than .05 is significant and indicates a real difference among experimental conditions. Bandura et al.'s findings go against most of the research reported prior to the study, which maintained that film-mediated aggression reduces aggressive drives through a cathartic process. The research reported in this selection suggests that filmed aggression can facilitate aggression in children. What are the implications of this study for aggression and violence in movies and on television today?

Key Concept: observation learning of aggression

In a test of the hypothesis that exposure of children to film-mediated aggressive models would increase the probability of Ss' [Subjects—i.e., children] aggression to subsequent frustration, 1 group of experimental Ss observed real-life aggressive models, a 2nd observed these same models portraying aggression on film, while a 3rd group viewed a film depicting an aggressive cartoon character. Following the exposure treatment, Ss were mildly frustrated and tested for the amount of imitative and nonimitative aggression in a different experimental setting. The overall results provide evidence for both the facilitating and the modeling influence of film-mediated aggressive stimulation. In addition, the findings reveal that the effects of such exposure are to some extent a function of the sex of the model, sex of the child, and the reality cues of the model. . . .

A recent incident (San Francisco Chronicle, 1961) in which a boy was seriously knifed during a re-enactment of a switchblade knife fight the boys had seen the previous evening on a televised rerun of the James Dean movie, *Rebel Without a Cause,* is a dramatic illustration of the possible imitative influence of film stimulation. Indeed, anecdotal data suggest that portrayal of aggression through pictorial media may be more influential in shaping the form aggression will take when a person is instigated on later occasions, than in altering the level of instigation to aggression.

In an earlier experiment (Bandura & Huston, 1961), it was shown that children readily imitated aggressive behavior exhibited by a model in the presence of the model. A succeeding investigation (Bandura, Ross, & Ross, 1961), demonstrated that children exposed to aggressive models generalized aggressive responses to a new setting in which the model was absent. The present study sought to determine the extent to which film-mediated aggressive models may serve as an important source of imitative behavior.

Aggressive models can be ordered on a reality-fictional stimulus dimension with real-life models located at the realty end of the continuum, nonhuman cartoon characters at the fictional end, and films portraying human models occupying an intermediate position. It was predicted, on the basis of saliency and similarity of cues, that the more remote the model was from reality, the weaker would be the tendency for subjects to imitate the behavior of the model. . . .

To the extent that observation of adults displaying aggression conveys a certain degree of permissiveness for aggressive behavior, it may be assumed that such exposure not only facilitates the learning of new aggressive responses but also weakens competing inhibitory responses in subjects and thereby increases the probability of occurrence of previously learned patterns of aggression. It was predicted, therefore, that subjects who observed aggressive models would display significantly more aggression when subsequently frustrated than subjects who were equally frustrated but who had no prior exposure to models exhibiting aggression.

The subjects were 48 boys and 48 girls enrolled in the Stanford University Nursery School. They ranged in age from 35 to 69 months, with a mean age of 52 months.

Two adults, a male and a female, served in the role of models both in the real-life and the human film-aggression condition, and one female experimenter conducted the study for all 96 children.

General Procedure

Subjects were divided into three experimental groups and one control group of 24 subjects each. One group of experimental subjects observed real-life aggressive models, a second group observed these same models portraying aggression on film, while a third group viewed a film depicting an aggressive cartoon character. The experimental groups were further subdivided into male and female subjects so that half the subjects in the two conditions involving human models were exposed to same-sex models, while the remaining subjects viewed models of the opposite sex.

Following the exposure experience, subjects were tested for the amount of imitative and nonimitative aggression in a different experimental setting in the absence of the models.

The control group subjects had no exposure to the aggressive models and were tested only in the generalization situation.

Subjects in the experimental and control groups were matched individually on the basis of ratings of their aggressive behavior in social interactions in the nursery school. The experimenter and a nursery school teacher rated the subjects on four five-point rating scales which measured the extent to which subjects displayed physical aggression, verbal aggression, aggression toward inanimate objects, and aggression inhibition. The latter scale, which dealt with the subjects' tendency to inhibit aggressive reactions in the face of high instigation, provided the measure of aggression anxiety. Seventy-one percent of the subjects were rated independently by both judges so as to permit an assessment of interrater agreement. The reliability of the composite aggression score, estimated by means of the Pearson product-moment correlation, was .80. . . .

Experimental Conditions

Subjects in the Real-Life Aggressive condition were brought individually by the experimenter to the experimental room and the model, who was in the hallway outside the room, was invited by the experimenter to come and join in the game. The subject was then escorted to one corner of the room and seated at a small table which contained potato prints, multicolor picture stickers, and colored paper. After demonstrating how the subject could design pictures with the materials provided, the experimenter escorted the model to the opposite corner of the room which contained a small table and chair, a tinker toy set, a mallet, and a 5-foot inflated Bobo doll. The experimenter explained that this was the model's play area and after the model was seated, the experimenter left the experimental room.

The model began the session by assembling the tinker toys but after approximately a minute had elapsed, the model turned to the Bobo doll and spent the remainder of the period aggressing toward it with highly novel responses which are unlikely to be performed by children independently of the observation of the model's behavior. Thus, in addition to punching the Bobo doll, the model exhibited the following distinctive aggressive acts which were to be scored as imitative responses:

The model sat on the Bobo doll and punched it repeatedly in the nose.

The model then raised the Bobo doll and pommeled it on the head with a mallet.

Following the mallett aggression, the model tossed the doll up in the air aggressively and kicked it about the room. This sequence of physically aggressive acts was repeated approximately three times, interspersed with verbally aggressive responses such as, "Sock him in the nose . . . ," "Hit him down . . . ," "Throw him in the air . . . ," "Kick him . . . ," and "Pow."

Subjects in the Human Film-Aggression condition were brought by the experimenter to the semi-darkened experimental room, introduced to the picture materials, and informed that while the subjects worked on potato prints, a movie would be shown on a screen, positioned approximately 6 feet from the subject's table. The movie projector was located in a distant corner of the room and was screened from the subject's view by large wooden panels.

The color movie and a tape recording of the sound track was begun by a male projectionist as soon as the experimenter left the experimental room and was shown for a duration of 10 minutes. The models in the film presentations were the same adult males and females who participated in the Real-Life condition of the experiment. Similarly, the aggressive behavior they portrayed in the film was identical with their real-life performances.

For subjects in the Cartoon Film-Aggression condition, after seating the subject at the table with the picture construction material, the experimenter walked over to a television console approximately 3 feet in front of the subject's table, remarked, "I guess I'll turn on the color TV," and ostensibly tuned in a cartoon program. The experimenter then left the experimental room. The cartoon was shown on a glass lens screen in the television set by means of a rear projection arrangement screened from the subject's view by large panels. . . .

In both film conditions, at the conclusion of the movie the experimenter entered the room and then escorted the subject to the test room.

Aggression Instigation

In order to differentiate clearly the exposure and test situations subjects were tested for the amount of imitative learning in a different experimental room which was set off from the main nursery school building.

The degree to which a child has learned aggressive patterns of behavior through imitation becomes most evident when the child is instigated to aggression on later occasions. Thus, for example, the effects of viewing the movie, *Rebel Without a Cause*, were not evident until the boys were instigated to aggression the following day, at which time they re-enacted the televised switchblade knife fight in considerable detail. For this reason, the children in the experiment, both those in the control group, and those who were exposed to the aggressive models, were mildly frustrated before they were brought to the test room.

Following the exposure experience, the experimenter brought the subject to an anteroom which contained a varied array of highly attractive toys. The experimenter explained that the toys were for the subject to play with, but, as soon as the subject became sufficiently involved with the play material, the experimenter remarked that these were her very best toys, that she did not let just anyone play with them, and that she had decided to reserve these toys for some other children. However, the subject could play with any of the toys in the next room. The experimenter and the subject then entered the adjoining experimental room. . . .

Test for Delayed Imitation

The experimental room contained a variety of toys, some of which could be used in imitative or nonimitative aggression, and others which tended to elicit predominantly nonaggressive forms of behavior. The aggressive toys included a 3-foot Bobo doll, a mallet and peg board, two dart guns, and a tether ball with a face painted on it which hung from the ceiling. The nonaggressive toys, on the other hand, included a tea set, crayons and coloring paper, a ball, two dolls, three bears, cars and trucks, and plastic farm animals. . . .

The subject spent 20 minutes in the experimental room during which time his behavior was rated in terms of predetermined response categories by judges who observed the session through a one-way mirror in an adjoining observation room. The 20-minute session was divided in 5-second intervals by means of an electric interval timer, thus yielding a total number of 240 response units for each subject. . . .

RESULTS

The mean imitative and nonimitative aggression scores for subjects in the various experimental and control groups are presented in Table 1.

Since the distributions of scores departed from normality and the assumption of homogeneity of variance could not be made for most of the measures, the Freidman two-way analysis of variance by ranks was employed for testing the significance of the obtained differences.

TABLE 1

*Mean Aggression Scores for Subgroups of Experimental and
Control Subjects*

| Response category | Experimental groups | | | | | |
| | Real-life aggressive | | Human film aggressive | | Cartoon film aggressive | Control group |
	F Model	M Model	F Model	M Model		
Total aggression						
Girls	65.8	57.3	87.0	79.5	80.9	36.4
Boys	76.8	131.8	114.5	85.0	117.2	72.2
Imitative aggression						
Girls	19.2	9.2	10.0	8.0	7.8	1.8
Boys	18.4	38.4	34.3	13.3	16.2	3.9
Mallet aggression						
Girls	17.2	18.7	49.2	19.5	36.8	13.1
Boys	15.5	28.8	20.5	16.3	12.5	13.5
Sits on Bobo doll[a]						
Girls	10.4	5.6	10.3	4.5	15.3	3.3
Boys	1.3	0.7	7.7	0.0	5.6	0.6
Nonimitative aggression						
Girls	27.6	24.9	24.0	34.3	27.5	17.8
Boys	35.5	48.6	46.8	31.8	71.8	40.4
Aggressive gun play						
Girls	1.8	4.5	3.8	17.6	8.8	3.7
Boys	7.3	15.9	12.8	23.7	16.6	14.3

[a]This response category was not included in the total aggression score.

Total Aggression

The mean total aggression scores for subjects in the real-life, human film, cartoon film, and the control groups are 83, 92, 99, and 54 respectively. The results of the analysis of variance performed on these scores reveal that the main effect of treatment conditions is significant ($Xr^2 = p < .05$), confirming the prediction that exposure of subjects to aggressive models increases the probability that subjects will respond aggressively when instigated on later occasions. Further analyses of pairs of scores by means of the Wilcoxon matched-pairs signed-ranks test show that subjects who viewed the real-life models and the film-mediated models do not differ from each other in total aggressiveness but all three experimental groups expressed significantly more aggressive behavior than the control subjects. . . .

*Albert Bandura
et al.*

In order to determine the influence of sex of model and sex of child on the expression of imitative and nonimitative aggression, the data from the experimental groups were combined and the significance of the differences between groups was assessed by t tests for uncorrelated means. In statistical comparisons involving relatively skewed distributions of scores the Mann-Whitney U test was employed.

Sex of subjects had a highly significant effect on both the learning and the performance of aggression. Boys, in relation to girls, exhibited significantly more total aggression ($t = 2.69$, $p < .01$), more imitative aggression ($t = 2.82$, $p < .005$), more aggressive gun play ($z = 3.38$, $p < .001$), and more nonimitative aggressive behavior ($t = 2.98$, $p < .005$). Girls, on the other hand, were more inclined than boys to sit on the Bobo doll but refrained from punching it ($z = 3.47$, $p < .001$).

The analyses also disclosed some influences of the sex of the model. Subjects exposed to the male model, as compared to the female model, expressed significantly more aggressive gun play ($z = 2.83$, $p < .005$). The most marked differences in aggressive gun play ($U = 9.5$, $p < .001$), however, were found between girls exposed to the female model ($M = 2.9$) and males who observed the male model ($M = 19.8$). Although the overall model difference in partially imitative behavior, Sits on Bobo, was not significant, Sex $\times$ Model subgroup comparisons yielded some interesting results. Boys who observed the aggressive female model, for example, were more likely to sit on the Bobo doll without punching it than boys who viewed the male model ($U = 33$, $p < .05$). Girls reproduced the nonaggressive component of the male model's aggressive pattern of behavior (i.e., sat on the doll without punching it) with considerably higher frequency than did boys who observed the same model ($U = 21.5$, $p < .02$). The highest incidence of partially imitative responses was yielded by the group of girls who viewed the aggressive female model ($M = 10.4$), and the lowest values by the boys who were exposed to the male model ($M = 0.3$). This difference was significant beyond the .05 significance level. These findings, along with the sex of child and sex of model differences reported in the preceding sections, provide further support for the view that the influence of models in promoting social learning is determined, in part, by the sex appropriateness of the model's behavior (Bandura et al., 1961). . . .

DISCUSSION

The results of the present study provide strong evidence that exposure to filmed aggression heightens aggressive reactions in children. Subjects who viewed the aggressive human and cartoon models on film exhibited nearly twice as much aggression than did subjects in the control group who were not exposed to the aggressive film content. . . .

Filmed aggression, not only facilitated the expression of aggression, but also effectively shaped the form of the subjects' aggressive behavior. The finding that children modeled their behavior to some extent after the film characters suggests that pictorial mass media, particularly television, may serve as an important source of social behavior. In fact, a possible generalization of responses originally learned in the television situation to the experimental film may account for the significantly greater amount of aggressive gun play displayed by subjects in the film condition as compared to subjects in the real-life and control groups. It is unfortunate that the qualitative features of the gun behavior were not scored since subjects in the film condition, unlike those in the other two groups, developed interesting elaborations in gun play (for example, stalking the imaginary opponent, quick drawing, and rapid firing), characteristic of the Western gun fighter.

REFERENCES

1. Bandura, A., & Huston, Aletha C. Identification as a process of incidental learning. *J. abnorm. soc. Psychol.*, 1961, **63**, 311–318.
2. Bandura, A., Ross, Dorothea, & Ross, Sheila A. Transmission of aggression through imitation of aggressive models. *J. abnorm. soc. Psychol.*, 1961, **63**, 575–582.
3. San Francisco Chronicle. "James Dean" knifing in South City. *San Francisco Chron.*, March 1, 1961, 6.

6.4 KONRAD Z. LORENZ

Poor Fish

Scientists study animals both to better understand them and to provide insight into human behavior. The study of the behavior of animals, especially in a natural setting, is called "ethnology." In the 1930s, Konrad Z. Lorenz became a leader of this approach. He often brought animals into his home so he could carefully observe their behavior patterns.

Lorenz (1903–1989) received his M.D. in 1928 and his Ph.D. in 1933 from the University of Vienna. He spent his career at the University of Vienna and the Institute for the Physiology of Behavior. He is perhaps best known by American students for his work in the 1930s on imprinting in geese. He wrote a number of books, including *On Aggression* (Harcourt Brace Jovanovich, 1966) and *King Solomon's Ring: New Light on Animal Ways* (Thomas Y. Crowell, 1952). In 1973, the Nobel Prize for physiology was awarded to Lorenz, Niko Tinbergen, and Karl von Frisch for their work in animal behavior.

This selection is from chapter 4, "Poor Fish," in Lorenz's 1952 animal behavoir book *King Solomon's Ring*. Lorenz was a delightful writer, and this selection shows how entertaining yet how educating he could be. Although he is describing the behavior of fish in this chapter, he is also writing about some fundamental principles of human behavior. As you read this selection, note the care with which he describes his subjects and the enjoyment with which he communicates with the reader.

Key Concept: animal behavior

*S*trange what blind faith is placed in proverbs, even when what they say is false or misleading. The fox is not more cunning than other beasts of prey and is much more stupid than wolf or dog, the dove is certainly not peaceful, and of the fish, rumour spreads only untruth: it is neither so cold-blooded as one says of dull people, nor is the "fish in water" nearly so happily situated as the converse saying would imply. In reality there is no other group of animals that, even in nature, is so plagued with infectious diseases as the fish. I have never yet known a newly caught bird, reptile or mammal bring an infectious disease into my animal population; but every newly acquired fish must, as a routine measure, go into the quarantine aquarium, otherwise you may bet a hundred to one that within a very short time the dreaded minute white spots, the sign of infection with the parasite *Ichthyophtirius multifiliis*, will appear on the fins of the previously installed aquarium dwellers.

And regarding the alleged cold-bloodedness of fishes; I am familiar with many animals and with their behaviour in the most intimate situations of their life, in the wild ecstasies of the fight and of love, but, with the exception of the wild canary, I know of no animal that can excel in hot-bloodedness a male stickleback, a Siamese fighting-fish or a cichlid. No animal becomes so completely transformed by love, none glows, in such a literal sense, with passion as a stickleback or fighting-fish. Who could reproduce in words, what artist in colour, that glowing red that makes the sides of the male stickleback glassy and transparent, the iridescent blue-green of its back whose colour and brilliance can only be compared with the illuminating power of neon lighting, or finally, the brilliant emerald green of its eyes? According to the rules of artistic taste, these colours should clash horribly, and yet what a symphony they produce, composed by the hand of nature.

In the fighting-fish, this marvel of colour is not continually present. For the little brown-grey fish that lies with folded fins in one corner of the aquarium reveals nothing of it for the moment. It is only when another fish, equally inconspicuous at first, approaches him and each sights the other, that they begin gradually to light up in all their incandescent glory. The glow pervades their bodies almost as quickly as the wire of an electric heater grows red. The fins unfold themselves like ornamental fans, so suddenly that one almost expects to hear the sound of an umbrella being opened quickly. And now follows a dance of burning passion, a dance which is not play but real earnest, a dance of life or death, of be-all or end-all. To begin with, strangely enough, it is uncertain whether it will lead to love overtures and mating, or whether it will develop, by an equally flowing transition, into a bloody battle. Fighting-fish recognize the sex of a member of their own species not simply by seeing it but by watching the way in which it responds to the severely ritualized, inherited, instinctive movements of the dancer.

The meeting of two previously unacquainted fighting-fish begins with a mutual "showing-off," a swaggering act of self-display in which every luminous colour-spot and every iridescent ray of the wonderful fins is brought into maximum play. Before the glorious male, the modestly garbed female lowers the flag—by folding her fins—and, if she is unwilling to mate, flees immediately. Should she be willing to mate, she approaches the male . . . in an attitude directly opposed to that of the swaggering male. And now begins a love ceremonial which, if it cannot compare in grandeur with the male war-dance, can emulate it in grace of movement.

When two males meet face to face, veritable orgies of mutual self-glorification take place. There is a striking similarity between the war-dance of these fish and the corresponding ceremonial dances of Japanese and other Indonesian peoples. In both man and fish the minutest detail of every movement is laid down by immutable and ancient laws, the slightest gesture has its own deeply symbolic meaning. There is a close resemblance between man and fish in the style and exotic grace of their movements of restrained passion.

The beautifully refined form of the movements betrays the fact that they have a long historical development behind them and that they owe their elaborateness to an ancient ritual. It is, however, not so obvious that though in man this ritual is a ceremony which has been handed down from generation to generation by a thousand-year-old tradition, in the fish it represents the result of an evolutional development of innate instinctive activities, at least a hundred times older. Genealogical research into the origin of such ritual expression, and the comparison of such ceremonies in related species are exceedingly illuminating. We know more of the evolutionary history of these movements than of all other instincts.

After this digression, let us return to the war-dance of the male fighting-fish. This has exactly the same meaning as the duel of words of the Homeric heroes, or of our Alpine farmers which, even today, often precedes the traditional Sunday brawl in the village inn. The idea is to intimidate one's opponent and at the same time to stimulate oneself to a state of fearlessness. In the fish, the long duration of these preliminaries, their ritual character and above all their great show of colour finery and fin development which at first only serve to subdue the opponent, mask, for the uninitiated, the seriousness of the situation. On account of their beauty, the fighters appear less malevolent than they really are and one is just as loth to ascribe to them embittered courage and contempt of death as one is to associate head-hunting with the almost effeminately beautiful Indonesian warriors. Nevertheless both are capable of fighting to the death. The battles of the fighting-fish often end in the death of one of the adversaries. When they are stimulated to the point of inflicting the first sword-thrust, it is only a matter of minutes till wide slits are gaping in their fins, which in a few more minutes are reduced to tatters. The method of attack of a fighting-fish, as of nearly all fish that fight, is literally the sword-thrust and not the bite. The fish opens its jaws so wide that all its teeth are directed forwards and, in this attitude, it rams them, with all the force of its muscular body, into the side of its adversary. The ramming of a fighting-fish is so strong and hard that its impact is clearly audible if, in the confusion of the fight, one of the antagonists happens to hit the glass side of the tank. The self-display-dance can last for hours but, should it develop into action, it is often only a matter of minutes before one of the combatants lies mortally wounded on the bottom.

The fights of our European sticklebacks are very different from those of the Siamese fighting-fish. In contrast to the latter, the stickleback, at mating time, glows not only when it sees an opponent or a female, but does so as long as it is in the vicinity of its nest, in its own chosen territory. The basic principle of his fighting is, "my home is my castle." Take his nest from a stickleback or remove him from the tank where he built it and put him with another male and he will not dream of fighting but, on the contrary, will make himself small and ugly. It would be impossible to use sticklebacks for exhibition battles as the Siamese have done, for hundreds of years, with fighting-fish. It is only when he has founded his home that the stickleback becomes physically capable of reaching a state of full sexual excitement; therefore, a real stickleback fight can only be seen when two males are kept together in a large tank where they are both building their nests. The fighting inclinations of a stickleback, at any given moment, are in direct proportion to his proximity to his nest. At the nest itself, he is a raging fury and with a fine contempt of death will recklessly ram the strongest opponent, or even the human hand. The further he strays from his headquarters in the course of his swimming, the more his courage wanes. When two sticklebacks meet in battle, it is possible to predict with a high degree of certainty how the fight will end: the one which is further from his nest will lose the match. In the immediate neighbourhood of his nest, even the smallest male will defeat the largest one, and the relative fighting potential of the individual is shown by the size of the territory which he can keep clear of rivals. The vanquished fish invariably flees homeward and the victor, carried away by his successes, chases the other furiously, far into its domain. The further the victor goes from home, the more his courage ebbs, while that of the vanquished rises in proportion. Arrived in the precincts of his nest, the fugitive gains new strength, turns right about and dashes with gathering fury at his pursuer. A new battle begins, which ends with absolute certainty in the defeat of the former victor, and off goes the chase again in the opposite direction. The pursuit is repeated a few times in alternating directions, swinging to and fro like a pendulum which at last reaches a state of equilibrium at a certain point. The line at which the fighting potentials of the individuals are thus equally balanced marks the border of their territories. This same principle is of great importance in the biology of many animals, particularly that of birds. Every bird lover has seen two male redstarts chasing each other in exactly the same manner.

Once on this borderline, both sticklebacks hesitate to attack. Taking on a peculiar threatening attitude, they incessantly stand on their heads and . . . they do it again and again. At the same time they turn broadside on towards each other and each erects threateningly the ventral spine on the side nearer his opponent. All the while they seem to be "pecking" at the bottom for food. In reality, however, they are executing a ritualized version of the activity normally used in nest-digging. If an animal finds the outlet for some instinctive action blocked by a conflicting drive, it often finds relief by discharging an entirely different instinctive movement. In this case, the stickleback, not quite daring to attack, finds an outlet in nest digging. This type of phenomenon, which is of great theoretical interest both from the physiological and psychological point of view, is termed in comparative ethology a "displacement activity."

Unlike the fighting-fish, the sticklebacks do not waste time by threatening before starting to fight, but will do so after or between battles. This, in itself, implies that they never fight to a finish, although from their method of fighting, the contrary might be expected. Thrust and counter-thrust follow each other so quickly that the eye of the observer can scarcely follow them. The large ventral spine, that appears so ominous, plays in reality quite a subordinate role. In older aquarium literature, it is often stated that these spines are used so effectively that one of the fighters may sink down dead, perforated by the spine of his opponent. Apparently the writers of these works have never tried to "perforate" a stickleback; for even a dead stickleback will slip from under the sharpest scalpel before one is able to penetrate its tough skin, even in places where it is not reinforced by bony armour. Place a dead stickleback on a soft surface—which certainly offers a much better resistance than water—and try to run it through with a sharp needle. You will be surprised at the force required to do so. Owing to the extreme toughness of the sticklebacks' skin, no serious wounds can be inflicted in their natural battles which, as compared with those of the fighting-fish, are absurdly harmless. Of course, in the confined space of a small tank, a stronger male stickleback may harry a weaker one to death, but rabbits and turtle doves, in analogous conditions, will do the same thing to each other.

The stickleback and the fighting-fish are as different in love as they are in fight, yet, as parents, they have much in common. In both species, it is the male and not the female that undertakes the building of the nest and the care of the young, and the future father only then begins to think of love when the cradle for the expected children is ready. But here the similarities end and the differences begin. The cradle of the stickleback lies, in a manner of speaking, under the floor, that of the fighting-fish above the ceiling: that is to say, the former digs a little hollow in the bottom and the latter builds his nest on the surface of the water; the one uses, for nest construction, plant strands and a special sticky kidney secretion, the other uses air and spittle. The castle-in-the-air of the fighting-fish, as also that of his nearer relations, consists of a little pile of air bubbles, stuck closely together, which protrudes somewhat over the water surface; the bubbles are coated with a tough layer of spittle and are very resistant. Already while building, the male radiates the most gorgeous colours, which gain in depth and iridescence when a female approaches. Like lightning, he shoots towards her and glowing, halts. If the female is prepared to accept him, she demonstrates it by investing herself with a characteristic, if modest colouring consisting of light grey vertical stripes on a brown background. With fins closely folded, she swims towards the male who, trembling with excitement, expands all his fins to breaking point and holds himself in such a position that the dazzling brilliance of his full broadside is presented to his bride. Next moment he swims off with a sweeping, gracefully sinuous movement, in the direction of the nest. The beckoning nature of this gesture is at once apparent even when seen for the first time. The essentially ritual nature of this swimming movement is easily understood: everything that enhances its optical effect is exaggerated in mimic, as the sinuous movements of the body or the waving of the tail fin, whereas all the means of making it mechanically effective are decreased. The movement says: "I am swimming away from you, hurry up and follow me!" At the same time, the fish swims neither fast nor far and turns back immediately to the female who is following . . . in his wake.

In this way the female is enticed under the bubble nest and now follows the wonderful love-play which resembles, in delicate grace, a minuet, but in general style, the trance dance of a Balinese temple dancer. In this love dance, by age-old law, the male must always exhibit his magnificent broadside to his partner, but the female must remain constantly at right angles to him. The male must never obtain so much as a glimpse of her flanks, otherwise he will immediately become angry and unchivalrous; for, standing broadsides means, in these fishes as in many others, aggressive masculinity and elicits instantaneously in every male a complete change of mood: hottest love is transformed to wildest hate. Since the male will not now leave the nest, he moves in circles round the female and she follows his every movement by keeping her head always turned towards him; the love-dance is thus executed in a small circle, exactly under the middle of the nest. Now the colours become more glowing, more frantic the movements, ever smaller the circles, until the bodies touch. Then, suddenly, the male slings his body tightly round the female, gently turns her on her back and, quivering, both fulfil the great act of reproduction. Ova and semen are discharged simultaneously.

The female remains, for a few seconds, . . . but the male has . . . things to attend to at once. The minute, glass-clear eggs are considerably heavier than water and sink at once to the ground. Now the posture of the bodies in spawning is such that the sinking eggs are bound to drift past the downward directed head of the male and thus catch his attention. He gently releases the female, glides downwards in pursuit of the eggs and gathers them up, one after the other, in his mouth. Turning upwards again, he blows the eggs into the nest. They now miraculously float instead of sinking. This sudden and amazing change of density is caused by a coating of buoyant spittle in which the male has enveloped every egg while carrying it in his mouth. He has to hurry in this work, for not only would he soon be unable to find the tiny, transparent globules in the mud, but, if he should delay a second longer, the female would wake from her trance and, also swimming after the eggs, would likewise proceed to engulf them. From these actions, it would appear, at first sight, that the female has the same intentions as her mate. But if we wait to see her packing the eggs in the nest, we will wait in vain, for these eggs will disappear, irrevocably swallowed. So the male knows very well why he is hurrying, and he knows, too, why he no longer allows the female near the nest when, after ten to twenty matings, all her eggs have been safely stored between the air bubbles.

CHAPTER 7 Memory

7.1 LLOYD R. PETERSON AND MARGARET JEAN PETERSON

Short-Term Retention of Individual Verbal Items

Memory involves mentally storing information that we learn so we can retrieve and use it at a later time. Short-term memory is the process by which we hold the information we are aware of at any particular moment. Because people tend to rehearse information in short-term memory (for example, repeating a phone number until the number is dialed), psychologists found it difficult to accurately determine how long a person could keep information in short-term memory; that is, until Lloyd R. Peterson and Margaret J. Peterson developed the procedure described in this selection.

Lloyd Peterson (b. 1922) earned his Ph.D. from the University of Minnesota in 1954. He then began teaching at Indiana University, where he is currently a professor of psychology. Margaret Peterson earned her Ph.D. from the University of Minnesota in 1955, and she is also a professor at Indiana University.

This selection, "Short-Term Retention of Individual Verbal Items," was published in the *Journal of Experimental Psychology* in 1959, and it provides an excellent opportunity to read original research in the area of memory. Experiment 1 (Experiment 2 is not included here) presents a useful technique for measuring the duration of a verbal stimulus in short-term memory. Keep in mind that statistical tests determine if we can conclude that real differences occur between experimental conditions. Also note that statistical significance (a real difference) is obtained when the probability (*p*) is less than .05. As you read this article, consider how quickly information fades from your short-term memory.

Key Concept: short-term memory

It is apparent that the acquisition of verbal habits depends on the effects of a given occasion being carried over into later repetitions of the situation. Nevertheless, textbooks separate acquisition and retention into distinct categories. The limitation of discussions of retention to long-term characteristics is necessary in large part by the scarcity of data on the course of retention over intervals of the order of magnitude of the time elapsing between successive repetitions in an acquisition study. The presence of a retentive function within the acquisition process was postulated by Hull (1940) in his use of the stimulus trace to explain serial phenomena. Again, Underwood (1949) has suggested that forgetting occurs during the acquisition process. But these theoretical considerations have not led to empirical investigation. . . .

Two studies have shown that the effects of verbal stimulation can decrease over intervals measured in seconds. Pillsbury and Sylvester (1940) found marked decrement with a list of items tested for recall 10 sec. after a single presentation. However, it seems unlikely that this traditional presentation of a list and later testing for recall of the list will be useful in studying intervals near or shorter than the time necessary to present the list. Of more interest is a recent study by Brown (1958) in which among other conditions a single pair of consonants was tested after a 5-sec. interval. Decrement was found at the one recall interval, but no systematic study of the course of retention over a variety of intervals was attempted.

EXPERIMENT I

The present investigation tests recall for individual items after several short intervals. An item is presented and tested without related items intervening. The initial study examines the course of retention after one brief presentation of the item.

Method

Subjects.—The *S*s [subjects] were 24 students from introductory psychology courses at Indiana University. Participation in experiments was a course requirement.

Materials.—The verbal items tested for recall were 48 consonant syllables with Witmer association value no greater than 33%* (Hilgard, 1951). Other materials were 48 three-digit numbers obtained from a table of random numbers. One of these was given to S after each presentation under instructions to count backward from the number. It was considered that continuous verbal activity during the time between presentation and signal for recall was desirable in order to minimize rehearsal behavior. The materials were selected to be categorically dissimilar and hence involve a minimum of interference.

Procedure.—The S was seated at a table with E [experimenter] seated facing in the same direction on S's right. A black plywood screen shielded E from S. On the table in front of S were two small lights mounted on a black box. The general procedure was for E to spell a consonant syllable and immediately speak a three-digit number. The S then counted backward by three or four from this number. On flashing of a signal light S attempted to recall the consonant syllable. The E spoke in rhythm with a metronome clicking twice per second and S was instructed to do likewise. As E spoke the third digit, he pressed a button activating a Hunter interval timer. At the end of a preset interval the timer activated a red light and an electric clock. The light was the signal for recall. The clock ran until E heard S speak three letters, when E stopped the clock by depressing a key. This time between onset of the light and completion of a response will be referred to as a latency. It is to be distinguished from the interval from completion of the syllable by E to onset of the light, which will be referred to as the recall interval.

The instructions read to S were as follows: "Please sit against the back of your chair so that you are comfortable. You will not be shocked during this experiment. In front of you is a little black box. The top or green light is on now. This green light means that we are ready to begin a trial. I will speak some letters and then a number. You are to repeat the number immediately after I say it and begin counting backwards by 3's (4's) from that number in time with the ticking that you hear. I might say, ABC 309. Then you say, 309, 306, 303, etc., until the bottom or red light comes on. When you see this red light come on, stop counting immediately and say the letters that were given at the beginning of the trial. Remember to keep your eyes on the black box at all times. There will be a short rest period and then the green light will come on again and we will start a new trial." The E summarized what he had already said and then gave S two practice trials. During this practice S was corrected if he hesitated before starting to count, or if he failed to stop counting on signal, or if he in any other way deviated from the instructions.

Each S was tested eight times at each of the recall intervals, 3, 6, 9, 12, 15, and 18 sec. A given consonant syllable was used only once with each S. Each syllable occurred equally often over the group at each recall interval. A specific recall interval was represented once in each successive block of six presentations. The S counted backward by three on half of the trials and by four on the

*[A low Witmer association value means that the consonant syllables used by the experimenters to test the subjects were nonsensical. It is a measure of the syllables' lack of meaning.—Ed.]

FIGURE 1 *Correct Recalls With Latencies Below 2.83 Sec. as a Function of Recall Interval*

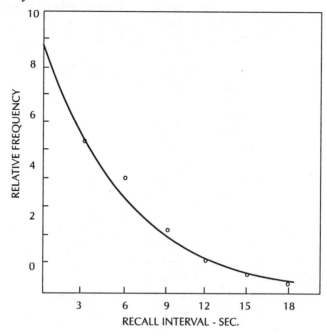

remaining trials. No two successive items contained letters in common. The time between signal for recall and the start of the next presentation was 15 sec.

Results and Discussion

Responses occurring any time during the 15-sec. interval following signal for recall were recorded. . . .

The feasibility of an interpretation by a statistical model was explored by fitting to the data the exponential curve of Fig. 1. The empirical points plotted here are proportions of correct responses with latencies shorter than 2.83 sec. Partition of the correct responses on the basis of latency is required by considerations developed in detail by Estes (1950). A given probability of response applies to an interval of time equal in length to the average time required for the response under consideration to occur. The mean latency of correct responses in the present experiment was 2.83 sec. Differences among the proportions of correct responses with latencies shorter than 2.83 sec. were evaluated by sign tests. The difference between the 3- and 18-sec. conditions was found to be significant at the .01 level. All differences among the 3-, 6-, 9-, 12-, and 18-sec. conditions were significant at the .05 level.

The general equation of which the expression for the curve of Figure 1 is a specific instance is derived from the stimulus fluctuation model developed by Estes (1955). In applying the model to the present experiment it is assumed that the verbal stimulus produces a response in *S* which is conditioned to a set of elements contiguous with the response. The elements thus conditioned are a sample of a larger population of elements into which the conditioned elements disperse as time passes. The proportion of conditioned elements in the sample determining *S*'s behavior thus decreases and with it the probability of the response. Since the fitted curve appears to do justice to the data, the observed decrement could arise from stimulus fluctuation.

The independence of successive presentations might be questioned in the light of findings that performance deteriorates as a function of previous learning (Underwood, 1957). The presence of proactive interference was tested by noting the correct responses within each successive block of 12 presentations. The short recall intervals were analyzed separately from the long recall intervals in view of the possibility that facilitation might occur with the one and interference with the other. The proportions of correct responses for the combined 3- and 6-sec. recall intervals were in order of occurrence .57, .66, .70, and .74. A sign test [statistical test] showed the difference between the first and last blocks to be significant at the .02 level. The proportions correct for the 15- and 18-sec. recall intervals were .08, .15, .09, and .12. The gain from first to last blocks is not significant in this case. There is no evidence for proactive interference. There is an indication of improvement with practice. . . .

SUMMARY

The investigation differed from traditional verbal retention studies in concerning itself with individual items instead of lists. Forgetting over intervals measured in seconds was found. The course of retention after a single presentation was related to a statistical model. . . . It was concluded that short-term retention is an important, though neglected, aspect of the acquisition process.

REFERENCES

BROWN, J. Some tests of the decay theory of immediate memory. *Quart. J. exp. Psychol.*, 1958, 10, 12–21.

ESTES, W. K. Toward a statistical theory of learning. *Psychol. Rev.* 1950, 57, 94–107.

ESTES, W. K. Statistical theory of spontaneous recovery and regression. *Psychol. Rev.*, 1955, 62, 145–154.

HILGARD, E. R. Methods and procedures in the study of learning. In S. S. Stevens (Ed.), *Handbook of experimental psychology.* New York: Wiley, 1951.

HULL, C. L., HOVLAND, C. I., ROSS, R. T., HALL, M., PERKINS, D. T., & FITCH, F. B. *Mathematico-deductive theory of rote learning: A study in scientific methodology.* New Haven: Yale Univer. Press, 1940.

PILLSBURY, W. B., & SYLVESTER, A. Retroactive and proactive inhibition in immediate memory. *J. exp. Psychol.*, 1940, 27, 532–545.

UNDERWOOD, B. J. *Experimental psychology,* New York: Appleton-Century-Crofts, 1949.

UNDERWOOD, B. J. Interference and forgetting. *Psychol. Rev.*, 1957, 64, 49–60.

How Many Memory Systems Are There?

Ultimately, what we learn must enter our long-term memory, which appears to have an unlimited capacity and is relatively permanent. During the past two decades, psychologists have debated the structure of long-term memory with respect to the number of memory systems that exist. One theory comes from psychologist Endel Tulving, who supports a classification scheme that consists of three memory systems: procedural, semantic, and episodic.

Tulving (b. 1927) received his B.A. from the University of Toronto in 1953 and his Ph.D. from Harvard University in 1957. He is currently a professor of psychology at the University of Toronto. Tulving, a leader in the area of long-term memory, has many publications in this area, including *Elements of Episodic Memory* (Oxford University Press, 1983).

This selection, "How Many Memory Systems Are There?" is based on a Distinguished Scientific Contribution Award address presented at the 1984 American Psychological Association meeting and was published in *American Psychologist* in 1985. In it, Tulving provides some of the theoretical considerations important to the area of long-term memory. He also provides a review of past research findings, and he challenges researchers to become involved in the search for a better understanding of human memory. As you read this selection, try to think of situations in which you have used procedural, semantic, and episodic memory.

Key Concept: types of long-term memory

Solving puzzles in science has much in common with solving puzzles for amusement, but the two differ in important respects. Consider, for instance, the jigsaw puzzle that scientific activity frequently imitates. The everyday version of the puzzle is determinate: It consists of a target picture and jigsaw pieces that, when properly assembled, are guaranteed to match the picture. Scientific puzzles are indeterminate: The number of pieces required to complete a picture is unpredictable; a particular piece may fit many pictures or none; it may fit only one picture, but the picture itself may be unknown; or the hypothetical picture may be imagined, but its component pieces may remain undiscovered.

This article is about a current puzzle in the science of memory. It entails an imaginary picture and a search for pieces that fit it. The picture, or the hypothesis, depicts memory as consisting of a number of systems, each system serving somewhat different purposes and operating according to somewhat different principles. Together they form the marvelous capacity that we call by the single name of *memory*, the capacity that permits organisms to benefit from their past experiences. Such a picture is at variance with conventional wisdom that holds memory to be essentially a single system, the idea that "memory is memory." . . .

PRETHEORETICAL CONSIDERATIONS

Why Multiple Memory Systems?

It is possible to identify several a priori reasons why we should break with long tradition (Tulving, 1984a) and entertain thoughts about multiple memory systems. I mention five here.

The first reason in many ways is perhaps the most compelling: No profound generalizations can be made about memory as a whole, but general statements about particular kinds of memory are perfectly possible. Thus, many questionable claims about memory in the literature, claims that give rise to needless and futile arguments, would become noncontroversial if their domain was restricted to parts of memory.

Second, memory, like everything else in our world, has become what it is through a very long evolutionary process. Such a process seldom forms a continuous smooth line, but is characterized by sudden twists, jumps, shifts, and turns. One might expect, therefore, that the brain structures and mechanisms that (together with their behavioral and mental correlates) go to make up memory will also reflect such evolutionary quirks (Oakley, 1983).

The third reason is suggested by comparisons with other psychological functions. Consider, for instance, the interesting phenomenon of *blindsight:* People with damage to the visual cortex are blind in a part of their visual field in that they do not see objects in that part, yet they can accurately point to and discriminate these objects in a forced-choice situation (e.g., Weiskrantz, 1980; Weiskrantz, Warrington, Sanders, & Marshall, 1974). Such facts imply that different brain mechanisms exist for picking up information about the visual environment. Or consider the massive evidence for the existence of two separate cortical pathways involved in vision, one mediating recognition of objects, the other their location in space (e.g., Mishkin, Ungerleider, & Macko, 1983; Ungerleider & Mishkin, 1982). If "seeing" things—something that phenomenal experience tells us is clearly unitary—is subserved by separable neural–cognitive systems, it is possible that learning and remembering, too, appear to be unitary only because of the absence of contrary evidence.

The fourth general reason derives from what I think is an unassailable assumption that most, if not all, of our currently held ideas and theories about mental processes are wrong and that sooner or later in the future they will be replaced with more adequate concepts, concepts that fit nature better (Tulving, 1979). Our task, therefore, should be to hasten the arrival of such a future. Among other things, we should be willing to contemplate the possibility that the "memory-is-memory" view is wrong and look for a better alternative.

The fifth reason lies in a kind of failure of imagination: It is difficult to think how varieties of learning and memory that appear to be so different on inspection can reflect the workings of one and the same underlying set of structures and processes. It is difficult to imagine, for instance, that perceptual-motor adaptations to distorting lenses and their aftereffects (e.g., Kohler, 1962) are mediated by the same memory system that enables an individual to answer affirmatively when asked whether Abraham Lincoln is dead. It is equally difficult to imagine that the improved ability to make visual acuity judgments, resulting from many sessions of practice without reinforcement or feedback (e.g., Tulving, 1958), has much in common with a person's ability to remember the funeral of a close friend.

If we reflect on the limits of generalizations about memory, think about the twists and turns of evolution, examine possible analogies with other biological and psychological systems, believe that most current ideas we have about the human mind are wrong, and have great difficulty apprehending sameness in different varieties of learning and memory, we might be ready to imagine the possibility that memory consists of a number of interrelated systems. But what exactly do we mean by a *memory system*?

The Concept of System

We could think of a system simply as a set of correlated processes: Processes within a system are more closely related to one another than they are to processes outside the system. Such an abstract and relatively innocuous definition could be used by those students of memory who, for whatever reasons, are reluctant to consider biology when they think about psychology. It would not distort too many claims I will make about memory systems. However, a more concrete conceptualization—one that refers to the correlation of behavior and thought with brain processes and postulates the verifiable, real existence of memory systems (e.g., Tulving, 1984a)—is preferable because it points to stronger tests of such existence.

Memory systems constitute the major subdivisions of the overall organization of the memory complex. They are organized structures of more elementary operating components. An operating component of a system consists of a neural substrate and its behavioral or cognitive correlates. Some components are shared by all systems, others are shared only by some, and still others are unique to individual systems. Different learning and memory situations involve different concatenations of components from one or more systems. The relatedness of such situations in a natural classification scheme of learning and memory varies directly with the extent to which they entail identical components (Tulving, in press).

Although there is no one-to-one correspondence between tasks and systems (e.g., Kinsbourne, 1976; Tulving, in press), they are nonetheless systematically related: A given memory system makes it possible for organisms to perform memory tasks that entail operating components unique to that system. This means, among other things, that intervention with the operation of a system—even if it occurs through a single component of the system—affects all those learning and memory performances that depend on that system. The widespread but systematic effects of a single toxin or microorganism, for example (Rozin, 1976), reflect the fact that many specific memory performances are subserved by the affected system.

Different systems have emerged at different stages in the evolution of the species, and they emerge at different stages in the development of individual organisms. Thus, they can be ordered from "lower" to "higher" systems (or from less to more advanced), provided that it is clearly understood that such attributions are meaningful only with respect to comparisons between combinations of systems, on the one hand, and individual systems alone, on the other (Schiller, 1952). When a new memory system with specialized novel capabilities evolves or develops, it enables the organism to increase the number, and the sophistication, of its memory functions. In this sense, the combination of the new system and the older ones is "higher," or more advanced than the older ones alone. As an analogy, we can think of an airplane with an autopilot as a more advanced or higher system than one without it, but we would not think of the autopilot alone as a higher system than the airplane.

PROCEDURAL, SEMANTIC, AND EPISODIC MEMORIES

A Ternary [Three-part] Classification

Let me now switch gears and discuss a classification scheme according to which memory consists of three major systems. I will refer to them as procedural, semantic, and episodic, primarily for the sake of continuity with previous usage, although these are not necessarily the best terms. The three systems constitute what might be called a *monohierarchical* arrangement (cf. Engelien, 1971). The system at the lowest level of the hierarchy, procedural memory, contains semantic memory as its single specialized subsystem, and semantic memory, in turn, contains episodic memory as its single specialized subsystem. In this scheme, each higher system depends on, and is supported by, the lower system or systems, but it possesses unique capabilities not possessed by the lower systems.

Procedural memory enables organisms to retain learned connections between stimuli and responses, including those involving complex stimulus patterns and response chains, and to respond adaptively to the environment. Semantic memory is characterized by the additional capability of internally representing states of the world that are not perceptually present. It permits the organism to construct mental models of the world (Craik, 1943), models that can be manipulated and operated on covertly, independently of any overt behaviour. Episodic memory affords the additional capability of acquisition and retention of knowledge about personally experienced events and their temporal relations in subjective time and the ability to mentally "travel back" in time.

The monohierarchical relation among the systems means that only procedural memory can operate completely independently of the other systems. This necessarily happens when an organism does not possess either of the two more advanced systems, and it may happen with higher organisms when situations do not call for the use of the other systems. Semantic memory can function independently of episodic memory but not independently of procedural memory. And episodic memory depends on both procedural and semantic memory in its workings, although, as already mentioned, it also possesses its own unique capabilities. The monohierarchical arrangement also implies that certain kinds of double dissociations between learning and memory tasks are precluded (Tulving, in press). . . .

Each system differs in its methods of acquisition, representation, and expression of knowledge. Each also differs in the kind of conscious awareness that characterizes its operations. Let us briefly consider these differences, taking each in turn.

Acquisition in the procedural system requires overt behavioral responding, whereas covert responding—cognitive activity, or "mere observation"—may be sufficient for the other two. We could also say that the characteristic mode of learning is *tuning* in the procedural system, *restructuring* in the semantic system, and *accretion* in the episodic system, along the general lines suggested by Rumelhart and Norman (1978), as long as we keep in mind the implications of the monohierarchical relation among the systems.

The representation of acquired information in the procedural system is prescriptive rather than descriptive: It provides a blueprint for future action without containing information about the past (Dretske, 1982). It may be conceptualized in terms of the "stage-setting" metaphor of Bransford, McCarrell, Franks, and Nitsch (1977), a metaphor akin to Craik's (1983) suggestion that the consequences of learning may take the form of "subtle alterations of the system" (p. 345). It can also be specified in terms of changing probabilities of specific responses to specific stimuli (Mishkin, Malamut, & Bachevalier, 1984). When we are dealing with procedural memory, I agree with Bransford et al. (1977) and with Craik (1983) that it is inappropriate to talk about discrete "memory traces."

Representations in the semantic system, however, are different from those in the procedural system; they describe the world without prescribing any particular action. Representations in both the semantic and episodic systems are isomorphic with the information they represent (Dretske, 1982). Representations in episodic memory additionally carry information about the relations of represented events in the rememberer's personal identity as it exists in subjective time and space (e.g., Claparede, 1911/1951; Tulving, 1983).

Expression of knowledge (Spear, 1984) also differs in the three systems. Only direct expression is possible in procedural memory; overt responding according to a relatively rigid format determined at the time of learning is obligatory (Hirsh, 1974; Mishkin & Petri, 1984). On the other hand, acquired knowledge in both semantic and episodic memory can be expressed flexibly, in different behavioral forms. Such knowledge may manifest itself, under conditions far removed from those of original learning, in behaviors quite dissimilar to the behavior entailed in such learning. Overt behavior corresponding to actualized knowledge is only an optional form of expression. In episodic memory, the typical mode of "expression" of remembering is recollective experience, based on synergistic ecphory. It occurs when the organism is in the "retrieval mode" (Tulving, 1983) or has a particular "attitude" (Bartlett, 1932).

The three memory systems are characterized by different kinds of consciousness (Tulving, 1985). Procedural memory is associated with anoetic (nonknowing) consciousness, semantic memory with noetic (knowing) consciousness, and episodic memory with autonoetic (self-knowing) consciousness. . . .

Anoetic (nonknowing) consciousness represents one of the end points of the continuum: It refers to an organism's capability to sense and to react to external and internal stimulation, including complex stimulus patterns. Plants and very simple animals possess anoetic consciousness as do computers and learning machines that have knowledge and that can improve it (e.g., Hayes-Roth, Klahr, & Mostow, 1980).

Noetic (knowing) consciousness is an aspect of the semantic memory system. It makes possible introspective awareness of the internal and external world. We can say that the object of noetic consciousness is the organism's knowledge of its world. Noetic consciousness is to such knowledge as the knowledge is to the world. Lower animals, very young children, and people suffering from brain damage may lack episodic memory and autonoetic consciousness but may have fully developed noetic consciousness.

Autonoetic (self-knowing) consciousness is a necessary correlate of episodic memory. It allows an individual to become aware of his or her own identity and existence in subjective time that extends from the past through the present to the future. It provides the familiar phenomenal flavor of recollective experience characterized by "pastness" and subjective veridicality [truthfulness]. It can be impaired or lost without impairment or loss of other forms of consciousness. . . .

HOW MANY SYSTEMS?

The puzzle of memory systems is not and will not be an easy one to solve. Many difficulties have to be overcome before we can expect more rapid progress. We assume that both memory systems and memory tasks (performances, manifestations, achievements) are composed of, or can be broken down into, more elementary constituents (I have referred to them in this article as operating components), but we do not yet know how to relate one to the other in the world of empirical observations. In the absence of such rules of the game, interpretation of existing evidence from the point of view of multiple memory systems is uncertain and frustrating. The difficulty is compounded by the clever and inventive strategies that learners and remembers frequently use when confronted with laboratory tasks, strategies that drive wedges between what the experimenter thinks he or she is observing and what the observed organism is in fact doing. A familiar bane of learning and memory researchers is the omnipresent possibility that identical behaviors and responses are produced by different underlying processes and mechanisms. Sometimes crucial theoretical distinctions may depend on fine differences in observed patterns of data, requiring discriminations beyond the resolving power of conventional methodology.

How then, with few facts yet available to guide us and many intractable problems to dampen our enthusiasm, can we expect to answer the question posed in the title of this article? We follow the same procedure that we use when we tackle other puzzles in our science: We exercise our imagination, trying to see beyond the visible horizon, reaching beyond what is given. As long as our imagination is eventually bridled and disciplined by nature's facts, we need not worry about thinking thoughts that transcend our knowledge.

Because I have discussed three systems in this article, in agreement with a number of other friends of multiple learning and memory systems, the answer "three" to our main question would not be entirely amiss at the present time. But if we try to imagine what might lie beyond our currently limited horizon we may decide that a better answer might be "at least three and probably many more."

Whether this or some other answer will prove to come closest to "carving nature at its joints" is something that only the future will show. What matters for the present is that the question is being asked by an increasing number of students of memory. There is no guarantee, of course, that just by asking the question we will get an answer that is acceptable to science. What is absolutely guaranteed, however, is that we will not get the answer unless we pose the question. We cannot solve puzzles that do not exist.

REFERENCES

Bartlett, F. C. (1932). *Remembering: A study in experimental and social psychology*. Cambridge, MA: University Press.

Bransford, J. D., McCarrell, N. S., Franks, J. J., & Nitsch, K. E. (1977). Toward unexplaining memory. In R. Shaw & J. Bransford (Eds.), *Perceiving, acting and knowing* (pp. 431–466). Hillsdale, NJ: Erlbaum.

Claparede, E. (1911). Reconnaissance et moiite. [Recognition and me-ness]. *Archives de Psychologie, 11*, 79–90. (English translation in D. Rapaport [Ed. and Trans.], *Organization and pathology of thought*, 1951, New York: Columbia University Press.)

Craik, K. (1943). *The nature of explanation*. Cambridge, MA: University Press.

Craik, F. I. M. (1983). On the transfer of information from temporary to permanent memory. *Philosophical Transactions of the Royal Society London, B302*, 341–359.

Dretske, F. (1982). The informational character of representations. *Behavioral and Brain Sciences, 5*, 376–377.

Engelien, G. (1971). *Der Begriff der Klassifikation* [The concept of classification]. Hamburg: Helmut Buske Verlag.

Hayes-Roth, F., Klahr, P., & Mostow, D. J. (1980, May). *Knowledge acquisition, knowledge programming, and knowledge refinement* (Report No. R-2540-NSF). Santa Monica, CA: Rand Corporation.

Hirsch, R. (1974). The hippocampus and contextual retrieval of information from memory: A theory. *Behavioral Biology, 12,* 421–444.

Kohler, I. (1962). Experiments with goggles. *Scientific American, 206,* 62–72.

Mishkin, M., Malamut, B., & Bachevalier, J. (1984). Memories and habits: Two neural systems. In G. Lynch, J. L. McGaugh, & N. M. Weinberger, (Eds.), *The neurobiology of learning and memory* (pp. 65–77). New York: Guilford Press.

Mishkin, M., & Petri, H. L. (1984). Memories and habits: Some implications for the analysis of learning and retention. In L. Squire & N. Butters (Eds.), *Neuropsychology of memory* (pp. 287–296). New York: Guilford Press.

Mishkin, M., Ungerleider, L. G., & Macko, K. A. (1983). Object vision and spatial vision: Two cortical pathways. *Trends in Neurosciences, 6,* 414–417.

Oakley, D. A. (1983). The varieties of memory: A phylogenetic approach. In A. Mayes (Ed.), *Memory in animals and humans* (pp. 20–82). Wokingham, England: Van Nostrand Reinhold.

Rozin, P. (1976). The psychobiological approach to human memory. In M. R. Rosenzweig & E. L. Bennett (Eds.), *Neural mechanisms of learning and memory* (pp. 3–46). Cambridge, MA: MIT Press.

Rumelhart, D. E., & Norman, D. A. (1978). Accretion, tuning, and restructuring: Three modes of learning. In J. W. Cotton & R. Klatzky (Eds.), *Semantic factors in cognition* (pp. 37–53). Hillsdale, NJ: Erlbaum.

Schiller, F. (1952). Consciousness reconsidered. *Archives of Neurology and Psychiatry, 67,* 199–227.

Spear, N. E. (1984). Behaviors that indicate memory: Levels of expression. *Canadian Journal of Psychology, 38,* 348–367.

Tulving, E. (1958). The relation of visual acuity to convergence and accommodation. *Journal of Experimental Psychology, 55,* 530–534.

Tulving, E. (1979). Memory research: What kind of progress? In L.-G. Nilsson (Ed.), *Perspectives on memory research: Essays in honor of Uppsala University's 500th anniversary* (pp. 19–34). Hillsdale, NJ: Erlbaum.

Tulving, E. (1983). *Elements of episodic memory.* New York: Oxford University Press.

Tulving, E. (1984a). Multiple learning and memory systems. In K. M. J. Lagerspetz & P. Niemi (Eds.), *Psychology in the 1990's* (pp. 163–184). North Holland: Elsevier Science Publishers B. V.

Tulving, E. (1985). Memory and consciousness. *Canadian Psychology, 26,* 1–12.

Tulving, E. (in press). On the classification problem in learning and memory. In L.-G. Nilsson & T. Archer (Eds.), *Perspectives on learning and memory.* Hillsdale, NJ: Erlbaum, in press.

Ungerleider, L. G., & Mishkin, M. (1982). Two cortical visual systems. In D. J. Ingle, M. A. Goodale, & R. J. W. Mansfield (Eds.), *Analysis of visual behavior* (pp. 549–586). Cambridge, MA: MIT Press.

Weiskrantz, L. (1980). Varieties of residual experience. *Quarterly Journal of Experimental Psychology, 32,* 365–386.

Weiskrantz, L., Warrington, E. K., Sanders, M. D., & Marshall, J. (1974). Visual capacity in the hemianopic field following a restricted occipital ablation. *Brain, 97,* 709–728.

Leading Questions and the Eyewitness Report

Most people want to believe that they have perfect memories. Psychologists have discovered, however, that memory is subject to a wide variety of distortions. Elizabeth F. Loftus, for example, has studied how asking certain questions of eyewitnesses to an event affects their later recall of the incident.

Loftus (b. 1944) earned her Ph.D. in psychology from Stanford University in 1970. She is currently a professor of psychology at the University of Washington. Loftus is one of the leading legal consultants in the United States in the area of eyewitness testimony in trials. She has written several books, including *Eyewitness Testimony* (Harvard University Press, 1979) in which she describes how leading questions can have a permanent effect on the memory of a witness.

This selection, "Leading Questions and the Eyewitness Report," published in *Cognitive Psychology* in 1975, clearly demonstrates how easy it is to modify eyewitness memory. This article consists of several different but related experiments, and for each one, the methods, the results, and a discussion section are provided. The chi-square (X^2) and the t-test are statistical tests used to determine significance (differences between conditions). A probability (p) less than .05 is significant. As you read this article, consider the implications that Loftus's research has for everyday situations.

Key Concept: eyewitness memory

A total of 490 subjects, in four experiments, saw films of complex, fast-moving events, such as automobile accidents or classroom disruptions. The purpose of these experiments was to investigate how the wording of questions asked immediately after an event may influence responses to questions asked considerably later. It is shown that when the initial question contains either either true presuppositions (e.g., it postulates the existence of an object that did exist in the scene) or false presuppositions (e.g., postulates the existence of an object that did not exist), the likelihood is increased that subjects will later report having seen the presupposed object. The results suggest that questions asked immediately after an event can introduce new—not necessarily correct—information, which is then added to the memorial representation of the event, thereby causing its reconstruction or alteration.

161

*Elizabeth F.
Loftus*

Although current theories of memory are derived largely from experiments involving lists of words or sentences, many memories occurring in everyday life involve complex, largely visual, and often fast-moving events. Of course, we are rarely required to provide precise recall of such experiences—though as we age, we often volunteer them—but on occasion such recall is demanded, as when we have witnessed a crime or an accident. Our theories should be able to encompass such socially important forms of memory. It is clearly of concern to the law, to police and insurance investigators, and to others to know something about the completeness, accuracy, and malleability of such memories.

When one has witnessed an important event, one is sometimes asked a series of questions about it. Do these questions, if asked immediately after the event, influence the memory of it that then develops? This paper first summarizes research suggesting that the wording of such initial questions can have a substantial effect on the answers given, and then reports four new studies showing that the wording of these initial questions can also influence the answers to different questions asked at some later time. The discussion of these findings develops the thesis that questions asked about an event shortly after it occurs may distort the witness' memory for that event.

ANSWERS DEPEND ON THE WORDING OF QUESTIONS

An example of how the wording of a question can affect a person's answer to it has been reported by Harris (1973). His subjects were told that "the experiment was a study in the accuracy of guessing measurements, and that they should make as intelligent a numerical guess as possible to each question" (p. 399). They were then asked either of two questions such as, "How tall was the basketball player?", or, "How short was the basketball player?" Presumably the former form of the question presupposes nothing about the height of the player, whereas the latter form involves a presupposition that the player is short. On the average, subjects guessed about 79 and 69 in. (190 and 175 mm), respectively. Similar results appeared with other pairs of questions. For example, "How long was the movie?", led to an average estimate of 130 min, whereas, "How short was the movie?" led to 100 min. While it was not Harris' central concern, his study clearly demonstrates that the wording of a question may affect the answer.

In one study (Loftus, unpublished), 40 people were interviewed about their headaches and about headache products under the belief that they were participating in market research on these products. Two of the questions were crucial to the experiment. One asked about products other than that currently being used, in one of two wordings:

(1a) In terms of the total number of products, how many other products have you tried? 1? 2? 3?

(1b) In terms of the total number of products, how many other products have you tried? 1? 5? 10?

The 1/2/3 subjects claimed to have tried an average of 3.3 other products, whereas the 1/5/10 subjects claimed an average of 5.2; $t(38) = 3.14$, $\sigma = .61$, $p < .01$.

The second key question asked about frequency of headaches in one of two ways:

(2a) Do you get headaches frequently, and, if so, how often?

(2b) Do you get headaches occasionally, and, if so, how often?

The "frequently" subjects reported an average of 2.2 headaches/wk, whereas the "occasionally" group reported only 0.7/wk; $t(38) = 3.19$, $\sigma = .47$, $p < .01$.

Recently Witnessed Events

Two examples from the published literature also indicate that the wording of a question put to a person about a recently-witnessed event can affect a person's answer to that question. In one study (Loftus, 1974; Loftus & Zanni, 1975), 100 students viewed a short file segment depicting a multiple-car accident. Immediately afterward, they filled out a 22-item questionnaire which contained six critical questions. Three of these asked about items that had appeared in the film whereas the other three asked about items not present in the film. For half the subjects, all the critical questions began with the words, "Did you see a . . ." as in, "Did you see a broken headlight?" For the remaining half, the critical questions began with the words, "Did you see the . . ." as in, "Did you see the broken headlight?"

Thus, the questions differed only in the form of the article, *the* or *a*. One uses "the" when one assumes the object referred to exists and may be familiar to the listener. An investigator who asks, "Did you see the broken headlight?" essentially says, "There was a broken headlight. Did you happen to see it?" His assumption may influence a witness' report. By contrast, the article "a" does not necessarily convey the implication of existence.

The results showed that witnesses who were asked "the" questions were more likely to report having seen something, whether or not it had really appeared in the film, than those who were asked "a" questions. Even this very subtle change in wording influences a witness' report.

In another study (Loftus & Palmer, 1974), subjects saw films of automobile accidents and then answered questions about the accidents. The wording of a question was shown to affect a numerical estimate. In particular, the question, "About how fast were the cars going when they smashed into each other?" consistently elicited a higher estimate of speed than when "smashed" was replaced by "collided," "bumped," "contacted," or "hit."

We may conclude that in a variety of situations the wording of a question about an event can influence the answer that is given. This effect has been observed when a person reports about his own experiences, about events he has recently witnessed, and when answering a general question (e.g., "How short was the movie?") not based on any specific witnessed incident.

QUESTION WORDING AND ANSWERS TO SUBSEQUENT QUESTIONS

Our concern in this paper is not on the effect of the wording of a question on its answer, but rather on the answers to other questions asked some time afterward. We will interpret the evidence to be presented as suggesting a memorial phenomenon of some importance.

In the present experiments, a key [set of] initial questions contains a *presupposition,* which is simply a condition that must hold in order for the question to be contextually appropriate. For example, the question, "How fast was the car going when it ran the stop sign?" presupposes that there was a stop sign. If a stop sign actually did exist, then in answering this question a subject might review, strengthen, or make more available certain memory representations corresponding to the stop sign. This being the case, the initial question might be expected to influence the answer to a subsequent question about the stop sign, such as the question, "Did you see the stop sign?" A simple extension of the argument of Clark and Haviland (in press) can be made here: When confronted with the initial question, "How fast was the car going when it ran the stop sign?", the subject might treat the presupposed information as if it were an address, a pointer, or an instruction specifying where information related to that presupposition may be found (as well as where new information is to be integrated into the previous knowledge). In the process the presupposed information may be strengthened.

What if the presupposition is false? In that case it will not correspond to any existing representation, and the subject may treat it as new information and enter it into his memory. Subsequently, the new "false" information may appear in verbal reports solicited from the subject.

To explore these ideas, subjects viewed films of complex, fast-moving events. Viewing of the film was followed by initial questions which contained presuppositions that were either true (Experiment 1) or false (Experiments 2–4). In Experiment 1, the initial questions either did or did not mention an object that was in fact present in the film. A subsequent question, asked a few minutes later, inquired as to whether the subject has seen the existing object. In

Experiments 2–4, the initial questions were again asked immediately after the film, whereas the subsequent questions were asked after a lapse of 1 wk.

EXPERIMENT 1

Method

One hundred and fifty University of Washington students, in groups of various sizes, were shown a film of a multiple-car accident in which one car, after failing to stop at a stop sign, makes a right-hand turn into the main stream of traffic. In an attempt to avoid a collision, the cars in the oncoming traffic stop suddenly and a five-car, bumper-to-bumper collision results. The film lasts less than 1 min, and the accident occurs within a 4-sec period.

At the end of the film, a 10-item questionnaire was administered. A diagram of the situation labeled the car that ran the stop sign as "A," and the cars involved in the collision as "B" through "F." The first question asked about the speed of Car A in one of two ways:

(1) How fast was Car A going when it ran the stop sign?

(2) How fast was Car A going when it turned right? Seventy-five subjects received the "stop sign" question and 75 received the "turned right" question. The last question was identical for all subjects: "Did you see a stop sign for Car A?" Subjects responded by circling "yes" or "no" on their questionnaires.

Results and Discussion

Fifty-three percent of the subjects in the "stop sign" group responded "yes" to the question, "Did you see a stop sign for Car A?", whereas only 35% in the "turn right" group claimed to have seen the stop sign; $x^2(1) = 4.98$, $p < .05$. The wording of a presupposition into a question about an event, asked immediately after that event has taken place, can influence the answer to a subsequent question concerning the presupposition itself, asked a very short time later, in the direction of conforming with the supplied information.

There are at least two possible explanations of this effect. The first is that when a subject answers the initial stop sign question, he somehow reviews, or strengthens, or in some sense makes more available certain memory representations corresponding to the stop sign. Later, when asked, "Did you see a stop sign . . . ?", he responds on the basis of the strengthened memorial representation.

A second possibility may be called the "construction hypothesis." In answering the initial stop sign question, the subject may "visualize" or "reconstruct " in his mind that portion of the incident needed to answer the question, and so, if he accepts the presupposition, he introduces a stop sign into his visualization whether or not it was in memory. When interrogated later about the existence of the stop sign, he responds on the basis of his earlier supplementation of the actual incident. In other words, the subject may "see" the stop sign that he has himself constructed. This would not tend to happen when the initial question refers only to the right turn.

The construction hypothesis has an important consequence. If a piece of true information supplied to the subject after the accident augments his memory, then, in a similar way, it should be possible to introduce into memory something that was not in fact in the scene, by supplying a piece of false information. For example, Loftus and Palmer (1974, Expt. 2) showed subjects a film of an automobile accident and followed it by questions about events that occurred in the film. Some subjects were asked "About how fast were the cars going when they smashed into each other?", whereas others were asked the same question with "hit" substituted for "smashed." On a retest 1 wk later, those questioned with "smashed" were more likely than those questioned with "hit" to agree that they had seen broken glass in the scene, even though none was present in the film. In the present framework, we assume that the initial representation of the accident the subject has witnessed is modified toward greater severity when the experimenter uses the term "smashed" because the question supplies a piece of new information, namely, that the cars did indeed *smash* into each other. On hearing the "smashed" question, some subjects may reconstruct the accident, integrating the new information into the existing representation. If so, the result is a representation of an accident in memory that is more severe than, in fact, it actually was. In particular, the more severe accident is more likely to include broken glass.

The presupposition that the cars smashed into each other may be additional information, but it can hardly be said to be false information. It is important to determine whether it is also true that false presuppositions can affect a witness' answer to a later question about that presupposition. Such a finding would imply that a false presupposition can be accepted by a witness, that the hypothesis of a strengthening of an existing memorial representation is untenable (since there should be no representation corresponding to nonexistent objects), and that the construction hypothesis discussed above is supported. Experiment 2 was designed to check this idea.

EXPERIMENT 2

Method

Forty undergraduate students at the University of Washington, again in groups of various sizes, were shown a 3-min videotape taken from the film *Diary of a Student Revolution*. The sequence depicted the disruption of a class by eight demonstrators; the confrontation, which was relatively noisy, resulted in the demonstrators leaving the classroom.

At the end of the videotape, the subjects received one of two questionnaires containing one key and nineteen filler questions. Half of the subjects were asked, "Was the leader of the four demonstrators who entered the classroom a male?", whereas the other half were asked, "Was the leader of the twelve demonstrators who entered the classroom a male?" The subjects responded by circling "yes" or "no."

One week later, all subjects returned and, without reviewing the videotape, answered a series of 20 new questions about the disruption. The subjects were urged to answer the questions from memory and not to make inference. The critical question here was, "How many demonstrators did you see entering the classroom?"

Results and Discussion

Subjects who had previously been asked the "12" question reported having seen an average 8.85 people 1 wk earlier, whereas those asked the "4" question recalled 6.40 people, $t(38) = 2.50$, $\sigma = .98$ $p < .01$. The actual number was, it will be recalled, eight. One possibility is that some fraction of the subjects remembered the number 12 or the number 4 from the prior questionnaire and were responding to the later question with that number, whereas the remainder had the correct number. An analysis of the actual responses given reveals that 10% of the people who had been interrogated with "12" actually responded "12," and that 10% of those interrogated with "4" actually responded with "4." A recalculation of the means, excluding those subjects in the "12" condition who responded "12" and those in the "4" condition who responded "4," still resulted in a significant difference between the two conditions (8.50 versus 6.67), $t(34) = 1.70$, $p < .05$. This analysis demonstrates that recall of the specific number given in the initial questionnaire is not an adequate alternative explanation of the present results.

The result shows that a question containing a false numerical presupposition can, on the average, affect a witness' answer to a subsequent question about that quantitative fact. The next experiment was designed to test whether the same is true for the existence of objects when the false presupposition concerns one that did not actually exist.

EXPERIMENT 3

Method

One hundred and fifty students at the University of Washington, in groups of various sizes, viewed a brief videotape of an automobile accident and then answered ten questions about the accident. The critical one concerned the speed of a white sports car. Half of the subjects were asked, "How fast was the white sports car going when it passed the barn while traveling along the country road?", and half were asked, "How fast was the white sports car going while traveling along the country road?" In fact, no barn appeared in the scene.

All of the subjects returned 1 wk later and, without reviewing the videotape, answered ten new questions about the accident. The final one was, "Did you see a barn?" The subjects responded by circling "yes" or "no" on their questionnaires.

167

Elizabeth F. Loftus

Results and Discussion

Of the subjects earlier exposed to the question containing the false presupposition of a barn, 17.3% responded "yes" when later asked, "Did you see a barn?", whereas only 2.7% of the remaining subjects claimed to have seen it; $x^2(1) = 8.96$, $p < .01$. An initial question containing a false presupposition can, it appears, influence a witness' later tendency to report the presence of the nonexistent object corresponding to the presupposition.

The last experiment not only extends this finding beyond the single example, but asks whether or not the effect is wholly due to the word "barn" having occurred or not occurred in the earlier session. Suppose an initial question merely asks about, instead of presupposing, a nonexistent object; for example, "Did you see a barn?," when no barn existed. Presumably subjects will mostly respond negatively to such questions. But, what if that same question is asked again some time later? It is possible that a subject will reflect to himself, "I remember something about a barn, so I guess I must have seen one." If this were the case, then merely asking about a nonexistent object could increase the tendency to report the existence of that object at some later time, thereby accounting for the results of Expt III.

EXPERIMENT 4

Method

One hundred and fifty subjects from the University of Washington, run in groups of various sizes, viewed a 3-min 8 mm film clip taken from inside of an automobile which eventually collides with a baby carriage being pushed by a man. Following presentation of the film, each subject received one of three types of booklets corresponding to the experimental conditions. One hundred subjects received booklets containing five key and 40 filler questions. In the "direct" version, the key questions asked, in a fairly direct manner, about items that were not present in the film. One example was, "Did you see a school bus in the film?" In the "False presupposition" version, the key questions contained false presuppositions referring to an item that did not occur in the film. The corresponding example was, "Did you see the children getting on the school bus?" The third group of 50 subjects received only the 40 filler questions and no key questions. The goal of using so many filler items was to minimize the possibility that subjects would notice the false presuppositions.

All subjects returned 1 wk later and, without reviewing the film clip, answered 20 new questions about the incident. Five of these questions were critical: They were direct questions that had been asked a wk earlier in identical form, of only one of the three groups of subjects. The subjects responded to all questions by circling "yes" or "no" on their questionnaires.

Results and Discussion

. . . Overall, of those who had been exposed to questions including a false presupposition, 29.2% said "yes" to the key nonexistent items; of those who had been exposed to the direct questions, 15.6% said "yes" and of those in the control group, 8.4% said "yes."

For each question individually, the type of prior experience significantly influenced the percentage of "yes" responses, with all chi-square values having $p < .05$. Additional chi-square tests were performed to test for the significance of the differences between the pairs of groups. For each of the five questions, the differences were all significant between the control group and the group exposed to false presuppositions, all chi-square values having $p < .025$. Summing over all five questions, a highly significant chi-square resulted, $x^2(5) = 40.79$, $p < 001$. Similarly, over all five questions, the difference between the group exposed to direct questions and the group exposed to false presuppositions was significant, $x^2(5) = 14.73$, $p < .025$. The difference between the control group and the group exposed to direct questions failed to reach significance, $x^2(5) = 9.24$, $p > .05$.

REFERENCES

Clark, H. H., & Haviland, S. E. Psychological processes as linguistic explanation. In D. Cohen (Ed.), *The nature of explanation in linguistics*. Milwaukee: University of Wisconsin Press, in press.

Harris, R. J. Answering questions containing marked and unmarked adjectives and adverbs. *Journal of Experimental Psychology*, 1973, 97, 399–401.

Loftus, E. F. Reconstructing memory. The incredible eyewitness. *Psychology Today*, 1974, 8, 116–119.

Loftus, E. F., & Palmer, J. C. Reconstruction of automobile destruction: An example of the interaction between language and memory. *Journal of Verbal Learning and Verbal Behavior*, 1974, 13, 585–589.

Loftus, E. F., & Zanni, G. Eyewitness testimony: The influence of the wording of a question. *Bulletin of the Psychonomic Society*, 1975, 5, 86–88.

CHAPTER 8 Intelligence and Language

8.1 ROBERT J. STERNBERG

Ability Tests, Measurements, and Markets

The measurement of mental abilities has been an objective of psychologists since the turn of the century, when the French psychologist Alfred Binet designed the first intelligence test. Developing an intelligence test that is valid, reliable, standardized, fair, and easy to use has proven to be a very difficult task. Indeed, over the years many controversies have arisen over perceived biases in intelligence testing of various groups of people. One of the current authorities on theories of intelligence is Robert J. Sternberg, who has been developing his own intelligence test.

Sternberg (b. 1949) earned his Ph.D. in psychology from Stanford University in 1975. He is currently a professor of psychology at Yale University, where he has been since 1975. His research has focused on defining and measuring intelligence, and he is the author of the award-winning book *Beyond IQ: A Triarchic Theory of Human Intelligence* (Cambridge University Press, 1985).

This selection, "Ability Tests, Measurements, and Markets," was published in 1992 in the *Journal of Educational Psychology,* an American Psychological Association journal. It provides an overview of the current state of affairs in intelligence testing from a leading theorist. Sternberg's criticisms of intelligence testing and his theory of intelligence are currently considered to be making major contributions to the field. As you read this article, think about how you would define intelligence and what the function of an intelligence test should be. Try to get a sense of intelligence testing from the point of view of both the test publisher and the test taker.

Key Concept: intelligence testing

*A*t the turn of the century, an enterprising young man departed on a journey to parts unknown in a primitive vehicle that he had invented. Although he had only an ill-formed sense of where he was going and how he would get there, the journey was a success by almost any standard. So successful was the trip that others started to follow. At time went on, the vehicles these travelers used became increasingly fancy, and every few years some new bells and whistles would be added. Yet, strangely enough little changed. The vehicles became a little faster, they went a little farther, but then they either ran out of gas, got lost in the wilderness, or both. As is so often true in life, the more things changed, the more they remained the same.

Just as the automobile we drive today is quite similar in conception to the Model T, the intelligence test of today is quite similar to that of Alfred Binet (Binet & Simon, 1916), the "enterprising young man" in the field of ability testing. Autos of today look fancier (some would say better, others would not), go faster, and are more comfortable than the Model T. Nevertheless, they still have four wheels, a basic body frame, seats to hold driver and passengers, an internal combustion engine, and the goal of transporting a passenger from one destination to another. Similarly, the tests of today are more valid and reliable than they were in the past, and can often be administered more efficiently (in less time for a given amount of information). Yet the basic test has changed little. If anything, its development is less obvious to a viewer than that of an automobile. Also, like the automobile, the test of today takes one to pretty much the same places as did its progenitors.

Few people outside the testing business itself are much impressed with the advances that have been made in testing since the time of Alfred Binet. In terms of the metaphor at the beginning of the article, we are still taking pretty much the same trip to the same places in the same vehicles. This is not to say that there have been no changes any more than one would want to say that automobiles have not changed. Scoring can now be done by machine, administration is occasionally computerized, and sometimes use of tailored tests can shorten testing time by administration of test items at appropriate levels of difficulty for each individual. In general, however, the kinds of items have changed little, and when one considers the public relations effort made by the College Board in the recent cosmetic changes in their Scholastic Aptitude Test (SAT), one can understand the frustration some people feel over the lack of progress in the field. . . .

MARKET FORCES IN THE SCIENCE AND TECHNOLOGY OF INTELLIGENCE TESTING

Testing is today, and has been for many years, a market-driven industry. Testing companies are no different from any other businesses in their desire to maximize both the top line (sales) and the bottom line (profit). Even a nonprofit company such as the Educational Testing Service finds itself in the position of needing very high revenues to support its huge overhead, which a visit to its sprawling "campus" quickly reveals to be quite substantial. My own background as a consultant to publishers and as a test author has made clear to me—sometimes painfully so—just how profit driven testing companies are. One needs to realize that virtually all businesses are this way, or else they do not survive. Some companies have more vision than others (and testing companies probably have not, for the most part, been at or near the top of the scale on this dimension) and some can predict better than others what the future holds, but all need revenues to survive. . . .

Ironically scientists, as well as those in many if not most other fields, are as susceptible in their own way to marketing issues as are business people. Their market of scientific peers may be different from that of most businesses, but it is a market nevertheless. When a scientist writes an article (his or her product), he or she learns to think in terms of what journal reviewers and editors will and will not accept (buy) (see Wagner & Sternberg, 1985). Almost inevitably there are some miscalculations, and the article is rejected or at least returned for revisions. Again, the scientist finds himself or herself pondering the changes that need to be made and that will be acceptable, given the feedback received. Similarly, in giving a talk, the scientist needs to take into account the audience to whom he or she is speaking and needs to pitch his or her talk accordingly. Indeed, anyone who writes or who gives speeches needs to do the same. Grant proposals are even more shamelessly pitched at the consumers of the products because scholars quickly learn that if the proposals are not so pitched, they do not get funded. . . .

If testing is driven largely by market considerations, a true understanding of the progress that has or has not been made in testing would require an understanding of the market forces that drive the testing industry. What do customers want? If test developers imagine themselves as the typical school-based consumer of intelligence tests, they can imagine what their needs might be.

1. *Predicting achievement:* The main use of intelligence tests has always been, and continues to be, prediction of school achievement, whether measured in terms of grades or of scores on standardized achievement tests.
2. *Test-retest or alternate-forms reliability:* Test scores are relatively stable over time. No one can afford the time or money to give the tests again and again on a frequent basis, so test scores need to be relatively stable to be useful.
3. *Accurate standardization:* Administrators are very concerned about how performance in their school (or district) compares with performance in

171

other schools (or districts). Thus, they need accurate and representative norms.

4. *High correlation with other, similar tests:* When records are sent from one school to another or from one district to another, or when a decision is made to switch tests one year, the administration wants to know that the tests used in the past will provide scores that are at least roughly comparable to the tests of the present.

5. *Ease of administration:* For the most part, group tests need to be administered by teachers with little or no training in psychological testing. Tests must therefore be simple to administer, with no hidden surprises.

6. *Ease of interpretation:* The interpreters of the test scores, with the general exception of the interpreters of tests for special educational children and children with problems of various kinds, have little or no knowledge about psychological testing. The test score or scores should thus be easily interpretable by a novice.

7. *Objectivity of scoring.* Administrators do not want to get into arguments with parents or with anyone else over "right answers" or how many points a given answer is worth. Nor do they want their own interpretation of the test scores to be compromised by ambiguities of various kinds. Objectivity is therefore important.

8. *Perceived fairness:* The tests should be perceived to be fair and hence not biased in favor of performance by one group over another. Often, the perception of fairness is more important than any kind of statistically measured fairness.

9. *Cost effectiveness:* In the venacular, the tests should give the maximum bargain for the buck. They should be as cheap as possible and yield information worth at least what they cost.

10. *Legal defensibility:* Given the litigiousness of the society in which we live, the tests should be legally defensible should their use be brought to court.

Although this list of criteria is certainly not exhaustive, nor applicable in every instance in which tests are used, it is at least representative of the kinds of considerations consumers have in mind when they purchase tests. Of course other criteria might be put forth that would be relevant, such as theoretical or empirical backing, and those who are simply "anti-test" might look for miracles, at least with respect to the present state of technology in testing. However, the criteria described above are pretty well aligned with the criteria of most purchasers, who cannot afford the luxury of scientific backing (which if available would be more of a bonus than a necessity) or the luxury of vain hopes for miracles that are presently unattainable.

If one considers current tests in light of the aforementioned criteria, even those (such as myself) who are less than enchanted with current tests cannot fail to realize how well they meet the criteria listed. This is not to say that there are not other lists of criteria on which they would fare much worse. Rather, it is to say that on this particular set of market-oriented criteria (given the market to which the tests are pitched), the tests do surprisingly well.

First, the tests predict achievement fairly well at the elementary school and secondary school levels, although less well in later grades. Even at the college level, they predict about as well as anything else. Second, their reliability over time has historically been good. Third, the tests have had a reputation for accurate standardization, although this reputation has been called into question as of late. As one successively considers each other criterion, current tests appear to meet them. If the tests are failing these days to meet any of the criteria, it is probably the criterion of perceived fairness. Although much has been written about the alleged lack of bias in intelligence tests (e.g., Jensen, 1980), many people remain unconvinced that the bias has been eliminated, for a variety of reasons, not the least of which is the possibility of criterion bias that is shared with the bias of the predictor.

If the tests, for the most part, are fulfilling the criteria of their actual marketplace, then is it any wonder that they should have been so slow to evolve? Of course there are dissatisfactions, and if anything these dissatisfactions seem to be on the increase. At the same time, it is important to realize (especially for those who are in favor of or are trying to instigate change) that there is more than a little smugness in the testing field. Meetings I have attended that were sponsored, for example, by the College Board have been characterized by a high degree of self-congratulation. Moreover, the president of the College Board himself made clear at one recent meeting I attended that he was quite pleased with what his organization is doing. The recent cosmetic changes in the SAT do not bode well for those who were hoping for either a genuine "face-lift," or better, a "new face."

RECENT DEVELOPMENTS FROM A MARKETING STANDPOINT

I now consider some of the recent developments that have been made in testing and how they appear from a marketing standpoint. The thesis of this section is simple: Most of the developments look worse than what they have been designed to replace. This does not mean that they are worse tests, merely that they are less marketable to the people who actually make the purchasing decisions.

Computerized Testing

Computerized testing, which is required for tailored testing, may well be the wave of the future. It is not here yet. People have been hearing for a number of years that computers are the direction in which things are going, but computerized testing has not yet arrived on a broad scale. Most schools do all their testing of all their students (or at least the large majority) at the same time, but few schools have enough computers to go around so that everyone can use a computer at the same time. Many teachers do not know how to use computers, especially how to administer tests on them. Moreover, the appearance of enhanced fairness is somewhat of a myth. Whereas almost all students have considerable experience with paper-and-pencil tasks, their experience with computers is likely to be much more variable. Some students adapt easily to the medium; others do not. The differential experience of the students with the medium of testing creates an unwanted source of bias. Also, if things are going wrong in terms of the student's ability to use the computer, one will probably be unable to separate the medium problem from the message: a low test score.

Quick-Fix Tests

There exists a class of what might be called quick-fix tests, which make enticing but elusive (and in some cases illusory) claims. For example, one such test promises to cut racial differences roughly in half but does so at the cost of emphasizing measurement of abilities that are rather peripheral to most conceptions of intelligence (Kaufman & Kaufman, 1983). Another test measures knowledge of ghetto slang, but it is clear that such a test has not found a ready market in the schools (Williams, 1972). Yet another test essentially gives the test taker points for being a member of a particular racial or ethnic group, a less than compelling way of solving the problem of fair assessments of individual differences in abilities (Mercer et al., 1986). Quick-fix tests may appeal to some market segments, but they are probably even less scientifically defensible than what is currently on the market.

Cognitive Batteries

With the revolution in cognitive psychology of the past 30 years, it is little surprise that cognitive psychologists have attempted to construct test batteries on the basis of current cognitive theories (e.g., Rose, 1978). . . . The result is that 30 years or so after the beginning of the cognitive revolution, there still is no viable test of intelligence based on modern cognitive theory. This is not to say that such a test could not be constructed, merely that it has not been yet.

Theories of Multiple Intelligences

Theories of multiple intelligences (e.g., Gardner, 1983; Sternberg, 1985) have a certain attraction to those who believe that there is more to intelligence than the relatively narrow range of abilities measured by conventional intelligence tests. I am a believer in this point of view. Constructing assessments though proves to be no easy task. . . .

I and colleagues have tried to create a more objective test on the basis of my triarchic theory of intelligence (see Sternberg, 1991), but the road has not been smooth. Items requiring coping with novelty are quite difficult, especially for young children, and practical intelligence items can be difficult to construct because the tacit knowledge that constitutes much of "common sense" is so contextually bound by place and time. Moreover, the full test is quite long (3 hr) by current standards and thus would be likely to sell only to those with a serious interest in broad intellectual assessment. Regrettably the publisher is not currently pursuing further piloting and standardization of the test. . . .

Robert J.
Sternberg

WHAT NEEDS TO BE MEASURED

Given that there is no quick fix in sight, test developers at least ought to be thinking about what they will want to measure in the future. . . . There are probably countless things that could be measured, so I concentrate on the four that I believe to be most important for diagnosis, prediction, and placement.

The first concerns the analytic side of the intellect (see Sternberg, 1985). Current tests measure to some extent this side of thinking. However, they measure it in a confounded and sometimes misleading way. For example, tests such as verbal analogies measure vocabulary and sometimes general information at least as much as they measure verbal reasoning ability (see Sternberg, 1977). Even spatial relations tests involve a variety of ability factors that are nonspatial (e.g., Lohman, 1988). We do not yet know how to measure individual component processes of thought for individuals in a way that is time efficient as well as reliable. However, it is not unrealistic to set as an aspiration measuring at least groupings of these components that will enable the examiner to separate out various kinds of information processing. In analogical reasoning, for example, one might separate out the "reasoning" components of inference, mapping, and application from the nonreasoning components of encoding and response (Sternberg & Gardner, 1983) and perhaps separate encoding and response from each other as well. By grouping together similar components that individually are likely to have less diagnostic value, it may become possible to obtain realistic information about processing from tests in a reliable and cost-efficient way. Such testing might yield more information than is currently available, although less than test developers might have if they were able to separate out all the components. Whereas separating all the components is probably unrealistic as a practical goal at this time, with the advent of various techniques for componential decomposition (e.g., Hunt, 1978; Pellegrino & Glaser, 1980; Snow, 1980; Sternberg, 1985), separating groupings of components seems to be a realistic goal.

Second is the creative side of the intellect: the person's ability to generate new ideas, to cope with novelty, to redefine ordinary problems in extraordinary ways. Traditional measurements have tended to focus on what some, including myself, believe to be a rather trivial side of creativity, and the hope would be that more modern theories of creativity might yield new dividends in terms of measurement (see Sternberg, 1988; Sternberg & Lubart, 1991a, 1991b). . . .

Third is the practical side of the intellect: the person's ability to function in social interactions, at work and in the daily activities that occur outside the school, as well as sometimes within. I (Sternberg, 1985) referred to this as the contextual aspect of intelligence; Gardner (1983) referred to it as interpersonal and intrapersonal intelligences. There are many other terms for it as well (see Sternberg & Wagner, 1986). To survive in the world, one ultimately needs more than academic skills, and there has been at least some progress toward measuring these skills.

A variety of steps have been taken to measure the practical aspect of intelligence (see Rogoff & Lave, 1984; Sternberg, 1991; Sternberg & Wagner, 1986). Some of these have already been used in practical settings; others have not. Practical intelligence is almost certainly domain specific to some degree, so it is doubtful that there will ever be any global measure of the construct. For example, the kind of practical intelligence one needs in a school setting may be somewhat different from the practical intelligence one needs on the job, and different jobs seem to require different kinds of practical intelligence (see Ceci, 1990; Sternberg, Okagaki, & Jackson, 1990; Sternberg, Wagner, & Okagaki, in press). Nevertheless, there is so much evidence that there is more to practical intelligence than what is tested by conventional tests that at least some steps in this direction seem essential. In my and my colleagues' work, for example, measures of tacit knowledge for management do not correlate with conventional ability measures (e.g., Wagner & Sternberg, 1985), and this finding appears to be the rule rather than the exception.

The fourth thing I believe we need to assess is the student's pattern of thinking and learning styles (see Sternberg, 1990). It is common knowledge that students think and learn in different ways, and an understanding of a student's preferred style of learning can facilitate the presentation of optimum instruction. Ultimately, I would like to see educators teaching the styles themselves, in order to maximize students' flexibility in using their intelligence in their work, both within school and outside of school.

In my theory of mental self-government, for example, I make a number of distinctions that are relevant to teaching and learning (Sternberg, 1990). A *legislative* individual—the kind who prefers to come up with his or her own ways of thinking and doing things—does not learn optimally well in the same kind of environment as does an *executive* individual, the kind who prefers more structure and essentially prefers to be told what to do and how to do it. An *oligarchic* individual, who has trouble setting priorities, needs guidance of a kind that a *hierarchical* individual, who is able to set priorities, may not need. Regardless of the theory one prefers, one needs to take into account the differences in the ways in which people learn and think that are not directly intelligence related, and this is something that, at the present time, is not done adequately.

Even these three modest changes in testing would yield far more information about students than is currently available and help forge more closely the link between instruction and assessment. However, I am not claiming that superb measures of any of these things are available, although I do not believe that superb measures of the more conventional memory and analytic sides of the intellect are available either. If educational researchers set their sights low, as I believe they have in testing, they will continue to market products that look like the ones that were available at the turn of the century. Technology, like science, progresses through vision. It is time that those involved in testing and those who buy tests seek out truly relevant technological innovations in their products. Trivial changes in tests make little difference to anyone other than those who concern themselves with marketing strategies.

The best thing that could happen to testing is that the publishers of tests would begin to lead rather than follow the market. Other industries have recognized the importance of basic research to the future development of products, and many of the greatest innovations have followed from basic research. Although the Educational Testing Service once had an active, cutting-edge basic research program, neither they nor any of the other test publishers currently have such a program. Although applied research is important, it is less likely than basic research to lead to fundamental innovations. Moreover, the fundamental innovations—the IBM Personal Computer, the Macintosh computer, or the ballpoint pen for that matter—have led rather than followed markets. Test publishers have become so reactive, perhaps because of the onslaughts of legal challenges to which they have been exposed, that they have lost whatever productive edge they might once have had in the development of products that lead rather than respond to markets. I believe that if educational researchers adopt a longer term perspective on ability testing and look at the vast horizons in front of them, they will be capable of making serious advances that the current shorter term perspective does not enable them to make.

Robert J.
Sternberg

REFERENCES

Binet, A. & Simon, T. (1916). *The development of intelligence in children* (E. S. Kite, Trans.). Baltimore, MD: Williams & Wilkins. (Reprinted from *L'Annee psychologique*, 1905, pp. 163–336; 1908, pp. 1–90; 1911, pp. 145–201).

Ceci, S. J. (1990). *On intelligence . . . more or less.* Englewood Cliffs, NJ: Prentice-Hall.

Gardner, H. (1983). *Frames of mind: The theory of multiple intelligences.* New York: Basic Books.

Hunt, E. B. (1978). Mechanics of verbal ability. *Psychological Review, 85,* 109–130.

Jensen, A. R. (1980). *Bias in mental testing.* New York: Free Press.

Kaufman, A. S., & Kaufman, N. L. (1983). *Kaufman Assessment Battery for Children.* Circle Pines, MN: American Guidance Service.

Lohman, D. F. (1988). Spatial abilities as traits, processes, and knowledge. In R. J. Sternberg (Ed.), *Advances in the Psychology of Human Intelligence* (Vol. 4, pp. 181–248). Hillsdale, NJ: Erlbaum.

Mercer, J. R., Gomez-Palacio, M., & Padilla, E. (1986). The development of intelligence in cross-cultural perspective. In R. J. Sternberg & R. K. Wagner (Eds.), *Practical intelligence: Nature and origins of competence in the everyday world* (pp. 307–337). New York: Cambridge University Press.

Pellegrino, J. W., & Glaser, R. (1980). Components of inductive reasoning. In R. Snow, P. A. Federico, & W. Montague (Eds.), *Aptitude, learning, and instruction: Cognitive process analysis of aptitude* (Vol. 1, pp. 177–217). Hillsdale, NJ: Erlbaum.

Rogoff, B., & Lave, J. (Eds.) (1984). *Everyday cognition: Its development in social context.* Cambridge, MA: Harvard University Press.

Rose, A. M. (1978). *An information processing approach to performance assessment* (NR 150–391 ONR Report). Washington, DC: American Institutes for Research.

Snow, R. E. (1980). Aptitude processes. In R. E. Snow, P. A. Federico, & W. E. Montague (Eds.), *Aptitude, learning, and instruction: Cognitive process and analysis of aptitude* (Vol. 1, pp. 27–63). Hillsdale, NJ: Erlbaum.

Sternberg, R. J. (1977). *Intelligence, information processing, and analogical reasoning: The componential analysis of human abilities.* Hillsdale, NJ: Erlbaum.

Sternberg, R. J. (1985). *Beyond IQ: A triarchic theory of human intelligence.* New York: Cambridge University Press.

Sternberg, R. J. (Ed.). (1988). *The nature of creativity.* New York: Cambridge University Press.

Sternberg, R. J. (1990). Thinking styles: Keys to understanding student performance. *Phi Delta Kappan, 71,* 366–371.

Sternberg, R. J. (1991). Theory-based testing of intellectual abilties: Rationale for the Sternberg Triarchic Abilities Test. In H. Rowe (Ed.), *Intelligence: Reconceptualization and measurement* (pp. 183–201). Hillsdale, NJ: Erlbaum.

Sternberg, R. J., & Gardner, M. K. (1983). Unities in inductive reasoning. *Journal of Experimental Psychology: General, 112,* 80–116.

Sternberg, R. J., & Lubart, T. I. (1991a). Creating creative minds. *Phi Delta Kappan, 72,* 608–614.

Sternberg, R. J., & Lubart, T. I. (1991b). An investment theory of creativity and its development. *Human Development, 34,* 1–25.

Sternberg, R. J., Okagaki, L., & Jackson, A. (1990). Practical intelligence for success in school. *Educational Leadership, 48,* 35–39.

Sternberg, R. J., & Wagner, R. K. (Eds.) (1986). *Practical intelligence: Nature and origins of competence in the everyday world.* New York: Cambridge University Press.

Sternberg, R. J., Wagner, R. K., & Okagaki, L. (in press). Practical intelligence: The nature and role of tacit knowledge in work and at school. In H. Reese & J. Puckett (Eds.), *Advances in lifespan development.* Hillsdale, NJ: Erlbaum.

Wagner, R. K., & Sternberg, R. J. (1985). Practical intelligence in real-world pursuits: The role of tacit knowledge. *Journal of Personality and Social Psychology, 49,* 436–458.

Williams, D. S. (1972). Computer program organization induced from problem examples. In H. A. Simon & L. Siklossy (Eds.), *Representation and meaning: Experiments with information processing systems.* Englewood Cliffs, NJ: Prentice-Hall.

8.2 SANDRA SCARR AND RICHARD A. WEINBERG

The Minnesota Adoption Studies: Genetic Differences and Malleability

Because of ethical and methodological constraints, it is often difficult to conduct research on how heredity and environment affect human cognitive abilities such as intelligence. One research technique that has been used in this area is the adoption method. With this method, psychologists look at the cognitive similarities between adopted children and their adoptive parents, as well as their biological parents, and, thus, distinguish between likely genetic and environmental influences. The adoption method is evident in the Minnesota adoption studies, designed by Sandra Scarr and Richard A. Weinberg, part of which was used to investigate racial differences in intelligence.

Scarr (b. 1936) earned her Ph.D. in psychology from Harvard University in 1965. She has taught at Yale University and the University of Minnesota, and she has been teaching at the University of Virginia since 1983. Weinberg obtained his Ph.D. from the University of Minnesota in 1968, where he is currently a professor of child psychology.

This selection, "The Minnesota Adoption Studies: Genetic Differences and Malleability," was published in *Child Development* in 1983. In it, Scarr and Weinberg review two long-term adoption studies that were begun in 1974. As you read this article, keep in mind that intelligence is influenced by many variables and that it is extremely difficult to isolate specific genetic and environmental factors. What do the results of these studies suggest about the relative importance of heredity and environment on intelligence?

Key Concept: intelligence, heredity, and adoption studies

*S*ocial sciences have been plagued by the controversy over nature and nurture, as though the conjunction were "or." At the core of the controversy is the idea that genetic variation fixes individual and group differences in human behavior. Opponents of the idea believe that genetic differences are antithetical to malleability or change in behavior. A common error underlying this belief is a failure to distinguish environmental and genetic sources of individual differences in behavior from the necessary roles of both genes and environments in behavioral development. One cannot assess the relative impact of heredity or environment in behavioral domains because everyone must have both a viable gene complement and an environment in which the genes can be expressed over development.

Behavioral differences among individuals, on the other hand, can arise in any population from genetic differences, from variations among their environments, or both. Imagine a population of genetically identical clones who are reared in family environments that vary from working to upper middle class. Any behavioral differences among the clones would necessarily arise from developing within those different environments. Next, imagine a genetically diverse human population reared in laboratory cages. All members experience exactly the same environments. Naturally, all differences among those individuals are accounted for by their genetic variability. Notice, however, that in the two fantasies the organisms all have both genes and environments for development (Scarr & Weinberg, 1980, p. 859). Because nearly all families share both genes and environments, it is usually impossible to know why individuals are similar or different from one another.

THE ADOPTION MODEL

The adoption of children with biological backgrounds that are different from both their adopting parents and each other provides an opportunity to evaluate the impact of environments on children's development. If differences among the child-rearing environments provided by families determine differences in children's development, then the differences among adopted children ought to be correlated with differences among their adoptive families. Theoretically, regressions of adopted-child outcomes on adoptive-family characteristics will provide genetically unbiased estimates of true environmental effects in the population from which they are drawn.

Unfortunately, adoptive families are selected by agencies for being above average in many virtues, including socioeconomic status [SES]. Children in adoptive families are reared in nondeprived, nonabusive environments. However, the fact that the SES range of adoptive families usually includes at least two-thirds of the U.S. white population makes results of adoption studies compelling.

Comparisons of adopted and biological relatives assume that the greater behavioral similarity usually found among biological relatives is a result of their greater genetic similarity. Critics of the adoption model assert to the contrary that important biases can creep into comparisons of genetically related and unrelated families through parental and child expectations of greater similarity among biological than adopted relatives. Fortunately for the adoption model, knowledge of adoptive or biological relatedness does not constitute a bias in comparisons of measured behavioral differences in biological and adoptive families, because there are no correlations between perceived and actual similarities in intelligence or personality (Scarr, Scarf, & Weinberg, 1980).

THE MINNESOTA ADOPTION STUDIES

Following in the tradition of Alice M. Leahy (1935), who conducted a pioneering adoption study in Minnesota, we launched two large adoption studies in 1974 for two quite different purposes. The Transracial Adoption Study was carried out from 1974 through 1976 in Minnesota to test the hypothesis that black and interracial children reared by white families (in the culture of the tests and the schools) would perform on IQ tests and school achievement measures as well as other adopted children (Scarr & Weinberg, 1976). A second investigation, the Adolescent Adoption Study, was conceived to assess the cumulative impact of differences in family environments on children's development at the end of the child-rearing period (Scarr & Weinberg, 1978; Scarr & Yee, 1980). In both studies, we examined the levels of intellectual and personality development, as well as the degree of resemblance among family members, by comparing adoptive and biological relatives. The focus of this review is on IQ and school achievement tests. . . .

TRANSRACIAL ADOPTION STUDY

Sample

The 101 transracial adoptive families included 176 adopted children, of whom 130 were socially classified as black. All of the adopted children were unrelated to the adoptive parents and to each other, with a few exceptions who were excluded from analyses. The sample also included 143 biological children of the adoptive parents. Among the adoptees, 111 were adopted in the first year of life and 65 after 12 months of age.

Results and Discussion

IQ levels of family members.—Both the parents and the biological children of the families scored in the bright average to superior range on age-appropriate IQ tests. The black and interracial adopted children were also found to

TABLE 1

*Comparisons of Biological and Unrelated Parent-Child IQ Correlations
in 101 Transracial Adoptive Families*

	N (pairs)	r
Parents–unrelated children:		
Adoptive mother–adopted child	174	.21 (.23)[a]
Natural mother–own child of adoptive family[b]	217	.15
Adoptive father–adopted child	170	.27 (.15)[a]
Natural father–own child of adoptive family[b]	86	.19
Parents–biological children:		
Adoptive mother–own child	141	.34
Natural mother–adopted child[b]	135	.33
Adoptive father–own child	142	.39
Natural father–adopted child[b]	46	.43

[a]Early adopted only (N = 111).
[b]Educational level, not IQ scores.

score above the average of the white population, regardless of when they had
been adopted. The black children adopted in the first 12 months of life scored
on the average at IQ 110 (Scarr & Weinberg, 1976), 20 points above comparable
children being reared in the black community. We interpreted the high IQ
scores of the black and interracial children to mean that *(a)* genetic racial differences do not account for a major portion of the IQ performance difference
between racial groups, and *(b)* black and interracial children reared in the
culture of the tests and the schools perform as well as other adopted children in
similar families (Burks, 1928; Horn, Loehlin, & Willerman, 1979; Leahy, 1935;
Scarr & Weinberg, 1978). The adopted children scored 6 points below the natural children of the same families, however, as Burks (1928) and our second
adoption study also found.

Parent-child correlations.—Table 1 shows the correlations of the parents
and children in the transracial adoption study. The adoptive families had
adopted at least one black child, but there were also other adopted children
and many biological offspring of these same parents. The children ranged in
age from 4 to about 18. Because of the age range, children from 4 to 7 years
were given the Stanford-Binet (1973 norms), children from 8 to 16 the WISC,
and older children and all parents the WAIS. The average age of the adopted
children was 7, and of the natural children about 10. Table 1 gives the parent-
child IQ correlations for all of the adopted children in the transracial adoptive
families, regardless of when they had been adopted. The total sample of
adopted children is just as similar to their adoptive parents as the early-
adopted group is to theirs. The midparent–child IQ correlation for all adoptees
is .29;[1] for the early adoptees it is .30. Mothers are equally similar to all adopted

children, and fathers are more similar to the total sample than they are to the early-adopted children.

Table 1 also shows the correlations between all adopted children's IQ scores and their natural parents' educational levels. Because we did not have IQ assessments of the natural parents, education is used here as proxy. Despite this limitation, the correlations of natural parents' education with their adopted-away offspring's IQ scores are as high as the IQ correlations of biological parent–child pairs and exceed those of the adoptive parent–child IQ scores. The natural midparent–child correlation of .43 is significantly greater than the adopted midparent–child correlation of .29. . . .

The correlations between natural parents of adopted children and the biological children of the same adoptive families is an estimate of the effects of selective placement (entries 2 and 4 in Table 1). If agencies match educational and social class characteristics of the natural mothers with similar adoptive parents, then the resemblance between adoptive parents and children is enhanced by the genetic resemblance of natural and adoptive parents in intelligence. Selective placement also enhances the correlation between natural parents and their adopted-away offspring, because the adoptive parents carry out the genotype-environment correlation that would have characterized the natural parent–child pairs, had the children been retained by their natural parents. Thus, neither the adoptive parent–child correlations nor the natural parent–adopted child correlations deserve to be as high as they are (Scarr & Weinberg, 1977). From the comparison of biological and adoptive parent–child correlations, each corrected for selective placement, we estimated that 40%–70% of the IQ variance in this sample was due to genetic differences among the children.

Sibling correlation.— . . .[T]he sibling correlations reveal a different picture. Young siblings are similar to each other, whether genetically related to each other or not. The IQ correlations of adopted siblings [.44] are as high as those of the biological siblings reared together [.42]. Children reared in the same family environments and who are still under the major influence of their parents score at similar levels on IQ tests. The IQ correlations of the adopted siblings result in small part from their correlations in background, such as their natural mothers' educational levels (.16) and age at placement in the adoptive home (.37), which are in turn related to the present intellectual functioning of the children—the earlier the placement, the higher the IQ score. Age of placement is itself correlated with many other background characteristics of the child and is a complex variable (Scarr & Weinberg, 1976). But note that the correlation among the early adopted siblings is .39. Even among the families who had early adoptees, differences in family environments and selective placement account for a substantial resemblance between unrelated children. . . .

The major point is that the heritabilities (percentage of genetic variance) calculated from young-sibling data in the Minnesota Transracial Adoption Study are very different from those calculated from the parent–child data. As Christopher Jencks pointed out in his earlier book (1972), the correlations of unrelated young siblings reared together do not fit any biometrical model because they are too high. This study of young children confirms his point. Our second study, of older adolescents, however, does not.

ADOLESCENT ADOPTION STUDY

Sample

The adolescents in this study had spent an average of 18 years in their families—194 adopted children in 115 adoptive families and a comparison group of 237 biological children in 120 other families. All of the adoptees were placed in their families in the first year of life, the median being 2 months of age. From 1975 to 1977 both groups of children were 16–22 years old. Both samples of parents were of similar SES, from working to upper middle class, and of similar IQ levels on the WAIS. The IQ scores of parents in both adoptive and biological families averaged 115, approximately 1 SD [standard deviation] above the population mean. The biological children scored, on the average, an IQ of 113, and the adopted children 7 points lower at 106.

Results and Discussion

Parent–child and sibling correlations.—The parent–child IQ correlations in the biological families were what we were led to expect from the Transracial Adoption Study and others—about .40 when corrected for restriction of range in the parents' scores. The biological midparent–child correlation was .52. The adoptive parent–child correlations were lower than those of the younger adoptive parents and their children—about .13; the adoptive midparent–child correlation was only .14.

The adopted children's IQ scores were more closely correlated with the educational levels of their natural mothers (.28) and fathers (.43) than with those of their adoptive mothers (.09) and fathers (.11). In fact, adopted children's IQ scores were as highly correlated with their natural parents' education as were those of the adolescents in the biological sample (.17 and .26, respectively) (Scarr & Weinberg, 1980).

The IQ correlation of the biologically related siblings was .35, similar to that of the siblings in the Transracial Adoption Study. However, the IQ correlation of adopted children reared together for 18 years was zero! Unlike the younger siblings, who are of different races, these white adolescents reared together from infancy did not resemble their genetically unrelated siblings. The heritabilities calculated from the adolescent IQ data varied from .38 to .61, much like the parent–child data in the study of younger, transracial adoptees but unlike data on these younger siblings. . . .

Our interpretation of these results (Scarr & Weinberg, 1978) is that older adolescents are largely liberated from their families' influences and have made choices and pursued courses that are in keeping with their own talents and interests. Thus, the unrelated siblings have grown less and less alike. This hypothesis cannot be tested fully without longitudinal data on adopted siblings; to date all of the other adoption studies sampled much younger children, at the average age of 7 or 8. We can think of no other explanation for the markedly low correlations between the adopted siblings at the end of the child-rearing period, in contrast to the several studies of younger adopted siblings, who are embarrassingly similar.

185

*Sandra Scarr
and Richard A.
Weinberg*

DISCUSSION

We interpret the results of the two studies to mean that younger children, regardless of their genetic relatedness, resemble each other intellectually because they share a similar rearing environment. Older adolescents, on the other hand, resemble one another only if they share genes. Our interpretation is that older children escape the influences of the family and are freer to select their own environments. Parental influences are diluted by the more varied mix of adolescent experiences.

The results support the idea that older children and adolescents build their own niches, which can be seen as an active genotype-environment correlation (Plomin, DeFries, & Loehlin, 1977). Different people select different aspects of their environments that they find compatible. Choices of environments are influenced by genetic differences in what individuals enjoy and at which they are competent. Adopted children, not genetically related to their parents or to one another, build niches that are related to their own genotypes but not to those of their family members. Biologically related children also create niches that are correlated with their genotypes, but their choices are also correlated with those of their genetically related family members (see Scarr & McCartney, in this issue).

Malleability.—What are the implications of these results for developmental plasticity? First, it is clear from the IQ scores of the transracially adopted children that they, like other adoptees, are responsive to the rearing environments in adoptive families, which as a group provide intellectual stimulation and exposure to the skills and knowledge sampled on IQ tests. The mean IQ scores of both samples of adoptees are above the average of age-mates, primarily because they benefit from their rearing environments.

Second, individual adoptees differ in their responses to the environmental advantages of adoptive families. Those with natural parents of higher educational levels, and by implication higher intellectual abilities, are more responsive to the rearing environments of adoptive families than are those with natural parents of more limited intellectual skills. Children adopted into families of adoptive parents at and above the average educational and IQ levels of adoptive parents score higher on the WAIS than children of comparable natural mothers adopted into families with less bright adoptive parents. . . . [T]he adolescents whose natural mothers and adoptive parents are both below average score 10.4 IQ points below those whose natural mothers and adoptive parents are both above average.

Individual differences among the adopted children at both younger and older ages are related to intellectual variation among adoptive parents and their biological parents, even though the average IQ of adoptees most likely exceeds that of their natural parents. Human beings are not infinitely plastic;

malleability does not mean that given the same environment, all individuals will end up alike.

REFERENCES

Burks, B. S. The relative influence of nature and nurture upon mental development: A comparative study of foster parent–foster child resemblance and true parent–true child resemblance. *Yearbook of the National Society for the Study of Education*, 1928, **27**, 219–316.

Horn, J. M., Loehlin, J. C., & Willerman, L. Intellectual resemblance among adoptive and biological relatives: The Texas Adoption Project. *Behavior Genetics*, 1979, **9**, 177–207.

Jencks, C. *Inequality: A reassessment of the effects of family and schooling in America*. New York: Basic, 1972.

Leahy, A. M. Nature-nurture and intelligence. *Genetic Psychology Monographs*, 1935, **17**, 237–308.

Plomin, R., DeFries, J. C., & Loehlin, J. C. Genotype-environment interaction and correlation in the analysis of human behavior. *Psychological Bulletin*, 1977, **84**(2), 309–322.

Scarr, S., Scarf, E., & Weinberg, R. A. Perceived and actual similarities in biological and adoptive families: Does perceived similarity bias genetic influence? *Behavior Genetics*, 1980, **10**, 445–458.

Scarr, S., & Weinberg, R. A. IQ test performance of black children adopted by white families. *American Psychologist*, 1976, **31**, 726–739.

Scarr, S., & Weinberg, R. A. Intellectual similarities within families of both adopted and biological children. *Intelligence*, 1977, **1**, 170–191.

Scarr, S., & Weinberg, R. A. The influence of "family background" on intellectual attainment. *American Sociological Review*, 1978, **43**, 674–692.

Scarr, S., & Weinberg, R. A. Calling all camps! The war is over. *American Sociological Review*, 1980, **45**, 859–865.

Scarr, S., & Yee, D. Heritability and educational policy: Genetic and environmental effects on IQ, aptitude, and achievement. *Educational Psychologist*, 1980, **15**(1), 1–22.

NOTE

1. The midparent value is the average of the two parents' scores.

8.3 DAVID PREMACK

The Education of Sarah: A Chimp Learns the Language

One difference between humans and other animals is the ability to use language. Other primates cannot speak verbally as we do; however, a number of studies have been done to investigate the ability of nonhuman primates to learn to communicate with language. Researchers have seemingly taught primates to communicate through various means, such as with sign language or, as David Premack demonstrates in this selection, with plastic symbols.

Premack (b. 1925) earned his Ph.D. from the University of Minnesota and began his research with chimpanzees in 1954 at the Yerkes Laboratories for Primate Biology in Florida. He taught psychology at the University of California prior to teaching at the University of Pennsylvania, and he coauthored *The Mind of an Ape* (W. W. Norton, 1983) with his wife, Ann.

This selection, "The Education of Sarah: A Chimp Learns the Language," was published in *Psychology Today* in 1970. Although it is written in an informal, conversational style, it conveys the rigorous scientific research that Premack performed to examine language development in a chimpanzee. Each question about the chimp's ability and understanding is carefully tested. Research on teaching language to primates is controversial as well as difficult to conduct. Premack helps us understand how he went about investigating this fascinating phenomenon. As you read the article, consider what criteria you would require to conclude that nonhuman primates can learn language.

Key Concept: teaching language to a chimpanzee

*I*n order to have a psychological theory of language, we must replace the structural emphasis of linguists with a functional emphasis. The general functions an organism carries out when it is engaged in language need to be separated from the specific form those functions take in man. Some aspects of human phonology and syntax might be unique to man, but it may be that the

187

basic functions of language depend on other mechanisms—logic and semantics—that are more widely distributed.

The functional approach requires two things: 1) a list of functions, the behaviors an organism must show to give evidence of language; 2) a parallel list of strict training procedures, giving one way—preferably several ways—to produce each function. A training procedure is actually no more than an ordered series of steps, each small enough to be manageable by our languageless subject. It is not an explanation of how the organism learns the function; training procedure, at this stage, is a method in search of a theory. . . .

Our drawing board will be the chimpanzee, close to man phylogenetically, if not linguistically. Meet Sarah, age seven, who has been our eager and delightful subject for two years at the University of California, Santa Barbara.

Attempts to teach simians to talk have failed consistently; speech appears to be anatomically impossible for them. So we decided to establish a nonvocal language for Sarah. Each "word" is a metal-backed plastic bit, varying in shape, size, color and texture, that adheres to a magnetized slate. Words and sentences are placed on the slate vertically, simply because at first this seemed to be the style Sarah preferred.

Man & Dog. The word is an essential unit of language. It reflects, among other things, the consensus that perceptual events can be divided into stable elements. In the occurrence "man bites dog," for instance, there are three clear units: someone doing the biting, the action of biting (as opposed to hitting or petting, perhaps), and something being bitten. Most functions of language serve to represent and distinguish the elements of experience.

But teaching first words to a totally naive animal is far different from introducing new words to a person who already has some language. The first step was to establish a simple social transaction between trainer and chimp—giving Sarah fruit—and it was this transaction that we set out to map with language.

At first, one of the trainers—Mary Morgan, Deborah Petersen, Randy Runk or Jim Olson—would place a banana on the table and watch benevolently as Sarah took it and ate it. This routine continued until one day the trainer introduced an element from the language system, a piece of colored plastic. The banana was now further back than usual, out of reach, while the plastic chip was easily within grasp. The trainer introduced Sarah to make a specific response with the "word": she had to place it on the language board before she got the banana. Sarah quickly learned to play this little game.

Variety. Now we began to introduce new fruits and new plastic words for them. In each case Sarah had to put the plastic on the board before she could get the apple, orange, or other fruit.

Then we gave her two words but only one piece of fruit, to see whether she could match the correct word to the food. Sarah was generally successful in this task, but she could occasionally be using the "wrong" word as a request for the fruit not being offered. To detect this, we allowed her to choose between all possible pairs of fruits, and then between all possible pairs of plastic words. If her fruit preferences agreed with her word preferences, we reasoned, then she must know what word goes with what fruit. And she did.

Matches. Next we began to change other aspects of the transaction, adding appropriate words. We varied the person giving the fruit. When Mary was present and the fruit was apple, Sarah had to write *Mary apple* on the board in order to get the food. If Randy was the donor, she had to write *Randy apple*, and so on. We used the same tests to see whether Sarah understood the association between persons and symbols and indeed Sarah did.

Sarah easily learned the fruit and donor classes. It was harder to vary the recipient of the fruit, since Sarah was understandably reluctant to write sentences calling for someone else to get the goodies. Similarly, the attempt to change the verb—*giving, cutting* or *inserting* the fruit—met with the same resistance: Sarah, childlike, only wanted to take it. These problems turned out to be practical matters, however; we handled them by arranging proper rewards. For example, when Sarah wrote *Mary give apple Randy*, thereby denying herself the apple, she got a tidbit she likes even more than apple. Altruism, properly rewarded, soon becomes quite reliable.

Classes. The basic training procedure for the function *word* is thus very simple. We establish a transaction between chimp and trainer, and divide the event into perceptual classes: in this case donor, action, fruit, recipient. Then each class is rotated through a series of values, holding the other classes constant. With each variation a corresponding change is made in the language element. Ultimately, the whole transaction is mapped: Sarah can fully describe the event by writing *Mary give apple Sarah*.

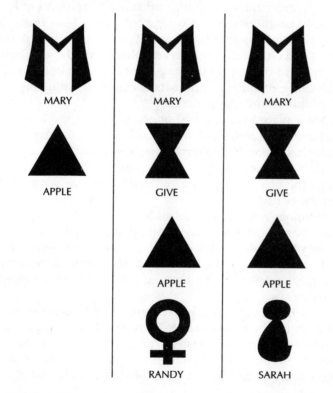

But the chimp may produce a properly ordered string of words without understanding that the string is a sentence. Unlike a string of words, a sentence has internal organization—syntax—in which each word depends on all the others. Perhaps the simplest condition requiring syntax is the symmetrical two-term relation found in geometrical propositions (A on C but also C on A) and in some verbs of social behavior (X talks to Y but also Y talks to X). In cases of this kind, the A's and C's can be completely interchanged and the sentence will still have meaning; the only way to distinguish them is by the order of appearance.

By contrast, in closed relations there is a clear difference between items that appear in one position and those that appear in another. For example, *insert*, as a verb, involves a closed relation: we can insert fruit in dishes, but pieces of fruit do not insert us. If I were to give you three words—Sarah, banana, insert—you would know, regardless of their order, who does the inserting and what is to be inserted. We can therefore treat *insert* as a relation between two classes—inserters and insertables—that are defined by their physical or functional properties. This is an example of a semantic covariation rule, since as one class varies the other must also.

Order. We began Sarah's lesson in sentence structure with symmetrical relations, using the preposition *on.* To make sure that she was learning on a syntactic basis, we used sentences in which one order made as much sense as another. Colors provided a good example: *red on green* has no necessary edge over *green on red*—unlike *fly on horse*, which is notably more probable than the reverse. Thus if Sarah could learn to recognize when one color is *on* another, we might infer that she can understand one contribution of syntax, word order.

We had previously taught Sarah four colors: red, green, blue and yellow; each appeared on a two-inch-by-four-inch card. These four colors make 12 possible combinations: red on green, green on red, blue on yellow, etc. Training consisted of three steps: 1) teaching Sarah one pair of colors, in both orders; 2) seeing whether she could generalize to other sets of colors; 3) testing her ability to produce, as well as understand, the sentences.

Switch. First, Mary placed the red card on the table, put the words *green on red* on the board, handed Sarah the green card and induced her to place it on the red one. After she had done this several times and Sarah was getting the idea, Mary reversed the sentence: she put *red on green* on the board and gave Sarah the red card as the one to be placed on top. Sarah was soon adept at doing what either sentence called for.

In step two, the trainer wrote sentences with the 10 other possible combinations of colors, and Sarah's task was the same. If she wrote *yellow on blue*, Sarah had to place the yellow card on the blue one, and not vice-versa. She did just as well on the 10 new cases as she had on red and green, demonstrating that she had not simply memorized the training colors but could apply the preposition to new sentences.

In the last step, the trainer gave Sarah three words, two colors and *on*, and required her to put them on the board so as to correspond to her placement of the cards. If Mary put the blue card on the green one, Sarah had to write *blue on green*. Sarah was able to do this eight or nine times out of 10, her usual performance level. She has since been taught "side" and "front of," using essentially the same procedure.

Agent. Now consider the sentence, in chimp language, *Sarah insert banana pail apple dish*, which means that Sarah must put the banana in the pail and the apple in the dish. This example carries us beyond word order to a second contribution of syntax: hierarchical organization of a sentence. It would be impossible to carry out the instruction without understanding that banana goes with pail, apple with dish, that insert applies to both cases, and that Sarah is the agent of both actions.

Sarah's previous levels of comprehension would not permit her to understand this complicated instruction. Word knowledge alone, for instance, would tell her that she is to be the agent, that she must insert something; and that the objects are fruits and containers. But from here there would be great latitude as to what was inserted in what; the dish could end up in the pail as often as the banana. Only knowledge of the hierarchical organization of the sentence would insure the outcome we wanted.

Choice. Sarah's training on this problem again proceeded in three stages. First we taught her each of the four simple statements that could be derived from the target sentence:

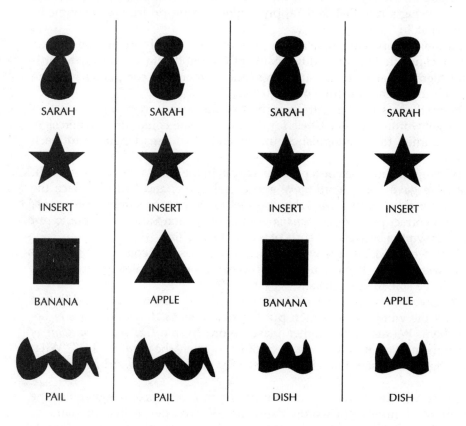

The trainer wrote each of these statements on the board, while offering Sarah a choice of fruits and containers, and required her to place the specified fruit in its proper container.

When Sarah had mastered this step, we gave her all possible pairs of the four statements, side by side. We included this step merely to accustom her to carrying out two acts of insertion, as required by the target sentence.

Finally, we combined all possible pairs of simple statements, this time one immediately above the other. . . .

Neither the deletion of the second use of *Sarah* nor the deletion of *insert* disrupted Sarah's performance. She carried out the instructions 80 to 90 per cent of the time, her usual level, even when we omitted the redundant words. Nor was she the least bit disturbed by our generalization tests. We substituted fruits (grape, apricot, orange); we replaced *insert* with *take out;* her performance remained highly accurate.

Outburst. To rule out the possibility that Sarah was using a semantic rule, such as "apply the container word to the fruit word immediately above it," we tried some modifications of the original sentence, such as *Sarah insert apple dish apple banana pail,* or *Sarah insert apple red dish apple banana green dish.* Although the last sentence was extremely difficult for her—judged by the emotional outbursts and the slow pace of her work—she was nevertheless able to do it. She put both apple and banana in the correct dish, proving that she could not simply be using a rule that said "apply container word to fruit word immediately above it."

Proving competence in syntax is, of course, a highly inferential matter. Still we feel justified in concluding that Sarah can understand some symmetrical and hierarchical sentence structures, and is therefore competent to some degree in the sentence function of language. . . .

Pairs. Sarah's language training had so far been a mapping of existing knowledge; words gave her labels for distinctions she could already perceive. Next we turned to metalinguistics, the function that uses language to teach language.

We taught Sarah the concept *is the name of* in the same way that we taught identity. We gave her a word *apple* and a real apple, and had her place the symbol *name of* between them. Likewise she had to put the symbol *not-name of* between incorrect pairs (word *banana* with apple). Soon Sarah was able to put the correct symbol between all sorts of word-object pairs.

Then we decided to see whether Sarah could use the concept *name of* in a more powerful way. If we taught her the name of a completely novel item, would she be able to use it in sentences thereafter?

We gave Sarah a new treat, figs. We placed a fig next to a plastic chip that was to be the word fig, and then put the newly learned symbol *name of* between them. We also put another plastic word by the fig, with *not-name of* between them. We gave Sarah a variety of tests ("Is *fig* the name of fig?" "What is *fig* to fig?"), and saw that she could clearly associate the word *fig* with the fruit.

To see whether Sarah could now use *fig* in a sentence, we gave her the real fruit and a number of words: the names of two other fruits, the name of fig, the word we told her was not the name of fig, and the familiar symbols *give, Sarah,* and *Mary.* We allowed Sarah to eat the fig when she wrote *Mary give fig Sarah.* To our delight she was highly successful on this test. She was equally good at learning other new words by this same metalinguistic procedure.

Condition. When does a piece of plastic become a word? We answer: when it is used as a word. For example, we consider a bit of blue plastic to be the name for apple because 1) it is the symbol used when Sarah requests apple, and 2) it is the answer Sarah gives to "what is the name for apple?" We can add that the plastic becomes a word when the properties ascribed to it are not those of the plastic, but those of the object it names.

We could see whether this condition was true for Sarah by use of matching-to-sample procedures. We gave her the apple and a pair of descriptive alternatives, and she had to tell us which of these was more like the apple. We began with four sets: red vs. green, round vs. square, square with stem vs. plain square, and plain circle vs. square with stem. Sarah gave consistent answers that tended to agree with those you and I would give.

Then we repeated the procedure exactly, but we replaced the real apple with the name for apple, a piece of blue plastic. Sarah assigned to the plastic the same properties that she had just ascribed to the apple: it was round, not square; red, not green, and so on. This is evidence that the chimp thinks of the word not as its literal form (blue plastic) but as the thing it represents (red apple).

Sarah's Turn. Our studies suggest that Sarah, who knows more than 120 words, has mastered . . . important functions of language. This does not mean that she can produce all the functions of language, or that she can do everything a human can; but then, we have only been working with her a relatively short while.

To cynics who doubt that Sarah understands language, we can say only that she understands well enough to teach her teachers. During a preposition test one day, Sarah, who became restless, gave Mary what amounted to a sentence-completion test. Sarah put up a partial statement on one side of the language board (A is on . . .) and then arranged alternate answers on the other side. Sarah would point to each possible answer, and Mary's task (which took her a good while to figure out) was to nod when Sarah pointed to the right one. "The little devil would pass by the solution quickly and try to trick me into a mistake," Mary reported.

PART FOUR

Motivation and Emotion

CHAPTER 9

Motivation

9.1 ABRAHAM H. MASLOW

A Theory of Human Motivation

Motivation, a core concept in psychology, has been studied from a wide variety of perspectives. One intriguing perspective is the humanistic theory, which proposes that there is a hierarchy of human needs that, when satisfied, leads to self-actualization, or the realization of one's potential.

Abraham H. Maslow (1908–1970), who first proposed the humanistic theory of motivation, earned his Ph.D. in experimental psychology from the University of Wisconsin in 1934. He taught at Brooklyn College and Brandeis University before going to the Laughlin Foundation in Menlo Park, California, in 1969. A leading proponent of the humanistic approach in psychology, Maslow wrote a number of books, including *Toward a Psychology of Being,* 2d ed. (Van Nostrand Reinhold, 1968) and *Motivation and Personality* (1954).

This selection, "A Theory of Human Motivation," was published in the *Psychological Review* in 1943. In it, Maslow presents his original thinking in developing his "positive" humanistic theory. He perceives human needs as composing a hierarchy, with self-actualization—becoming what one is capable of becoming—as the ultimate need. Maslow writes in a straightforward style, but he deals with issues that are complex and that, in many ways, form the essence of being human. As you read this article, consider what motivates you in your everyday life.

Key Concept: humanistic theory of motivation

*I*t is far easier to perceive and to criticize the aspects in motivation theory than to remedy them. Mostly this is because of the very serious lack of sound data in this area. I conceive this lack of sound facts to be due primarily to the absence of a valid theory of motivation. The present theory then must be considered to be a suggested program or framework for future research and must stand or fall, not so much on facts available or evidence presented, as upon researches yet to be done, researches suggested perhaps, by the questions raised in this paper.

THE BASIC NEEDS

The 'physiological' needs.—The needs that are usually taken as the starting point for motivation theory are the so-called physiological drives. Two recent lines of research make it necessary to revise our customary notions about these needs, first, the development of the concept of homeostasis, and second, the finding that appetites (preferential choices among foods) are a fairly efficient indication of actual needs or lacks in the body.

Homeostasis refers to the body's automatic efforts to maintain a constant, normal state of the blood stream. Cannon (2) has described this process for (1) the water content of the blood, (2) salt content, (3) sugar content, (4) protein content, (5) fat content, (6) calcium content, (7) oxygen content, (8) constant hydrogen-ion level (acid-base balance) and (9) constant temperature of the blood. Obviously this list can be extended to include other minerals, the hormones, vitamins, etc.

Young in a recent article (21) has summarized the work on appetite in its relation to body needs. If the body lacks some chemical, the individual will tend to develop a specific appetite or partial hunger for that food element.

Thus it seems impossible as well as useless to make any list of fundamental physiological needs for they can come to almost any number one might wish, depending on the degree of specificity of description. We can not identify all physiological needs as homeostatic. That sexual desire, sleepiness, sheer activity and maternal behavior in animals, are homeostatic, has not yet been demonstrated. Furthermore, this list would not include the various sensory pleasures (tastes, smells, tickling, stroking) which are probably physiological and which may become the goals of motivated behavior. . . .

It should be pointed out again that any of the physiological needs and the consummatory behavior involved with them serve as channels for all sorts of other needs as well. That is to say, the person who thinks he is hungry may actually be seeking more for comfort, or dependence, than for vitamins or proteins. Conversely, it is possible to satisfy the hunger need in part by other activities such as drinking water or smoking cigarettes. In other words, relatively isolable as these physiological needs are, they are not completely so.

Undoubtedly these physiological needs are the most prepotent of all needs [they exceed all others in power]. What this means specifically is, that in the human being who is missing everything in life in an extreme fashion, it is most likely that the major motivation would be the physiological needs rather than any others. A person who is lacking food, safety, love, and esteem would most probably hunger for food more strongly than for anything else. . . .

Abraham H. Maslow

Obviously a good way to obscure the 'higher' motivations, and to get a lopsided view of human capacities and human nature, is to make the organism extremely and chronically hungry or thirsty. Anyone who attempts to make an emergency picture into a typical one, and who will measure all of man's goals and desires by his behavior during extreme physiological deprivation is certainly being blind to many things. It is quite true that man lives by bread alone—when there is no bread. But what happens to man's desires when there *is* plenty of bread and when his belly is chronically filled?

At once other (and 'higher') needs emerge and these, rather than physiological hungers, dominate the organism. And when these in turn are satisfied, again new (and still 'higher') needs emerge and so on. This is what we mean by saying that the basic human needs are organized into a hierarchy of relative prepotency.

One main implication of this phrasing is that gratification becomes as important a concept as deprivation in motivation theory, for it releases the organism from the domination of a relatively more physiological need, permitting thereby the emergence of other more social goals. The physiological needs, along with their partial goals, when chronically gratified cease to exist as active determinants or organizers of behavior. They now exist only in a potential fashion in the sense that they may emerge again to dominate the organism if they are thwarted. But a want that is satisfied is no longer a want. The organism is dominated and its behavior organized only by unsatisfied needs. If hunger is satisfied, it becomes unimportant in the current dynamics of the individual. . . .

The safety needs.—If the physiological needs are relatively well gratified, there then emerges a new set of needs, which we may categorize roughly as the safety needs. All that has been said of the physiological needs is equally true, although in lesser degree, of these desires. The organism may equally well be wholly dominated by them. They may serve as the almost exclusive organizers of behavior, recruiting all the capacities of the organism in their service, and we may then fairly describe the whole organism as a safety-seeking mechanism. Again we may say of the receptors, the effectors, of the intellect and the other capacities that they are primarily safety-seeking tools. Again, as in the hungry man, we find that the dominating goal is a strong determinant not only of his current world-outlook and philosophy but also of his philosophy of the future. Practically everything looks less important than safety, (even sometimes the physiological needs which being satisfied, are now underestimated). A man, in this state, if it is extreme enough and chronic enough, may be characterized as living almost for safety alone.

Although in this paper we are interested primarily in the needs of the adult, we can approach an understanding of his safety needs perhaps more efficiently by observation of infants and children, in whom these needs are much more simple and obvious. One reason for the clearer appearance of the threat or danger reaction in infants, is that they do not inhibit this reaction at all, whereas adults in our society have been taught to inhibit it at all costs. Thus even when adults do feel their safety to be threatened we may not be able to see this on the surface. Infants will react in a total fashion and as if they were endangered, if they are disturbed or dropped suddenly, startled by loud noises, flashing light, or other unusual sensory stimulation, by rough handling, by general loss of support in the mother's arms, or by inadequate support. . . .

From these and similar observations, we may generalize and say that the average child in our society generally prefers a safe, orderly, predictable, organized world, which he can count on, and in which unexpected, unmanageable or other dangerous things do not happen, and in which, in any case, he has all-powerful parents who protect and shield him from harm. . . .

The healthy, normal, fortunate adult in our culture is largely satisfied in his safety needs. The peaceful, smoothly running, 'good' society ordinarily makes its members feel safe enough from wild animals, extremes of temperature, criminals, assault and murder, tyranny, etc. Therefore, in a very real sense, he no longer has any safety needs as active motivators. Just as a sated man no longer feels hungry, a safe man no longer feels endangered. If we wish to see these needs directly and clearly we must turn to neurotic or near-neurotic individuals, and to the economic and social underdogs. In between these extremes, we can perceive the expressions of safety needs only in such phenomena as, for instance, the common preference for a job with tenure and protection, the desire for a savings account, and for insurance of various kinds (medical, dental, unemployment, disability, old age).

Other broader aspects of the attempt to seek safety and stability in the world are seen in the very common preference for familiar rather than unfamiliar things, or for the known rather than the unknown. The tendency to have some religion or world-philosophy that organizes the universe and the men in it into some sort of satisfactorily coherent, meaningful whole is also in part motivated by safety-seeking. Here too we may list science and philosophy in general as partially motivated by the safety needs. . . .

The love needs.—If both the physiological and the safety needs are fairly well gratified, then there will emerge the love and affection and belongingness needs, and the whole cycle already described will repeat itself with this new center. Now the person will feel keenly, as never before, the absence of friends, or a sweetheart, or a wife, or children. He will hunger for affectionate relations with people in general, namely, for a place in his group, and he will strive with great intensity to achieve this goal. He will want to attain such a place more than anything else in the world and may even forget that once, when he was hungry, he sneered at love. . . .

One thing that must be stressed at this point is that love is not synonymous with sex. Sex may be studied as a purely physiological need. Ordinarily sexual behavior is multi-determined, that is to say, determined not only by sexual but also by other needs, chief among which are the love and affection needs. Also not to be overlooked is the fact that the love needs involve both giving *and* receiving love.

The esteem needs.—All people in our society (with a few pathological exceptions) have a need or desire for a stable, firmly based, (usually) high evaluation of themselves, for self-respect, or self-esteem, and for the esteem of others. By firmly based self-esteem, we mean that which is soundly based upon realty capacity, achievement and respect from others. These needs may be classified into two subsidiary sets. These are, first, the desire for strength, for achievement, for adequacy, for confidence in the face of the world, and for independence and freedom. Secondly, we have what we may call the desire for reputation or prestige (defining it as respect or esteem from other people), recognition, attention, importance or appreciation. . . .

Satisfaction of the self-esteem need leads to feelings of self-confidence, worth, strength, capability and adequacy of being useful and necessary in the world. But thwarting of these needs produces feelings of inferiority, of weakness and of helplessness. These feelings in turn give rise to either basic discouragement or else compensatory or neurotic trends. An appreciation of the necessity of basic self-confidence and an understanding of how helpless people are without it, can be easily gained from a study of severe traumatic neurosis (8).

The need for self-actualization.—Even is all these needs are satisfied, we may still often (if not always) expect that a new discontent and restlessness will soon develop, unless the individual is doing what he is fitted for. A musician must make music, an artist must paint, a poet must write, if he is to be ultimately happy. What a man *can* be, he *must* be. This need we may call self-actualization.

This term, first coined by Kurt Goldstein, is being used in this paper in a much more specific and limited fashion. It refers to the desire for self-fulfillment, namely, to the tendency for him to become actualized in what he is potentially. This tendency might be phrased as the desire to become more and more what one is, to become everything that one is capable of becoming.

The specific form that these needs will take will of course vary greatly from person to person. In one individual it may take the form of the desire to be an ideal mother, in another it may be expressed athletically, and in still another it may be expressed in painting pictures or in inventions. It is not necessarily a creative urge although in people who have any capacities for creation it will take this form.

The clear emergence of these needs rests upon prior satisfaction of the physiological, safety, love and esteem needs. We shall call people who are satisfied in these needs, basically satisfied people, and it is from these that we may expect the fullest (and healthiest) creativeness. Since, in our society, basically satisfied people are the exception, we do not know much about self-actualization, either experimentally or clinically. It remains a challenging problem for research.

The preconditions for the basic need satisfactions.—There are certain conditions which are immediate prerequisites for the basic need satisfactions. Danger to these is reacted to almost as if it were a direct danger to the basic needs themselves. Such conditions as freedom to speak, freedom to do what one wishes so long as no harm is done to others, freedom to express one's self, freedom to investigate and seek for information, freedom to defend one's self, justice, fairness, honesty, orderliness in the group are examples of such preconditions for basic need satisfactions. Thwarting in these freedoms will be reacted to with a threat or emergency response. These conditions are not ends in themselves but they are *almost* so since they are so closely related to the basic needs, which are apparently the only ends in themselves. These conditions are defended because without them the basic satisfactions are quite impossible, or at least, very severely endangered.

If we remember that the cognitive capacities (perceptual, intellectual, learning) are a set of adjustive tools, which have, among other functions, that of satisfaction of our basic needs, then it is clear that any danger to them, any deprivation or blocking of their free use, must also be indirectly threatening to the basic needs themselves. Such a statement is a partial solution of the general problems of curiosity, the search for knowledge, truth and wisdom, and the ever-persistent urge to solve the cosmic mysteries. . . .

The desires to know and to understand.—So far, we have mentioned the cognitive needs only in passing. Acquiring knowledge and systematizing the universe have been considered as, in part, techniques for the achievement of basic safety in the world, or, for the intelligent man, expressions of self-actualization. Also freedom of inquiry and expression have been discussed as preconditions of satisfactions of the basic needs. True though these formulation may be, they do not constitute definitive answers to the question as to the motivation role of curiosity, learning, philosophizing, experimenting, etc. They are, at best, no more than partial answers. . . .

FURTHER CHARACTERISTICS OF THE BASIC NEEDS

The degree of fixity of the hierarchy of basic needs.—We have spoken so far as if this hierarchy were a fixed order but actually it is not nearly as rigid as we may have implied. It is true that most of the people with whom we have worked have seemed to have these basic needs in about the order that has been indicated. However, there have been a number of exceptions. . . .

Degrees of relative satisfaction.—So far, our theoretical discussion may have given the impression that these five sets of needs are somehow in a step-wise, all-or-none relationships to each other. We have spoken in such terms as the following: "If one need is satisfied, then another emerges." This statement might give the false impression that a need must be satisfied 100 percent before the next need emerges. In actual fact, most members of our society who are normal, are partially satisfied in all their basic needs and partially unsatisfied in all their basic needs at the same time. A more realistic description of the hierarchy would be in terms of decreasing percentages of satisfaction as we go up the hierarchy of prepotency. For instance, if I may assign arbitrary figures for the sake of illustration, it is as if the average citizen is satisfied perhaps 85 percent in his physiological needs, 70 percent in his safety needs, 50 percent in his love needs, 40 percent in his self-esteem needs, and 10 percent in his self-actualization needs.

As for the concept of emergence of a new need after satisfaction of the prepotent need, this emergence is not a sudden saltatory phenomenon but rather a gradual emergence by slow degrees from nothingness. For instance, if prepotent need A is satisfied only 10 percent then need B may not be visible at all. However, as this need A becomes satisfied 25 percent, need B may emerge 5 percent, as need A becomes satisfied 75 percent need B may emerge 90 percent, and so on.

Unconscious character of needs.—These needs are neither necessarily conscious nor unconscious. On the whole, however, in the average person, they are more often unconscious rather than conscious. It is not necessary at this point to overhaul the tremendous mass of evidence which indicates the crucial importance of unconscious motivation. It would by now be expected, on a priori grounds alone, that unconscious motivations would on the whole be rather more important than the conscious motivations. What we have called the basic needs are very often largely unconscious although they may, with suitable techniques, and with sophisticated people become conscious.

Cultural specificity and generality of needs.—This classification of basic needs makes some attempt to take account of the relative unity behind the superficial differences in specific desires from one culture to another. Certainly in any particular culture an individual's conscious motivational content will usually be extremely different from the conscious motivational content of an individual in another society. However, it is the common experience of anthropologists that people, even in different societies, are much more alike than we would think from our first contact with them, and that as we know them better we seem to find more and more of this commonness. We then recognize the most startling differences to be superficial rather than basic, *e.g.,* differences in style of hairdress, clothes, tastes in food, etc. Our classification of basic needs is in part an attempt to account for this unity behind the apparent diversity from culture to culture. No claim is made that it is ultimate or universal for all cultures. The claim is made only that it is relatively *more* ultimate, more universal, more basic, than the superficial conscious desires from culture to culture, and makes a somewhat closer approach to common-human characteristics. Basic needs are *more* common-human than superficial desires or behaviors.

Multiple motivations of behavior.—These needs must be understood *not* to be *exclusive* or single determiners of certain kinds of behavior. An example may be found in any behavior that seems to be physiologically motivated, such as eating, or sexual play or the like. The clinical psychologists have long since found that any behavior may be a channel through which flow various determinants. Or to say it in another way, most behavior is multi-motivated. Within the sphere of motivational determinants any behavior tends to be determined by several or *all* of the basic needs simultaneously rather than by only one of them. The latter would be more an exception than the former. Eating may be partially for the sake of filling the stomach, and partially for the sake of comfort and amelioration of other needs. One may make love not only for pure sexual release, but also to convince one's self of one's masculinity, or to make a conquest, to feel powerful, or to win more basic affection. As an illustration, I may point out that it would be possible (theoretically if not practically) to analyze a single act of an individual and see in it the expression of his physiological needs, his safety needs, his love needs, his esteem needs and self-actualization. This contrasts sharply with the more naive brand of trait psychology in which one trait or one motive accounts for a certain kind of act, *i.e.,* an aggressive act is traced solely to a trait of aggressiveness. . . .

Goals as centering principle in motivation theory.—It will be observed that the basic principle in our classification has been neither the instigation nor the motivated behavior but rather the functions, effects, purposes, or goals of the behavior. It has been proven sufficiently by various people that this is the most suitable point for centering in any motivation theory.

REFERENCES

2. CANNON, W. B. *Wisdom of the body.* New York: Norton, 1932.

8. KARDINER, A. *The traumatic neuroses of war.* New York: Hoeber, 1941.

20. YOUNG, P. T. *Motivation of behavior.* New York: John Wiley & Sons, 1936.

21. ____. The experimental analysis of appetite. *Psychol. Bull.*, 1941, 38, 129–164.

9.2 JUDITH RODIN

Current Status of the Internal–External Hypothesis for Obesity: What Went Wrong?

Obesity, a state of being extremely overweight, is a problem for many people. It is especially frustrating because common wisdom does not appear to be able to explain the causes of obesity. In the 1960s, researchers proposed that overweight people were strongly influenced by external cues (such as the taste or sight of food). Consequent research, however, has made it apparent that the explanation is not that straightforward. Judith Rodin has been a leading authority in this area.

Rodin (b. 1944) received her Ph.D. from Columbia University in 1970. She is currently a professor of psychology and a provost at Yale University, and she is the author of many publications on obesity, including *Exploding the Obesity Myth* (1981).

This selection, "Current Status of the Internal–External Hypothesis for Obesity: What Went Wrong?" was published in the *American Psychologist* in 1981. In it, Rodin points out the difficulty in identifying external and internal cues in hunger and obesity and in demonstrating how they interact. Obesity, having a surplus of body fat, is a complex and puzzling problem, and Rodin's work has helped explode many myths about obese people.

Key Concept: obesity

*A*lmost any overweight person can lose weight; few can keep it off. It is this fact that makes the study and treatment of obesity so intriguing. What makes obesity unique, unlike many other disorders? First, heavy people are forced to wear the consequences of their affliction on their body and have probably built up a whole armamentarium of defenses to deal with that circumstance. No other physical characteristic except skin color is so stigmatized in our society (Allon, 1975; Cahnman, 1968). Second is the delightful but problematic fact that food is a positive and reinforcing stimulus for most of us. Since we have to eat to survive, the problem behavior can never be eliminated completely. Third, and probably most unfair of all, obesity is unusual because being fat is one of the factors that may keep one fat (Rodin, in press; Rodin, Note 1). Indeed, we have all heard the familiar refrain of many an overweight person who complains, "But I eat so little." Despite the disbelieving and reproachful looks of their lean friends, the perverse fact is that it often does take fewer calories to keep people fat than it did to get them fat in the first place. This occurs because obesity itself changes the fat cells and body chemistry and alters level of energy expenditure. Each of these factors operates to maintain obesity once it has developed.

SOME CONSEQUENCES OF OBESITY

First, people's metabolic machinery is constituted in such a way that the fatter they are, the fatter they are primed to become. This unfortunate state of affairs occurs because the larger a fat cell gets, the greater its capacity to store fat and become still larger (Salans, Knittle, & Hirsch, 1968). In addition, overweight people tend to have higher basal levels of insulin than people of normal weight (Rabinowitz & Zierler, 1962). This condition, which is called hyperinsulinemia, enhances fat storage because it accelerates the entry of sugar into the fat cell and actually speeds the conversion of sugar into fat. Humans in a state of natural or induced hyperinsulinemia report hunger (Crain & Thorn, 1949; Grossman & Stein, 1948; Janowitz & Ivy, 1949; Williams, 1960). Thus, the enlarged fat cells found in all overweight individuals, and the hyperinsulinemia found in most, may make them hungrier and prime their metabolic apparatus to make and store more fat.

Second, obesity also affects the degree of energy expenditure the overweight person is capable of. This occurs through its impact on activity level and resting metabolism. But metabolism is actually more interesting because metabolic processes use two thirds of all the energy expenditure of an individual. Even if one did nothing but lie in bed, basal metabolism (which keeps the internal life maintenance systems going) would account for an expenditure of about one calorie a minute. Fat tissue is more metabolically inert than lean tissue, so fatness itself can directly lower metabolic rate if fat tissue begins to replace lean tissue. This may be one of the reasons why some overweight people seem to need fewer calories to maintain a high level of body weight than people who are overeating for the first time to achieve the same weight (Sims et al., 1973). Metabolic rate also decreases during food deprivation, so when overweight people are dieting, their basal metabolism and thus their overall level of energy expenditure may slow down, making dieting both difficult and frustrating (Apfelbaum, 1975; Garrow, 1978). This fact suggests that dieting itself may be a critical factor in promoting the maintenance of overweight. In addition, this energy-saving slowdown of metabolism becomes more pronounced with each weight loss attempt (S. C. Wooley, Wooley, & Dyrenforth, 1979). It is as if the body has learned from earlier periods of deprivation and begins to slow down and decrease energy expenditure sooner and more efficiently after still another diet is begun.

The remaining third of a person's energy expenditure, the part not used for metabolism, is used for physical activity and exercise. Ever since Jean Mayer and his colleagues documented the popular assumption that obese people are less active than slender ones (Bullen, Reed, & Mayer, 1964), most people have concluded that laziness breeds plumpness. But actually, this process, too, may have occurred in reverse. Obesity makes physical activity more difficult and probably less pleasurable than average weight does, and it may encourage people to be sedentary. With less exercise, overweight people burn fewer calories. Moreover, inactivity can lead to a lowering of metabolic rate (Garrow, 1978).

It thus seems clear that a variety of factors serve to maintain and enhance obesity once it has developed. But the elements that cause obesity in the first place remain the subject of considerable current debate.

CAUSES OF OBESITY

What is certain is that obesity is a complex disorder with multiple levels of metabolic and behavioral characteristics which interact with one another. Getting fat involves some combination of food intake, energy expenditure, and the cellular tissue in which fat is stored, but the nature of the contribution of each and the way that they are involved vary greatly. The plump baby, the chubby adolescent boy, the woman who gets fatter after pregnancy, the overweight business executive—all have fatness in common—but it is doubtful that the cause or natural history of their fatness is the same (Bray, 1979). This is hardly surprising because our current views of eating generally see food-relevant behavior as a multiply regulated process that is influenced by interactions among physiological, cognitive, social, and cultural variables in a control system to which they are all essential, even in the disordered state of obesity (Booth, Toates, & Platt, 1976; Lytle, 1977; Rodin, Note 1). Thus, attempts to provide simplistic explanations of obesity or descriptions of the characteristics of all obese people may often be misleading. Unfortunately, this is the state of affairs in current applications of the "internal–external" hypothesis for obesity.

The Internal–External Distinction

This formulation developed in the late 1960s, when Schachter, Nisbett, and their associates reported a provocative series of studies suggesting that the eating behavior of their overweight subjects was greatly influenced by the apparent passage of time, the taste and sight of food, and the number of highly palatable food cues present (Nisbett, 1968a, 1968b; Schachter & Gross, 1968). These studies implied a dichotomy between internal and external control of feeding, suggesting that the eating behavior of normal weight people was responsive to internal stimuli (cf. Schachter, Goldman, & Gordon, 1968) and that, in contrast, the eating behavior of overweight people was unresponsive to internal stimuli and instead was primarily controlled by external cues.

The internal–external distinction is a widely held and cited framework. It appears, for example, in almost every introductory psychology textbook published in the last eight years. Because of its elegance and simplicity, it also attracted a considerable number of researchers to the area of human eating behavior and obesity. Yet, many investigators who pursued this dichotomy after Schachter seem to have greatly overextended its applicability. Indeed, it now appears that the injunction of extreme discontinuity between internal–physiological and external–environmental stimuli is wrong, especially for eating behavior. In addition, there are now many indications that the internal versus external view is far too simple a description of differences between different weight groups.

USE OF THE INTERNAL–EXTERNAL DISTINCTION TO EXPLAIN DIFFERENCES BETWEEN OBESE AND NORMAL WEIGHT PEOPLE

First, consider the argument that obese individuals are more responsive to environmental cues than are people of average weight. Although Schachter and I reported that many overweight subjects are highly responsive to external food and nonfood stimuli (Schachter & Rodin, 1974), these studies have not always been easy to replicate. Many experiments have failed to demonstrate that overweight individuals are more responsive to external food and nonfood cues than are their normal weight peers (e.g., Goldman, 1969; Nisbett & Storms, 1975; Nisbett & Temoshok, 1976; Shaw, 1973; Stunkard & Levitz [cited in Levitz, 1975]; S. Wooley, 1972).

The inconsistency of these results is not surprising for several reasons. First, it would be most unusual if the wide variety of manipulations of external cues that have been used were shown to have uniform effects. The seeming inconsistencies also arise from a failure to have developed a very good definition of external responsiveness. It now seems clear that external responsiveness is most easily defined as the extent to which a greater magnitude response (e.g., increased eating, increased emotionality, increased attention) is evoked by highly salient cues, as compared with cues of low salience, in the external environment. In other words, it should be calculated as the difference score for each subject between his or her response to a high- versus a low-intensity cue, with intensity determined on the basis of independent criteria (e.g., *number* of food cues, *decibels* of noise, *degree* of proximity of food) and not the subject's response. Comparing responses when there are not cues versus when there are some cues would not be a reasonable test in this case.

A second reason for these inconsistent findings relates to issues of sampling. My own early studies with colleagues were among those that failed to show reliable overweight/normal weight differences consistently from subject population to subject population, or even from study to study within the same population (Rodin, 1975; Moskowitz, & Bray, 1976; Rodin, Slochower, & Fleming, 1977). The evidence is now quite clear, however, that *all* overweight individuals are not externally responsive; neither are *all* normal weight individuals internally sensitive. Therefore, mean differences in any single study depend on how many individuals of each type wind up in samples divided according to weight. This assertion comes from experiments in which the internal or external responsiveness of several hundred individuals who also varied in degree of overweight were tested. These studies found that in every weight category there were people who were externally responsive and people who were not (e.g., Nisbett & Storms, 1975; Nisbett & Tomoshok, 1976; Rodin & Slochower, 1976; Tom & Rucker, 1975). The same was true for internal responsiveness (e.g., Hibscher & Herman, 1977; Price & Grinker, 1973; Speigel, 1973; S. Wooley, 1972). Moreover, across all weight groups, degree of overweight was not strongly related to the degree of external or internal responsiveness demonstrated in these studies (Nisbett, 1972; Price & Grinker, 1973; Rodin et al., 1977). In fact, at extreme degrees of obesity, some individuals showed very little responsiveness to external cues. . . .

Internal Responsiveness and Body Weight

It now seems clear that the opposite component of the internal–external hypothesis is also not easily demonstrated. The original evidence for a lack of internal responsiveness in the obese came from studies showing their failure to regulate their intake as accurately as normal weight people did (Nisbett, 1968b; Pliner, 1973; Schachter et al., 1968). These studies are widely cited, although the greater number of studies has failed to find obese–normal differences in response to manipulations that varied the caloric value of a preload given prior to the test meal (Herman & Mack, 1975; Hibscher & Herman, 1977; Hill & McCutcheon, 1975; Nisbett & Storms, 1975; Price & Grinker, 1973; Ruderman & Wilson, 1979; Singh, 1973). These inconsistent findings are readily explained, since there is now a great deal of evidence that even normal weight people show poor regulation when they only have internal signals to go on (Jordan, 1975; Speigel, 1973; S. Wooley, 1972). It is simply not true that people who are of average weight can interpret hunger pangs, low blood sugar, and other physiological signals which tell them when they are hungry and that overweight people cannot, and that this is why they are fat. In fact, most people are pretty inadequate at knowing how many calories they have consumed or how much food their bodies really need on the basis of internal cues alone. Studies using disguised caloric dilution have shown that only some normal weight subjects are able to compensate over several days for changes in the caloric density of their diets, and in nearly all cases compensation is incomplete (Campbell, Hashim, & Van Itallie, 1971; Jordan, 1969; Speigel, 1973; O. Wooley, 1971).

The problem is that there are as yet no clear-cut measures of internal sensitivity, in part because it has not been possible to identify unequivocally the unconditioned stimuli for hunger and satiety, although there are currently some interesting leads (cf. Booth et al., 1976; Friedman & Stricker, 1976). Vast individual differences exist in the bodily cues that people use as signals of hunger and satiety, and much of the relevant data suggest strongly that these differences are not at all correlated with overweight (Leon & Roth, 1977; O. W. Wooley & Wooley, 1975; Rodin, Note 1). No doubt they have to do more with learning histories than with any characteristics related to weight per se. . . .

INTERACTION OF EXTERNAL AND INTERNAL SIGNALS

The second point that changes one's view about the internal versus external hypothesis is that internal and external cues interact in the regulation of eating. For example, external cues may exert some of their effects by triggering internal, physiological signals that motivate the individual to eat. In this way, salient external cues could affect internal state, doing so even before food enters the mouth.

Arousal

External food cues such as the smell and sight of food are arousing. Many investigators have argued that this physiological arousal plays a crucial role in the control of feeding in both people and animals (Marshall, 1976; Rowland & Antelman, 1976; Wolgin, Cytawa, & Teitelbaum, 1976; Rodin, Note 1). Hyperarousal in response to external stimuli appears to be related to overeating in ventromedial-hypothalamic-lesioned animals and in many people (e.g., Marshall, 1975; White, 1973). In each of these groups, heightened responsiveness to external stimuli can be shown to produce physiological arousal, which leads to overeating and weight gain over time. An external stimulus can thus be seen as having two effects: a specific one that elicits some appropriate motivational state and a nonspecific one that arouses the organism and thereby permits the responses to occur (Stricker & Zigmond, 1976). Organisms could literally be turned on by an external stimulus, and at the same time, this arousal would make them even more likely to eat, perhaps because arousal reciprocally increases responsiveness to external cues. The neurochemical link among responsivity, arousal, and feeding systems that has been so beautifully worked out for animals in the past few years (Antelman, Szechtman, Chin, & Fisher, 1975; Marshall, 1976) has exciting implications for the study of external responsiveness in human obesity. . . .

In addition to general arousal, a second interaction of external cues and internal factors may arise from the effects of the external cues on metabolic events or digestive processes. Here one's own experience can validate what has now been demonstrated in the laboratory. Tempted by external stimuli, people tend to salivate, which is the first internal response in the digestive process. The Wooleys and their co-workers have shown that salivation is much greater when subjects are presented with a food as opposed to a nonfood stimulus in their visual field and that these salivary responses to food stimuli vary as a function of the imagined palatability of the food and whether or not it will be available for subsequent ingestion (O. Wooley, Wooley, & Dunham, 1976; S. Wooley & Wooley, 1973).

Insulin release is another major candidate for an intervening physiological mechanism that might be responsive to external stimuli. As indicated earlier, insulin is involved in promoting increased ingestion and in increased storage of nutrients as fat. It is thus a critical internal response in the digestive and fat-storing process. The important role of insulin responses to the sight and taste of food in animals has been explored by Powley (1977) and Woods et al. (1977), who have showed that rats develop the tendency to secrete insulin in the presence of stimuli which reliably predict the opportunity to eat (time of day or odor). The relationship of increased insulin to overeating and weight gain (Lovett & Booth, 1970; MacKay, Calloway, & Barnes, 1940; Steffens, 1975) appears to hold despite the fact that insulin is secreted by the pancreas following the intestinal absorption of glucose (McIntyre, Holdsworth, & Turner, 1965), suggesting that increased insulin levels should actually correlate with satiety. . . .

CLARIFYING WHAT CONSTITUTES AN EXTERNAL CUE

The more precise definition of external cue responsiveness suggested here, which focuses on differential responsiveness to high- versus low-intensity stimuli, should be useful in further research endeavors. But the notion of what constitutes an external cue itself has to be reconsidered. Manipulations of putative external cues for eating have even included whether or not the experimenter was dressed as a scientist (Stalling & Friedman, Note 2) or variations of the color of the granulated sugar glaze on the top of cookies (Cheung, Barnes, & Barnes, 1980). There is also reason to argue that responsiveness to taste and other oropharyngeal stimuli should be different from responsiveness to visual or cognitive cues. First, the receptor sites of stimulation by taste and smell are quite different from those of visual cues (Pfaffmann, 1960). In the hypothalamic region, Rolls (1976) found specific and different neurons firing to the sight of food and to the taste of food in deprived animals. Second, taste can serve as an unconditioned stimulus for learning and appears to have more direct biological significance for the organism (Garcia & Hankins, 1974; Rozin & Kalat, 1971).

There exists empirical support for the assertion that responsiveness to taste and responsiveness to external visual cues are linked to different factors. Milstein (1980) found increased taste responsiveness to be associated with greater body mass index and skinfold thickness in newborn infants, but neither of these indices related to visual cue responsiveness. Rodin et al. (1977) found that overweight subjects were more responsive to differences between good- and bad-tasting ice milk than were normal weight subjects prior to weight loss, and the former became even more so following weight reduction. By contrast, weight loss in the overweight subjects did not reliably change the degree of responsiveness to manipulations of high versus low *visual* salience of food cues. Thus, long-term factors related to energy reserves do appear to influence hedonic responsiveness to taste but not responsiveness to visual cues. . . .

CONCLUSION

To conclude I would like to reiterate that onset and degree of overweight are determined by a combination of genetic, metabolic, psychological, and environmental events. Considerable data arguing against the simplistic notion that all overweight people are externally responsive and lack internal sensitivity, and that people of average weight show the opposite pattern, have been reviewed. It may never be possible to find the "magic bullet," since obesity is not a single syndrome, has no single cause, and therefore probably does not have a single cure. Medicine is frequently condemned by behavioral scientists because it usually focuses on changing the body—the internal processes—and forgets the role of the environment. With this I agree. However, some behavioral scientists are trying to change responses to the environment without examining its effects on internal processes. This too is one-sided. I believe the answers must come from a model that appreciates the integration of these processes, and psychology may now be approaching it.

REFERENCE NOTES

1. Rodin, J. *Obesity: Why the losing battle?* Master Lecture on Brain–Behavior Relationships presented at the meeting of the American Psychological Association, San Francisco, August 1977.
2. Stalling, R. B. & Friedman, L. *Effect of fictitious food ratings and experimenter's attire on eating behavior of obese and normal people.* Unpublished manuscript, Bradley University, 1978.

REFERENCES

Allon, N. The stigma of overweight in everyday life. In G. A. Bray et al. (Eds.), *Obesity in perspective* (Vol. 2, DHEW Publication No. NIH 75–708). Washington, D.C.: U.S. Government Printing Office, 1975.

Antelman, S. M., Szechtman, H., Chin, P., & Fisher, A. E. Tail pinch-induced eating, gnawing and licking behavior in rats: Dependence on the nigrostriatal dopamine system. *Brain Research*, 1975, 99, 319–337.

Apfelbaum, M. Influence of level of energy intake on energy expenditure in man: Effects of spontaneous intake, experimental starvation and experimental overeating. In G. A. Bray et al. (Eds.), *Obesity in perspective* (Vol. 2, DHEW Publication No. NIH 75-708). Washington, D.C.: U.S. Government Printing Office, 1975.

Booth, D. A., Toates, F. M., & Platt, S. V. Control system for hunger and its implications in animals and man. In D. Novin, W. Wyrwicks, & G. A. Bray (Eds.), *Hunger: Basic mechanisms and clinical implications.* New York: Raven Press, 1976.

Bray, G. A. (Ed.). *Obesity in America* (DHEW Publication No. NIH 79-359). Washington, D.C.: U.S. Government Printing Office, 1979.

Bullen, B. A., Reed, R. B., & Mayer, J. Physical activity of obese and nonobese adolescent girls, appraised by motion picture sampling. *American Journal of Clinical Nutrition*, 1964, 14, 211–223.

Cahnman, W. J. The stigma of obesity. *Sociological Quarterly*, 1968, 9, 283–299.

Campbell, R. G., Hashim, S. A., & Van Itallie, T. B. Studies of food-intake regulation in man: Responses to variations in nutritive density in lean and obese subjects. *New England Journal of Medicine*, 1971, 285, 1402–1407.

Cheung, R. C., Barnes, T. R., & Barnes, M. J. Relationship between visually based food preference and amount eaten. *Perceptual and Motor Skills*, 1980, 50, 780–782.

Crain, E. L., Jr., & Thorn G. W. Functioning pancreatic islet cell adenomas. *Medicine*, 1949, 28, 427–447.

Friedman, M. I., & Stricker, E. M. The physiological psychology of hunger: A physiological perspective. *Psychological Review*, 1976, 83, 409–431.

Garcia, J., & Hankins, W. G. The evolution of bitter and the acquisition of toxaphobia. In D. Denton (Ed.), *Fifth International Symposium on Olfaction and Taste* (DHEW Publication No. NIH 74-563). Washington, D.C.: U.S. Government Printing Office, 1974.

Garrow, J. The regulation of energy expenditure. In G. A. Bray (Ed.), *Recent advances in obesity research* (Vol. 2). London: Newman, 1978.

Goldman, R. L. *The effects of the manipulation of the visibility of food on the eating behavior of obese and normal subjects* (Doctoral dissertation, Columbia University, 1968). *Dissertation Abstracts International*, 1969 30, 807A.

Grossman, M. I., & Stein, I. F. The effect of vagotomy on the hunger producing action of insulin in man. *Journal of Applied Physiology*, 1948, 1, 263–269.

Herman, C. P., & Mack, D. Restrained and unrestrained eating. *Journal of Personality*, 1975, 43, 647–660.

Hibscher, J. A., & Herman, C. P. Obesity, dieting, and the expression of "obese" characteristics. *Journal of Comparative and Physiological Psychology*, 1977, 91, 374–380.

Hill, S., & McCutcheon, N. Eating responses of obese and nonobese humans during dinner meals. *Psychosomatic Medicine*, 1975, 37, 395–401.

Janowitz, H. D., & Ivy, A. C. Role of blood sugar levels in spontaneous and insulin-induced hunger in man. *Journal of Applied Physiology*, 1949, 2, 643–645.

Jordan, H. Voluntary intragastric feeding: Oral and gastric contributions to food intake and hunger in man. *Journal of Comparative and Physiological Psychology*, 1969, 68, 498–506.

Jordan, H. A. Physiological control of food intake in man. In G. A. Bray et al. (Eds.), *Obesity in perspective* (Vol. 2, DHEW Publication No. NIH 75-708). Washington, D.C.: U.S. Government Printing Office, 1975.

Leon, G. R., & Roth, L. Obesity: Psychological causes, correlations, and speculations. *Psychological Bulletin*, 1977, 84, 117–139.

Levitz, L. The susceptibility of human feeding to external controls. In G. A. Bray et al. (Eds.), *Obesity in perspective* (Vol 2, DHEW Publication No. NIH 75-708). Washington, D.C.: U.S. Government Printing Office, 1975.

Lovett, D., & Booth, D. A. Four effects of exogenous insulin on food intake. *Quarterly Journal of Experimental Psychology*, 1970, 22, 406–419.

Lytle, L. D. Control of eating behavior. In R. J. Wurtman & J. J. Wurtman (Eds.), *Nutrition and the brain* (Vol. 2). New York: Raven Press, 1977.

MacKay, E. M., Calloway, J. W., & Barnes, R. H. Hyperalimentation in normal animals produced by protamine insulin. *Journal of Nutrition*, 1940, 20, 59–66.

Marshall, J. Increased orientation to sensory stimuli following medial hypothalamic damage in rats. *Brain Research*, 1975, 86, 373–387.

Marshall, J. Neurochemistry of central monoamine systems as related to food intake. In T. Silverstone (Ed.), *Appetite and food intake*. Braunschweig, West Germany: Pergamon Press, 1976.

McIntyre, N., Holdsworth, C. D., & Turner D. S. *Journal of Clinical Endocrinology*, 1965, 25, 1317.

Milstein, R. M. Responsiveness in newborn infants of overweight and normal weight parents. *Appetite*, 1980, 1, 65–74.

Nisbett, R. E. Determinants of food intake in human obesity. *Science*, 1968, 159, 1254–1255. (a)

Nisbett, R. E. Taste, deprivation and weight determinants of eating behavior. *Journal of Personality and Social Psychology*, 1968, 10, 107–116. (b)

Nisbett, R. E. Hunger, obesity, and the ventromedial hypothalamus. *Psychological Review*, 1972, 79, 433–453.

Nisbett, R. E., & Storms, M. D. Cognitive, social, psychological determinants of food intake. In H. London & R. E. Nisbett (Eds.), *Cognitive modification of emotional behavior*. Chicago: Aldine, 1975.

Nisbett, R. E., & Temoshok, L. Is there an external cognitive style? *Journal of Personality and Social Psychology*, 1976, 33, 36–47.

Pfaffman, C. The pleasures of sensation. *Psychological Review*, 1960, 65, 253–268.

Pliner, P. L. Effect of liquid and solid preloads on eating behavior of obese and normal persons. *Physiology & Behavior*, 1973, 11, 285–290.

Powley, T. The ventromedial hypothalamic syndrome, satiety, and a cephalic phase hypothesis. *Psychological Review*, 1977, 84, 89.

Price, J. M., & Grinker, J. Effects of degree of obesity, food deprivation, and palatability on eating behavior of humans. *Journal of Comparative and Physiological Psychology*, 1973, 85, 256–271.

Rabinowitz, D., & Zierler, K. L. Forearm metabolism in obesity and its response to intra-arterial insulin: Characterization of insulin resistance and evidence for adaptive hyperinsulinism. *Journal of Clinical Investigation*, 1962, 41, 2173–2181.

Rodin, J. The effects of obesity and set point on taste responsiveness and intake in humans. *Journal of Comparative and Physiological Psychology*, 1975, 89, 1003–1009.

Rodin, J. *Exploding the obesity myth*. London: Multimedia, in press.

Rodin, J., Moskowitz, H. R., & Bray, G. A. Relationship between obesity, weight loss, and taste responsiveness. *Physiology & Behavior*, 1976, 17, 591–597.

Rodin, J., & Slochower, J. Externality in the nonobese: The effects of environmental responsiveness on weight. *Journal of Personality and Social Psychology*, 1976, 29, 557–565.

Rodin, J., Slochower, J., & Fleming, B. The effects of degree of obesity, age of onset, and energy deficit on external responsiveness. *Journal of Comparative and Physiological Psychology*, 1977, 91, 586–597.

Rolls, E. T. Neurophysiology of feeding. In T. Silverstone (Ed.), *Appetite and food intake*. Braunschweig, West Germany: Pergamon Press, 1976.

Rowland, N., & Antelman, S. Stress-induced hyperphagia and obesity in rats: A possible model for understanding human obesity. *Science*, 1976, 191, 310–312.

Rozin, P., & Kalat, J. W. Specific hungers and poison avoidance as adaptive specializations of learning. *Psychological Review*, 1971, 78, 459–486.

Ruderman, A. J., & Wilson, G. T. Weight restraint, cognitions and counterregulation. *Behaviour Research and Therapy*, 1979, 17, 581–590.

Salans, L. B., Knittle, J. L., & Hirsch, J. The role of adipose cell size and adipose tissue insulin sensitivity in the carbohydrate intolerance of human obesity. *Journal of Clinical Investigation*, 1968, 47, 153–165.

Schachter, S., Goldman, R., & Gordon, A. Effects of fear, food deprivation, and obesity on eating. *Journal of Personality and Social Psychology*, 1968, 10, 91–97.

Schachter, S., & Gross, R. Manipulated time and eating behavior. *Journal of Personality and Social Psychology*, 1968, 10, 98–106.

Schachter, S., & Rodin, J. *Obese humans and rats*. Washington, D.C.: Erlbaum/Halsted, 1974.

Shaw, J. C. *The influence of food type and method of presentation on human ingestive behavior*. Unpublished doctoral dissertation, University of Pennsylvania, 1973.

Sims, E., Danforth, E., Horton, E., Bray, G., Glennon, J., & Salans, L. Endocrine and metabolic effects of experimental obesity in man. *Recent Progress in Hormonal Research*, 1973, 29, 457–496.

Singh, D. Role of response habits and cognitive factors in determination of behavior of obese humans. *Journal of Personality and Social Psychology*, 1973, 27, 220–238.

Speigel, T. A. Caloric regulation of food intake in man. *Journal of Comparative and Physiological Psychology*, 1973, 84, 24–37.

Steffens, A. B. Influence of reversible obesity on eating behavior, blood glucose, and insulin in the rat. *American Journal of Physiology*, 1975, 228, 1738–1744.

Stricker, E., & Zigmond, M. Brain catecholamines and the lateral hypothalamic syndrome. In D. Novin, W. Wyrwicka, & G. A. Bray (Eds.), *Hunger: Basic mechanisms and clinical implications*. New York: Raven Press, 1976.

Tom, G., & Rucker, M. Fat, full, and happy. *Journal of Personality and Social Psychology*, 1975, 32, 761–766.

White, E. The effects of viewing film of different arousal content on the eating behavior of obese and normal weight subjects (Doctoral dissertation, University of Miami, 1973). *Dissertation Abstracts International*, 1973, 34, 2324B.

Williams, R. H. Hypoglycemosis. In R. H. Williams (Ed.), *Diabetes*. New York: Hoeber, 1960.

Wolgin, E., Cytawa, J., & Teitelbaum, P. The role of activation in the regulation of food intake. In D. Novin, W. Wyrwicka, & G. A. Bray (Eds.), *Hunger: Basic mechanisms and clinical implications*. New York: Raven Press, 1976.

Woods, S. C., Vaselli, J. R., Kaestner, E., Szakmary, G. A., Milburn, P., & Vitiello, M. V. Conditioned insulin secretion and meal feeding in rats. *Journal of Comparative and Physiological Psychology*, 1977, 91, 128–133.

Wooley, O. Long-term food regulation in the obese and nonobese. *Psychosomatic Medicine*, 1971, 33, 436.

Wooley, O., Wooley, S., & Dunham, R. Deprivation, expectation and threat: Effects on salivation in the obese and nonobese. *Physiology & Behavior*, 1976, 17, 187–193.

Wooley, O. W., & Wooley, S. C. The experimental psychology of obesity. In T. Silverstone & J. Findham (Eds.), *Obesity: Its pathogenesis and management*. Lancaster, England: Medical and Technical Publishing, 1975.

Wooley, S. Physiologic versus cognitive factors in short-term food regulation in the obese and nonobese. *Psychosomatic Medicine*, 1972, 34, 62.

Wooley, S. & Wooley, O. Salivation to the sight and thought of food: A new measure of appetite. *Psychosomatic Medicine*, 1973, 35, 136.

Wooley, S. C., Wooley, O. W., & Dyrenforth, S. R. Theoretical, practical, and social issues in behavior treatments of obesity. *Journal of Applied Behavior Analysis*, 1979, 12, 3–25.

9.3 EDWARD L. DECI

Work: Who Does Not Like It and Why

Psychologists have always been interested in why people do what they do—in short, their motivation. Sometimes people do things for extrinsic or outside reasons (such as for money or for praise), and sometimes they do things for intrinsic or internal reasons (simply because they enjoy the activities). There are a number of situations, however, in which people are *expected* to work, such as in school or on the job. Teachers and employers are especially interested in work motivation. Edward L. Deci has spent much of his career trying to determine the influences on intrinsic and extrinsic motivation.

Deci (b. 1942) earned his Ph.D. in psychology from Carnegie-Mellon University in 1970. He is a professor of psychology at the University of Rochester, where he has been teaching since 1970. A leader in the study of intrinsic motivation, he has authored or coauthored a number of books, including *Intrinsic Motivation and Self-Determination in Human Behavior* (Plenum, 1985), with Richard M. Ryan.

This selection, "Work: Who Does Not Like It and Why," published in *Psychology Today* in 1972, is an informal discussion of the influences on intrinsic motivation and work. In this selection, Deci provides some practical advice to anyone who wants to enjoy what he or she does. In his later research, Deci has found that self-determination is an important variable in intrinsic motivation. As you read this article, notice how each experiment leads to the next one. Also, think about what you enjoy doing most and what motivates you to do it.

Key Concept: intrinsic motivation

I am fascinated with a child's unflagging curiosity. He explores everything; for him objects exist to be touched, smelled, tasted, and where possible, eaten. He learns, and learning excites and delights him. Yet by the time he reaches seventh grade, he is likely to complain that he doesn't like school and having to "learn stuff." And when he is out of school he may give up reading books entirely.

The work I have done over the last three years may account for some of this loss of curiosity. I began with the distinction that psychologists make between intrinsic and extrinsic motivation. When a person does a thing solely for the pleasure of the activity, we say that he is intrinsically motivated: the activity is its own reward. (I once spent a solid 12 hours doing a jigsaw puzzle. No one forced me; no one even knew that I had done it. I was intrinsically motivated.) By contrast, when a person does something for an outside reward—money, a better job—or to avoid a punishment—loss of money, censure—we say that he is extrinsically motivated.

Joy. Many psychologists have documented such intrinsically motivated acts as exploration and curiosity. Harry Harlow reports that monkeys will spend hours working on a puzzle for no apparent reward; they seem to like to work on the puzzle, much as I do. Robert W. White has suggested that man strives to deal effectively with his environment: we are, he says, intrinsically motivated to be creative, spontaneous and curious. Daniel Berlyne and other researchers have written about play, another intrinsic activity. In all, it is clear that human beings do many things for the simple joy of the activity.

Now consider a person who is involved in an intrinsically interesting task for which he is also receiving extrinsic rewards. This situation marks the child's development: he is eager to learn, but the school soon controls his learning with grades, threats of failure, gold stars, and so on. One must wonder what happens—whether extrinsic reinforcements increase a person's intrinsic motivation, decrease it, or leave it unchanged.

Puzzle. In quest of answers, I have observed hundreds of college students at work on an intrinsically interesting task. I used a popular puzzle called Soma, which consists of seven three-dimensional pieces, all variously shaped. We asked students to use the pieces to reproduce several configurations that were outlined on paper. Our pilot tests showed clearly that the students thought the puzzle was intrinsically interesting.

The outline for our series of experiments was the same. We gave each student four configurations to solve, allowing him 10 minutes for each puzzle. If he could not solve a puzzle in the allotted time, we stopped him and showed him the solution. After completing the four puzzles, the student remained alone in the experimental room, free to do what he wished: read magazines, solve more puzzles, or whatever. We reasoned that the students were intrinsically motivated if they continued to work on puzzles when they were alone, since there were other things they could do in that situation. Thus the additional amount of time they spent with the Soma game was our measure of their intrinsic motivation for that activity.

Pay. Our first experiment looked at the effect of money. We told half of the 64 student subjects at the outset that they would receive one dollar for each correct solution; the most they could win, then, was four dollars (the average was over two dollars). The money reward was therefore contingent upon their performance. The other half of the students also worked on the four puzzles, but we did not pay them for the correct answer.

Money made a difference. Those students whom we had paid spent significantly less time with the puzzles when they were alone later than did those who had done the same puzzles for free. Once they got money for doing a fun game, their intrinsic motivation decreased; to an extent, they had become dependent on the external reward.

Buzzer. In a second experiment, Wayne Cascio and I sought to determine whether threats of punishment would have the same effect. We told half of the 32 students that if they were unable to solve a puzzle within 10 minutes a buzzer would sound, indicating that their time was up for that puzzle. We gave them a short sample blast of the noise, so they knew that it was truly obnoxious—to be avoided if at all possible. This group, then, worked on Soma partly to avoid a punishment, the buzzer. We found that these students, like those who had worked for money, were less intrinsically interested in the puzzle later than students who had not been threatened with the unpleasant sound. Actually, few students had to endure the punishment of the buzzer, since most were able to solve all the problems. So it seems to have been the *threat* of punishment that was critical in decreasing their intrinsic motivation.

Locus. In our third variation, we paid each student two dollars for participating in the experiment regardless of performance, instead of paying for each solution. This time they showed no change in degree of intrinsic motivation.

We can explain these findings in terms of locus of causality. That is, when a person does a thing for no apparent reward, he explains his behavior in terms of internal causes: *I am doing this because I like to,* he seems to say. When we give him external reasons, however, he begins to attribute his behavior to other causes: *I am doing this for the money, or to avoid punishments.* When we paid our students for each solution the locus of causality for their behavior shifted from internal motives to external ones. They readily came to perceive of the money as the reason for their behavior. However, when we did not tie payments directly to their performance—when we gave the flat fee to everyone—the students were less likely to think that the money was the reason for working. Doing the puzzles was not instrumental in getting the money, so they were less likely to think of the money as their reason for doing the puzzle.

A change in locus of causality is one of two processes that affect intrinsic motivation. The other concerns verbal feedback. We found, for instance, that if we rewarded a student for each correct solution with statements such as "good, that's very fast for that one," his intrinsic motivation increased markedly. The 48 students told us that they liked the puzzle more, and spent more free time working on it, than the 48 students whom we had not so praised.

Why did verbal rewards increase intrinsic motivation, while money rewards decreased it? The answer, we think, is that an intrinsically motivated activity is one that provides feelings of competence and self-determination for a person. I stayed with that 12-hour jigsaw partly out of furious resolve to beat the damned thing, and my success reinforced my feelings of competence. Verbal feedback does much the same thing: it reaffirms the individual's confidence in himself; it makes him feel competent and self-determining.

Pair. Thus external rewards have at least two functions: one is a controlling function that makes a person dependent on the reward; the other is a feedback function that affects his feelings of competence and self-determination. Money and threats are common controllers; we do not generally think of them as reassurance about our competence. Praise and compliments, however, make a person feel good. In this sense, verbal feedback from someone else may not differ phenomenologically from the feedback an individual gives himself; both help him feel that he is worthy and capable. Both, therefore, maintain one's intrinsic motivation.

Of course it is possible that a heavy dosage of verbal reward would make a person dependent on praise, just as he becomes dependent on money or threats; and it also is possible that this type of dependency too would decrease intrinsic motivation. So far, however, we can conclude that feedback rewards differ significantly from controlling rewards.

Offset. In our next experiment, we gave our subjects both money (one dollar per correct puzzle) and praise. Apparently, the two kinds of reward offset each other: this group showed the same level of intrinsic motivation that we found with students who received neither reward.

Finally, we wondered what would happen when feedback was negative. Cascio and I gave 32 students new puzzles that were much more difficult. They failed miserably at solving them; and later they were indeed less likely to spend time working on them than the 24 students who had worked on somewhat easier puzzles with higher success rates. The negative feelings associated with failure counteracted the positive feelings associated with the puzzle. Failure won: failing at a task, it seems, reduces our motive to stay with it. Similarly, Cascio and I found that negative verbal feedback also decreases intrinsic motivation.

Toy. Another area of social psychology that fits nicely with our research is that of insufficient justification. This line of theory suggests that when persons do not have sufficient external reasons to explain their actions, they develop internal reasons; attitudes change accordingly.

For example, Elliot Aronson and J. Merrill Carlsmith gave one group of children strong warnings against playing with a particular toy, and gave another group milder warnings. The first group had a clear, external reason for avoiding the attractive toy; hence they felt no need for internal justification for not playing with it. But the second group, those who were warned mildly, changed their attitudes toward the toy significantly: they decided that they really didn't want to play with the "dumb old thing" anyway. Since there were insufficient outside threats, they developed internal reasons. Jonathan Freedman reported similar findings. Children who developed internal reasons for not playing with the toy were less likely to play with the toy in a free situation even two months later. Intrinsic controls, it appears, have lasting effect.

Controls. When we apply the results of these experiments to the real world, we begin to see why curiosity and pleasure in learning decrease as the child grows up. When the child enters school he immediately becomes subject to numerous extrinsic controls. Teachers grade him, and warn him that he will fail if he does not do what he is told to do. Teachers determine what the child should learn, and at what pace he must learn it. Some parents compound the process by promising money or gifts for good marks. So the child begins to work for the grade, or the gift, or to avoid the consequences of failure. The result is a student who works only for external rewards.

John Holt has described this process beautifully. Children fail, he says, because they are afraid of punishment and bored by the dull and trivial tasks they must perform. The school provides little that is intrinsically interesting, and then teachers control the student's behavior in such a way that they destroy any intrinsic motivation that may sneak through.

Systems. Educators are not the only ones who want to know how to maintain intrinsic motivation. Organizations and businesses have become concerned. Managerial psychologists have begun to focus on factors that promote the worker's intrinsic motivation and ego-involvement with his job. They stress the kinds of work that promote creativity and they argue that workers should participate in the decision-making processes of the company.

Yet others look more at reward systems that tie money and other benefits to performance—sales commissions and piece-rate payments are examples. My research indicates, however, that such pay systems will *decrease* the intrinsic motivation that is aroused by the interesting jobs and sharing of decision-making. (Straight salaries, however, which are not directly tied to workers' performances, run less risk of this.)

Chaos. There are many individuals who argue that if we remove external controls, people will flounder about in their new-found freedom and abuse it. Lift curfews, say the administrators, and students will carouse all night. Lift threats, says the employer, and employees will stop working. Lift grades, says the parent, and my child will not strive for college.

In fact, they are probably right. The external controls which they have used have co-opted internal control, so the initial response to the breakdown of external controls can be chaotic or destructive behavior. However, I think that the internal control can be reestablished. Forced to rely on his own resources, a person establishes internal controls and limits. This is especially so if the administrators, the employers, and the parents are supportive.

Intrinsic motivation and internal controls have the advantage of being operative when no one is looking. More importantly, they help to maintain a person's sense of self-esteem and personal worth. Abraham Maslow, in *Eupsychian Management*, argues that internal controls also produce less anxiety and are more conducive to strong mental health than external controls are.

Level. It is clear to me that if we want individuals to enjoy what they do, to derive joy and satisfaction from their work as well as their play, we must do two things. We must create more activities that are inherently interesting and gratifying; and we must not use extrinsic rewards in a way that will lower the interest level of those activities that are intrinsically motivated. We should learn to give verbal support to our friends, colleagues and children, and not rely on tendencies to reward or threaten. External controls may get others to act the way we want them to, but such controls absolve them of the feeling of responsibility for those acts. Controlling others seems to insure that others will not control themselves.

10.1 STANLEY SCHACHTER AND
JEROME E. SINGER

Cognitive, Social, and Physiological Determinants of Emotional State

Emotions are generally defined as responses that include physiological arousal, subjective feeling, cognitive interpretation, and overt behavior. Psychologists have been debating the exact definition for years, and the role of cognition in emotion is still not agreed upon today. In the early 1960s, Stanley Schachter and Jerome E. Singer set out to determine whether or not environmental conditions influence emotions.

Schachter (b. 1922) earned his Ph.D. from the University of Michigan in 1950. He is currently a professor of psychology at Columbia University, where he has been teaching since 1960. Singer received his Ph.D. in psychology from the University of Minnesota in 1961. He is currently at the Uniformed Services University of the Health Sciences in Bethesda, Maryland.

This selection, "Cognitive, Social, and Physiological Determinants of Emotional State," was published in the *Psychological Review* in 1962. The authors' experimental procedures are described in great detail, and although it is important to note the precise conditions that needed to be included in order to rule out other influences on the subjects' reactions, do not get so

bogged down in detail that you miss the major points. As you read this
article, consider how important your surroundings are to your emotional
feelings.

Key Concept: arousal-cognitive theory of emotion

*T*he problem of which cues, internal or external, permit a person to label
and identify his own emotional state has been with us since the days that
James (1890) first tendered his doctrine that "the bodily changes follow directly
the perception of the exciting fact, and that our feeling of the same changes as
they occur *is* the emotion" (p. 449). Since we are aware of a variety of feeling
and emotion states, it should follow from James' proposition that the various
emotions will be accompanied by a variety of differentiable bodily states. Following James' pronouncement, a formidable number of studies were undertaken in search of the physiological differentiators of the emotions. The results,
in these early days, were almost uniformly negative. All of the emotional states
experimentally manipulated were characterized by a general pattern of excitation of the sympathetic nervous system but there appeared to be no clear-cut
physiological discriminators of the various emotions. . . .

More recent work, however, has given some indication that there may be
differentiators. Ax (1953) and Schachter (1957) studied fear and anger. On a
large number of indices both of these states were characterized by a similarly
high level of autonomic activation but on several indices they did differ in the
degree of activation. . . .

This rather ambiguous situation has led Ruckmick (1936), Hunt, Cole,
and Reis (1958), Schachter (1959) and others to suggest that cognitive factors
may be major determinants of emotional states. Granted a general pattern of
sympathetic excitation as characteristic of emotional states, granted that there
may be some differences in pattern from state to state, it is suggested that one
labels, interprets, and identifies this stirred-up state in terms of the characteristics of the precipitating situation and one's apperceptive mass. This suggests, then, that an emotional state may be considered a function of a state of
physiological arousal and of a cognition appropriate to this state of arousal.
The cognition, in a sense, exerts a steering function. Cognitions arising from the
immediate situation as interpreted by past experience provide the framework
within which one understands and labels his feelings. It is the cognition which
determines whether the state of physiological arousal will be labeled as "anger," "joy," "fear," or whatever.

In order to examine the implications of this formulation let us consider
the fashion in which these two elements, a state of physiological arousal and
cognitive factors, would interact in a variety of situations. In most emotion
inducing situations, of course, the two factors are completely interrelated.
Imagine a man walking alone down a dark alley, a figure with a gun suddenly
appears. The perception-cognition "figure with a gun" in some fashion initiates
a state of physiological arousal; this state of arousal is interpreted in terms of

knowledge about dark alleys and guns and the state of arousal is labeled "fear." Similarly a student who unexpectedly learns that he has made Phi Beta Kappa may experience a state of arousal which he will label "joy." . . .

Consider now a person in a state of physiological arousal for which no immediately explanatory or appropriate cognitions are available. Such a state could result were one covertly to inject a subject with adrenalin or, unknown to him, feed the subject a sympathomimetic drug such as ephedrine. Under such conditions a subject would be aware of palpitations, tremor, face flushing, and most of the battery of symptoms associated with a discharge of the sympathetic nervous system. . . . [H]e would, at the same time, be utterly unaware of why he felt this way. What would be the consequence of such a state?

Schachter (1959) has suggested that precisely such a state would lead to the arousal of "evaluative needs" (Festinger, 1954), that is, pressures would act on an individual in such a state to understand and label his bodily feelings. His bodily state grossly resembles the condition in which it has been at times of emotional excitement. How would he label his present feelings? It is suggested, of course, that he will label his feelings in terms of his knowledge of the immediate situation. Should he at the time be with a beautiful woman he might decide that he was wildly in love or sexually excited. Should he be at a gay party [i.e., one that is lively, upbeat] he might, by comparing himself to others, decide that he was extremely happy and euphoric. Should he be arguing with his wife, he might explode in fury and hatred. Or, should the situation be completely inappropriate he could decide that he was excited about something that had recently happened to him or, simply, that he was sick. In any case, it is our basic assumption that emotional states are a function of the interaction of such cognitive factors with a state of physiological arousal. . . .

PROCEDURE

The experimental test of these propositions requires (*a*) the experimental manipulation of a state of physiological arousal, (*b*) the manipulation of the extent to which the subject has an appropriate or proper explanation of his bodily state, and (*c*) the creation of situations from which explanatory cognitions may be derived.

In order to satisfy the first two experimental requirements, the experiment was cast in the framework of a study of the effects of vitamin supplements on vision. As soon as a subject arrived, he was taken to a private room and told by the experimenter:

In this experiment we would like to make various tests of your vision. We are particularly interested in how certain vitamin compounds and vitamin supplements affect the visual skills. In particular, we want to find out how the vitamin compound called 'Suproxin' affects your vision.

What we would like to do, then, if we can get your permission, is to give you a small injection of Suproxin. The injection itself is mild and harmless; however, since some people do object to being injected we don't want to talk you into anything. Would you mind receiving a Suproxin injection?

If the subject agrees to the injection (and all but 1 of 185 subjects did) the experimenter continues with instructions we shall describe shortly, then leaves the room. In a few minutes a physician enters the room, briefly repeats the experimenter's instructions, takes the subject's pulse and then injects him with Suproxin.

Depending upon condition, the subject receives one of two forms of Suproxin—epinephrine or a placebo.

Epinephrine or adrenalin is a sympathomimetic drug whose effects, with minor exceptions, are almost a perfect mimicry of a discharge of the sympathetic nervous system. Shortly after injection systolic blood pressure increases markedly, heart rate increases somewhat, cutaneous blood flow decreases, while muscle and cerebral blood flow increase, blood sugar and lactic acid concentration increase, and respiration rate increases slightly. As far as the subject is concerned the major subjective symptoms are palpitation, tremor, and sometimes a feeling of flushing and accelerated breathing. With a subcutaneous injection (in the dosage administered to our subjects), such effects usually begin within 3–5 minutes of injection and last anywhere from 10 minutes to an hour. For most subjects these effects are dissipated within 15–20 minutes after injection. . . .

Manipulating an Appropriate Explanation

By "appropriate" we refer to the extent to which the subject has an authoritative, unequivocal explanation of his bodily condition. Thus, a subject who had been informed by the physician that as a direct consequence of the injection he would feel palpitations, tremor, etc. would be considered to have a completely appropriate explanation. A subject who had been informed only that the injection would have no side effects would have no appropriate explanation of his state. This dimension of appropriateness was manipulated in three experimental conditions which shall be called: Epinephrine Informed (Epi Inf), Epinephrine Ignorant (Epi Ign), and Epinephrine Misinformed (Epi Mis).

Immediately after the subject had agreed to the injection and before the physician entered the room, the experimenter's spiel in each of these conditions went as follows:

> *Epinephrine Informed.* I should also tell you that some of our subjects have experienced side effects from the Suproxin. These side effects are transitory, that is, they will only last for about 15 to 20 minutes. What will probably happen is that your hand will start to shake, your heart will start to pound, and your face may get warm and flushed. Again these are side effects lasting about 15 or 20 minutes.

While the physician was giving the injection, she told the subject that the injection was mild and harmless and repeated this description of the symptoms that the subject could expect as a consequence of the shot. In this condition, then, subjects have a completely appropriate explanation of their bodily state. They know precisely what they will feel and why.

Epinephrine Ignorant. In this condition, when the subject agreed to the injection, the experimenter said nothing more relevant to side effects and simply left the room. While the physician was giving the injection, she told the subject that the injection was mild and harmless and would have no side effects. In this condition, then, the subject has no experimentally provided explanation for his bodily state.

> *Epinephrine Misinformed*. I should also tell you that some of our subjects have experienced side effects from the Suproxin. These side effects are transitory, that is, they will only last for about 15 or 20 minutes. What will probably happen is that your feet will feel numb, you will have an itching sensation over parts of your body, and you may get a slight headache. Again these are side effects lasting 15 or 20 minutes.

And again, the physician repeated these symptoms while injecting the subject.

None of these symptoms, of course, are consequences of an injection of epinephrine and, in effect, these instructions provide the subject with a completely inappropriate explanation of his bodily feelings. This condition was introduced as a control condition of sorts. . . .

Subjects in all of the above conditions were injected with epinephrine. Finally, there was a placebo condition in which subjects, who were injected with saline solution, were given precisely the same treatment as subjects in the Epi Ign condition.

Producing an Emotion Inducing Cognition

Our initial hypothesis has suggested that given a state of physiological arousal for which the individual has no adequate explanation, cognitive factors can lead the individual to describe his feelings with any of a diversity of emotional labels. [*At this point, the experimenters describe their attempt to prove this hypothesis by manipulating two emotional states: euphoria and anger. In both conditions, after the injection, the experimenter left the subject alone with a stooge (an accomplice pretending to be another subject) who had been trained to act euphorically or angrily, depending on which emotion was to be manipulated. (Subjects in the epinephrine misinformed group were not run in the anger condition.) To measure the subject's emotional reaction, the experimenters observed the behavior of the subject through a one-way mirror during the stooge's act; after the stooge was dismissed, the experimenters had the subject provide a self-report inventory of mood. They also measured the subject's pulse rate to determine the effects of the drug.—Ed.*]

Subjects

The subjects were all male, college students taking classes in introductory psychology at the University of Minnesota. Some 90% of the students in these classes volunteer for a subject pool for which they receive two extra points on their final exam for every hour that they serve as experimental subjects. For this study the records of all potential subjects were cleared with the Student

Health Service in order to insure that no harmful effects would result from the injections. . . .

RESULTS

Effects of the Injections on Bodily State

Let us examine first the success of the injections at producing the bodily state required to examine the propositions at test. Does the injection of epinephrine produce symptoms of sympathetic discharge as compared with the placebo injection? [*Schachter and Singer's data, not included here, show that the injection of epinephrine did cause a significant physiological arousal in the subjects in the Epinephrine Informed, the Epinephrine Misinformed, and the Epinephrine Ignorant groups. In assessing the emotional levels of each group, the experimenters found that for both the euphoria and anger conditions, the emotional levels in the Epinephrine Misinformed and the Epinephrine Ignorant conditions were considerably greater than that in the Epinephrine Informed condition. For the euphoria condition, physiologically aroused subjects were happiest when they were not informed of the cause of their arousal, especially as measured by self-report. Similarly, according to the observational data, physiologically aroused subjects became angriest in the anger condition when they were not informed of the cause of their arousal.—Ed.*]

DISCUSSION

Let us summarize the major findings of this experiment and examine the extent to which they support the propositions offered in the introduction of this paper. It has been suggested, first, that given a state of physiological arousal for which an individual has no explanation, he will label this state in terms of the cognitions available to him. This implies, of course, that by manipulating the cognitions of an individual in such a state we can manipulate his feelings in diverse directions. Experimental results support this proposition for following the injection of epinephrine, those subjects who had no explanation for the bodily state thus produced, gave behavioral and self-report indications that they had been readily manipulable into the disparate feeling states of euphoria and anger.

From this first proposition, it must follow that given a state of physiological arousal for which the individual has a completely satisfactory explanation, he will not label this state in terms of the alternative cognitions available. Experimental evidence strongly supports this expectation. In those conditions in which subjects were injected with epinephrine and told precisely what they would feel and why, they proved relatively immune to any effects of the manipulated cognitions. In the anger condition, such subjects did not report or show anger; in the euphoria condition, such subjects reported themselves as far less happy than subjects with an identical bodily state but no adequate knowledge of why they felt the way they did.

Finally, it has been suggested that given constant cognitive circumstances, an individual will react emotionally only to the extent that he experiences a state of physiological arousal. Without taking account of experimental artifacts, the evidence in support of this proposition is consistent but tentative. When the effects of "self-informing" tendencies in epinephrine subjects and of "self-arousing" tendencies in placebo subjects are partialed out, the evidence strongly supports the proposition. . . .

SUMMARY

It is suggested that emotional states may be considered a function of a state of physiological arousal and of a cognition appropriate to this state of arousal. From this follows these propositions:

1. Given a state of physiological arousal for which an individual has no immediate explanation, he will label this state and describe his feelings in terms of the cognitions available to him. To the extent that cognitive factors are potent determiners of emotional states, it should be anticipated that precisely the same state of physiological arousal could be labeled "joy" or "fury" or "jealousy" or any of a great diversity of emotional labels depending on the cognitive aspects of the situation.

2. Given a state of physiological arousal for which an individual has a completely appropriate explanation, no evaluative needs will arise and the individual is unlikely to label his feelings in terms of the alternative cognitions available.

3. Given the same cognitive circumstances, the individual will react emotionally or describe his feeling as emotions only to the extent that he experiences a state of physiological arousal.

An experiment is described which, together with the results of other studies, supports these propositions.

NOTE

This experiment is part of a program of research on cognitive and physiological determinants of emotional state which is being conducted at the Department of Social Psychology at Columbia University under PHS Research Grant M-2584 from the National Institute of Mental Health, United States Public Health Service. This experiment was conducted at the Laboratory for Research in Social Relations at the University of Minnesota.

The authors wish to thank Jean Carlin and Ruth Hase, the physicians in the study, and Bibb Latané and Leonard Weller who were the paid participants.

REFERENCES

Stanley Schachter and Jerome E. Singer

Ax, A. F. Physiological differentiation of emotional states. *Psychosom. Med.,* 1953, **15,** 433–442.

Festinger, L. A theory of social comparison processes. *Hum. Relat.,* 1954, **7,** 114–140.

Hunt, J. McV., Cole, M. W., & Reis, E. E. Situational cues distinguishing anger, fear, and sorrow. *Amer. J. Psychol.,* 1958, **71,** 136–151.

James, W. *The principles of psychology.* New York: Holt, 1890.

Ruckmick, C. A. *The psychology of feeling and emotion.* New York: McGraw-Hill. 1936.

Schachter, J. Pain, fear and anger in hypertensives and normotensives: A psychophysiologic study. *Psychosom. Med.,* 1957, **19,** 17–29.

Schachter, S. *The psychology of affiliation.* Stanford, Calif.: Stanford Univer. Press, 1959.

Facial Expressions of Emotion: New Findings, New Questions

During the past two decades, researchers have discovered that facial expressions for a number of emotions are universally recognizable—that is, people from a wide variety of cultures will attribute certain facial expressions to the same emotions. More recently, psychologists have reported that facial muscular actions associated with specific emotions (such as frowning, which indicates sadness) cause changes in physiological arousal as well as enhance feelings of the emotion associated with the muscular movements. Paul Ekman has been at the cutting edge of research on facial expression of emotion.

Ekman (b. 1934) earned his Ph.D. from Adelphi University in 1958. He is currently a professor of psychology and the director of the Human Interaction Laboratory at the University of California at San Francisco. He has written a number of books, including *Emotion in the Human Face,* 2d ed. (Cambridge University Press, 1983) and *Telling Lies* (Berkeley, 1985).

This selection, "Facial Expressions of Emotion: New Findings, New Questions," was published in the American Psychological Society journal *Psychological Science* in 1992. In it, Ekman offers a glimpse of an active and relevant research program concerning observable facial expressions of emotion. In one part of the original article not included in this selection, Ekman demonstrates that there are differences among smiles and that it is possible to distinguish a smile of enjoyment from other kinds of smiling (such as a smile of embarrassment). As you read this selection, consider how easy it is to detect a person's emotions by observing his or her facial expressions. Does Ekman's evidence suggest that it is possible to modify your emotional state by exercising certain facial muscles?

Key Concept: facial expression of emotion

This paper focuses on the evidence and issues regarding observable facial expression of emotion. . . . I will focus on two new findings and one set of studies dating back 20 years. I will begin with those older studies, of universals in facial expression, because they provide the background for the newer research and also because there is renewed controversy about universals, as well as some new findings and a number of unanswered questions.

Paul Ekman

UNIVERSAL FACIAL EXPRESSIONS

From 1920 through 1960 many influential psychologists maintained that facial expressions are socially learned and culturally variable, with no fixed relationship between an expression and what it signifies. In the early 1970s there were two challenges: a critical reevaluation of the experiments which had supported that position (Ekman, Friesen, & Ellsworth, 1972) and, more important, new data. Izard and also Friesen and I conducted similar studies of literate cultures, working independently but at the same time. Izard's work and ours was influenced by Tomkins's writings on emotion (1962) and his advice on the conduct of the research we performed.

In each culture subjects chose the emotion terms which fit photographs of posed Caucasian facial expressions. Although Izard (1971) and I (Ekman, Sorenson, & Friesen, 1969) showed different photographs, gave our subjects somewhat different lists of emotion terms, and examined people in different cultures, we both obtained consistent evidence of agreement across more than a dozen Western and non-Western literate cultures in the labeling of enjoyment, anger, fear, sadness, disgust, and surprise facial expressions.

In order to rule out the possibility that such agreement could be due to members of every culture having learned expressions from a shared mass media input, Friesen and I (Ekman, 1972; Ekman & Friesen, 1971; Ekman et al., 1969) also studied a visually isolated preliterate culture in New Guinea. We replicated our findings for literate cultures, as did Heider and Rosch a few years later in another visually isolated culture in what is now West Irian. Although surprise expressions were distinguished from anger, sadness, disgust, and enjoyment expressions in both preliterate cultures, surprise was not distinguished from fear expressions in one of these cultures. Friesen and I also reversed the research design and found that when New Guineans posed facial expressions they were understandable to Western observers (Ekman & Friesen, 1971).

To reconcile these findings of universality with the many reports by cultural anthropologists of dissimilar facial expressions, we (Ekman & Friesen, 1969) postulated *display rules* to refer to what we presume each culture teaches its members about the management of expression in social contexts. Cultural differences in display rules could explain how universal expressions might be modified to create, on occasion, the appearance of culture-specific facial expressions of emotion. We tested this idea in a study comparing the spontaneous expressions shown by Japanese and Americans when they were alone, and presumably no display rules should operate, and when they were with another person (Ekman, 1972; Friesen, 1972). As predicted, there was no difference between cultures in the expressions shown in response to films of unpleasant scenes when the subjects thought they were alone. However, when an authority figure was present the Japanese more than the Americans masked negative expressions with the semblance of smile.

We, like Izard, interpreted the evidence in terms of universal facial expressions as posited by Tomkins (1962) and (much earlier) by Darwin (1872). Consistent with an evolutionary view of expression were other reports of similarities in expression in other primates and in early appearance developmentally. Recently, there have been some challenges to that interpretation. Lutz and White (1986) cited anthropologists who regard emotions as social constructions and reported cultures in which the emotions proposed as universal are neither named nor expressed. Unfortunately, such reports are not substantiated by quantitative methods nor protected against the potential for bias or error when the information is obtained by the single observer who formulated the hypothesis under study. Ortony and Turner (1990) provided a different challenge, speculating that it is only the components of expressions, not the full emotional expressions, which are universal: but see my rebuttal (Ekman, in press-a) and one by Izard (in press).

A new line of studies has found consistent evidence of cultural differences in the perception of the strength of an emotion rather than of which emotion is shown in a facial expression. Japanese make less intense attributions than do Americans (Ekman et al., 1987) regardless of whether the person showing the emotion is Japanese or American, male or female (Matsumoto & Ekman, 1989). This difference appears to be specific to the interpretation of facial expressions of emotions, since it was not found in the judgment of either nonfacial emotional stimuli or facial nonemotional stimuli (Matsumoto & Kudoh, 1991).

A number of empirical questions remain about universals in facial expression. Although there is evidence of more than one different expression for each emotion (up to five visibly different expressions for some emotions) in Western cultures, we do not know how many of those different expressions which signal a single emotion are shown universally (Ekman & Friesen, 1975, 1978). Nor is there certain knowledge about whether there are other emotions in addition to anger, fear, disgust, sadness, enjoyment, and surprise that have universal expressions. There is some evidence, although it is contradictory, for universal facial expressions for contempt, interest, shame, and guilt. Little is known also about cross-cultural differences in display rules, as a function of sex, role, age, and social context (but see recent work by Matsumoto, in press). These and other questions about universals have recently been reviewed (Ekman, 1989b).

FACIAL ACTION GENERATES EMOTION PHYSIOLOGY

Most emotion theorists emphasize the involuntary nature of emotional experience, ignoring those instances when people choose to generate an emotion through reminiscence or by adopting the physical actions associated with a particular emotion (e.g., speaking more softly to deintensify anger or smiling to generate enjoyment). Facial expression from this vantage point is seen as one of a number of emotional responses that are generated centrally when an emotion is called forth by, for example, an event, memory, or image.

A new role for facial expression was found in my collaborative study with Levenson and Friesen (Ekman, Levenson, & Friesen, 1983). Voluntarily performing certain facial muscular actions generated involuntary changes in autonomic nervous system (ANS) activity. We did not ask subjects to pose emotions, but instead to follow muscle-by-muscle instructions to create on their faces one of the expressions which had been found to be universal. For example, rather than ask a subject to pose anger we said: "Pull your eyebrows down and together; raise your upper eyelids and tighten your lower eyelids; narrow your lips and press them together." Different patterns of ANS activity occurred when subjects made the muscular movements which had been found universally for the emotions of anger, fear, sadness, and disgust.

This work has since been replicated in three more experiments (Levenson, Carstensen, Frisen, & Ekman, 1991; Levenson, Ekman, & Friesen, 1990), and a number of possible artifacts which could have been responsible for this phenomenon have been ruled out. The findings were again obtained in a very different culture—the Minangkabau of Sumatra, Indonesia, who are fundamentalist Moslem and matrilineal—suggesting that this phenomenon may be pan-cultural (Ekman, 1989a).

It appears that the specific patterns of ANS activity that were generated by making the different facial expressions are not unique to this task, but are the same as are found in more conventional emotion-arousing tasks. This lack of specificity confirms my proposal (Ekman, 1984, in press-b) that emotions are characterized by patterned changes in both expression and physiology, changes which are distinctive for each emotion, and which are not (in large part) specific to the means by which the emotion was aroused. This latter point is most readily noted with facial expression, which can signal that someone is angry, for example, without providing any clue as to what made the person angry.

When subjects followed our instructions to make these facial expressions, most reported not simply a physiological change but the experience of an emotion. In response to an open-ended question about what emotions, sensations, or memories they experienced, there were few reports of memories or sensations, while on 78% of the trials the subjects reported feeling an emotion. More information on this point, on the issue of generality, and on the details of the emotion-specific patterns of ANS activity can be found in . . . Levenson et al. (1990).

Before turning to the question of *how* voluntarily making different facial configurations generates different patterns of physiology, let me broaden our focus to consider central nervous system (CNS), not just ANS, physiology. In a study employing the same muscle-by-muscle instructions used to study ANS activity, subjects created the various facial configurations while left and right frontal, temporal, and parietal electroencephalographic (EEG) activity was measured. Different patterns of EEG activity occurred when subjects made the muscular movements which had been found universally for the emotions of happiness, anger, fear, sadness, and disgust (Davidson & Ekman, 1991; Ekman & Davidson, 1991).

In an unpublished research Friesen, Levenson, and I have formulated nine different explanations of how voluntary facial action generates emotion-specific physiology. Here I will indicate only three broad divisions among these explanations, leaving out the specific details relevant to subdistinctions within each of these divisions. The first explanation, which is the one we endorse, posits a central, hard-wired connection between the motor cortex and other areas of the brain involved in directing the physiological changes which occur during emotion. The second group of explanations proposes that such a connection is learned, not hard-wired. Such learning could be common to all members of our species or culture-specific. (Our findings in Indonesia raise questions but cannot rule out the viability of the culture-specific variation.) The third set of explanations emphasizes peripheral feedback from the facial actions themselves, rather than a central connection between the brain areas which direct those facial movements and other brain areas. This view includes variations in terms of whether feedback comes from the muscles, the skin, or temperature changes and whether it is hard-wired or requires learning. This explanation is consistent with the view of Izard (in press), Laird (Laird, 1971; Duclos et al., 1989), Tomkins (1962), and Zajonc (1985).

For now, there is no clear empirical basis for a definitive choice among these explanations. Through studies of people with facial paralysis who have no possibility of peripheral facial action or feedback we hope to challenge the third category of explanations, but this work is not yet complete, and the results may not be unambiguous. . . .

OTHER ISSUES ABOUT EXPRESSION

In closing let me mention three major questions about observable facial expressions. Every student who examines expression itself, not its recognition, must be impressed with individual differences in the speed, magnitude, and duration of expression as well as variations in which facial expression of emotion occurs in response to a particular event. It is not known whether such differences are consistent across emotions or situations, or over time. We also do not know whether a facial activity is a necessary part of any emotional experience. Under what circumstances, and with what kinds of people, might there be evidence of physiological changes relevant to emotion and the subjective experience of emotion with no evidence of visible expression or nonvisible electromyographic facial activity? Another issue requiring study is whether personality traits, moods, and psychopathology have facial markers or are second-order inferences drawn from the occurrence of facial expressions of emotion.

Darwin, C. (1972). *The expression of the emotions in man and animals.* New York: Philosophical Library.

Davidson, R. J., & Ekman, P. (1991). *Differences in regional brain activity among different emotions.* Unpublished manuscript.

Duclos, S. E., Laird, J. D., Schneider, E., Sexter, M., Stern, L., & Van Leighten, O. (1989). Emotion-specific effects of facial expressions and postures on emotional experience. *Journal of Personality and Social Psychology, 57,* 100–108.

Ekman, P. (1972). Universals and cultural differences in facial expressions of emotion. In J. Cole (Ed.), *Nebraska symposium on motivation, 1971* (pp. 207–283). Lincoln: University of Nebraska Press.

Ekman, P. (1984). Expression and the nature of emotion. In K. Scherer & P. Ekman (Eds.), *Approaches to emotion* (pp. 319–344). Hillsdale, NJ: Erlbaum.

Ekman, P. (1989a). The argument and evidence about universals in facial expressions of emotion. In H. Wagner & A. Manstead (Eds.), *Handbook of social psychophysiology* (pp. 143–164). Chichester, England: Wiley.

Ekman, P. (1989b, January). *A cross cultural study of emotional expression, language and physiology.* Symposium conducted at the annual meeting of the American Association for the Advancement of Science, San Francisco.

Ekman, P. (in press-a). Are there basic emotions? A reply to Ortony and Turner. *Psychological Review.*

Ekman, P. (in press-b). An argument for basic emotions. *Cognition and Emotion.*

Ekman, P., & Davidson, R. J. (1991). *Hemispheric activation in different types of smiles.* Unpublished manuscript.

Ekman, P., & Friesen, W. V. (1969). The repertoire of nonverbal behavior: Categories, origins, usage, and coding. *Semiotica, 1,* 49–98.

Ekman, P., & Friesen, W. V. (1971). Constants across cultures in the face and emotion. *Journal of Personality and Social Psychology, 17,* 124–129.

Ekman, P., & Friesen, W. V. (1975). *Unmasking the face: A guide to recognizing emotions from facial clues.* Englewood Cliffs, NJ: Prentice-Hall.

Ekman, P., & Friesen, W. V. (1978). *The Facial Action Coding System: A technique for the measurement of facial movement.* Palo Alto, CA: Consulting Psychologists Press.

Ekman, P., Friesen, W. V., & Ellsworth, P. (1972). *Emotion in the human face: Guidelines for research and an integration of findings.* New York: Pergamon Press.

Ekman, P., Friesen, W. V., O'Sullivan, M., Chan, A., Diacoyanni-Tarlatzis, I., Heider, K., Krause, R., LeCompte, W. A., Pitcairn, T., Ricci-Bitti, P. E., Scherer, K. R., Tomita, M., & Tzavaras, A. (1987). Universals and cultural differences in the judgments of facial expressions of emotion. *Journal of Personality and Social Psychology, 53,* 712–717.

Ekman, P., Levenson, R. W., & Friesen, W. V. (1983). Autonomic nervous system activity distinguishes between emotions. *Science, 221,* 1208–1210.

Ekman, P., Sorenson, E. R., & Friesen, W. V. (1969). Pan-cultural elements in facial displays of emotions. *Science, 164,* 86–88.

Friesen, W. V. (1972). *Cultural differences in facial expression in a social situation: An experimental test of the concept of display rules.* Unpublished doctoral dissertation, University of California, San Francisco.

Izard, C. E. (1971). *The face of emotion.* New York: Appleton-Century-Crofts.

Izard, C. E. (in press). Basic emotions, relation among emotions and emotion-cognition relation. *Psychological Review.*

Laird, J. D. (1974). Self-attribution of emotion: The effects of expressive behavior on the quality of emotional experience. *Journal of Personality and Social Psychology, 29,* 475–486.

Levenson, R. W., Carstensen, L. L., Friesen, W. V., & Ekman, P. (1991). Emotion, physiology, and expression in old age. *Psychology and Aging, 6,* 28–35.

Levenson, R. W., Ekman, P., & Friesen, W. V. (1990). Voluntary facial action generates emotion-specific autonomic nervous system activity. *Psychophysiology, 27,* 363–384.

Lutz, C., & White, G. M. (1986). The anthropology of emotions. *Annual Review of Anthropology, 15,* 405–436.

Matsumoto, D. (in press). Cultural similarities and differences in display rules. *Motivation and Emotion.*

Matsumoto, D., & Ekman, P. (1989). American-Japanese cultural differences in rating the intensity of facial expressions of emotion. *Motivation and Emotion, 13,* 143–157.

Matsumoto, D., & Kudoh, T. (1991). *Cultural differences in judgments of emotion and other personal attributes: What's in a smile?* Manuscript submitted for publication.

Ortony, A., & Turner, T. J. (1990). What's basic about basic emotions? *Psychological Review, 97,* 315–331.

Tomkins, S. S. (1962). *Affect, imagery, consciousness: Vol. 1. The positive affects.* New York: Springer.

Zajonc, R. B. (1985). Emotion and facial efference: A theory reclaimed. *Science, 228,* 15–21.

10.3 ROBERT J. STERNBERG

The Ingredients of Love

Love is one of the most important human emotions. Although it has been the subject of countless poems and works of art, it has only recently become the focus of research by psychologists. Researchers recognize that there are different kinds of love, making it difficult to generalize the results of love studies. In an attempt to make such a generalization, Yale psychologist Robert J. Sternberg has proposed a triangular theory of love in which love consists of intimacy, passion, and decision/commitment.

Sternberg (b. 1949) earned his Ph.D. from Stanford University in 1975. He has been very influential in psychology in the cognitive area of intelligence and in the emotional area of love. The American Psychological Association awarded him the Distinguished Scientific Award for Early Career Contribution to Psychology in 1981. Sternberg has written much about his research on love, including his book *Triangle of Love: Intimacy, Passion, and Commitment* (Basic Books, 1988).

This selection is from chapter 2, "The Ingredients of Love," of Sternberg's *Triangle of Love.* In it, Sternberg describes, in an informal, practical style, how the three ingredients intimacy, passion, and commitment combine to form eight possible kinds of love. He provides many examples, some of which should seem familiar to you. Sternberg's objective is to help you more fully understand the characteristics of love. As you read this selection, evaluate Sternberg's theory of love. Are there any other ingredients that he may have left out of his theory?

Key Concept: love

A substantial body of evidence suggests that the components of intimacy, passion, and commitment play a key role in love over and above other attributes. Even before I collected the first bit of data to test my theory, I had several reasons for choosing these three components as the building blocks for it.

First, many of the other aspects of love prove, on close examination, to be either parts or manifestations of these three components. Communication, for example, is a building block of intimacy, as is caring or compassion. Were one to subdivide intimacy and passion and commitment into their own subparts, the theory would eventually contain so many elements as to become unwieldy. There is no one, solely correct fineness of division. But a division into three components works well in several ways. . . .

Second, my review of the literature on couples in the United States, as well as in other lands, suggested that, whereas some elements of love are fairly time-bound or culture-specific, the three I propose are general across time and place. The three components are not equally weighted in all cultures, but each component receives at least some weight in virtually any time or place.

Third, the three components do appear to be distinct, although, of course, they are related. You can have any one without either or both of the others. In contrast, other potential building blocks for a theory of love—for example, nurturance and caring—tend to be difficult to separate, logically as well as psychologically.

Fourth, . . . many other accounts of love seem to boil down to something similar to my own account, or a subset of it. If we take away differences in language and tone, the spirit of many other theories converges with mine.

Finally, and perhaps most important, the theory works. . . .

INTIMACY

In the context of the triangular theory, intimacy refers to those feelings in a relationship that promote closeness, bondedness, and connectedness. My research with Susan Grajek . . . indicates that intimacy includes at least ten elements:

1. *Desiring to promote the welfare of the loved one.* The lover looks out for the partner and seeks to promote his or her welfare. One may promote the other's welfare at the expense of one's own—but in the expectation that the other will reciprocate when the time comes.

2. *Experiencing happiness with the loved one.* The lover enjoys being with his or her partner. When they do things together, they have a good time and build a store of memories upon which they can draw in hard times. Furthermore, good times shared will spill over into the relationship and make it better.

3. *Holding the loved one in high regard.* The lover thinks highly of and respects his or her partner. Although the lover may recognize flaws in the partner, this recognition does not detract from the overall esteem in which the partner is held.

4. *Being able to count on the loved one in times of need.* The lover feels that the partner is there when needed. When the chips are down, the lover can call on the partner and expect that he or she will come through.

5. *Having mutual understanding with the loved one.* The lovers understand each other. They know each other's strengths and weaknesses and how to respond to each other in a way that shows genuine empathy for the loved one's emotional states. Each knows where the other is "coming from."

6. *Sharing oneself and one's possessions with the loved one.* One is willing to give of oneself and one's time, as well as one's things, to the loved one. Al-

though all things need not be joint property, the lovers share their property as the need arises. And, most important, they share themselves.

7. *Receiving emotional support from the loved one.* The lover feels bolstered and even renewed by the loved one, especially in times of need.

8. *Giving emotional support to the loved one.* The lover supports the loved one by empathizing with, and emotionally supporting, him or her in times of need.

9. *Communicating intimately with the loved one.* The lover can communicate deeply and honestly with the loved one, sharing innermost feelings.

10. *Valuing the loved one.* The lover feels the great importance of the partner in the scheme of life.

These are only some of the possible feelings one can experience through the intimacy of love; moreover, it is not necessary to experience all of these feelings in order to experience intimacy. To the contrary, our research indicates that you experience intimacy when you sample a sufficient number of these feelings, with that number probably differing from one person and one situation to another. You do not usually experience the feelings independently, but often as one overall feeling. . . .

Intimacy probably starts in self-disclosure. To be intimate with someone, you need to break down the walls that separate one person from another. It is well known that self-disclosure begets self-disclosure: if you want to get to know what someone else is like, let him or her learn about you. But self-disclosure is often easier in same-sex friendships than in loving relationships, probably because people see themselves as having more to lose by self-disclosure in a loving relationship. And odd as it may sound, there is actually evidence that spouses may be less symmetrical in self-disclosure than are strangers, again probably because the costs of self-disclosure can be so high in love. . . .

Intimacy, then, is a foundation of love, but a foundation that develops slowly, through fits and starts, and is difficult to achieve. Moreover, once it starts to be attained, it may, paradoxically, start to go away because of the threat it poses. It poses a threat in terms not only of the dangers of self-disclosure but of the danger one starts to feel to one's existence as a separate, autonomous being. Few people want to be "consumed" by a relationship, yet many people start to feel as if they are being consumed when they get too close to another human being. The result is a balancing act between intimacy and autonomy which goes on throughout the lives of most couples, a balancing act in which a completely stable equilibrium is often never achieved. But this in itself is not necessarily bad: the swinging back and forth of the intimacy pendulum provides some of the excitement that keeps many relationships alive.

PASSION

The passion component of love includes what Elaine Hatfield and William Walster refer to as a "state of intense longing *for union* with the other." Passion is largely the expression of desires and needs—such as for self-esteem, nurturance, affiliation, dominance, submission, and sexual fulfillment. The strengths of these various needs vary across persons, situations, and kinds of loving relationship. For example, sexual fulfillment is likely to be a strong need in romantic relationships but not in filial ones. These needs manifest themselves through psychological and physiological arousal, which are often inseparable from each other.

Passion in love tends to interact strongly with intimacy, and often they fuel each other. For example, intimacy in a relationship may be largely a function of the extent to which the relationship meets a person's need for passion. Conversely, passion may be aroused by intimacy. In some close relationships with members of the opposite sex, for example, the passion component develops almost immediately; and intimacy, only after a while. Passion may have drawn the individuals into the relationship in the first place, but intimacy helps sustain the closeness in the relationship. In other close relationships, however, passion, especially as it applies to physical attraction, develops only after intimacy. Two close friends of the opposite sex may find themselves eventually developing a physical attraction for each other once they have achieved a certain emotional intimacy. . . .

Most people, when they think of passion, view it as sexual. But any form of psychophysiological arousal can generate the experience of passion. For example, an individual with a high need for affiliation may experience passion toward an individual who provides him or her with a unique opportunity to affiliate. For example, Debbie grew up in a broken home, with no extended family to speak of, and two parents who were constantly at war with each other and eventually divorced when she was an adolescent. Debbie felt as though she never had a family, and when she met Arthur, her passion was kindled. What he had to offer was not great sex but a large, warm, closely knit family that welcomed Debbie with open arms. Arthur was Debbie's ticket to the sense of belongingness she had never experienced but had always craved, and his ability to bring belongingness into her life aroused her passion for him. . . .

For other people, the need for submission can be the ticket to passion. . . . Social workers are often frustrated when, after months spent getting a battered woman to leave her husband, the woman ultimately goes back to the batterer. To some observers, her return may seem incomprehensible; to others, it may seem like a financial decision. But often it is neither. Such a woman has had the misfortune to identify abuse with being loved and, in going back to the abuse, is returning to what is, for her, love as she has learned it.

These patterns of response have been established through years of observation and sometimes first-hand experience, which cannot be easily undone by a social worker or anyone else in a few months. Probably the strangest learning mechanism for the buildup of passionate response is the mechanism of *intermittent reinforcement*, the periodic, sometimes random rewarding of a particular response to a stimulus. If you try to accomplish something, and sometimes are rewarded for your efforts and sometimes not, you are being intermittently reinforced. Oddly enough, intermittent reinforcement is even more powerful at developing or sustaining a given pattern of behavior than is continuous reinforcement. You are more likely to lose interest in or desire for something, and to become bored, if you are always rewarded when you seek it than if you are sometimes rewarded, but sometimes not. Put another way, sometimes the fun is in wanting something rather than in getting it. And if you are never re-warded for a given pattern of behavior, you are likely to give up on it ("extin-guish," as learning theorists would say), if only because of the total frustration you experience when you act in that particular way.

Passion thrives on the intermittent reinforcement that is intense at least in the early stages of a relationship. When you want someone, sometimes you feel as if you are getting closer to him or her, and sometimes you feel you are not—an alternation that keeps the passion aroused. . . .

DECISION AND COMMITMENT

The decision/commitment component of love consists of two aspects—one short-term and one long-term. The short-term aspect is the decision to love a certain other, whereas the long-term one is the commitment to maintain that love. These two aspects of the decision/commitment component of love do not necessarily occur together. The decision to love does not necessarily imply a commitment to that love. Oddly enough, the reverse is also possible, where there is a commitment to a relationship in which you did not make the deci-sion, as in arranged marriages. Some people are committed to loving another without ever having admitted their love. Most often, however, a decision pre-cedes the commitment both temporally and logically. Indeed, the institution of marriage represents a legalization of the commitment to a decision to love another throughout life.

While the decision/commitment component of love may lack the "heat" or "charge" of intimacy and passion, loving relationships almost inevitably have their ups and downs, and in the latter, the decision/commitment compo-nent is what keeps a relationship together. This component can be essential for getting through hard times and for returning to better ones. In ignoring it or separating it from love, you may be missing exactly that component of a loving relationship that enables you to get through the hard times as well as the easy ones. Sometimes, you may have to trust your commitment to carry you through to the better times you hope are ahead.

The decision/commitment component of love interacts with both inti-macy and passion. For most people, it results from the combination of intimate involvement and passionate arousal; however, intimate involvement or pas-sionate arousal can follow from commitment, as in certain arranged marriages or in close relationships in which you do not have a choice of partners. For example, you do not get to choose your mother, father, siblings, aunts, uncles, or cousins. In these close relationships, you may find that whatever intimacy or passion you experience results from your cognitive commitment to the rela-tionship, rather than the other way around. Thus, love can start off as a decision.

The expert in the study of commitment is the UCLA psychologist Harold Kelley. . . . For Kelley, commitment is the extent to which a person is likely to stick with something or someone and see it (or him or her) through to the finish. A person who is committed to something is expected to persist until the goal underlying the commitment is achieved. A problem for contemporary relationships is that two members of a couple may have different ideas about what it means to stick with someone to the end or to the realization of a goal. These differences, moreover, may never be articulated. One person, for example, may see the "end" as that point where the relationship is no longer working, whereas the other may see the end as the ending of one of the couple's lives. In a time of changing values and notions of commitment, it is becoming increasingly common for couples to find themselves in disagreement about the exact nature and duration of their commitment to each other. When marital commitments were always and automatically assumed to be for life, divorce was clearly frowned upon. Today, divorce is clearly more acceptable than it was even fifteen years ago, in part because many people have different ideas about how durable and lasting the marital commitment need be.

Difficulties in mismatches between notions of commitment cannot always be worked out by discussing mutual definitions of it, because these may change over time and differently for the two members of a couple. Both may intend a life-long commitment at the time of marriage, for example; but one of them may have a change of mind—or heart—over time. . . .

KINDS OF LOVING

How do people love, and what are some examples of ways in which they love? A summary of the various kinds of love captured by the triangular theory is shown in table 1.

TABLE 1

Taxonomy of Kinds of Love

Kind of Love	Intimacy	Passion	Decision/ Commitment
Non-love	-	-	-
Liking	+	-	-
Infatuated love	-	+	-
Empty love	-	-	+
Romantic love	+	+	-
Companionate love	+	-	+
Fatuous love	-	+	+
Consummate love	+	+	+

Note: + = component present; - = component absent.

Robert J. Sternberg

. . . Liking results when you experience only the intimacy component of love without passion or decision/commitment. The term *liking* is used here in a nontrivial sense, to describe not merely the feelings you have toward casual acquaintances and passers-by, but rather the set of feelings you experience in relationships that can truly be characterized as friendships. You feel closeness, bondedness, and warmth toward the other, without feelings of intense passion or long-term commitment. Stated another way, you feel emotionally close to the friend, but the friend does not arouse your passion or make you feel that you want to spend the rest of your life with him or her.

It is possible for friendships to have elements of passionate arousal or long-term commitment, but such friendships go beyond mere liking. You can use the absence test to distinguish mere liking from love that goes beyond liking. If a typical friend whom you like goes away, even for an extended period of time, you may miss him or her but do not tend to dwell on the loss. You can pick up the friendship some years later, often in a different form, without even having thought much about the friendship during the intervening years. When a close relationship goes beyond liking, however, you actively miss the other person and tend to dwell on or be preoccupied with his or her absence. The absence has a substantial and fairly long-term effect on your life. When the absence of the other arouses strong feelings of intimacy, passion, or commitment, the relationship has gone beyond liking.

Passion Alone: Infatuated Love

Tom met Lisa at work. One look at her was enough to change his life: he fell madly in love with her. Instead of concentrating on his work, which he hated, he would think about Lisa. She was aware of this, but did not much care for Tom. When he tried to start a conversation with her, she moved on as quickly as possible. . . .

Tom's "love at first sight" is infatuated love or, simply, infatuation. It results from the experiencing of passionate arousal without the intimacy and decision/commitment components of love. Infatuation is usually obvious, although it tends to be somewhat easier for others to spot than for the person who is experiencing it. An infatuation can arise almost instantaneously and dissipate as quickly. Infatuations generally manifest a high degree of psychophysiological arousal and bodily symptoms such as increased heartbeat or even palpitations of the heart, increased hormonal secretions, and erection of genitals. . . .

Decision/Commitment Alone: Empty Love

John and Mary had been married for twenty years, for fifteen of which Mary had been thinking about getting a divorce, but could never get herself to go through with it. . . .

Mary's kind of love emanates from the decision that you love another and are committed to that love even without having the intimacy or the passion associated with some loves. It is the love sometimes found in stagnant relationships that have been going on for years but that have lost both their original mutual emotional involvement and physical attraction. Unless the commitment to the love is very strong, such love can be close to none at all. Although in our society we see empty love generally as the final or near-final stage of a long-term relationship, in other societies empty love may be the first stage of a long-term relationship. As I have said, in societies where marriages are arranged, the marital partners start with the commitment to love each other, or to try to do so, and not much more. Here, *empty* denotes a relationship that may come to be filled with passion and intimacy, and thus marks a beginning rather than an end.

Intimacy + Passion: Romantic Love

Susan and Ralph met in their junior year of college. Their relationship started off as a good friendship, but rapidly turned into a deeply involved romantic love affair. They spent as much time together as possible, and enjoyed practically every minute of it. But Susan and Ralph were not ready to commit themselves permanently to the relationship: both felt they were too young to make any long-term decisions, and that until they at least knew where they would go after college, it was impossible to tell even how much they could be together. . . .

Ralph and Susan's relationship combines the intimacy and passion components of love. In essence, it is liking with an added element: namely, the arousal brought about by physical attraction. Therefore, in this type of love, the man and woman are not only drawn physically to each other but are also bonded emotionally. This is the view of romantic love found in classic works of literature, such as *Romeo and Juliet*. . . .

Intimacy + Commitment: Companionate Love

In their twenty years of marrige, Sam and Sara had been through some rough times. They had seen many of their friends through divorces, Sam through several jobs, and Sara through an illness that at one point had seemed as though it might be fatal. Both had friends, but there was no doubt in either of their minds that they were each other's best friend. When the going got rough, each of them knew he or she could count on the other. Neither Sam nor Sara felt any great passion in their relationship, but they had never sought out others. . . .

Sam and Sara's kind of love evolves from a combination of the intimacy and decision/commitment components of love. It is essentially a long-term, committed friendship, the kind that frequently occurs in marriages in which physical attraction (a major source of passion) has waned. . . .

Passion + Commitment: Fatuous Love

When Tim and Diana met at a resort in the Bahamas, they were each on the rebound. Tim's fiancée had abruptly broken off their engagement. . . . Diana was recently divorced, the victim of the "other woman." Each felt desperate for love, and when they met each other, they immediately saw themselves as a match made in heaven. . . . The manager of the resort, always on the lookout for vacation romances as good publicity, offered to marry them at the resort and to throw a lavish reception at no charge, other than cooperation in promotional materials. After thinking it over, Tim and Diana agreed. . . .

Fatuous love, as in the case of Tim and Diana, results from the combination of passion and decision/commitment without intimacy, which takes time to develop. It is the kind of love we sometimes associate with Hollywood, or with a whirlwind courtship, in which a couple meet one day, get engaged two weeks later, and marry the next month. This love is fatuous in the sense that the couple commit themselves to one another on the basis of passion without the stabilizing element of intimate involvement. Since passion can develop almost instantaneously, and intimacy cannot, relationships based on fatuous love are not likely to last.

Intimacy + Passion + Commitment: Consummate Love

Harry and Edith seemed to all their friends to be the perfect couple. And what made them distinctive from many such "perfect couples" is that they pretty much fulfilled the notion. They felt close to each other, they continued to have great sex after fifteen years, and they could not imagine themselves happy over the long term with anyone else. . . .

Consummate, or complete, love like Edith and Harry's results from the combination of the three components in equal measure. It is a love toward which many of us strive, especially in romantic relationships. Attaining consummate love is analogous, in at least one respect, to meeting your goal in a weight-reduction program: reaching your ideal weight is often easier than maintaining it. Attaining consummate love is no guarantee that it will last; indeed, one may become aware of the loss only after it is far gone. Consummate love, like other things of value, must be guarded carefully. . . .

The Absence of the Components: Non-Love

Jack saw his colleague Myra at work almost every day. They interacted well in their professional relationship, but neither was particularly fond of the other.

Neither felt particularly comfortable talking to the other about personal matters; and after a few tries, they decided to limit their conversations to business.

Non-love, as in the relationship of Jack and Myra, refers simply to the absence of all three components of love. Non-love characterizes many personal relationships, which are simply casual interactions that do not partake of love or even liking.

PART FIVE

Personality and Adjustment

CHAPTER 11 Personality

11.1 SIGMUND FREUD

The Psychical Apparatus

In many ways, personality is the sum total of who you are and what you do. There are many different approaches to studying personality; some researchers stress overt behavior, while others focus on internal processes. Sigmund Freud's psychoanalytic theory of personality, which is discussed in this selection, represents an early attempt to describe the unseen structures of personality.

Freud (1856–1939), an Austrian neurologist, obtained his M.D. in 1881 from the University of Vienna. Through his medical practice, he began to study patients' mental disorders by employing his theory of psychoanalysis, which emphasizes past experiences and unconscious motivations as the determinants of personality. Freud thought of personality as an iceberg, with only the tip showing above the water (i.e., revealed in outward behavior). Personality, he believed, is the result of the interaction of the three personality structures that he dubbed the id, ego, and superego.

This selection is from chapter 1, "The Psychical Apparatus," of Freud's *An Outline of Psycho-Analysis*, which was originally published in 1940 and which was intended to be a very concise summary of a very complicated theory. In this selection, Freud describes the characteristics of personality and briefly defines the id, ego, and superego. Notice that Freud begins by stating that we do not really know what the apparatus of personality is, but by observing people we can make a prediction. As you read this selection, think about how Freud's theory of personality could be tested.

Key Concept: psychoanalytic theory of personality

*P*sycho-analysis makes a basic assumption, the discussion of which is reserved to philosophical thought but the justification for which lies in its results. We know two kinds of things about what we call our psyche (or mental life): firstly, its bodily organ and scene of action, the brain (or nervous system) and, on the other hand, our acts of consciousness, which are immediate data and cannot be further explained by any sort of description. Everything that lies between is unknown to us, and the data do not include any direct relation between these two terminal points of our knowledge. If it existed, it would at the most afford an exact localization of the processes of consciousness and would give us no help towards understanding them.

Our two hypotheses start out from these ends or beginnings of our knowledge. The first is concerned with localization. We assume that mental life is the function of an apparatus to which we ascribe the characteristics of being extended in space and of being made up of several portions—which we imagine, that is, as resembling a telescope or microscope or something of the kind. Notwithstanding some earlier attempts in the same direction, the consistent working-out of a conception such as this is a scientific novelty.

We have arrived at our knowledge of this psychical apparatus by studying the individual development of human beings. To the oldest of these psychical provinces or agencies we give the name of *id*. It contains everything that is inherited, that is present at birth, that is laid down in the constitution—above all, therefore, the instincts, which originate from the somatic organization and which find a first psychical expression here [in the id] in forms unknown to us.

Under the influence of the real external world around us, one portion of the id has undergone a special development. From what was originally a cortical layer, equipped with the organs for receiving stimuli and with arrangements for acting as a protective shield against stimuli, a special organization has arisen which henceforward acts as an intermediary between the id and the external world. To this region of our mind we have given the name of *ego*.

Here are the principal characteristics of the ego. In consequence of the pre-established connection between sense perception and muscular action, the ego has voluntary movement at its command. It has the task of self-preservation. As regards *external* events, it performs that task by becoming aware of stimuli, by storing up experiences about them (in the memory), by avoiding excessively strong stimuli (through flight), by dealing with moderate stimuli (through adaptation) and finally by learning to bring about expedient changes in the external world to its own advantage (through activity). As regards *internal* events, in relation to the id, it performs that task by gaining control over the demands of the instincts, by deciding whether they are to be allowed satisfaction, by postponing that satisfaction to times and circumstances favourable in the external world or by suppressing their excitations entirely. It is guided in its activity by consideration of the tensions produced by stimuli, whether these tensions are present in it or introduced into it. The raising of these tensions is in general felt as *unpleasure* and their lowering as *pleasure*. It is probable, however, that what is felt as pleasure or unpleasure is not the *absolute* height of this tension but something in the rhythm of the changes in them. The ego strives after pleasure and seeks to avoid unpleasure. An increase in unpleasure that is expected and foreseen is met by a *signal of anxiety*; the occasion of such an increase, whether it threatens from without or within, is known as a *danger*. From time to time the ego gives up its connection with the external world and withdraws into the state of sleep, in which it makes far-reaching changes in its organization. It is to be inferred from the state of sleep that this organization consists in a particular distribution of mental energy.

The long period of childhood, during which the growing human being lives in dependence on his parents, leaves behind it as a precipitate the formation in his ego of a special agency in which this parental influence is prolonged. It has received the name of *super-ego*. In so far as this super-ego is differentiated from the ego or is opposed to it, it constitutes a third power which the ego must take into account.

An action by the ego is as it should be if it satisfies simultaneously the demands of the id, of the super-ego and of reality—that is to say, if it is able to reconcile their demands with one another. The details of the relation between the ego and the superego become completely intelligible when they are traced back to the child's attitude to its parents. This parental influence of course includes in its operation not only the personalities of the actual parents but also the family, racial and national traditions handed on through them, as well as the demands of the immediate social *milieu* which they represent. In the same way, the super-ego, in the course of an individual's development, receives contributions from later successors and substitutes of his parents, such as teachers and models in public life of admired social ideals. It will be observed that, for all their fundamental difference, the id and the super-ego have one thing in common: they both represent the influences of the past—the id the influence of heredity, the super-ego the influence, essentially, of what is taken over from other people—whereas the ego is principally determined by the individual's own experience, that is by accidental and contemporary events.

This general schematic picture of a psychical apparatus may be supposed to apply as well to the higher animals which resemble man mentally. A super-ego must be presumed to be present wherever, as is the case with man, there is a long period of dependence in childhood. A distinction between ego and id is an unavoidable assumption. Animal psychology has not yet taken in hand the interesting problem which is here presented.

External Control and Internal Control

Psychologists do not all agree on what determines personality, but many accept that reinforcement can shape behaviors that ultimately may influence personality. The social learning theory of personality suggests that behavior that is rewarded leads to the expectancy that the behavior will continue to produce rewards in the future. According to Julian B. Rotter's locus of control personality theory, which is based in the social learning theory, two personality types exist: People with an internal locus of control, who perceive that reinforcement is due to their own behavior; and people with an external locus of control, who perceive that reinforcement is independent of their behavior.

Rotter (b. 1916) earned his Ph.D. from Indiana University in 1941. He taught at several schools, including Ohio State University, before going to the University of Connecticut in 1963, where he is currently a professor of clinical psychology. Rotter's social learning theory (proposed in his 1954 book *Social Learning and Clinical Psychology*) has greatly influenced modern psychologists.

This selection, "External Control and Internal Control," was published in *Psychology Today* in 1971. It contains a straightforward description of Rotter's theory of personality as well as some fascinating applications. Note the development of Rotter's thinking as he describes how the idea of locus of control came to him. As you read the article, think about the implications for people who have an internal or external locus of control. Which one, if either, do you think you have?

Key Concept: internal and external locus of control

Some social scientists believe that the impetus behind campus unrest is youth's impatient conviction that they can control their own destinies, that they can change society for the better.

My research over the past 12 years has led me to suspect that much of the protest, outcry and agitation occurs for the opposite reason—because students feel they *cannot* change the world, that the system is too complicated and too much controlled by powerful others to be changed through the students' efforts. They feel more powerless and alienated today than they did 10 years ago, and rioting may be an expression of their hostility and resentment.

Dog. One of the most pervasive laws of animal learning is that a behavior followed by a reward tends to be repeated, and a behavior followed by a punishment tends not to be repeated. This seems to imply that reward and punishment act directly on behavior, but I think this formulation is too simplistic to account for many types of human behavior.

For example, if a dog lifts its leg at the exact moment that someone throws a bone over a fence, the dog may begin to lift its leg more often than usual when it is in the same situation—whether or not anyone is heaving a bone. Adult human beings are usually not so superstitious—a person who finds a dollar bill on the sidewalk immediately after stroking his hair is not likely to stroke his hair when he returns to the same spot.

It seemed to me that, at least with human beings who have begun to form concepts, the important factors in learning were not only the strength and frequency of rewards and punishments but also whether or not the person believed his behavior produced the reward or punishment.

According to the social-learning theory that I developed several years ago with my colleagues and students, rewarding a behavior strengthens an *expectancy* that the behavior will produce future rewards.

In animals, the expectation of reward is primarily a function of the strength and frequency of rewards. In human beings, there are other things that can influence the expectation of reward—the information others give us, our knowledge generalized from a variety of experiences, and our perceptions of causality in the situation.

Consider the ancient shell game. Suppose I place a pea under one of three shells and quickly shuffle the shells around the table. A player watches my movements carefully and then, thinking that he is using his fine perceptual skills, he tells me which shell the pea is under. If his choice is correct, he will likely choose the same shell again the next time he sees me make those particular hand movements. It looks like a simple case of rewarding a response.

But suppose I ask the subject to turn his back while I shuffle the shells. This time, even if his choice is rewarded by being correct, he is not so likely to select the same shell again, because the outcome seems to be beyond his control—just a lucky guess.

Chips. In 1957, E. Jerry Phares tried to find out if these intuitive differences between chance-learning and skill-learning would hold up in the laboratory. Phares would give each subject a small gray-colored chip and ask him to select one of 10 standard chips that had exactly the same shade of gray. The standards were all different but so similar in value that discrimination among them was very difficult. Phares told half of his subjects that matching the shades required great skill and that some persons were very good at it. He told the rest that the task was so difficult that success was a matter of luck. Before

(continued on p. 255)

Internal Control—External Control
A Sampler

Julian B. Rotter is the developer of a forced-choice 29-item scale for measuring an individual's degree of internal control and external control. This I-E test is widely used. The following are sample items taken from an earlier version of the test, but not, of course, in use in the final version. The reader can readily find for himself whether he is inclined toward internal control or toward external control, simply by adding up the choices he makes on each side

I more strongly believe that:	OR
Promotions are earned through hard work and persistence.	Making a lot of money is largely a matter of getting the right breaks.
In my experience I have noticed that there is usually a direct connection between how hard I study and the grades I get.	Many times the reactions of teachers seem haphazard to me.
The number of divorces indicates that more and more people are not trying to make their marriages work.	Marriage is largely a gamble.
When I am right I can convince others.	It is silly to think that one can really change another person's basic attitudes.
In our society a man's future earning power is dependent upon his ability.	Getting promoted is really a matter of being a little luckier than the next guy.
If one knows how to deal with people they are really quite easily led.	I have little influence over the way other people behave.
In my case the grades I make are the results of my own efforts; luck has little or nothing to do with it.	Sometimes I feel that I have little to do with the grades I get.
People like me can change the course of world affairs if we make ourselves heard.	It is only wishful thinking to believe that one can really influence what happens in society at large.
I am the master of my fate.	A great deal that happens to me is probably a matter of chance.
Getting along with people is a skill that must be practiced.	It is almost impossible to figure out how to please some people.

the experiment began, Phares arbitrarily decided which trials would be "right" and which would be "wrong"; the schedule was the same for everyone. He found that because of the difficulty of the task all subjects accepted his statements of right and wrong without question.

Phares gave each subject a stack of poker chips and asked him to bet on his accuracy before each trial as a measure of each subject's expectancy of success.

The subjects who thought that success depended on their own skills shifted and changed frequently—their bets would rise after success and drop after failure, just as reinforcement-learning theory would predict. But subjects who thought that a correct match was a matter of luck reacted differently. In fact, many of them raised their bets after failure and lowered them after success—the "gambler's fallacy." Thus, it appeared that traditional laws of learning could not explain some types of human behavior. . . .

I decided to study internal and external control (I-E), the beliefs that rewards come from one's own behavior or from external sources. The initial impetus to study internal-external control came both from an interest in individual differences and from an interest in explaining the way human beings learn complex social situations. There seemed to be a number of attitudes that would lead a person to feel that a reward was not contingent upon his own behavior, and we tried to build all of these attitudes into a measure of individual differences. A person might feel that luck or chance controlled what happened to him. He might feel that fate had preordained what would happen to him. He might feel that powerful others controlled what happened to him or he might feel that he simply could not predict the effects of this behavior because the world was too complex and confusing.

Scale. Phares first developed a test of internal-external control as part of his doctoral dissertation, and [William H.] James enlarged and improved on Phares' scale as part of his doctoral dissertation. Later scales were constructed with the important help of several of my colleagues including Liverant, Melvin Seeman and Crowne. In 1962 I developed a final 29-item version of the I-E scale and published it in *Psychological Monographs* in 1966. This is a forced-choice scale in which the subject reads a pair of statements and then indicates with which of the two statements he more strongly agrees. The scores range from zero (the consistent belief that individuals can influence the environment—that rewards come from *internal* forces) to 23 (the belief that all rewards come from *external* forces). . . .

Degree. One conclusion is clear from I-E studies: people differ in the tendency to attribute satisfactions and failures to themselves rather than to external causes, and these differences are relatively stable. For the sake of convenience most investigators divide their subjects into two groups—internals and externals—depending on which half of the distribution a subject's score falls into. This is not meant to imply that there are two personality types and that everyone can be classified as one or the other, but that there is a continuum, and that persons have varying degrees of internality or externality.

Many studies have investigated the differences between internals and externals. For example, it has been found that lower-class children tend to be external; children from richer, better-educated families tend to have more belief in their own potential to determine what happens to them. The scores do not seem to be related to intelligence, but young children tend to become more internal as they get older.

Esther Battle and I examined the attitudes of black and white children in an industrialized Ohio city. The scale we used consisted of five comic-strip cartoons; the subjects told us what they thought one of the children in the cartoon would say. We found that middle-class blacks were only slightly more external in their beliefs than middle-class whites but that among children from lower socioeconomic levels blacks were significantly more external than whites. Herbert Lefcourt and Gordon Ladwig also found that among young prisoners in a Federal reformatory, blacks were more external than whites.

Ute. It does not seem to be socioeconomic level alone that produces externality, however. Theodore Graves, working with Richard and Shirley L. Jessor, found that Ute Indians were more external than a group of Spanish-Americans, even though the Indians had higher average living standards than the Spanish-Americans. Since Ute tradition puts great emphasis on fate and unpredictable external forces, Graves concluded that internality and externality resulted from cultural training. A group of white subjects in the same community were more internal than either the Indians or the Spanish-Americans.

A measure of internal-external control was used in the well-known Coleman Report on Equality of Educational Opportunity. The experimenters found that among disadvantaged children in the sixth, ninth and 12th grades, the students with high scores on an achievement test had more internal attitudes than did children with low achievement scores.

One might expect that internals would make active attempts to learn about their life situations. To check on this, Seeman and John Evans gave the I-E scale to patients in a tuberculosis hospital. The internal patients knew more details about their medical conditions and they questioned doctors and nurses for medical feedback more often than did the external patients. The experimenters made sure that in their study there were no differences between the internals and externals in education, occupational status or ward placement. . . .

Bet. Highly external persons feel that they are at the mercy of the environment, that they are being manipulated by outside forces. When they *are* manipulated, externals seem to take it in stride. Internals are not so docile. For example, Crowne and Liverant set up an experiment to see how readily their subjects would go along with a crowd. In a simple . . . conformity experiment in which there is one true subject plus several stooges posing as subjects, Crowne and Liverant found that neither internals nor externals were more likely to yield to an incorrect majority judgment. But when the experimenters gave money to the subjects and allowed them to bet on their own judgments, the externals yielded to the majority much more often than did the internals. When externals did vote against the majority they weren't confident about their independence—they bet less money on being right than they did when they voted along with the crowd. . . .

Suspicion. Some externals, who feel they are being manipulated by the outside world, may be highly suspicious of authorities. With Herbert Hamsher and Jesse Geller, I found that male subjects who believed that the Warren

Commission Report was deliberately covering up a conspiracy were significantly more external than male subjects who accepted the report.

To some degree externality may be a defense against expected failure but internals also have their defenses. In investigating failure defenses, Jay Efran studied high-school students' memories for tasks they had completed or failed. He found that the tendency to forget failures was more common in internal subjects than in external ones. This suggests that external subjects have less need to repress past failures because they have already resigned themselves to the defensive position that failures are not their responsibility. Internals, however, are more likely to forget or repress their failures.

Today's activist student groups might lead one to assume that our universities are filled with internals—people with strong belief in their ability to improve conditions and to control their own destinies. But scores on the same I-E test involving large numbers of college students in many localities show that between 1962 and 1971 there was a large increase in externality on college campuses. Today the average score on the I-E scale is about 11. In 1962 about 80 per cent of college students had more internal scores than this. The increase in externality has been somewhat less in Midwest colleges than in universities on the coasts, but there is little doubt that, overall, college students feel more powerless to change the world and control their own destinies now than they did 10 years ago.

Clearly, we need continuing study of methods to reverse this trend. Our society has so many critical problems that it desperately needs as many active, participating internal-minded members as possible. If feelings of external control, alienation and powerlessness continue to grow, we may be heading for a society of dropouts—each person sitting back, watching the world go by.

Validation of the Five-Factor Model of Personality Across Instruments and Observers

Over the years, there have been numerous attempts to classify personality traits. Little agreement was reached among psychologists until the five-factor model became popular. The five-factor model of personality was originally proposed in the early 1960s, but it did not become popular among psychologists until the 1980s. The five factors of this model are extraversion (sociability), agreeableness (friendliness), conscientiousness (dependability), emotional stability (versus neuroticism), and openness (liberalism). Psychologists do not all agree on the specific labels, but there is some consensus on the five areas of personality. Robert R. McCrae and Paul T. Costa, Jr., are among the leaders in the quest to understand these factors and how they can explain personality.

McCrae earned his Ph.D. from Boston University in 1976. He has since been an associate of the Gerontology Research Center of the National Institute of Aging, National Institutes of Health. Costa (b. 1942) received his Ph.D. from the University of Chicago in 1970. He is also with the National Institute on Aging, National Institutes of Health.

This selection, "Validation of the Five-Factor Model of Personality Across Instruments and Observers," was published in the American Psychological Association's *Journal of Personality and Social Psychology* in 1987. In it, McCrae and Costa describe the history and interpretation of each of the five factors in this model. In one part of the original article, which is not included here, the authors report an experiment in which they used self-reports, peer ratings, and questionnaire scales to measure the five factors. The results of this study validated the five-factor model. As you read this selection, note which characteristics best describe your personality. Can you think of any other major factors of personality that might be included in this model?

Key Concept: five-factor model of personality

Perhaps in response to critiques of trait models (Mischel, 1968) and to rebuttals that have called attention to common inadequacies in personality research (Block, 1977), personologists in recent years have devoted much of their attention to methodological issues.... As a body, these studies have simultaneously increased the level of methodological sophistication in personality research and restored confidence in the intelligent use of individual difference models of personality.

Robert R. McCrae and Paul T. Costa, Jr.

In contrast, there has been relatively little interest in the substance of personality—the systematic description of traits. The variables chosen as vehicles for tests of methodological hypotheses often appear arbitrary.... Indeed, Kenrick and Dantchik (1983) complained that "catalogs of convenience" have replaced meaningful taxonomies of personality traits among "most of the current generation of social/personality researchers" (p. 299).

This disregard of substance is unfortunate because substance and method are ultimately interdependent. Unless methodological studies are conducted on well-defined and meaningful traits their conclusions are dubious; unless the traits are selected from a comprehensive taxonomy, it is impossible to know how far or in what ways they can be generalized.

Fortunately, a few researchers have been concerned with the problem of structure and have recognized the need for a consensus on at least the general outlines of a trait taxonomy (H. J. Eysenck & Eysenck, 1984; Kline & Barrett, 1983; Wiggins, 1979). One particularly promising candidate has emerged. The five-factor model—comprising extraversion or surgency, agreeableness, conscientiousness, emotional stability versus neuroticism, and culture—of Tupes and Christal (1961) was replicated by Norman in 1963 and heralded by him as the basis for "an adequate taxonomy of personality." Although it was largely neglected for several years, variations on this model have recently begun to re-emerge (Amelang & Borkenau, 1982; Bond, Nakazato, & Shiraishi, 1975; Conley, 1985; Digman & Takemoto-Chock, 1981; Goldberg, 1981, 1982; Hogan, 1983; Lorr & Manning, 1978; McCrae & Costa, 1985b)....

THE NATURE OF THE FIVE FACTORS

... A growing body of research has pointed to the five-factor model as a recurrent and more or less comprehensive taxonomy of personality traits. Theorists disagree, however, in precisely how to conceptualize the factors themselves. It seems useful at this point to review each of the factors and attempt to define the clear elements as well as disputed aspects....

Neuroticism versus emotional stability. There is perhaps least disagreement about neuroticism, defined here by such terms as worrying, insecure, self-conscious, and temperamental. Although adjectives describing neuroticism are relatively infrequent in English (Peabody, 1984), psychologists' concerns with psychopathology have led to the development of innumerable scales saturated

(continued on p. 261)

TABLE 1

80 Adjective Items From Peer Ratings

Adjectives	*Adjectives*
Neuroticism (N)	Agreeableness vs. antagonism (A)
Calm–worrying	Irritable–good natured
At ease–nervous	Ruthless–soft hearted
Relaxed–high-strung	Rude–courteous
Unemotional–emotional	Selfish–selfless
Even-tempered–temperamental	Uncooperative–helpful
Secure–insecure	Callous–sympathetic
Self-satisfied–self-pitying	Suspicious–trusting
Patient–impatient	Stingy–generous
Not envious–envious/jealous	Antagonistic–acquiescent
Comfortable–self-conscious	Critical–lenient
Not impulse ridden–impulse ridden	Vengeful–forgiving
Hardy–vulnerable	Narrow-minded–open-minded
Objective–subjective	Disagreeable–agreeable
	Stubborn–flexible
Extraversion (E)	Serious–cheerful
Retiring–sociable	Cynical–gullible
Sober–fun loving	Manipulative–straightforward
Reserved–affectionate	Proud–humble
Aloof–friendly	
Inhibited–spontaneous	Conscientiousness vs. undirectedness (C)
Quiet–talkative	Negligent–conscientious
Passive–active	Careless–careful
Loner–joiner	Undependable–reliable
Unfeeling–passionate	Lazy–hardworking
Cold–warm	Disorganized–well organized
Lonely–not lonely	Lax–scrupulous
Task oriented–person oriented	Weak willed–self-disciplined
Submissive–dominant	Sloppy–neat
Timid–bold	Late–punctual
	Impractical–practical
Openness (O)	Thoughtless–deliberate
Conventional–original	Aimless–ambitious
Down to earth–imaginative	Unstable–emotionally stable
Uncreative–creative	Helpless–self-reliant
Narrow interests–broad interests	Playful–businesslike
Simple–complex	Unenergetic–energetic
Uncurious–curious	Ignorant–knowledgeable
Unadventurous–daring	Quitting–persevering
Prefer routine–prefer variety	Stupid–intelligent
Conforming–independent	Unfair–fair
Unanalytical–analytical	Imperceptive–perceptive
Conservative–liberal	Uncultured–cultured
Traditional–untraditional	
Unartistic–artistic	

with neuroticism. Indeed, neuroticism is so ubiquitous an element of personality scales that theorists sometimes take it for granted.

Robert R.
McCrae and
Paul T. Costa, Jr.

A provocative view of neuroticism is provided by Tellegen (in press), who views it as negative emotionality, the propensity to experience a variety of negative affects, such as anxiety, depression, anger, and embarrassment. Virtually all theorists would concur in the centrality of negative affect to neuroticism; the question is whether other features also define it. Tellegen himself (in press) pointed out that his construct of negative emotionality has behavioral and cognitive aspects. Guilford included personal relations and objectivity in his emotional health factor (Guilford, Zimmerman, & Guilford, 1976), suggesting that mistrust and self-reference form part of neuroticism. We have found that impulsive behaviors, such as tendencies to overeat, smoke, or drink excessively, form a facet of neuroticism (Costa & McCrae, 1980), and *impulse-ridden* is a definer of the neuroticism factor in self-reports, although not in ratings. Others have linked neuroticism to irrational beliefs (Teasdale & Rachman, 1983; Vestre, 1984) or to poor coping efforts (McCrae & Costa, 1986).

What these behaviors seem to share is a common origin in negative affect. Individuals high in neuroticism have more difficulty than others in quitting smoking because the distress caused by abstinence is stronger for them. They may more frequently use inappropriate coping responses like hostile reactions and wishful thinking because they must deal more often with disruptive emotions. They may adopt irrational beliefs like self-blame because these beliefs are cognitively consistent with the negative feelings they experience. Neuroticism appears to include not only negative affect, but also the disturbed thoughts and behaviors that accompany emotional distress.

Extraversion or surgency. Sociable, fun-loving, affectionate, friendly, and talkative are the highest loading variables on the extraversion factor. This is not Jungian extraversion (see Guilford, 1977), but it does correspond to the conception of H. J. Eysenck and most other contemporary researchers, who concur with popular speech in identifying extraversion with lively sociability.

However, disputes remain about which elements are central and which are peripheral to extraversion. Most writers would agree that sociability, cheerfulness, activity level, assertiveness, and sensation seeking all covary, however loosely. But the Eysencks have at times felt the need to distinguish between sociability and what they call impulsiveness (S. B. G. Eysenck & Eysenck, 1963; Revelle, Humphreys, Simon, & Gilliland, 1980). Hogan (1983) believed that the five-factor model was improved by dividing extraversion into sociability and assertiveness factors. In Goldberg's analyses, surgency (dominance and activity) were the primary definers of extraversion, and terms like warm–cold were assigned to the agreeableness–antagonism factor. Tellegen (in press) emphasized the complementary nature of neuroticism and extraversion by labeling his extraversion factor positive emotionality.

These distinctions do seem to merge at a high enough level of analysis (H. J. Eysenck & Eysenck, 1976; McCrae & Costa, 1983a), and sociability—the enjoyment of others' company—seems to be the core. What is essential to recall, however, is that liking people does not necessarily make one likable. Salesmen, those prototypic extraverts, are generally happier to see you than you are to see them.

Openness to experience. The reinterpretation of Norman's culture as openness to experience was the focus of some of our previous articles (McCrae & Costa, 1985a, 1985b), and the replication of results in peer ratings was one of the purposes of the present article. According to adjective-factor results, openness is best characterized by original, imaginative, broad interests, and daring. In the case of this dimension, however, questionnaires may be better than adjectives as a basis for interpretation and assessment. Many aspects of openness (e.g., openness to feelings) are not easily expressed in single adjectives, and the relative poverty of the English-language vocabulary of openness and closedness may have contributed to confusions about this domain (McCrae & Costa, 1985a). We know from questionnaire studies that openness can be manifest in fantasy, aesthetics, feelings, actions, ideas, and values (Costa & McCrae, 1978, 1980), but only ideas and values are well represented in the adjective factor. Interestingly, questionnaire measures of openness give higher validity coefficients than do adjective-factor measures. . . .

Perhaps the most important distinction to be made here is between openness and intelligence. Open individuals tend to be seen by themselves and others as somewhat more intelligent. . . . However, joint factor analyses using Army Alpha intelligence subtests and either adjectives (McCrae & Costa, 1985b) or NEO Inventory scales (McCrae & Costa, 1985a) show that intelligence scales define a factor clearly separate from openness. Intelligence may in some degree predispose the individual to openness, or openness may help develop intelligence, but the two seem best construed as separate dimensions of individual differences.

Agreeableness versus antagonism. As a broad dimension, agreeableness–antagonism is less familiar than extraversion or neuroticism, but some of its component traits, like trust (Stark, 1978) and Machiavellianism (Christie & Geis, 1970), have been widely researched. The essential nature of agreeableness–antagonism is perhaps best seen by examining the disagreeable pole, which we have labeled antagonism. . . . [A]ntagonistic people seem always to set themselves against others. Cognitively they are mistrustful and skeptical; affectively they are callous and unsympathetic; behaviorally they are uncooperative, stubborn, and rude. It would appear that their sense of attachment or bonding with their fellow human beings is defective, and in extreme cases antagonism may resemble sociopathy (cf. H. J. Eysenck & Eysenck's, 1975, psychoticism).

An insightful description of antagonism in its neurotic form is provided by Horney's account of the tendency to move against people (1945, 1950). She theorized that a struggle for mastery is the root cause of this tendency and that variations may occur, including narcissistic, perfectionistic, and arrogant vindictive types. Whereas some antagonistic persons are overtly aggressive, other may be polished manipulators. The drive for mastery and the overt or inhibited hostility of antagonistic individuals suggests a resemblance to some formulations of Type A personality (Dembroski & MacDougall, 1983), and systematic studies of the relations between agreeableness–antagonism and measures of coronary-prone behavior should be undertaken.

Unappealing as antagonism may be, it is necessary to recognize that extreme scores on the agreeable pole may also be maladaptive. The person high in agreeableness may be dependent and fawning, and agreeableness has its neurotic manifestation in Horney's self-effacing solution of moving toward people.

Robert R. McCrae and Paul T. Costa, Jr.

Antagonism is most easily confused with dominance. Amelang and Borkenau (1982), working in German and apparently unaware of the Norman taxonomy, found a factor they called *dominance*. Among its key definers, however, were Hartnäckigkeit (*stubbornness*) and Erregbarkeit (*irritability*); scales that measure agreeableness and cooperation defined the opposite pole in their questionnaire factor. Clearly, this factor corresponds to antagonism. In self-reports (McCrae & Costa, 1985b), submissive–dominant is a weak definer of extraversion; from the peers' point of view, it is a definer of antagonism. The close etymological relationship of *dominant* and *domineering* shows the basis of the confusion.

Agreeableness–antagonism and conscientiousness–undirectedness are sometimes omitted from personality systems because they may seem too value laden. Indeed, the judgment of character is made largely along these two dimensions: Is the individual well or ill intentioned? Is he or she strong or weak in carrying out those intentions? Agreeableness–antagonism, in particular, has often been assumed to be an evaluative factor of others' perceptions rather than a veridical component of personality (e.g., A. Tellegen, personal communication, March 28, 1984).

However, the fact that a trait may be judged from a moral point of view does not mean that it is not a substantive aspect of personality. The consensual validation seen among peers and between peer-reports and self-reports demonstrates that there are some observable consistencies of behavior that underlie attributions of agreeableness and conscientiousness. They may be evaluated traits, but they are not mere evaluations.

Conscientiousness versus undirectedness. Conscientious may mean either governed by conscience or careful and thorough (Morris, 1976), and psychologists seem to be divided about which of these meanings best characterizes the last major dimension of personality. Amelang and Borkenau (1982) labeled their factor self-control versus impulsivity, and Conley (1985) spoke of impulse control. This terminology connotes an inhibiting agent, as Cattell (Cattell, Eber, & Tatsuoka, 1970) recognized when he named his Factor G *superego strength*. A conscientious person in this sense should be dutiful, scrupulous, and perhaps moralistic.

A different picture, however, is obtained by examining the adjectives that define this factor. In addition to conscientious and scrupulous, there are a number of adjectives that suggest a more proactive stance: hardworking, ambitious, energetic, persevering. Digman and Takemoto-Chock (1981) labeled this factor *will to achieve,* and it is notable that one of the items in the questionnaire measure of conscientiousness, "He strives for excellence in all he does," comes close to the classic definition of need for achievement (McClelland, Atkinson, Clark, & Lowell, 1953).

At one time, the purposefulness and adherence to plans, schedules, and requirements suggested the word *direction* as a label for this factor, and we have retained that implication in calling the opposite pole of conscientiousness *undirectedness*. In our view, the individual low in conscientiousness is not so much uncontrolled as undirected, not so much impulse ridden as simply lazy.

It seems probable that these two meanings may be related. Certainly individuals who are well organized, habitually careful, and capable of self-discipline are more likely to be able to adhere scrupulously to a moral code if they choose to—although there is no guarantee that they will be so inclined. An undirected individual may have a demanding conscience and a pervasive sense of guilt but be unable to live up to his or her own standards for lack of self-discipline and energy. In any case, it is clear that this is a dimension worthy of a good deal more empirical attention than it has yet received. Important real-life outcomes such as alcoholism (Conley & Angelides, 1984) and academic achievement (Digman & Takemoto-Chock, 1981) are among its correlates, and a further specification of the dimension is sure to be fruitful.

Some personality theorists might object that trait ratings, in whatever form and from whatever source, need not provide the best foundation for understanding individual differences. Experimental analysis of the psychophysiological basis of personality (H. J. Eysenck & Eysenck, 1984), examination of protypic acts and act frequencies (Buss & Craik, 1983), psychodynamic formulations (Horney, 1945), or behavioral genetics (Plomin, DeFries, & McClearn, 1980) provide important alternatives. But psychophysiological, behavioral, psychodynamic, and genetic explanations must eventually be related to the traits that are universally used to describe personality, and the five-factor model can provide a framework within which these relations can be systematically examined. The minor conceptual divergences noted in this article suggest the need for additional empirical work to fine-tune the model, but the broad outlines are clear in self-reports, spouse ratings, and peer ratings; in questionnaires and adjective factors; and in English and in German (Amelang & Borkenau, 1982; John, Goldberg, & Angleitner, 1984). Deeper causal analyses may seek to account for the structure of personality, but the structure that must be explained is, for now, best represented by the five-factor model.

REFERENCES

Amelang, M., & Borkenau, P. (1982). Über die faktorielle Struktur und externe Validität einiger Fragebogen-Skalen zur Erfasusng von Dimensionen der Extraversion und emotionalen Labilität [On the factor structure and external validity of some questionnaire scales measuring dimensions of extraversion and neuroticism]. *Zeitschrift für Differentielle und Diagnostische Psychologie, 3*, 119–146.

Block J. (1977). Advancing the psychology of personality: Paradigmatic shift or improving the quality of research? In D. Magnusson & N. S. Endler (Eds.), *Personality at the cross-roads: Current issues in interactional psychology* (pp. 37–63), Hillsdale, NJ: Erlbaum.

Bond, M. H., Nakazato, H., & Shiraishi, D. (1975). Universality and distinctiveness in dimensions of Japanese person perception. *Journal of Cross-Cultural Psychology, 6*, 346–357.

Buss, D. M., & Craik, K. H. (1983). The act frequency approach to personality. *Psychological Review, 90*, 105–126.

Cattell, R. B., Eber, H. W., & Tatsuoka, M. M. (1970). *The handbook for the Sixteen Personality Factor Questionnaire.* Champaign, IL: Institute for Personality and Ability Testing.

Christie, R., & Geis, R. L. (Eds.). (1970). *Studies in Machiavellianism.* New York: Academic Press.

Conley, J. J. (1985). Longitudinal stability of personality traits: A multitrait–multimethod–multioccasion analysis. *Journal of Personality and Social Psychology, 49,* 1266–1282.

Conley, J. J., & Angelides, M. (1984). *Personality antecedents of emotional disorders and alcohol abuse in men: Results of a forty-five year prospective study.* Manuscript submitted for publication.

Costa, P. T., Jr., & McCrae, R. R. (1978). Objective personality assessment. In M. Storandt, I. C. Siegler, & M. F. Elias (Eds.), *The clinical psychology of aging* (pp. 119–143). New York: Plenum Press.

Costa, P. T., Jr., & McCrae, R. R. (1980). Still stable after all these years: Personality as a key to some issues in adulthood and old age. In P. B. Baltes & O. G. Brim, Jr. (Eds.), *Life span development and behavior* (Vol. 3, pp. 65–102). New York: Academic Press.

Dembroski, T. M., & MacDougall, J. M. (1983). Behavioral and psychophysiological perspectives on coronary-prone behavior. In T. M. Dembroski, T. H. Schmidt, & G. Blumchen (Eds.), *Biobehavioral bases of coronary heart disease* (pp. 106–129). New York: Karger.

Digman, J. M., & Takemoto-Chock, N. K. (1981). Factors in the natural language of personality: Re-analysis, comparison, and interpretation of six major studies. *Multivariate Behavioral Research, 16,* 149–170.

Eysenck, H. J., & Eysenck, M. (1984). *Personality and individual differences.* London: Plenum Press.

Eysenck, H. J., & Eysenck, S. B. G. (1967). On the unitary nature of extraversion. *Acta Psychologica, 26,* 383–390.

Eysenck, H. J., & Eysenck, S. B. G. (1975). *Manual of the Eysenck Personality Questionnaire.* San Diego, CA: EdITS.

Eysenck, S. B. G., & Eysenck, H. J. (1963). On the dual nature of extraversion. *British Journal of Social and Clinical Psychology, 2,* 46–55.

Goldberg, L. R. (1981). Language and individual differences: The search for universals in personality lexicons. In L. Wheeler (Ed.), *Review of personality and social psychology* (Vol. 2, pp. 141–165). Beverly Hills, CA: Sage.

Goldberg, L. R. (1982). From ace to zombie: Some explorations in the language of personality. In C. D. Spielberger & J. N. Butcher (Eds.), *Advances in personality assessment* (Vol. 1, pp. 203–234). Hillsdale, NJ: Erlbaum.

Guilford, J. P. (1977). Will the real factor of extraversion–introversion please stand up? A reply to Eysenck. *Psychological Bulletin, 84,* 412–416.

Guilford, J. S. Zimmerman, W. S., & Guilford, J. P. (1976). *The Guilford–Zimmerman Temperament Survey handbook: Twenty-five years of research and application.* San Diego, CA: EdITS.

Hogan, R. (1983). Socioanalytic theory of personality. In M. M. Page (Ed.), *1982 Nebraska Symposium on Motivation: Personality—current theory and research* (pp. 55–89). Lincoln: University of Nebraska Press.

Horney, K. (1945). *Our inner conflicts.* New York: Norton.

Horney, K. (1950). *Neurosis and human growth.* New York: Norton.

John, O. P., Goldberg, L. R., & Angleitner, A. (1984). Better than the alphabet: Taxonomies of personality-descriptive terms in English, Dutch, and German. In H. J. C.

Bonarius, G. L. M. van Heck, & N. G. Smid (Eds.), *Personality psychology in Europe: Theoretical and empirical developments.* Lisse, Switzerland: Swets & Zeitlinger.

Kenrick, D. T., & Dantchik, A. (1983). Interactionism, idiographics, and the social psychological invasion of personality. *Journal of Personality, 51,* 286–307.

Kline, P., & Barrett, P. (1983). The factors in personality questionnaires among normal subjects. *Advances in Behaviour Research and Therapy, 5,* 141–202.

Lorr, M., & Manning, T. T. (1978). Higher-order personality factors of the ISI. *Multivariate Behavioral Research, 13,* 3–7.

McClelland, D. C., Atkinson, J. W., Clark, R. A., & Lowell, E. L. (1953). *The achievement motive.* New York: Appleton-Century-Crofts.

McCrae, R. R., & Costa, P. T., Jr. (1983a). Joint factors in self-reports and ratings: Neuroticism, extraversion, and openness to experience. *Personality and Individual Differences, 4,* 245–255.

McCrae, R. R., & Costa, P. T., Jr. (1985a). Openness to experience. In R. Hogan & W. H. Jones (Eds.), *Perspectives in personality: Theory, measurement, and interpersonal dynamics* (Vol. 1). Greenwich, CT: JAI Press.

McCrae, R. R., & Costa, P. T., Jr. (1985b). Updating Norman's "adequate taxonomy": Intelligence and personality dimensions in natural language and in questionnaires. *Journal of Personality and Social Psychology, 49,* 710–721.

McCrae, R. R., & Costa, P. T., Jr. (1986). Personality, coping, and coping effectiveness in an adult sample. *Journal of Personality, 54,* 385–405.

Mischel, W. (1968). *Personality and assessment.* New York: Wiley.

Morris, W. (Ed.). (1976). *The American Heritage dictionary of the English language.* Boston: Houghton Mifflin.

Peabody, D. (1984). Personality dimensions through trait inferences. *Journal of Personality and Social Psychology, 46,* 384–403.

Plomin, R., DeFries, J. C., & McClearn, G. E. (1980). *Behavior genetics: A primer.* San Francisco: Freeman.

Revelle, W., Humphreys, M. S., Simon, L., & Gilliland, K. (1980). The interactive effect of personality, time of day, and caffeine: A test of the arousal model. *Journal of Experimental Psychology: General, 109,* 1–31.

Stark, L., (1978). Trust. In H. London & J. E. Exner, Jr. (Eds.), *Dimensions of personality* (pp. 561–599). New York: Wiley.

Teasdale, J. D., & Rachman, S. (Eds.). (1983). Cognitions and mood: Clinical aspects and applications [Special issue]. *Advances in Behaviour Research and Therapy, 5,* 1–88.

Tellegen, A. (in press). Structures of mood and personality and their relevance to assessing anxiety, with an emphasis on self-report. In A. H. Tuma & J. D. Maser (Eds.), *Anxiety and the anxiety disorders.* Hillsdale, NJ: Erlbaum.

Tupes, E. C., & Christal, R. E. (1961). Recurrent personality factors based on trait ratings. *USAF ASD Technical Report* (No. 61–97).

Vestre, N. D. (1984). Irrational beliefs and self-reported depressed mood. *Journal of Abnormal Psychology, 93,* 239–241.

Wiggins, J. S. (1979). A psychological taxonomy of trait-descriptive terms: The interpersonal domain. *Journal of Personality and Social Psychology, 37,* 395–412.

CHAPTER 12 Stress and Adjustment

12.1 HANS SELYE

The Evolution of the Stress Concept

Only in the past couple of decades have psychologists become convinced that psychological as well as physiological variables can produce stress. However, as far back as the 1930s, Canadian physiologist Hans Selye was studying stress through the general adaptation syndrome (GAS). The general adaptation syndrome, first identified by Selye, is a consistent series of bodily reactions to stress that can be divided into three stages: the alarm reaction stage, the stage of resistance, and the stage of exhaustion. The GAS serves as a model for investigating the long-term effects of stress on the body.

Selye (1907–1982) received his D.Sc. from McGill University in 1942 and later earned a Ph.D. and an M.D. He spent most of his professional career at the Institute of Experimental Medicine and Surgery at the University of Montreal. As an endocrinologist, he dedicated his life to understanding the hormonal reactions in the stress syndrome. Selye wrote over 30 books on stress, including *The Stress of Life* (1976) and *Stress Without Distress* (1974).

This selection, "The Evolution of the Stress Concept," was published in the *American Scientist* in 1973. In it, Selye provides the history behind his famous general adaptation syndrome model of stress. Note how Selye's discoveries occurred in steps as he encountered different situations. As you read this selection, consider the definition of stress and how you measure the effects of stress in your life.

Key Concept: stress and the general adaptation syndrome

*E*verybody knows what stress is and nobody knows what it is. The word *stress*, like *success*, *failure*, or *happiness*, means different things to different people and, except for a few specialized scientists, no one has really tried to define it although it has become part of our daily vocabulary. . . .

Yet, how are we to cope with the stress of life if we cannot even define it? The businessman who is under constant pressure from his clients and employees alike, the air traffic controller who knows that a moment of distraction may mean death to hundreds of people, the athlete who desperately wants to win a race, and the husband who helplessly watches his wife slowly and painfully die of cancer—all suffer from stress. The problems they face are totally different, but medical research has shown that in many respects their bodies respond in a stereotyped manner with identical biochemical changes, meant fundamentally to cope with any type of increased demand upon the human machinery. The stress-producing factors—technically called *stressors*—are different, and yet they all produce essentially the same biologic stress response. This distinction between stressor and stress was perhaps the first important step in the scientific analysis of that most common biologic phenomenon that we all know only too well from personal experience.

But if we want to use what the laboratory has taught us about stress in formulating our own philosophy of life, if we want to avoid its bad effects and yet be able to enjoy the pleasures of accomplishment, we have to learn more about the nature and mechanism of stress. To succeed in this, we must concentrate on the fundamental technical data which the laboratory has given us as a basis for a scientific philosophy of conduct. Examination of the data seems to be the only way of finding purpose in life without having to fall back upon traditional beliefs whose acceptance depends primarily on indoctrination (1).

WHAT IS STRESS?

Stress is the nonspecific response of the body to any demand made upon it. In order to understand this definition we must first comprehend what is meant by "nonspecific." Each demand made upon our body is in a sense unique, that is, specific. When exposed to cold we shiver to produce more heat, and the blood vessels in our skin contract to diminish loss of heat from the body surface. When exposed to heat we sweat, because evaporation of perspiration from the surface of our skin has a cooling effect. When we eat so much sugar that the blood-sugar level rises above normal, we excrete some of it and try to activate chemical reactions which will enable us to store or burn up the rest so that the blood sugar may return to normal. A great muscular effort, such as running up many flights of stairs at full speed, makes increased demands upon our musculature and cardiovascular system: the muscles will need more energy to perform this unusual work; hence, the heart will beat more rapidly and strongly, and the blood pressure will rise to accelerate delivery of blood to the musculature.

Each drug and hormone has such specific actions: diuretics increase urine production; adrenalin augments the pulse rate and blood pressure, simultaneously increasing blood sugar, whereas insulin decreases blood sugar. Yet, no matter what kind of derangement is produced, all these agents have one thing in common: they also make an increased demand upon the body to readjust itself. This demand is nonspecific; it requires adaptation to a problem, regardless of what that problem may be. That is to say, in addition to their specific actions, all agents to which we are exposed produce a nonspecific increase in the need to perform certain adaptive functions and then to reestablish normalcy, which is independent of the specific activity that caused the rise in requirements. This nonspecific demand for activity as such is the essence of stress.

From the point of view of its stress-producing, or stressor, activity, it is even immaterial whether the agent or situation we face is pleasant or unpleasant; all that counts is the intensity of the demand for readjustment or adaptation. The mother who is suddenly told that her only son died in battle suffers a terrible mental shock; if years later it turns out that the news was false, and the son unexpectedly walks into her room alive and well, she experiences extreme joy. The *specific* results of the two events, sorrow and joy, are completely different, in fact, opposite to each other; yet their stressor effect—the *nonspecific* demand to readjust to an entirely new situation—may be the same.

It is difficult to see how such essentially different things as cold, heat, drugs, hormones, sorrow, and joy could provoke an identical biochemical reaction in the organism. Yet this is the case; it can now be demonstrated by highly objective quantitative biochemical determinations that certain reactions of the body are totally nonspecific and common to all types of exposure. . . .

WHAT STRESS IS NOT

Since the term stress has been used quite loosely, many confusing and often contradictory definitions have been formulated; hence, it will be useful to add a few remarks stating clearly what it is *not*. Stress is not simply nervous tension; stress reactions do occur in lower animals, which have no nervous system, and even in plants. Stress is not the nonspecific result of damage. We have seen that it is immaterial whether an agent is pleasant or unpleasant; its stressor effect depends merely on the intensity of the demand made upon the adaptive work of the body. As I have explained elsewhere (2), "normal activities—a game of tennis or even a passionate kiss—can produce considerable stress without causing conspicuous damage."

Stress is not something to be avoided. In fact, it is evident from the definition given earlier that it cannot be avoided; no matter what you do or what happens to you, there arises a demand to provide the necessary energy to perform the tasks required to maintain life and to resist and adapt to the changing external influences. Even while fully relaxed and asleep, you are under some stress: your heart must continue to pump blood, your intestines to digest last night's dinner, your muscles to move your chest to permit respiration; even your brain is not at complete rest while you are dreaming.

Complete freedom from stress is death. Contrary to public opinion, we must not—and indeed cannot—avoid stress, but we can meet it efficiently and enjoy it by learning more about its mechanism and adjusting our philosophy of life accordingly (1).

HISTORIC DEVELOPMENT

The concept of stress is very old; it must have occurred even to prehistoric man that the loss of vigor and feeling of exhaustion that overcame him after hard labor, prolonged exposure to cold or heat, loss of blood, agonizing fear, or any kind of disease had something in common. He may not have been consciously aware of this similarity in his response to anything that was just too much for him, but when the feeling came he must have realized that he had exceeded the limits of what he could reasonably handle, in other words that "he had had it."

Man soon must have discovered also that whenever faced with a prolonged and unaccustomed strenuous task—be it swimming in cold water, lifting rocks, or going without food—he passes through three stages: at first the experience is a hardship, then one gets used to it, and finally one cannot stand it any longer. . . .

How could different agents produce the same result? Is there a nonspecific adaptive reaction to change as such? In 1926, as a second-year medical student, I first came across this problem of a stereotyped response to any exacting task. I began to wonder why patients suffering from the most diverse diseases have so many signs and symptoms in common. Whether a man suffers from severe loss of blood, an infectious disease, or advanced cancer, he loses his appetite, his muscular strength, and his ambition to accomplish anything; usually the patient also loses weight, and even his facial expression betrays that he is ill. What is the scientific basis of what I thought of at the time as the "syndrome of just being sick"? Could the mechanism of this syndrome be analyzed by modern scientific techniques? Could it be reduced to its elements and expressed in the precise terms of biochemistry, biophysics, and morphology? Could this reaction be subject to scientific analysis?

It was not until 1936 that the problem presented itself again, now under conditions more suited to analysis. At that time, I was working in the biochemistry Department of McGill University, trying to find a new hormone in extracts of cattle ovaries. I injected the extracts into rats to see if their organs would show unpredictable changes that could not be attributed to any known hormone. Much to my satisfaction, the first and most impure extracts changed the rats in three ways: (1) the adrenal cortex became enlarged, (2) the thymus, spleen, lymph nodes, and all other lymphatic structures shrank, and (3) deep, bleeding ulcers appeared in the stomach and in the upper gut. Because the three types of change were closely interdependent they formed a definite syndrome. The changes varied from slight to pronounced, depending on the amount of extract I injected.

At first, I ascribed all these changes to a new sex hormone in the extract. But soon I found that all toxic substances—extracts of kidney, spleen, or even a toxin not derived from living tissue—produced the same syndrome. Gradually, my classroom concept of the "syndrome of just being sick" came back to me. I realized that the reaction I had produced with my impure extracts and toxic drugs was an experimental replica of this syndrome. Adrenal enlargement, gastrointestinal ulcers, and thymicolymphatic shrinkage were the omnipresent signs of damage to the body when under disease attack. The three changes thus became the objective indexes of stress and the basis for the development of the entire stress concept.

The reaction was first described in *Nature* (4 July 1936) as "A Syndrome Produced by Various Nocuous Agents" and, subsequently, it became known as the General Adaptation Syndrome (GAS) or biologic stress syndrome. In the same paper I also suggested the name *alarm reaction* for the initial response, arguing that it probably represents the somatic expression of a generalized "call to arms" of the body's defensive forces.

THE GENERAL ADAPTATION SYNDROME

The alarm reaction, however, was evidently not the entire response. Upon continued exposure to any noxious agent capable of eliciting this reaction, a stage of adaptation or resistance ensues. In other words, no organism can be maintained continuously in a state of alarm. If the agent is so drastic that continued exposure becomes incompatible with life, the animal dies during the alarm reaction within the first hours or days. If it can survive, this initial reaction is necessarily followed by the "stage of resistance." The manifestations of this second phase are quite different from—in many instances, the exact opposite of—those which characterize the alarm reaction. For example, during the alarm reaction, the cells of the adrenal cortex discharge their secretory granules into the bloodstream and thus become depleted of corticoid-containing lipid storage material; in the stage of resistance, on the other hand, the cortex becomes particularly rich in secretory granules. Whereas in the alarm reaction, there is hemoconcentration, hypochloremia, and general tissue catabolism, during the stage of resistance, there is hemodilution, hyperchloremia, and anabolism, with a return toward normal body weight.

Curiously, after still more exposure to the noxious agent, the acquired adaptation is lost again. The animal enters into a third phase, the "stage of exhaustion," which inexorably follows as long as the stressor is severe enough and applied for a sufficient length of time. Because of its great practical importance, it should be pointed out that the triphasic nature of the GAS gave us the first indication that the body's adaptability, or "adaptation energy," is finite since, under constant stress, exhaustion eventually ensues. We still do not know precisely what is lost, except that it is not merely caloric energy, since food intake is normal during the stage of resistance. Hence, one would think that once adaptation has occurred and ample energy is available, resistance should go on indefinitely. But just as any inanimate machine gradually wears out, so does the human machine sooner or later become the victim of constant wear and tear.

REFERENCES

1. H. Selye. In preparation. *Stress without Distress*. New York, Philadelphia: Lippincott.
2. H. Selye. 1956. *The Stress of Life*. New York: McGraw-Hill.

12.2 MEYER FRIEDMAN AND RAY H. ROSENMAN

The Key Cause—Type A Behavior Pattern

Scientists have become increasingly concerned about the effects of stress on health. In the late 1950s, physicians Meyer Friedman and Ray H. Rosenman began to investigate the possibility that a stress-producing personality pattern, which they called "Type A," might lead to cardiovascular disease and heart attacks.

Friedman (b. 1919) received his M.D. from the Johns Hopkins University in 1935. He currently works at the Mount Zion Hospital and Medical Center in San Francisco. Rosenman (b. 1920) earned his M.D. from the University of Michigan in 1944. He is also affiliated with the Mount Zion Hospital and Medical Center. Their popular book *Type A Behavior and Your Heart* (Fawcett Crest, 1974) represents their research findings on stress personalities and heart disease.

This selection is from chapter 6, "The Key Cause—Type A Behavior Pattern," of *Type A Behavior and Your Heart*. In it, Friedman and Rosenman give the background of their research and describe the classic symptoms of the Type A behavior pattern (which include a sense of time urgency, a quest to accumulate things, insecurity, aggression, and hostility). This book spurred a significant amount of research in the area of personality and stress, and, interestingly, some of the more recent research findings are in conflict with the original hypothesis. Although investigations are continuing, some authorities now suggest that hostility is the key to understanding stress and health. As you read this selection, consider how prevalent Type A behavior is in today's society.

Key Concept: Type A behavior pattern

We believe that the major cause of coronary artery and heart disease is a complex of emotional reactions, which we have designated Type A Behavior

Pattern. Such being our conviction, and also because less than a handful of medical investigators have concerned themselves with the possible relationship of your brain to your heart and its nourishing arteries, we mean to deal with the subject at thorough and, we trust, convincing length.

When, sometime between 1955 and 1958, we first began to approach the possibility that the brain and its functions might have some relevance to coronary artery and heart disease, we each had been seeing scores of coronary patients in our private consultation rooms for well over a decade. We greeted them, asked them how they felt, took their blood pressure, listened to their hearts, and then had a nurse take their electrocardiograms and obtain a blood sample for cholesterol analysis. Depending upon the results of these examinations, we might or might not have altered the dosage of their various drugs. Of course, each patient was routinely exhorted (1) to continue to eat his low animal fat/high unsaturated fat/low cholesterol diet, (2) to continue his exercise program, and (3) to avoid excess cigarette smoking. They in turn always asked what their blood pressure reading was, how high their last serum cholesterol measurement had been and whether their present electrocardiogram showed any "improvement." Having received such information (sometimes good, sometimes bad), they said good-bye, stopped at the secretary's desk to make their next appointment, and then departed.

Sometimes, however, we would ponder over the coronary status of some of these patients and wonder whether we really were helping them in any meaningful way. If we concluded—as we often did—that our therapeutic measures were actually far more impressive than helpful to a patient, we immediately rationalized that, after all, we had done the best that we could and no other physician could have done much more. . . .

We first began to consider the personality of these patients seriously when we had to search the medical literature prior to writing a review article on the role of dietary cholesterol in coronary heart disease. Too many finely executed studies suggested that neither the cholesterol nor the fat content of various diets could always explain the coronary heart disease developing in persons ingesting such diets. Other factors just had to be playing a part!

This impression grew to a certainty after we investigated the dietary habits of both a representative group of volunteers from the San Francisco Junior League and their husbands. We had expected (because American white women develop coronary heart disease much less frequently than their husbands) that our study would show that these women ate much less cholesterol and animal fat than their husbands. But the dietary intakes were exactly the same. What, then, was protecting the women? Their female sex hormones, that's what, most of our medical colleagues had been clamoring for a number of years. Yet if our colleagues had investigated and mulled over the total enigma in their minds, they would not have jumped to such a silly conclusion. They would have recalled that not only is the female laboratory animal as susceptible to experimentally induced coronary disease as her male counterpart, but also—and far more relevantly—white women of various countries other than the United States are as prone to coronary heart disease as their husbands. Also, in several separate studies done in different areas of the United States, the *black* woman was found to be slightly *more* susceptible than her black husband to coronary heart disease. If, then, the American white female owed her relative immunity to coronary heart disease to her female sex hormones, these hormones must be chemically and biologically different from those of most other women on our planet. We considered (and still consider) such a thesis to be ridiculous.

If we were in a mental stew following this dietary study, the then-president of the San Francisco Junior League wasn't confused at all. "I told you right from the first," she said, "that you would find that we are eating exactly as our husbands do. If you really want to know what is giving our husbands heart attacks, I'll tell you." . . .

"It's stress, the stress they receive in their work, that's what's doing it," she quickly responded.

And that's when our concept of Type A Behavior Pattern and its probable relationship to coronary heart disease was born. . . .

One of our earliest difficulties was to determine precisely which emotional traits had relevance. This determination has not been easy, and now, well over a decade since we first began this analysis, we are still adding features to the total complex of characteristics we have designated Type A Behavior Pattern. But from the beginning we did know that whatever else this pattern might encompass *in its entirety*, whenever any person felt within himself a chronic sense of time urgency and also exhibited *excessive* competitive drive, he invariably possessed the Type A Behavior Pattern. Knowing this, we were capable of performing various biochemical and epidemiological studies while we were still ferreting out the possible other traits making up the total pattern.

We discovered that time urgency and competitive overdrive were components of the behavior pattern by reconsidering our own private coronary patients. Almost invariably, if these patients were under sixty-five years of age, they exhibited an habitual sense of time urgency and *excessive* competitive drive. Often, perhaps because of their excessive competitive drive, these same individuals showed an easily aroused hostility, which was likely to flare up under very diverse conditions. Involuntarily, our patients had been trying to tell us about these traits for a long, long time, but we had been too busy or too preoccupied with other matters to receive, much less comprehend, these "signals." . . .

It has been a long and at times rather arduous scientific trek. We cannot truthfully assert that our course over these past fifteen years has been as direct as a crow is reputed to fly, but we believe we at least are beginning to home in on the true target responsible for the epidemic-like increase in coronary artery and heart disease during our own lifetime. We base this optimism on four findings: (1) the ubiquity of Type A Behavior Pattern in those already ill with coronary heart disease, (2) the extreme vulnerability of Type A subjects to this disease, (3) the identification of the cluster of coronary biochemical abnormalities in Type A subjects, and perhaps most important of all, (4) our success in experimentally inducing a facsimile of Type A Behavior Pattern, followed by emergence of the most dreaded of all coronary biochemical derangements. It is now appropriate that we explain to you precisely what it is that we have termed Type A Behavior Pattern, and its probable causes.

WHAT IS TYPE A BEHAVIOR PATTERN?

Type A Behavior Pattern is an action-emotion complex that can be observed in any person who is *aggressively* involved in a *chronic, incessant* struggle to achieve more and more in less and less time, and if required to do so, against the opposing efforts of other things or other persons. It is not psychosis or a complex of worries or fears or phobias or obsessions, but a socially accept-able—indeed often praised—form of conflict. Persons possessing this pattern also are quite prone to exhibit a free-floating but extraordinarily well-rational-ized hostility. As might be expected, there are degrees in the intensity of this behavior pattern. Moreover, because the pattern represents the reaction that takes place when particular personality traits of an afflicted individual are challenged or aroused by a specific environmental agent, the results of this reaction (that is, the behavior pattern itself) may not be felt or exhibited by him if he happens to be in or confronted by an environment that presents no chal-lenge. For example, a usually hard-driving, competitive, aggressive editor of an urban newspaper, if hospitalized with a trivial illness, may not exhibit a single sign of Type A Behavior Pattern. In short, for Type A Behavior Pattern to ex-plode into being, the *environmental challenge must always serve as the fuse for this explosion.*

The person with Type B Behavior Pattern is the exact opposite of the Type A subject. He, unlike the Type A person, is rarely harried by desires to obtain a wildly increasing number of things or participate in an endlessly growing series of events in an ever decreasing amount of time. His intelligence may be as good as or even better than that of the Type A subject. *Similarly, his ambition may be as great or even greater than that of his Type A counterpart.* He may also have a considerable amount of "drive," but its character is such that it seems to steady him, give confidence and security to him, rather than to goad, irritate, and infuriate, as with the Type A man.

In our experience, based on extensive practices in typing and then observ-ing many hundreds of individuals, the general run of urban Americans tend to fall into one or the other of these two groups. The Type A's, we have found, predominate; they usually represent somewhat over half of all those in the open samples we have tested. There are somewhat fewer true Type B individu-als, perhaps 40 percent of the whole. People in whom Type A and Type B characteristics are mixed account for about 10 percent. . . .

Again we should like to reiterate that, with exceedingly rare exception, the socioeconomic position of a man or woman does not determine whether he or she is a Type A or Type B subject. The presidents of many banks and corpo-rations (perhaps even the majority) may be Type B individuals. Conversely, many janitors, shoe salesmen, truck drivers, architects, and even florists may be Type A subjects. We have not found any clear correlation between occupa-tional position held and the incidence of Type A Behavior Pattern. Why is this so? Because (1) a sense of job or position responsibility is not synonymous with the Type A sense of time urgency; (2) excessive drive or competitive enthusi-asm may only too frequently be expended upon economic trivia rather than affairs of importance; and (3) promotion and elevation, particularly in corporate and professional organizations, usually go to those who are wise rather than to those who are merely hasty, to those who are tactful rather than to those who are hostile, and to those who are creative rather than to those who are merely agile in competitive strife. . . .

277

Meyer Friedman and Ray H. Rosenman

SENSE OF TIME URGENCY, OR THE MODERN DISEASE, "HURRY SICKNESS"

Overwhelmingly, the most significant trait of the Type A man is his habitual sense of time urgency or "hurry sickness." Why does the Type A man so often feel that he doesn't have enough time to do all the things that he either believes should be done or that he wishes to do, whereas the Type B man feels that he has quite enough time to do all that he believes ought to be done? The answer is quite a simple one. The Type A man incessantly strives to accomplish too much or to participate in too many events in the amount of time he allots for these purposes. Even if by some miracle time could be stretched adequately just once for his activities, the Type A man still would not be satisfied. He would then seek to stretch time a second or third or fourth time.

The fundamental sickness of the Type A subject consists of his peculiar failure to perceive, or perhaps worse, to accept the simple fact that a man's time can be exhausted by his activities. As a consequence, he never ceases trying to "stuff" more and more events in his constantly shrinking reserves of time. It is the Type A man's ceaseless striving, his everlasting *struggle* with time, that we believe so very frequently leads to his early demise from coronary heart disease.

In an attempt to save time the Type A man often creates deadlines for himself. He subconsciously believes that if he fixes a date for the execution of a particular task that is actually too soon, somehow or other he will succeed in triumphing over his inveterate enemy, time. Since he very often has created not one but as many as a dozen such deadlines, he is subjecting himself to a more or less continuous time pressure. This voluntary tyranny frequently forms the very essence of Type A Behavior Pattern. To fill a life with deadlines to the exclusion of life's lovelinesses is a peculiarly dreadful form of self-punishment.

If this ever-increasing harassment by a sense of time urgency is not checked, eventually the Type A subject begins to indulge in a phenomenon that can and only too often does subvert his creative and judgmental attributes. This phenomenon is stereotyped thinking and action. More and more, again to save time, the Type A subject tends to think and do things in exactly the same way. Consciously or not, the Type A man apparently feels that if he can bring the previously "coded" thought and action processes again to bear on a new task, he can accomplish it *faster*. He more and more substitutes "faster" for "better" or "different" in his way of thinking and doing. In other words, he indulges in stereotyped responses. He substitutes repetitive urgency for creative energy. . . .

Far more often than not, then, the Type A man, because he tries so desperately to accomplish more and more in less and less time, finally impairs his creative power and only too often the acuity of his judgment. Thus bereft, he desperately seeks to substitute speed of execution. If sometimes he still seems to display brilliance, it usually is due to those original and creative concepts which he may have formulated in his younger years—before he became *totally* enslaved to his Type A Behavior Pattern. But this earlier collected cache of concepts can serve him well only as long as the milieu and its demands remain relatively unchanged. . . .

THE QUEST FOR NUMBERS

Man's fascination with the quantitative accumulation of material objects is a trait, like speech or awareness of future time, which is not shared by any other species. Admittedly, squirrels accumulate nuts and bees honey, but they do so for strictly utilitarian reasons—to forestall winter's famine. They do not do so simply for the "human" joy of adding to that of which they already have enough.

This almost innate delight in acquisition probably begins quite early in our childhood. All of us have witnessed, for example, the delight a small boy takes in his first electric train set, even though it only consists of a locomotive and several freight cars. Later, as he experiences more birthdays and Christmases and receives more toy locomotives, freight cars, and tracks, he begins to *count* (rather than enjoy) the number of units he has. A similar process takes place when he begins to collect marbles, postage stamps, or anything else. . . .

Because of his obsession with numbers and because so many of the world's activities are expressed in currency units (that is, dollars, pounds, francs, and marks), the Type A subject more often than not appears to be absorbed in money. Before we thoroughly understood our own Type A patients and friends, we were inclined to believe that they were inordinately fond of making money for its own sake. This, however, is not true. The Type A businessman is not intrigued with money as such, nor is he miserly, nor is he necessarily eager to buy a better and bigger house or automobile than his friends (even if he frequently ends up doing just exactly that). Money for him merely represents the tokens or chips of the "numbers game" to which he has dedicated himself. "Last year my company grossed a profit before taxes of five million dollars," the Type A businessman proudly states. "Last year I performed one hundred fifty appendectomies," the Type A surgeon just as proudly announces. "Last year my laboratory published eighteen articles," the Type A scientist even more proudly announces. You will note that each is proud of his kind of "numbers." . . .

THE INSECURITY OF STATUS

Perhaps no man, at first glance, seems less insecure than the typical Type A man. He bristles with confidence and appears to exude lavish amounts of self-assurance and self-conviction. How can we indict a man as being insecure who is always so eager to ask, "What is your problem and how can I help *you*?" a man who is so loath to say, "I have a problem and I need your help"? We do so because we have found, after many years of studying the Type A man, that he either lost or never had any intrinsic "yardstick" by which he can gauge his own fundamental worth to his own satisfaction.

Somewhere in his development process he began to measure the value of his total personality or character by the *number* of his *achievements*. Moreover, these achievements invariably must be those he believes capture the respect and admiration of his peers and superiors. He does not, however, care whether these achievements gain him the love or affection of his fellow man, although he does not particularly care to be disliked.

Having chosen his yardstick, he has committed himself irretrievably to a life course that can never bring him true equanimity. The *number*, not the quality, of his achievements must constantly increase to satiate an appetite that, unchecked by other restraints, ceaselessly increases. Second, he believes that the number of his achievements are always being judged by his peers and subordinates, and since the latter are constantly changing as he ascends in the socioeconomic scale, he feels that the number of his achievements must continue to rise. . . .

From what we have written so far, it should be obvious that the Type A man isn't very concerned about simply sustaining himself. He feels that he always can obtain food, shelter, and clothing (and the modern welfare state, of course, buttresses his confidence in this regard). Nor is his insecurity exclusively focused solely upon his status at any given instant. Rather, it appears to be directly attuned to the *pace* at which his status *improves*. This brings us, then, to the key reason for the insecurity of the Type A man: he has staked his innermost security upon the *pace* of his status enhancement. This pace in turn depends upon a *maximal* number of achievements accomplished in a *minimal* amount of time, achievements recognized as significant by constantly changing groups of his peers and superiors.

His only possible surcease from this almost continuous self-harassment occurs at those fleeting moments when he believes that the number of his achievements are increasing at a satisfactory rate. These moments have to be rare. In his frenzy to accumulate achievements, he necessarily tends at the same time to subvert their quality. Noting unconsciously this fall-off in quality, he desperately attempts on a conscious level to make up for the deficit, by heaping up a still greater number of achievements. . . .

AGGRESSION AND HOSTILITY

No man who is eager to achieve is totally lacking in aggressive spirit. Certainly we have met few if any Type A subjects who are deficient in this trait. On the contrary, most Type A subjects possess so much aggressive drive that it frequently evolves into a free-floating hostility. But excess aggression and certainly hostility are not always easily detected in Type A men, if only because they so often keep such feelings and impulses under deep cover. Indeed, very few of these men are even aware of his hostility. Indeed, it is maybe only after fairly intimate acquaintance with a Type A man that his hostility becomes manifest.

Perhaps the prime index of the presence of aggression or hostility in almost all Type A men is the tendency always to compete with or to challenge other people, whether the activity consists of a sporting contest, a game of cards, or a simple discussion. If the aggression has evolved into frank hostility, more often than not one feels, even when talking casually to such men, that there is a note of rancor in their speech. They tend to bristle at points in a conversation where the ordinary person might either laugh self-deprecatingly or pass over the possibly contentious theme.

There are some persons whom we consider Type A, not because they are engaged in a struggle to achieve a maximal number of goals in a minimal amount of time (the usual complex making up this pattern), but because they are so hostile that they are almost continuously engaged in a struggle against other persons. Of course nature does not distinguish between a man struggling against time and one struggling against another man, but makes the organs of this struggling man discharge the same kinds of chemicals regardless of the exact causes of the struggle. No Type A man is more difficult to treat than one whose pattern stems directly and wholly from his free-floating hostility.

PART SIX

Psychological Disorders

CHAPTER 13 Abnormal Behavior

13.1 D. L. ROSENHAN

On Being Sane in Insane Places

Mental health workers have devised various classification schemes to help them diagnose abnormal behaviors. Although this may be beneficial in the vast majority of cases, some psychologists worry that misdiagnosis can result in inappropriate treatments or stigmatization and that mental health workers therefore need to be extremely careful about labeling mental patients. Social psychologist D. L. Rosenhan is a leading critic of the method in which patients are labeled in mental hospitals.

Rosenhan (b. 1929) earned his Ph.D. from Columbia University in 1958. He is currently a professor of psychology at Stanford University.

This selection, "On Being Sane in Insane Places," was published in *Science* in 1973. In it, Rosenhan describes his and others' experiences as pseudopatients (healthy people who secretly gained admission to mental hospitals as patients), and he discusses the implications of labeling mental patients as insane or as mentally ill. This article encouraged debate among mental health providers on diagnosis in clinical psychology that is still going on today. A readable article, it provides a good inside look at mental institutions as well as the labeling process. Although Rosenhan's research successfully persuaded psychologists to discuss the problems that come with diagnosing mental patients, some people have criticized the study as unethical. As you read this article, consider what it must be like for mental patients to live in an institution.

Key Concept: labeling and the diagnosis of abnormal behavior

*I*f sanity and insanity exist, how shall we know them?

The question is neither capricious nor itself insane. However much we may be personally convinced that we can tell the normal from the abnormal, the evidence is simply not compelling. It is commonplace, for example, to read about murder trials wherein eminent psychiatrists for the defense are contradicted by equally eminent psychiatrists for the prosecution on the matter of the defendant's sanity. More generally, there are a great deal of conflicting data on the reliability, utility, and meaning of such terms as "sanity," "insanity," "mental illness," and "schizophrenia." Finally, as early as 1934, Benedict suggested that normality and abnormality are not universal (*1*). What is viewed as normal in one culture may be seen as quite aberrant in another. Thus, notions of normality and abnormality may not be quite as accurate as people believe they are.

To raise questions regarding normality and abnormality is in no way to question the fact that some behaviors are deviant or odd. Murder is deviant. So, too, are hallucinations. Nor does raising such questions deny the existence of the personal anguish that is often associated with "mental illness." Anxiety and depression exist. Psychological suffering exists. But normality and abnormality, sanity and insanity, and the diagnoses that flow from them may be less substantive than many believe them to be.

At its heart, the question of whether the sane can be distinguished from the insane (and whether degrees of insanity can be distinguished from each other) is a simple matter: do the salient characteristics that lead to diagnoses reside in the patients themselves or in the environments and contexts in which observers find them? . . . [T]he belief has been strong that patients present symptoms, that those symptoms can be categorized, and, implicitly, that the sane are distinguishable from the insane. More recently, however, this belief has been questioned. Based in part on theoretical and anthropological considerations, but also on philosophical, legal, and therapeutic ones, the view has grown that psychological categorization of mental illness is useless at best and downright harmful, misleading, and pejorative at worst. Psychiatric diagnoses, in this view, are in the minds of the observers and are not valid summaries of characteristics displayed by the observed.

Gains can be made in deciding which of these is more nearly accurate by getting normal people (that is, people who do not have, and have never suffered, symptoms of serious psychiatric disorders) admitted to psychiatric hospitals and then determining whether they were discovered to be sane and, if so, how. If the sanity of such pseudopatients were always detected, there would be prima facie evidence that a sane individual can be distinguished from the insane context in which he is found. Normality (and presumably abnormality) is distinct enough that it can be recognized wherever it occurs, for it is carried within the person. If, on the other hand, the sanity of the pseudopatients were never discovered, serious difficulties would arise for those who support traditional modes of psychiatric diagnosis. Given that the hospital staff was not incompetent, that the pseudopatient had been behaving as sanely as he had been outside of the hospital, and that it had never been previously suggested that he belonged in a psychiatric hospital, such an unlikely outcome would support the view that psychiatric diagnosis betrays little about the patient but much about the environment in which an observer finds him.

This article describes such an experiment. Eight sane people gained secret admission to 12 different hospitals. Their diagnostic experiences constitute the data of the first part of this article; the remainder is devoted to a description of their experiences in psychiatric institutions. Too few psychiatrists and psychologists, even those who have worked in such hospitals, know what the experience is like. They rarely talk about it with former patients, perhaps because they distrust information coming from the previously insane. Those who have worked in psychiatric hospitals are likely to have adapted so thoroughly to the settings that they are insensitive to the impact of the experience. And while there have been occasional reports of researchers who submitted themselves to psychiatric hospitalization (3), these researchers have commonly remained in the hospitals for short periods of time, often with the knowledge of the hospital staff. It is difficult to know the extent to which they were treated like patients or like research colleagues. Nevertheless, their reports about the inside of the psychiatric hospital have been valuable. This article extends those efforts.

PSEUDOPATIENTS AND THEIR SETTINGS

The eight pseudopatients were a varied group. One was a psychology graduate student in his 20's. The remaining seven were older and "established." Among them were three psychologists, a pediatrician, a psychiatrist, a painter, and a housewife. Three pseudopatients were women, five were men. All of them employed pseudonyms, lest their alleged diagnoses embarrass them later. Those who were in mental health professions alleged another occupation in order to avoid the special attentions that might be accorded by staff, as a matter of courtesy or caution, to ailing colleagues. With the exception of myself (I was the first pseudopatient and my presence was known to the hospital administrator and chief psychologist and, so far as I can tell, to them alone), the presence of pseudopatients and the nature of the research program was not known to the hospital staffs.

The settings were similarly varied. In order to generalize the findings, admission into a variety of hospitals was sought. The 12 hospitals in the sample are located in five different states on the East and West coasts. Some were old and shabby, some were quite new. Some were research-oriented, others not. Some had good staff-patient ratios, others were quite understaffed. Only one was a strictly private hospital. All the others were supported by state or federal funds or, in one instance, by university funds.

After calling the hospital for an appointment, the pseudopatient arrived at the admissions office complaining that he had been hearing voices. Asked what the voices said, he replied that they were often unclear, but as far as he could tell they said "empty," "hollow," and "thud." The voices were unfamiliar and were of the same sex as the pseudopatient. The choice of these symptoms was occasioned by their apparent similarity to existential symptoms. Such symptoms were alleged to arise from painful concerns about the perceived meaninglessness of one's life. It is as if the hallucinating person were saying, "My life is empty and hollow." The choice of these symptoms was also determined by the *absence* of a single report of existential psychoses in the literature.

Beyond alleging the symptoms and falsifying name, vocation, and employment, no further alterations of person, history, or circumstances were made. The significant events of the pseudopatient's life history were presented as they had actually occurred. Relationships with parents and siblings, with spouse and children, with people at work and in school, consistent with the aforementioned exceptions, were described as they were or had been. Frustrations and upsets were described along with joys and satisfactions. These facts are important to remember. If anything, they strongly biased the subsequent results in favor of detecting sanity, since none of their histories or current behaviors were seriously pathological in any way.

Immediately upon admission to the psychiatric ward, the pseudopatient ceased simulating *any* symptoms of abnormality. In some cases, there was a brief period of mild nervousness and anxiety, since none of the pseudopatients really believed that they would be admitted so easily. Indeed their shared fear was that they would be immediately exposed as frauds and greatly embarrassed. Moreover, many of them had never visited a psychiatric ward; even those who had, nevertheless, had some genuine fears about what might happen to them. Their nervousness, then, was quite appropriate to the novelty of the hospital setting, and it abated rapidly.

Apart from that short-lived nervousness, the pseudopatient behaved on the ward as he "normally" behaved. The pseudopatient spoke to patients and staff as he might ordinarily. Because there is uncommonly little to do on a psychiatric ward, he attempted to engage others in conversation. When asked by staff how he was feeling, he indicated that he was fine, that he no longer experienced symptoms. He responded to instructions from attendants, to calls for medication (which was not swallowed), and to dining-hall instructions. Beyond such activities as were available to him on the admissions ward, he spent his time writing down his observations about the ward, its patients, and the staff. Initially these notes were written "secretly," but as it soon became clear that no one much cared, they were subsequently written on standard tablets of paper in such public places as the dayroom. No secret was made of these activities.

The pseudopatient, very much as a true psychiatric patient, entered a hospital with no foreknowledge of when he would be discharged. Each was told that he would have to get out by his own devices, essentially by convincing the staff that he was sane. The psychological stresses associated with hospitalization were considerable, and all but one of the pseudopatients desired to be discharged almost immediately after being admitted. They were, therefore, motivated not only to behave sanely, but to be paragons of cooperation. That their behavior was in no way disruptive is confirmed by nursing reports, which have been obtained on most of the patients. These reports uniformly indicate that the patients were "friendly," "cooperative," and "exhibited no abnormal indications."

287

D. L. Rosenhan

THE NORMAL ARE NOT DETECTABLY SANE

Despite their public "show" of sanity, the pseudopatients were never detected. Admitted, except in one case, with a diagnosis of schizophrenia, each was discharged with a diagnosis of schizophrenia "in remission." The label "in remission" should in no way be dismissed as a formality, for at no time during any hospitalization had any question been raised about any pseudopatient's simulation. Nor are there any indications in the hospital records that the pseudopatient's status was suspect. Rather, the evidence is strong that, once labeled schizophrenic, the pseudopatient was stuck with that label. If the pseudopatient was to be discharged, he must naturally be "in remission"; but he was not sane, nor, in the institution's view, had he ever been sane.

The uniform failure to recognize sanity cannot be attributed to the quality of the hospitals, for, although there were considerable variations among them, several are considered excellent. Nor can it be alleged that there was simply not enough time to observe the pseudopatients. Length of hospitalization ranged from 7 to 52 days, with an average of 19 days. The pseudopatients were not, in fact, carefully observed, but this failure clearly speaks more to traditions within psychiatric hospitals than to lack of opportunity.

Finally, it cannot be said that the failure to recognize the pseudopatients' sanity was due to the fact that they were not behaving sanely. While there was clearly some tension present in all of them, their daily visitors could detect no serious behavioral consequences—nor, indeed, could other patients. It was quite common for the patients to "detect" the pseudopatients' sanity. During the first three hospitalizations, when accurate counts were kept, 35 of a total of 118 patients on the admissions ward voiced their suspicions, some vigorously. "You're not crazy. You're a journalist, or a professor [referring to the continual note-taking]. You're checking up on the hospital." While most of the patients were reassured by the pseudopatient's insistence that he had been sick before he came in but was fine now, some continued to believe that the pseudopatient was sane throughout his hospitalization. The fact that the patients often recognized normality when staff did not raises important questions.

Failure to detect sanity during the course of hospitalization may be due to the fact that physicians operate with a strong bias toward what statisticians call the type 2 error (2). This is to say that physicians are more inclined to call a healthy person sick (a false positive, type 2) than a sick person healthy (a false negative, type 1). The reasons for this are not hard to find: it is clearly more dangerous to misdiagnose illness than health. Better to err on the side of caution, to suspect illness even among the healthy.

But what holds for medicine does not hold equally well for psychiatry. Medical illnesses, while unfortunate, are not commonly pejorative. Psychiatric

diagnoses, on the contrary, carry with them personal, legal, and social stigmas
(4). . . .

THE STICKINESS OF PSYCHODIAGNOSTIC LABELS

Beyond the tendency to call the healthy sick—a tendency that accounts better for diagnostic behavior on admission than it does for such behavior after a lengthy period of exposure—the data speak to the massive role of labeling in psychiatric assessment. Having once been labeled schizophrenic, there is nothing the pseudopatient can do to overcome this tag. The tag profoundly colors others' perceptions of him and his behavior. . . .

Once a person is designated abnormal, all of his other behaviors and characteristics are colored by that label. Indeed, that label is so powerful that many of the pseudopatients' normal behaviors were overlooked entirely or profoundly misinterpreted. . . .

All pseudopatients took extensive notes publicly. Under ordinary circumstances, such behavior would have raised questions in the minds of observers, as, in fact, it did among patients. Indeed, it seemed so certain that the notes would elicit suspicion that elaborate precautions were taken to remove them from the ward each day. But the precautions proved needless. The closest any staff member came to questioning these notes occurred when one pseudopatient asked his physician what kind of medication he was receiving and began to write down the response. "You needn't write it," he was told gently. "If you have trouble remembering, just ask me again."

If no questions were asked of the pseudopatients, how was their writing interpreted? Nursing records for three patients indicate that the writing was seen as an aspect of their pathological behavior. "Patient engages in writing behavior" was the daily nursing comment on one of the pseudopatients who was never questioned about his writing. Given that the patient is in the hospital, he must be psychologically disturbed. And given that he is disturbed, continuous writing must be a behavioral manifestation of that disturbance, perhaps a subset of the compulsive behaviors that are sometimes correlated with schizophrenia. . . .

A psychiatric label has a life and an influence of its own. Once the impression has been formed that the patient is schizophrenic, the expectation is that he will continue to be schizophrenic. When a sufficient amount of time has passed, during which the patient has done nothing bizarre, he is considered to be in remission and available for discharge. But the label endures beyond discharge, with the unconfirmed expectation that he will behave as a schizophrenic again. Such labels, conferred by mental health professionals, are as influential on the patient as they are on his relatives and friends, and it should not surprise anyone that the diagnosis acts on all of them as a self-fulfilling prophecy. Eventually, the patient himself accepts the diagnosis, with all of its surplus meanings and expectations, and behaves accordingly (5). . . . If it makes no sense to label ourselves permanently depressed on the basis of an occasional depression, then it takes better evidence than is presently available to label all patients insane or schizophrenic on the basis of bizarre behaviors or cognitions. It seems more useful, as Mischel (5) has pointed out, to limit our discussions to *behaviors*, the stimuli that provoke them, and their correlates. . . . I may hallucinate because I am sleeping, or I may hallucinate because I have ingested a peculiar drug. These are termed sleep-induced hallucinations, or dreams, and drug-induced hallucinations, respectively. But when the stimuli to my hallucinations are unknown, that is called craziness, or schizophrenia—as if that inference were somehow as illuminating as the others. . . .

SUMMARY AND CONCLUSIONS

It is clear that we cannot distinguish the sane from the insane in psychiatric hospitals. The hospital itself imposes a special environment in which the meanings of behavior can easily be misunderstood. The consequences to patients hospitalized in such an environment—the powerlessness, depersonalization, segregation, mortification, and self-labeling—seem undoubtedly counter-therapeutic.

I do not, even now, understand this problem well enough to perceive solutions. But two matters seem to have some promise. The first concerns the proliferation of community mental health facilities, of crisis intervention centers, of the human potential movement, and of behavior therapies that, for all of their own problems, tend to avoid psychiatric labels, to focus on specific problems and behaviors, and to retain the individual in a relatively nonpejorative environment. Clearly, to the extent that we refrain from sending the distressed to insane places, our impressions of them are less likely to be distorted. (The risk of distorted perceptions, it seems to me, is always present, since we are much more sensitive to an individual's behaviors and verbalizations than we are to the subtle contextual stimuli that often promote them. At issue here is a matter of magnitude. And, as I have shown, the magnitude of distortion is exceedingly high in the extreme context that is a psychiatric hospital).

The second matter that might prove promising speaks to the need to increase the sensitivity of mental health workers and researchers to the *Catch 22* position of psychiatric patients. Simply reading materials in this area will be of help to some such workers and researchers. For others, directly experiencing the impact of psychiatric hospitalization will be of enormous use. Clearly, further research into the social psychology of such total institutions will both facilitate treatment and deepen understanding.

REFERENCES AND NOTES

1. R. Benedict, *J. Gen. Psychol.* **10**, 59 (1934).
2. T. J. Scheff, *Being Mentally Ill: A Sociological Theory* (Aldine, Chicago, 1966).
3. A. Barry, *Bellevue Is a State of Mind* (Harcourt Brace Jovanovich, New York, 1971); . . .
4. J. Cumming and E. Cumming, *Community Ment. Health* **1**, 135 (1965); . . .
5. W. Mischel, *Personality and Assessment* (Wiley, New York, 1968).

Depression

Depression is a very serious mental disorder, and a number of different theoretical explanations of depression have been proposed. In the mid-1970s, Martin E. P. Seligman proposed the learned helplessness model of depression. This theory suggests that when people come to feel that they have no control over a situation, they feel helpless and tend to give up; they passively accept adverse stimuli. This helplessness can lead to depression.

Seligman (b. 1942) received his Ph.D. in psychology in 1967 from the University of Pennsylvania, where he is currently a professor of psychology. In addition to depression, Seligman has also had an impact on psychology in the areas of learning theory, phobias, and personality and adjustment.

This selection is from chapter 5, "Depression," of Seligman's *Helplessness: On Depression, Development, and Death* (W. H. Freeman, 1975). In it, Seligman describes the causes of, consequences of, and treatments for learned helplessness. Note the emphasis Seligman places on common, everyday occurrences and their role in inducing helplessness. As you read this selection, consider how you react to frustrating situations.

Key Concept: learned helplessness

*L*earned helplessness is caused by learning that responding is independent of reinforcement; so the model suggests that the cause of depression is the belief that action is futile. What kind of events set off reactive depressions? Failure at work and school, death of a loved one, rejection or separation from friends and loved ones, physical disease, financial difficulty, being faced with insoluble problems, and growing old. There are many others, but this list captures the flavor.

I believe that what links these experiences and lies at the heart of depression is unitary: the depressed patient believes or has learned that he cannot control those elements of his life that relieve suffering, bring gratification, or provide nurture—in short, he believes that he is helpless. Consider a few of the precipitating events: What is the meaning of job failure or incompetence at school? Often it means that all of a person's efforts have been in vain, that his responses have failed to achieve his desires. When an individual is rejected by someone he loves, he can no longer control this significant source of gratification and support. When a parent or lover dies, the bereaved is powerless to elicit love from the dead person. Physical disease and growing old are helpless conditions par excellence; the person finds his own responses ineffective and is thrown upon the care of others.

Endogenous depressions [caused by internal factors], while not set off by an explicit helplessness-inducing event, also may involve the belief in helplessness. I suspect that a continuum of susceptibility to this belief may underlie the endogenous-reactive continuum. At the extreme endogenous end, the slightest obstacle will trigger in the depressive a vicious circle of beliefs in how ineffective he is. At the extreme reactive ends, a sequence of disastrous events in which a person is actually helpless is necessary to force the belief that responding is useless. . . .

Is depression a cognitive or an emotional disorder? Neither and both. Clearly, cognitions of helplessness lower mood, and a lowered mood, which may be brought about physiologically, increases susceptibility to cognitions of helplessness; indeed, this is the most insidious vicious circle in depression. In the end, I believe that the cognition-emotion distinction in depression will be untenable. Cognition and emotion need not be separable entities in nature simply because our language separates them. When depression is observed close up, the exquisite interdependence of feelings and thought is undeniable: one does not *feel* depressed without depressing thoughts, nor does one have depressing thoughts without feeling depressed. I suggest that it is a failure of language, not a failure of understanding, that has fostered the confusion about whether depression is a cognitive or an emotional disorder. . . .

In the last few years, many of my students have come to tell me that they felt depressed. Often they attributed their depression to their belief that life had no intrinsic meaning, that the Vietnam war would never end, that the poor and the black are oppressed, or that our leaders are corrupt. These are legitimate concerns and to devote so much thought and energy to them is certainly justifiable. But was the feeling, the actual depression, caused directly by these issues? Clearly, for a poor person, a black, or a student about to be drafted, these propositions could directly cause depression. But most of those I saw were neither poor, nor black, nor about to be drafted; these propositions were remote from their daily lives. Yet they said they were depressed about them—not just concerned or angry, but depressed. To me, this meant that they were feeling bad about something much closer to home, bad about themselves, their capacities, and their daily lives. Such existential depressions are rampant today, I daresay much more than when I was a student ten years ago.

At first it seems paradoxical. More of the good things of life are available now than ever before: more sex, more records, more intellectual stimulation, more books, more buying power. On the other hand, there have always been wars, oppression, corruption, and absurdity; the human condition has been pretty stable along these lines. Why should this particularly fortunate generation find itself especially depressed?

I think the answer may lie in the lack of contingency between the actions of these students and the good things, as well as the negative events, that came their way. These reinforcers came about less through the efforts of the young individuals who benefited from them, than because our society is affluent. They have experienced a minimum of hard work followed by reward. From where does one get a sense of power, worth, and self-esteem? Not from what he owns, but from long experience watching his own actions change the world.

I am claiming, then, that not only trauma occurring independently of response, but noncontingent *positive* events, can produce helplessness and depression. After all, what is the evolutionary significance of mood? Presumably sentient organisms could just as well be constructed without mood—complex computers are. What selective pressure produced feeling and affect? It may be that the hedonic [pleasure] system evolved to goad and fuel instrumental action. I suggest that joy accompanies and motivates effective responding; and that in the absence of effective responding, an aversive state arises, which organisms seek to avoid. It is called depression. It is highly significant that when rats and pigeons are given a choice between getting free food and getting the same food for making responses, they choose to work. Infants smile at a mobile whose movements are contingent on their responses, but not at a noncontingent mobile. Do hunters hunt from a lust to kill or mountain climbers scale peaks for glory? I think not. These activities, because they entail effective instrumental responding, produce joy.

Dysphoria [a state of feeling unwell or unhappy] produced by the cessation of effective responding may explain "success depression." Not infrequently, when a person finally achieves a goal toward which he has been striving for years, depression ensues. Officials elected to public office after arduous campaigns, presidents of the American Psychological Association, successful novelists, and even men who land on the moon can become severely depressed soon after achieving the pinnacle. For a theory of depression by loss of reinforcers, these depressions are paradoxical, since successful individuals continue to receive most of their old reinforcers, plus more new reinforcers than ever before.

This phenomenon is not a paradox for the theory of helplessness. Depressed, successful people tell you that they are now rewarded not for what they're doing, but for who they are or what they *have* done. Having achieved the goal that they strove for, their rewards now come independently of any ongoing instrumental activity. . . .

In summary, I suggest that what produces self-esteem and a sense of competence, and protects against depression, is not only the absolute quality of experience, but the perception that one's own actions controlled the experience. To the degree that uncontrollable events occur, either traumatic or positive, depression will be predisposed and ego strength undermined. To the degree that controllable events occur, a sense of mastery and resistance to depression will result.

CURE OF DEPRESSION AND LEARNED HELPLESSNESS

Forced exposure to the fact that responding produces reinforcement is the most effective way of breaking up learned helplessness. Helplessness also dissipates in *time*. Furthermore, two physiological therapies seem to have an effect: electroconvulsive shock (ECS) broke up helplessness in three out of six dogs, and atropine cannulated to the septum broke it up in cats.

There is no scientifically established panacea for depression. Left alone, depression often dissipates in a few weeks or months; but there are therapies that are reported to alleviate depression and that are consistent with the theory of learned helplessness. According to this view, the central goal in successful therapy should be to have the patient come to believe that his responses produce the gratification he desires—that he is, in short, an effective human being. . . .

A. T. Beck's (1970, 1971) cognitive therapy is aimed at similar goals. In his view, successful manipulations change the negative cognitive set to a more positive one: he argues that the primary task of the therapist is to change the negative expectation of the depressed patient to a more optimistic one, in which the patient comes to believe that his responses will produce the outcomes he wants. . . .

Other therapies are claimed to be successful in alleviating depression and providing the patient with control over important outcomes. The "Tuscaloosa Plan" of a Veterans Administration hospital in Alabama puts severely depressed patients in an "anti-depression room." In this room the patient is subjected to an attitude of "kind firmness": He is told to sand a block of wood, and then reprimanded when he sands against the grain. He then sands with the grain, only to be reprimanded for that. Alternatively, he is told to begin counting about a million little seashells scattered about the room. This systematic harassment continues until the depressed patient finally tells the guard "Get off my back!" or says something like "I've counted my last seashell." He is then promptly let out of the room with apologies. The patient has been forced to emit one of the most powerful responses people have for controlling others— anger, and when this response is dragged out of his depleted repertoire, he is powerfully reinforced. This breaks up depression—lastingly.

Gradual exposure to the response-reinforcement contingencies of work reinforces active behaviors, and may be effective against depression. In a graded-task treatment of depression, E. P. Burgess (1968) first had her patients emit some minimal bit of behavior, like making a telephone call. She emphasizes that it is crucial that the patient succeed, rather than just start and give up. The task requirements were then increased, and the patient was reinforced for successfully completing the tasks by the attention and interest of the therapist. . . .

Individuals often adopt their own strategies for dealing with their own minor depressions. Asking for help and getting it or helping someone else (even caring for a pet) are two strategies that entail gaining control and may alleviate minor depressions. . . .

Many therapies . . . claim to be able to cure depression. But we do not yet have sufficient evidence from well-controlled studies to evaluate the effectiveness of any form of psychotherapy for depression. The evidence I have presented is selected: only those treatments that seem compatible with helplessness were discussed. It is possible that when other therapies work it is because they, too, restore the patient's sense of efficacy. What is needed now is experimental evidence isolating the effective variable in the psychological treatment of depression. It is also essential that untreated control groups be run, since depression dissipates in time, of its own accord.

PREVENTION OF DEPRESSION AND LEARNED HELPLESSNESS

Learned helplessness can be prevented if the subject first masters outcomes before being exposed to their uncontrollability. Can depression be prevented? Almost everyone loses control over some of the outcomes that are significant to him: parents die, loved ones reject him, failure occurs. Everyone becomes at least mildly and transiently depressed in the wake of such events, but why are some people hospitalized by depression for long periods, and others so resilient? . . .

The life histories of those individuals who are particularly resistant to depression, or resilient from depression, may have been filled with mastery; these people may have had extensive experience controlling and manipulating the sources of reinforcement in their lives, and may therefore see the future optimistically. Those people who are particularly susceptible to depression may have had lives relatively devoid of mastery; their lives may have been full of situations in which they were helpless to influence their sources of suffering and relief. . . .

A caveat is in order here, however. While it seems reasonable that extended experience with controllable outcomes will make a person more resilient from depression, how about the person who has met only with success? Is a person whose responses have always succeeded especially susceptible to depression when confronted with situations beyond his control? We all know of people who were stunningly successful in high school, but who collapsed on encountering their first failure in college. Everyone eventually confronts failure and anxiety; too much success with controlling reinforcers, just like too little, might not allow the development and use of responses for coping with failure.

Successful therapy should be preventative. Therapy must not focus just on undoing past problems; it should also arm the patient against future depressions. Would therapy for depression be more successful if it strove explicitly to provide the patient with a wide repertoire of coping responses that he could use at times when he found his usual responses ineffective?

14.1 TED AYLLON

Intensive Treatment of Psychotic Behaviour by Stimulus Satiation and Food Reinforcement

Behavior therapy—the application of reinforcement and punishment to modify behavior—became popular in the 1960s. Today there are many kinds of behavior therapy (behavior modification) methods available.

Researcher Ted Ayllon (b. 1929) was instrumental in the development of behavior therapy, as he was the first to demonstrate how reinforcement could be used to successfully treat mental patients. One of his best-known books is *The Token Economy: A Motivational System for Therapy and Rehabilitation* (1968), coauthored with Nathan Azrin, which describes an early study in behavior therapy in which the authors awarded tokens that were redeemable for privileges to mental patients who demonstrated desired behaviors.

This selection, "Intensive Treatment of Psychotic Behaviour by Stimulus Satiation and Food Reinforcement," was published in *Behaviour Research and Therapy* in 1963. It is based on a research project conducted by Ayllon at the Saskatchewan Hospital in Weyburn, Saskatchewan, Canada. This article describes three experiments in behavior therapy that were conducted with one mental patient. Note that Ayllon focuses on one specific behavior at a time. As you read this article, think about how you might use behavior modification techniques to eliminate unwanted traits in yourself or someone you know.

Key Concept: behavior therapy

INTRODUCTION

Until recently, the effective control of behaviour was limited to the animal laboratory. The extension of this control to human behaviour was made when Lindsley successfully adapted the methodology of operant conditioning to the study of psychotic behaviour (Lindsley, 1956). Following Lindsley's point of departure other investigators have shown that, in its essentials, the behaviour of mental defective individuals (Orlando and Bijou, 1960), stutterers (Flanagan, Goldiamond and Azrin, 1958), mental patients (Hutchinson and Azrin, 1961), autistic (Ferster and DeMyer, 1961), and normal children (Bijou, 1961; Azrin and Lindsley, 1956) is subject to the same controls.

Despite the obvious implications of this research for applied settings there has been a conspicuous lag between the research findings and their application. The greatest limitation to the direct application of laboratory principles has been the absence of control over the subjects' environment. Recently, however, a series of applications in a regulated psychiatric setting has clearly demonstrated the possibilities of behavioural modification (Ayllon and Michael, 1959; Ayllon and Haughton, 1962). Some of the behaviour studied has included repetitive and highly stereotyped responses such as complaining, pacing, refusal to eat, hoarding and many others.

What follows is a demonstration of behaviour techniques for the intensive individual treatment of psychotic behaviour. Specific pathological behaviour patterns of a single patient were treated by manipulating the patient's environment.

The Experimental Ward and Control Over the Reinforcement

This investigation was conducted in a mental hospital ward, the characteristics of which have been described elsewhere (Ayllon and Haughton, 1962). Briefly, this was a female ward to which only authorized personnel were allowed access. The ward staff was made up of psychiatric nurses and untrained aides who carried out the environmental manipulations under the direction of the experimenter. Using a time-sample technique, patients were observed daily every 30 minutes from 7:00 A.M. to 11:00 P.M.

The dining room was the only place where food was available and entrance to the dining room could be regulated. Water was freely available at a drinking fountain on the ward. None of the patients had ground passes or jobs outside the ward.

Subject

The patient was a 47-year-old female patient diagnosed as a chronic schizophrenic. The patient had been hospitalized for 9 years. Upon studying the patient's behaviour on the ward, it became apparent that the nursing staff spent considerable time caring for her. In particular, there were three aspects of her behaviour which seemed to defy solution. The first was stealing food. The second was the hoarding of the ward's towels in her room. The third undesirable aspect of her behaviour consisted in her wearing excessive clothing, e.g. a half-dozen dresses, several pairs of stockings, sweaters, and so on.

In order to modify the patient's behaviour systematically, each of these three types of behaviour (stealing food, hoarding, and excessive dressing) was treated separately.

EXPERIMENT I

Control of Stealing Food by Food Withdrawal

The patient had weighed over 250 pounds for many years. She ate the usual tray of food served to all patients, but, in addition, she stole food from the food counter and from other patients. Because the medical staff regarded her excessive weight as detrimental to her health, a special diet had been prescribed for her. However, the patient refused to diet and continued stealing food. In an effort to discourage the patient from stealing, the ward nurses had spent considerable time trying to persuade her to stop stealing food. As a last resort, the nurses would force her to return the stolen food.

To determine the extent of food stealing, nurses were instructed to record all behaviour associated with eating in the dining room. This record, taken for nearly a month, showed that the patient stole food during two thirds of all meals.

Procedure

The traditional methods previously used to stop the patient from stealing food were discontinued. No longer were persuasion, coaxing, or coercion used.

The patient was assigned to a table in the dining room, and no other patients were allowed to sit with her. Nurses removed the patient from the dining room when she approached a table other than her own, or when she picked up unauthorized food from the dining room counter. In effect, this procedure resulted in the patient missing a meal whenever she attempted to steal food.

Results

... [W]hen withdrawal of positive reinforcement (i.e. meal) was made dependent upon the patient's 'stealing', this response was eliminated in two weeks. Because the patient no longer stole food, she ate only the diet prescribed for her. The effective control of the stealing response is also indicated by the gradual reduction in the patient's body weight. At no time during the patient's 9 years of hospitalization had she weighed less than 230 pounds.... [A]t the conclusion of this treatment her weight stabilized at 180 pounds or 17 per cent loss from her original weight. At this time, the patient's physical condition was regarded as excellent.

Discussion

A principle used in the laboratory shows that the strength of a response may be weakened by the removal of positive reinforcement following the response (Ferster, 1958). In this case, the response was food-stealing and the reinforcer was access to meals. When the patient stole food she was removed from the dining room and missed her meal.

After one year of this treatment, two occasions of food stealing occurred. The first occasion, occurring after one year of not stealing food, took the nurses by surprise and, therefore the patient 'got away' with it. The second occasion occurred shortly thereafter. This time, however, the controlling consequences were in force. The patient missed that meal and did not steal again to the conclusion of this investigation.

Because the patient was not informed or warned of the consequences that followed stealing, the nurses regarded the procedure as unlikely to have much effect on the patient's behaviour. The implicit belief that verbal instructions are indispensable for learning is part of present day psychiatric lore. In keeping with this notion, prior to this behaviour treatment, the nurses had tried to persuade the patient to co-operate in dieting. Because there were strong medical reasons for her losing weight, the patient's refusal to follow a prescribed diet was regarded as further evidence of her mental illness.

EXPERIMENT II

Control of One Form of Hoarding Behaviour Through Stimulus Satiation

During the 9 years of hospitalization, the patient collected large numbers of towels and stored them in her room. Although many efforts had been made to discourage hoarding, this behaviour continued unaltered. The only recourse for the nursing staff was to take away the patient's towels about twice a week.

To determine the degree of hoarding behaviour, the towels in her room were counted three times a week, when the patient was not in her room. This count showed that the number of towels kept in her room ranged from 19 to 29 despite the fact that during this time the nurses continued recovering their towel supply from the patient's room.

Procedure

The routine removal of the towels from the patient's room was discontinued. Instead, a programme of stimulus satiation was carried out by the nurses. Intermittently, throughout the day, the nurses took a towel to the patient when she was in her room and simply handed it to her without any comment. The first week she was given an average of 7 towels daily, and by the third week this number was increased to 60.

Results

The technique of satiation eliminated the towel hoarding. Figure 1 shows the mean number of towels per count found in the patient's room. When the number of towels kept in her room reached the 625 mark, she started taking a few of them out. Thereafter, no more towels were given to her. During the next 12 months the mean number of towels found in her room was 1–5 per week. . . .

Discussion

The procedure used to reduce the amount of towel hoarding bears resemblance to satiation of a reinforcer. A reinforcer loses its effect when an excessive amount of that reinforcer is made available. Accordingly, the response maintained by that reinforcer is weakened. In this application, the towels constituted the reinforcing stimuli. When the number of towels in her room reached 625, continuing to give her towels seemed to make their collection aversive. The patient then proceeded to rid herself of the towels until she had virtually none.

During the first few weeks of satiation, the patient was observed patting her cheeks with a few towels, apparently enjoying them. Later, the patient was observed spending much of her time folding and stacking the approximately 600 towels in her room. A variety of remarks were made by the patient regarding receipt of towels. All verbal statements made by the patient were recorded by the nurse. The following represent typical remarks made during this experiment. First week: As the nurse entered the patient's room carrying a towel, the patient would smile and say, "Oh, you found it for me, thank you". Second week: When the number of towels given to patient increased rapidly, she told the nurses, "Don't give me no more towels. I've got enough". Third week: "Take them towels away. . . . I can't sit here all night and fold towels". Fourth

FIGURE 1

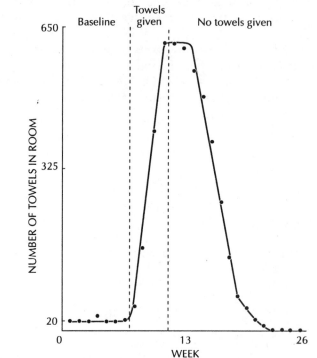

A response, towel hoarding, is eliminated when the patient is given towels in excess. When the number of towels reaches 625 the patient starts to discard them. She continues to do so until the number found in her room averages 1–5 compared to the previous 20 towels per week.

and fifth weeks: "Get these dirty towels out of here". Sixth week: After she had started taking the towels out of her room, she remarked to the nurse, "I can't drag any more of these towels, I just can't do it".

The quality of these remarks suggests that the initial effect of giving towels to the patient was reinforcing. However as the towels increased they ceased to be reinforcing, and presumably became aversive.

The ward nurses, who had undergone a three year training in psychiatric nursing, found it difficult to reconcile the procedure in this experiment with their psychiatric orientation. Most nurses subscribed to the popular psychiatric view which regards hoarding behaviour as a reflection of a deep 'need' for love and security. Presumably, no 'real' behavioural change was possible without meeting the patient's 'needs' first. Even after the patient discontinued hoarding towels in her room, some nurses predicted that the change would not last and that worse behaviour would replace it. Using a time-sampling technique the patient was under continuous observation for over a year after the termination of the satiation programme. Not once during this period did the patient return to hoarding towels. Furthermore, no other behaviour problem replaced hoarding.

Control of an Additional Form of Hoarding Through Food Reinforcement

Shortly after the patient had been admitted to the hospital she wore an excessive amount of clothing which included several sweaters, shawls, dresses, undergarments and stockings. The clothing also included sheets and towels wrapped around her body, and a turban-like head-dress made up of several towels. In addition, the patient carried two to three cups on one hand while holding a bundle of miscellaneous clothing, and a large purse on the other.

To determine the amount of clothing worn by the patient, she was weighed before each meal over a period of two weeks. By subtracting her actual body weight from that recorded when she was dressed, the weight of her clothing was obtained.

Procedure

The response required for reinforcement was stepping on a scale and meeting a predetermined weight. The requirement for reinforcement consisted of meeting a single weight (i.e. her body weight plus a specified number of pounds of clothing). Initially she was given an allowance of 23 pounds over her current body weight. This allowance represented a 2 pound reduction from her usual clothing weight. When the patient exceeded the weight requirement, the nurse stated in a matter-of-fact manner, "Sorry, you weigh too much, you'll have to weigh less". Failure to meet the required weight resulted in the patient missing the meal at which she was being weighed. Sometimes, in an effort to meet the requirement, the patient discarded more clothing than she was required. When this occurred the requirement was adjusted at the next weighing-time to correspond to the limit set by the patient on the preceding occasion.

Results

When food reinforcement is made dependent upon the removal of superfluous clothing the response increases in frequency. Figure 2 shows that the patient gradually shed her clothing to meet the more demanding weight requirement until she dressed normally. At the conclusion of this experiment her clothes weighed 3 pounds compared to the 25 pounds she wore before this treatment.

Some verbal shaping was done in order to encourage the patient to leave the cups and bundles she carried with her. Nurses stopped her at the dining room and said, "Sorry, no things are allowed in the dining room". No mention of clothing or specific items was made to avoid focusing undue attention upon them. Within a week, the patient typically stepped on the scale without her bundle and assorted objects. When her weight was over the limit, the patient was informed that she weighed "too much". She then proceeded to take off a

FIGURE 2

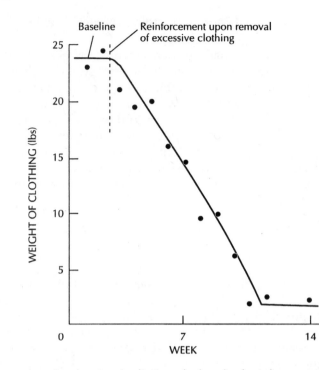

A response, excessive dressing, is eliminated when food reinforcement is made dependent upon removal of superfluous clothing. Once the weight of the clothing worn by the patient drops to 3 pounds it remains stable.

few clothes, stepped on the scale again, and upon meeting the weight requirement, gained access to the dining room. . . .

Discussion

According to the principle of reinforcement a class of responses is strengthened when it is followed by reinforcement. A reinforcer is such when it results in a response increase. In this application the removal of excessive clothing constituted the response and the reinforcer was food (i.e. access to meals). When the patient met the weight requirement she was reinforced by being given access to meals.

At the start of this experiment, the patient missed a few meals because she failed to meet the weight requirement, but soon thereafter she gradually discarded her superfluous clothing. First, she left behind odd items she had carried in her arms, such as bundles, cups and handbags. Next she took off the elaborate headgear and assorted capes or shawls she had worn over her shoulders. Although she had worn 18 pairs of stockings at one time, she eventually shed these also.

During the initial part of this experiment, the patient showed some emotional behaviour, e.g. crying, shouting and throwing chairs around. Because nurses were instructed to "ignore" this emotional behaviour, the patient obtained no sympathy or attention from them. The withholding of social reinforcement for emotional behaviour quickly led to its elimination.

At the conclusion of this behaviour treatment, the patient typically stepped on the scale wearing a dress, undergarments, a pair of stockings and a pair of light shoes. One of the behavioural changes concomitant with the current environmental manipulation was that as the patient began dressing normally she started to participate in small social events in the hospital. This was particularly new to the patient as she had previously remained seclusive spending most of the time in her room.

About this time the patient's parents came to visit her and insisted on taking her home for a visit. This was the first time during the patient's 9 years of hospitalization that her parents had asked to take her out. They remarked that previously they had not been interested in taking her out because the patient's excessive dressing in addition to her weight made her look like a "circus freak".

CONCLUSIONS

The research presented here was conducted under nearly ideal conditions. The variables manipulated (i.e. towels and food) were under full experimental control. Using a time-sample technique the patient was observed daily every 30 minutes from 7.00 A.M. to 11:00 P.M. Nurses and aides carried out these observations which were later analysed in terms of gross behaviour categories. These observations were in force for over a year during which time these three experiments were conducted. The results of these observations indicate that none of the three pathological behaviour patterns (i.e. food stealing, hoarding and excessive dressing) exhibited by the patient were replaced by any undesirable behaviour.

The patient displayed some emotional behaviour in each experiment, but each time it subsided when social reinforcement (i.e. attention) was not forthcoming. The patient did not become violent or seclusive as a consequence of these experiments. Instead, she became socially more accessible to patients and staff. She did not achieve a great deal of social success but she did begin to participate actively in social functions.

A frequent problem encountered in mental hospitals is overeating. In general this problem is solved by prescribing a reduction diet. Many patients, however, refuse to take a reduction diet and continue overeating. When confronted with this behaviour, psychiatric workers generally resort to two types of explanations.

One explanation of overeating points out that only with the active and sincere cooperation of the patient can weight reduction be accomplished. When the patient refuses to co-operate he is regarded as showing more signs of mental illness and all hopes of eliminating overeating come to an end.

Another type of explanation holds that overeating is not the behaviour to be concerned with. Instead, attention is focused on the psychological 'needs' of the patient. These 'needs' are said to be the cause of the observable behaviour, overeating. Therefore the emphasis is on the removal of the cause and not on the symptom or behaviour itself. Whatever theoretical merit these explanations may have, it is unfortunate that they fail to suggest practical ways of treating the behaviour itself. As a consequence, the patient continues to overeat often to the detriment of his health.

The current psychiatric emphasis on the resolution of the mental conflict that is presumably at the basis of the symptoms, is perhaps misplaced. What seems to have been forgotten is that behaviour problems such as those reported here, prevent the patient from being considered for discharge not only by the hospital personnel but also by the patient's relatives. Indeed, as far as the patient's relatives are concerned, the index of improvement or deterioration is the readily observable behaviour and not a detailed account of the mechanics of the mental apparatus.

Many individuals are admitted to mental hospitals because of one or more specific behaviour difficulties and not always because of a generalized 'mental' disturbance. For example, an individual may go into a mental hospital because he has refused to eat for several days, or because he talks to himself incessantly. If the goal of therapy were behavioural rehabilitation, these problems would be treated and normal eating and normal talking reinstated. However, the current emphasis in psychotherapy is on 'mental-conflict resolution' and little or no attention is given to dealing directly with the behavioural problems which prevent the patient from returning to the community.

REFERENCES

Ayllon, T. and Michael, J. (1959) The psychiatric nurse as a behavioural engineer. *J. exp. anal. Behav.* **2**, 323–334.

Ayllon, T. and Haughton, E. (1962) Control of the behaviour of schizophrenic patients by food. *J. Exp. anal. Behav.* **5**, 343–352.

Azrin, N. and Lindsley, O. (1956) The reinforcement of cooperation between children. *J. abnorm. (soc.) Psychol.* **52**, 100–102.

Bijou, S. (1961) Discrimination performance as a baseline for individual analysis of young children. *Child Develpm.* **32**, 160–163.

Ferster, C. B. (1958) Control of behaviour in chimpanzees and pigeons by time out from positive reinforcement. *Psychol. Monogr.* **72**, 1–38.

Ferster, C. and DeMyer, M. (1961) The development of performances in autistic children in an automatically controlled environment. *J. chron. Dis.* **13**, 312–345.

Flanagan, B., Goldiamond, I. and Azrin, N. (1958) Operant stuttering: The control of stuttering behaviour through response-contingent consequences. *J. exp. anal. Behav.* **56**, 49–56.

Hutchinson, R. R. and Azrin, N. H. (1961) Conditioning of mental hospital patients to fixed-ratio schedules of reinforcement. *J. exp. anal. Behav.* **4,** 87–95.

Lindsley, O. R. (1956) Operant conditioning methods applied to research in chronic schizophrenia. *Psychiat. Res. Rep.* **5,** 118–139.

Orlando, R. and Bijou, S. (1960) Single and multiple schedules of reinforcement in developmentally retarded children. *J. exp. anal. Behav.* **3,** 339–348.

The Foundations of a Person-centered Approach

Insight therapy is designed to help people gain an understanding of who they are and why they feel the way they do. One popular type of insight therapy is person-centered therapy (formerly called "client-centered therapy"), which was founded by personality theorist Carl R. Rogers. The main assumption of person-centered therapy is that everyone has the capacity to be psychologically healthy. The therapist's job is to provide a warm, nondirective atmosphere, to draw out the client's thoughts and feelings, and to help the client accept his or her true self.

Rogers (1902–1987), who helped develop the humanistic approach to psychology, earned his Ph.D. in clinical psychology from Columbia University in 1931. He taught at the Ohio State University, the University of Chicago, and the University of Wisconsin before settling at the Center for Studies of the Person in LaJolla, California. Rogers wrote numerous books, including *Client-centered Therapy* (Houghton Mifflin, 1951) and *On Becoming a Person* (Houghton Mifflin, 1961).

This selection is from chapter 6, "The Foundations of a Person-centered Approach," of *A Way of Being* (Houghton Mifflin, 1980). In it, Rogers presents the core characteristics of the person-centered approach to therapy. This book was written many years after Rogers first developed his humanistic approach to therapy; hence, he is able to present a broad view that includes information garnered from his vast experiences. Note how he focuses on both the individual's actualizing tendency and a formative tendency that he sees at work in the entire universe. Taken together, these are the central ideas that make up humanistic psychology. Do you think the person-centered approach works equally well for all people and problems, or do you see certain restrictions?

Key Concept: person-centered approach

I wish to point to two related tendencies which have acquired more and more importance in my thinking as the years have gone by. One of these is an actualizing tendency, a characteristic of organic life. One is a formative tendency in the universe as a whole. Taken together, they are the foundation blocks of the person-centered approach.

Carl R. Rogers

CHARACTERISTICS OF THE PERSON-CENTERED APPROACH

What do I mean by a person-centered approach? It expresses the primary theme of my whole professional life, as that theme has become clarified through experience, interaction with others, and research. I smile as I think of the various labels I have given to this theme during the course of my career—nondirective counseling, client-centered therapy, student-centered teaching, group-centered leadership. Because the fields of application have grown in number and variety, the label "person-centered approach" seems the most descriptive.

The central hypothesis of this approach can be briefly stated. (See Rogers, 1959, for a complete statement.) Individuals have within themselves vast resources for self-understanding and for altering their self-concepts, basic attitudes, and self-directed behavior; these resources can be tapped if a definable climate of facilitative psychological attitudes can be provided.

There are three conditions that must be present in order for a climate to be growth-promoting. These conditions apply whether we are speaking of the relationship between therapist and client, parent and child, leader and group, teacher and student, or administrator and staff. The conditions apply, in fact, in any situation in which the development of the person is a goal. I have described these conditions in previous writings; I present here a brief summary from the point of view of psychotherapy, but the description applies to all of the foregoing relationships.

The first element could be called genuineness, realness, or congruence. The more the therapist is himself or herself in the relationship, putting up no professional front or personal facade, the greater is the likelihood that the client will change and grow in a constructive manner. This means that the therapist is openly being the feelings and attitudes that are flowing within at the moment. The term "transparent" catches the flavor of this condition: the therapist makes himself or herself transparent to the client; the client can see right through what the therapist *is* in the relationship; the client experiences no holding back on the part of the therapist. As for the therapist, what he or she is experiencing is available to awareness, can be lived in the relationship, and can be communicated, if appropriate. Thus, there is a close matching, or congruence, between what is being experienced at the gut level, what is present in awareness, and what is expressed to the client.

The second attitude of importance in creating a climate for change is acceptance, or caring, or prizing—what I have called "unconditional positive regard." When the therapist is experiencing a positive, acceptant attitude toward whatever the client is at that moment, therapeutic movement or change is more likely to occur. The therapist is willing for the client to be whatever immediate feeling is going on—confusion, resentment, fear, anger, courage, love, or pride. Such caring on the part of the therapist is nonpossessive. The therapist prizes the client in a total rather than a conditional way.

The third facilitative aspect of the relationship is empathic understanding. This means that the therapist senses accurately the feelings and personal meanings that the client is experiencing and communicates this understanding to the client. When functioning best, the therapist is so much inside the private world of the other that he or she can clarify not only the meanings of which the client is aware but even those just below the level of awareness. This kind of sensitive, active listening is exceedingly rare in our lives. We think we listen, but very rarely do we listen with real understanding, true empathy. Yet listening, of this very special kind, is one of the most potent forces for change that I know.

How does this climate which I have just described bring about change? Briefly, as persons are accepted and prized, they tend to develop a more caring attitude toward themselves. As persons are empathically heard, it becomes possible for them to listen more accurately to the flow of inner experiencings. But as a person understands and prizes self, the self becomes more congruent with the experiencings. The person thus becomes more real, more genuine. These tendencies, the reciprocal of the therapist's attitudes, enable the person to be a more effective growth-enhancer for himself or herself. There is a greater freedom to be the true, whole person (Rogers, 1962). . . .

A DIRECTIONAL PROCESS IN LIFE

Practice, theory, and research make it clear that the person-centered approach rests on a basic trust in human beings, and in all organisms. There is evidence from many disciplines to support an even broader statement. We can say that there is in every organism, at whatever level, an underlying flow of movement toward constructive fulfillment of its inherent possibilities. In human beings, too, there is a natural tendency toward a more complex and complete development. The term that has most often been used for this is the "actualizing tendency," and it is present in all living organisms.

Whether we are speaking of a flower or an oak tree, of an earthworm or a beautiful bird, of an ape or a person, we will do well, I believe, to recognize that life is an active process, not a passive one. Whether the stimulus arises from within or without, whether the environment is favorable or unfavorable, the behaviors of an organism can be counted on to be in the direction of maintaining, enhancing, and reproducing itself. This is the very nature of the process we call life. This tendency is operative at all times. Indeed, only the presence or absence of this total directional process enables us to tell whether a given organism is alive or dead.

The actualizing tendency can, of course, be thwarted or warped, but it cannot be destroyed without destroying the organism. I remember that in my boyhood, the bin in which we stored our winter's supply of potatoes was in the basement, several feet below a small window. The conditions were unfavorable, but the potatoes would begin to sprout—pale white sprouts, so unlike the healthy green shoots they sent up when planted in the soil in the spring. But these sad, spindly sprouts would grow 2 or 3 feet in length as they reached toward the distant light of the window. The sprouts were, in their bizarre, futile growth, a sort of desperate expression of the directional tendency I have been describing. They would never become plants, never mature, never fulfill their real potential. But under the most adverse circumstances, they were striving to become. Life would not give up, even if it could not flourish. In dealing with clients whose lives have been terribly warped, in working with men and women on the back wards of state hospitals, I often think of those potato sprouts. So unfavorable have been the conditions in which these people have developed that their lives often seem abnormal, twisted, scarcely human. Yet, the directional tendency in them can be trusted. The clue to understanding their behavior is that they are striving, in the only ways that they perceive as available to them, to move toward growth, toward becoming. To healthy persons, the results may seem bizarre and futile, but they are life's desperate attempt to become itself. This potent constructive tendency is an underlying basis of the person-centered approach. . . .

The Trustworthy Base

Thus, to me it is meaningful to say that the substratum of all motivation is the organismic tendency toward fulfillment. This tendency may express itself in the widest range of behaviors and in response to a wide variety of needs. To be sure, certain basic wants must be at least partially met before other needs become urgent. Consequently, the tendency of the organism to actualize itself may at one moment lead to the seeking of food or sexual satisfaction, and yet, unless these needs are overpoweringly great, even these satisfactions will be sought in ways that enhance, rather than diminish, self-esteem. And the organism will also seek other fulfillments in its transactions with the environment. The need for exploration of and producing change in the environment, the need for play and for self-exploration—all of these and many other behaviors are basically expressions of the actualizing tendency.

In short, organisms are always seeking, always initiating, always "up to something." There is one central source of energy in the human organism. This source is a trustworthy function of the whole system rather than of some portion of it; it is most simply conceptualized as a tendency toward fulfillment, toward actualization, involving not only the maintenance but also the enhancement of the organism. . . .

THE FUNCTION OF CONSCIOUSNESS IN HUMAN BEINGS

What part does our awareness have in this formative function? I believe that consciousness has a small but very important part. The ability to focus conscious attention seems to be one of the latest evolutionary developments in our species. This ability can be described as a tiny peak of awareness, of symbolizing capacity, topping a vast pyramid of nonconscious organismic functioning.... It seems that the human organism has been moving toward the more complete development of awareness. It is at this level that new forms are invented, perhaps even new directions for the human species. It is here that the reciprocal relationship between cause and effect is most demonstrably evident. It is here that choices are made, spontaneous forms created. We see here perhaps the highest of the human functions.

Some of my colleagues have said that organismic choice—the nonverbal, subconscious choice of way of being—is guided by the evolutionary flow. I agree; I will even go one step further. I would point out that in psychotherapy we have learned something about the psychological conditions that are most conducive to increasing this highly important self-awareness. With greater self-awareness, a more informed choice is possible, a choice more free from introjects, a *conscious* choice that is even more in tune with the evolutionary flow. Such a person is more potentially aware, not only of the stimuli from outside, but of ideas and dreams, and of the ongoing flow of feelings, emotions, and physiological reactions that he or she senses from within. The greater this awareness, the more surely the person will float in a direction consonant with the directional evolutionary flow.

When a person is functioning in this way, it does not mean that there is a self-conscious awareness of all that is going on within, like the centipede whose movements were paralyzed when it became aware of each of its legs. On the contrary, such a person is free to live a feeling subjectively, as well as be aware of it. The individual might experience love, or pain, or fear, or just live in these experiences subjectively. Or, he or she might abstract self from this subjectivity and realize in awareness, "I am in pain;" "I am afraid;" "I do love." The crucial point is that when a person is functioning fully, there are no barriers, no inhibitions, which prevent the full experiencing of whatever is organismically present. This person is moving in the direction of wholeness, integration, a unified life. Consciousness is participating in this larger, creative, formative tendency.

ALTERED STATES OF CONSCIOUSNESS

But some go even further in their theories. Researchers such as Grof and Grof (1977) and Lilly (1973) believe that persons are able to advance beyond the ordinary level of consciousness. Their studies appear to reveal that in altered states of consciousness, persons feel they are in touch with, and grasp the meaning of, this evolutionary flow. They experience it as tending toward a transcending experience of unity. They picture the individual self as being dissolved in a whole area of higher values, especially beauty, harmony, and love. The person feels at one with the cosmos. Hard-headed research seems to be confirming the mystic's experience of union with the universal.

For me, this point of view is confirmed by my more recent experience in working with clients, and especially in dealing with intensive groups. I described earlier those characteristics of a growth-promoting relationship that have been investigated and supported by research. But recently, my view has broadened into a new area which cannot as yet be studied empirically.

When I am at my best, as a group facilitator or as a therapist, I discover another characteristic. I find that when I am closest to my inner, intuitive self, when I am somehow in touch with the unknown in me, when perhaps I am in a slightly altered state of consciousness, then whatever I do seems to be full of healing. Then, simply my *presence* is releasing and helpful to the other. There is nothing I can do to force this experience, but when I can relax and be close to the transcendental core of me, then I may behave in strange and impulsive ways in the relationship, ways which I cannot justify rationally, which have nothing to do with my thought processes. But these strange behaviors turn out to be *right*, in some odd way: it seems that my inner spirit has reached out and touched the inner spirit of the other. Our relationship transcends itself and becomes a part of something larger. Profound growth and healing and energy are present.

This kind of transcendent phenomenon has certainly been experienced at times in groups in which I have worked, changing the lives of some of those involved. One participant in a workshop put it eloquently: "I found it to be a profound spiritual experience. I felt the oneness of spirit in the community. We breathed together, felt together, even spoke for one another. I felt the power of the 'life force' that infuses each of us—whatever that is. I felt its presence without the usual barricades of 'me-ness' or 'you-ness'—it was like a meditative experience when I feel myself as a center of consciousness, very much a part of the broader, universal consciousness. And yet with that extraordinary sense of oneness, the separateness of each person present has never been more clearly preserved."

Again, as in the description of altered states of consciousness, this account partakes of the mystical. Our experiences in therapy and in groups, it is clear, involve the transcendent, the indescribable, the spiritual. I am compelled to believe that I, like many others, have underestimated the importance of this mystical, spiritual dimension. . . .

A HYPOTHESIS FOR THE FUTURE

As I try to take into account the scope of the various themes I have presented, along with some of the available evidence that appears to support them, I am led to formulate a broad hypothesis. In my mind, this hypothesis is very tentative. But, for the sake of clarity, I will state it in definite terms.

I hypothesize that there is a formative directional tendency in the universe, which can be traced and observed in stellar space, in crystals, in microorganisms, in more complex organic life, and in human beings. This is an evolutionary tendency toward greater order, greater complexity, greater interrelatedness. In humankind, this tendency exhibits itself as the individual moves from a single-cell origin to complex organic functioning, to knowing and sensing below the level of consciousness, to a conscious awareness of the organism and the external world, to a transcendent awareness of the harmony and unity of the cosmic system, including humankind.

It seems to me just possible that this hypothesis could be a base upon which we could begin to build a theory for humanistic psychology. It definitely forms a base for the person-centered approach.

CONCLUSIONS

What I have been saying is that in our work as person-centered therapists and facilitators, we have discovered the attitudinal qualities that are demonstrably effective in releasing constructive and growthful changes in the personality and behavior of individuals. Persons in an environment infused with these attitudes develop more self-understanding, more self-confidence, more ability to choose their behaviors. They learn more significantly, they have more freedom to be and become.

The individual in this nurturing climate is free to choose *any* direction, but actually selects positive and constructive ways. The actualizing tendency is operative in the human being.

It is still further confirming to find that this is not simply a tendency in living systems but is part of a strong formative tendency in our universe, which is evident at all levels.

Thus, when we provide a psychological climate that permits persons to *be*—whether they are clients, students, workers, or persons in a group—we are not involved in a chance event. We are tapping into a tendency which permeates all of organic life—a tendency to become all the complexity of which the organism is capable. And on an even larger scale, I believe we are tuning in to a potent creative tendency which has formed our universe, from the smallest snowflake to the largest galaxy, from the lowly amoeba to the most sensitive and gifted of persons. And perhaps we are touching the cutting edge of our ability to transcend ourselves, to create new and more spiritual directions in human evolution.

This kind of formulation is, for me, a philosophical base for a person-centered approach. It justifies me in engaging in a life-affirming way of being.

REFERENCES

Grof, S., & Grof, J. H. *The human encounter with death.* New York: E. P. Dutton Co., 1977.

Lilly, J. C. *The center of the cyclone.* New York: Bantam Books, 1973. (Originally Julian Press, 1972.)

Rogers, C. R. A theory of therapy, personality and interpersonal relationships. In S. Koch (Ed.), *Psychology: A study of a science* (Vol. 3). New York: McGraw-Hill, 1959, pp. 184–256.

Rogers, C. R. Toward becoming a fully functioning person. In *Perceiving, behaving, becoming,* 1962 Yearbook, Association for Supervision and Curriculum Development. Washington, D.C.: National Education Association, 1962, pp. 21–33.

14.3 AARON T. BECK

Principles of Cognitive Therapy

Aaron T. Beck developed cognitive therapy to help people with psychological disorders caused by negative, self-defeating thoughts and feelings. Cognitive therapists attempt to restructure these negative thoughts and modify the way people view the world. Beck originally developed cognitive therapy to treat depression, but recently he has extended it to the treatment of anxiety disorders.

Beck (b. 1921) earned his M.D. from the Yale University School of Medicine in 1946. He is currently a professor of psychiatry at the University of Pennsylvania. Beck's theories of depression and cognitive therapy have had a significant impact on clinical psychology. He has written a number of books in this area, including *Depression: Clinical, Experimental, and Theoretical Aspects* (1967) and *Anxiety Disorders and Phobias: A Cognitive Perspective* (Basic Books, 1985), coauthored with Gary Emery.

This selection is from chapter 9, "Principles of Cognitive Therapy," of Beck's *Cognitive Therapy and the Emotional Disorders* (International Universities Press, 1976). In it, Beck presents the basic concepts of cognitive therapy, and he provides several examples of how therapists apply these concepts in treating depressed patients. Note that cognitive therapy is effective only for those who are able to think and reason about their problems. Do you think the principles of cognitive therapy can be applied to everyday problems as well as to more serious psychological disorders?

Key Concept: cognitive therapy

We have seen that the common psychological disorders center around certain aberrations in thinking. The challenge to psychotherapy is to offer the patient effective techniques for overcoming his blindspots, his blurred perceptions, and his self-deceptions. A promising lead is provided by the observation that a person responds realistically and effectively to situations not related to his neurosis. His judgments and behavior in areas of experience beyond the boundaries of his specific vulnerability often reflect a high level of functioning. Furthermore, prior to the onset of illness, the neurotic frequently shows adequate development of his conceptual tools for dealing with the problems of living.

Psychological skills (integrating, labeling, and interpreting experience) can be applied to correcting the psychological aberrations. Since the central psychological problem and the psychological *remedy* are both concerned with the patient's thinking (or cognitions), we call this form of help cognitive therapy.

In the broadest sense, cognitive therapy consists of all the approaches that alleviate psychological distress through the medium of correcting faulty conceptions and self-signals. The emphasis on thinking, however, should not obscure the importance of the emotional reactions which are generally the immediate source of distress. It simply means that we get to the person's emotions through his cognitions. By correcting erroneous beliefs, we can damp down or alter excessive, inappropriate emotional reactions.

Many methods of helping a patient make more realistic appraisals of himself and his world are available. The "intellectual" approach consists of identifying the misconceptions, testing their validity, and substituting more appropriate concepts. Often the need for broad attitudinal change emerges with the patient's recognition that the rules he has relied on to guide his thinking and behavior have served to deceive and to defeat him.

The "experiential" approach exposes the patient to experiences that are in themselves powerful enough to change misconceptions. The interactions with other people in certain organized situations, such as encounter groups or conventional psychotherapy, may help a person to perceive others more realistically and consequently to modify his inappropriate maladaptive responses to them. In encounter groups, the interpersonal experiences may cut through maladaptive attitudes blocking the expression of intimate feelings. Similarly, a patient, in response to his psychotherapist's warmth and acceptance, often modifies his stereotyped conception of authority figures. Such a change has been labeled "corrective emotional experience" (Alexander, 1950). Sometimes the effectiveness of psychotherapy is implemented by motivating a patient to enter situations he had previously avoided because of his misconceptions.

The "behavioral" approach encourages the development of specific forms of behavior that lead to more general changes in the way the patient views himself and the real world. Practicing techniques for dealing with people who frighten him, as in "assertive training," not only enables him to regard other people more realistically but enhances his self-confidence. . . .

TARGETS OF COGNITIVE THERAPY

Cognitive techniques are most appropriate for people who have the capacity for introspection and for reflecting about their own thoughts and fantasies. This approach is essentially an extension and a refinement of what people have done to varying degrees since the early stages of their intellectual development. The particular techniques such as labeling objects and situations, setting up hypotheses, and weeding out and testing the hypotheses are based on skills that people apply automatically without being cognizant of the operations involved.

This kind of intellectual function is analogous to the formation of speech in which rules of pronunciation and grammatical construction are applied without consciousness of the rules or of their application. When an adult has to correct a speech disorder or attempts to learn a new language, then he has to concentrate on the formation of words and sentences. Similarly, when he has a problem in interpreting certain aspects of reality, it may be useful for him to focus on the rules he applies in making judgments. In examining a problem area, he finds that the rule is incorrect or that he has been applying it incorrectly.

Since making the incorrect judgments has probably become a deeply ingrained habit, which he may not be conscious of, several steps are required to correct it. First, he has to become aware of what he is thinking. Second, he needs to recognize what thoughts are awry. Then he has to substitute accurate for inaccurate judgments. Finally, he needs feedback to inform him whether his changes are correct. The same kind of sequence is necessary for making behavioral changes, such as improving form in a sport, correcting faults in playing an instrument, or perfecting techniques of persuasion.

To illustrate the process of cognitive change, let us take as a rather gross example a person who is afraid of all strangers. When we explore his reactions, we may find that he is operating under the rule, "All strangers are unfriendly or hostile." In this case, the rule is wrong. On the other hand, he may realize that strangers vary, but he may not have learned to discriminate among friendly strangers, neutral strangers, and unfriendly strangers. In such a case, his trouble is in applying the rule, that is, in converting the available information in a given situation into an appropriate judgment.

It is obvious that not all people who think erroneously need or want to get their thinking straightened out. When a person's erroneous ideation disrupts his life or makes him feel miserable, then he becomes a candidate for some form of help.

The troubles or problems that stimulate a person to seek help may be manifested by distress of a subjective nature (such as anxiety or depression), a difficulty in his overt behavior (such as disabling inhibition or overaggressiveness), or a deficiency in his responses (for example, inability to experience or express warm feelings). The kinds of thinking that underlie these problems may be summarized as follows.

Direct, Tangible Distortions of Reality

Distortions familiar to everybody are the thoughts of a paranoid patient who indiscriminately concludes when he sees other people (even people who are obviously friendly toward him): "Those people want to harm me." Or, as one patient once told me, "I killed President Kennedy."

Less obvious distortions of reality occur in all neuroses. For example, a depressed patient may say, "I have lost my ability to type, to read, to drive a car." However, when he becomes involved in the task, he may find his performance is still adequate. A depressed businessman complains that he is on the verge of bankruptcy, yet examination of his accounts indicates that he is completely solvent and, in fact, is prospering. The label "distortion of reality" is justified because an objective appraisal of the situation contradicts his appraisal.

Other examples of distortions that are relatively simple to check are ideas such as, "I am getting fat" or "I am a burden to my family." Some judgments require greater work to authenticate; for example, "Nobody likes me." The therapeutic sessions, particularly when the patient has been trained to report his automatic thoughts, provide an excellent laboratory for exposing distortions. The therapist may readily identify certain distortions, for instance, when a patient toward whom he has warm feelings reports the thought that he believes the therapist dislikes him.

Illogical Thinking

The patient's appraisal of reality may not be distorted, but his system of making inferences or drawing conclusions from his observations is at fault: He hears distant noise and concludes someone has fired a gun at him. In such instances, the basic premises may be erroneous or the logical processes may be faulty. A depressed patient observed that a faucet was leaking in a bathroom, that the pilot light was out in the stove, and that one of the steps in the staircase was broken. He concluded, "The whole house is deteriorating." The house was in excellent condition (except for these minor problems); he had made a massive overgeneralization. In the same way, patients who have difficulties as a result of their overt behavior often start from inaccurate premises. Someone who consistently alienates potential friends because of his overaggressiveness may operate according to the rule, "If I don't push people around, they will push me around." A timid, inhibited person may be indiscriminately applying the principle, "If I open my mouth, everybody will jump on me."

THE THERAPEUTIC COLLABORATION

Certain factors are important in practically all forms of psychotherapy, but are crucial in cognitive therapy. An obvious primary component of effective psychotherapy is genuine collaboration between the therapist and patient. Moving blindly in separate directions, as sometimes happens, frustrates the therapist and distresses the patient. It is important to realize that the dispenser of the service (the therapist) and the recipient (the patient) may envision the therapeutic relationship quite differently. The patient, for instance, may visualize therapy as a molding of a lump of clay by an omnipotent and omniscient God figure. To minimize such hazards, the patient and therapist should reach a consensus regarding what problem requires help, the goal of therapy, and how they plan to reach that goal. Agreement regarding the nature and duration of therapy is important in determining the outcome. One study has shown, for instance, that a discrepancy between the patient's expectations and the kind of therapy he actually receives militates against a successful outcome. On the other hand, preliminary coaching of the patient about the type of therapy selected appeared to enhance its effectiveness (Orne and Wender, 1968).

Furthermore, the therapist needs to be tuned in to the vicissitudes of the patient's problems from session to session. Patients frequently formulate an "agenda" of topics they want to discuss at a particular session; if the therapist disregards this, he may impose an unnecessary strain on the relationship. For instance, a patient who is disturbed by a recent altercation with his wife may be alienated by the therapist's rigid adherence to a predetermined format such as desensitizing him to his subway phobia.

It is useful to conceive of the patient-therapist relationship as a joint effort. It is not the therapist's function to try to reform the patient; rather, his role is working with the patient against "*it*," the patient's problem. Placing the emphasis on solving problems, rather than his presumed defects or bad habits, helps the patient to examine his difficulties with more detachment and makes him less prone to experience shame, a sense of inferiority, and defensiveness. The partnership concept helps the therapist to obtain valuable "feedback" about the efficacy of therapeutic techniques and further detailed information about the patient's thoughts and feelings. In employing systematic desensitization, for instance, I customarily ask for a detailed description of each image. The patient's report is often very informative and, on many occasions, reveals new problems that had not previously been identified. The partnership arrangement also reduces the patient's tendency to cast the therapist in the role of a superman. Investigators (Rogers, 1951; Truax, 1963) have found that if the therapist shows the following characteristics, a successful outcome is facilitated: genuine warmth, acceptance, and accurate empathy. By working with the patient as a collaborator, the therapist is more likely to show these characteristics than if he assumes a Godlike role.

ESTABLISHING CREDIBILITY

Problems often arise with regard to the suggestions and formulations offered by the therapist. Patients who view the therapist as a kind of superman are likely to accept his interpretations and suggestions as sacred pronouncements. Such bland ingestion of the therapist's hypotheses deprives the therapy of the corrective effect of critical evaluation by the patient.

A different type of problem is presented by patients who automatically react to the therapist's statements with suspicion or skepticism. Such a reaction is most pronounced in paranoid and severely depressed patients. In attempting to expose the distortions of reality, the therapist may become mired in the patient's deeply entrenched belief system. The therapist, therefore, must establish some common ground, find some point of agreement, and then attempt to extend the area of consensus from there. Depressed patients are often concerned that their emotional disorder will persist or get worse, and that they will not respond to therapy. If the therapist assumes a hearty optimistic attitude, the patient may decide that the therapist is either faking, doesn't really understand the gravity of the disorder, or is simply a fool. Similarly, trying to talk a paranoid patient out of his distorted views of reality may drive him to stronger belief in his paranoid ideas. Also, if the paranoid patient begins to regard the therapist as a member of the "opposition," he may assign the therapist a key role in his delusional system.

A more appropriate approach in establishing credibility is to convey a message such as: "You have certain ideas that upset you. They may or they may not be correct. Now let us examine some of them." By assuming a neutral stance, the therapist may then encourage the patient to express his distorted ideas and listen to them attentively. Later he sends up some "trial balloons" to determine whether the patient is ready to examine the evidence regarding these distortions. . . .

Many patients appear to agree with the therapist because of their fears of challenging him and their need to please him. A clue to such superficial consensus is provided by the patient who says, "I agree with you intellectually but not emotionally." Such a statement generally indicates that the therapist's comments or interpretations may seem logical to the patient, but that they do not penetrate the patient's basic belief system (Ellis, 1962). The patient continues to operate according to his faulty ideas. Moreover, strongly authoritative remarks that appeal to the patient's yearning for explanations for his misery may set the stage for disillusionment when the patient finds loopholes in the therapist's formulations. The therapist's confidence in his role as an expert requires a strong admixture of humility. Psychotherapy often involves a good deal of trial-and-error, experimenting with several approaches or formulations to determine which fit the best. . . .

In less extreme cases, it is possible to deal more directly with the irrational ideas. However, the therapist must assess the "latitude of acceptance" of the patient for statements challenging his distorted concepts. Being told that his ideas are wrong might antagonize the patient; but, he might respond favorably to a question such as "Is there another way of interpreting your wife's behavior?" As long as the therapist's attempts at clarification are within an acceptable range, the problem of a credibility gap is minimized.

PROBLEM REDUCTION

Many patients come to the therapist with a host of symptoms or problems. To solve each one of the problems in isolation from the others might very well take a lifetime. A patient may seek help for a variety of ailments such as headaches, insomnia, and anxiety, in addition to interpersonal problems. Identifying problems with similar causes and grouping them together is termed "problem reduction." Once the multifarious difficulties are condensed, the therapist can select the appropriate techniques for each group of problems.

Let us take as an example the patient with multiple phobias. A woman . . . was greatly handicapped by a fear of elevators, tunnels, hills, closed spaces, riding in an open car, riding in an airplane, swimming, walking fast or running, strong winds, and hot, muggy days. Treating each phobia separately with the technique of systematic desensitization might have required innumerable therapeutic sessions, However, it was possible to find a common denominator for her symptoms: an overriding fear of suffocation. She believed that each of the phobic situations presented substantial risk of deprivation of air and consequent suffocation. The therapy was focused directly on this central fear.

The principle of problem reduction is also applicable to a constellation of symptoms that comprise a specific disorder such as depression. By concentrating on certain key components of the disorder, such as low self-esteem or negative expectations, the therapy can produce improvement in mood, overt behavior, appetite, and sleeping pattern. One patient, for instance, revealed that whenever he was in a gratifying situation, he would get some kind of "kill-joy" thought: When he began to feel pleasure from listening to music, he would think, "This record will be over soon," and his pleasure would disappear. When he discovered that he was enjoying a movie, a date with a girl, or just walking, he would think: "This will end soon," and immediately his satisfaction was squelched. In this case, a thought pattern that he could not enjoy things because they would end became the focus of the therapy.

In another case the main focus was the patient's overabsorption in the negative aspects of her life and her selective inattention to positive occurrences. The therapy consisted of having her write down and report back positive experiences. She was surprised to find how many positive, gratifying experiences she had had and subsequently forgotten about.

Another form of problem reduction is the identification of the first link in a chain of symptoms. An interesting feature is that the first link may be a relatively small and easily eradicable problem that leads to consequences that are disabling. For analogy, a person may writhe with pain and be unable to walk, eat, talk at length, or perform minimal constructive activities—because of a speck in the eye. The "speck in the eye" syndrome probably occurs more frequently among psychiatric patients than is generally realized. Because of delay in identifying and dealing with the initial problem, however, the ensuing difficulties become deeply entrenched. A mother who was afraid to leave her children at home with a babysitter continued to be housebound long after the children reached maturity. . . .

LEARNING TO LEARN

. . . [I]t is not necessary for a psychotherapist to help a patient solve every problem that troubles him. Nor is it necessary to anticipate all the problems that may occur after the termination of therapy and to try to work them out in advance. The kind of therapeutic collaboration previously described is conducive to the patient's developing new ways to learn from his experiences and to solve problems. In a sense the patient is "learning to learn." This process has been labeled deutero-learning (Bateson, 1942).

The problem-solving approach to psychotherapy removes much of the responsibility from the therapist and engages the patient more actively in working on his difficulties. By reducing the patient's dependency on the therapist, this approach increases the patient's self-confidence and self-esteem. More important, perhaps, is the fact that the patient's active participation in defining the problem and considering various options yields more ample information than would otherwise be available. His participation in making the decision helps him implement it.

I have explained the problem-solving concept to patients in somewhat the following way: "One of the goals of therapy is to help you learn new ways of approaching problems. Then, as problems come up, you can apply the formulas that you have already learned. For instance, in learning arithmetic you simply learned the fundamental rules. It was not necessary to learn every single possible addition and subtraction. Once you had learned the operations, you could apply them to any arithmetic problem."

To illustrate "learning to learn," let us consider the practical and interpersonal problems that contribute to a patient's various symptoms. A woman, for instance, discovered she was constantly plagued with headaches, feelings of tension, abdominal pain, and insomnia. By focusing on her problems at work and at home, the patient was able to find some solutions for them and became less prone to experience symptoms. As was hoped, she was able to generalize these practical lessons to solving other problems of living, so that it was not necessary for us to work on all her problems in therapy. . . .

"Learning to learn" consists of much more than the patient's adopting a few techniques that can be used in a wide variety of situations. Basically, this approach attempts to remove obstacles that have prevented the patient from profiting from experience and from developing adequate ways of dealing with their internal and external problems. Most of the patients have been blocked in their psychosocial development by certain maladaptive attitudes and patterns of behavior. For instance, the woman with the numerous problems at work and at home had a characteristic response when she was confronted with sensitive interpersonal relations or new practical problems: "I don't know what to do." As a result of therapy, each successful experience tended to erode this negative attitude. Consequently, she was enabled to draw on her ingenuity in meeting and mastering completely different situations.

Patients generally try to avoid situations that cause them uneasiness. Consequently, they do not develop the trial-and-error techniques that are prerequisite to solving many problems. Or by staying out of difficult situations, they do not learn how to rid themselves of their tendency to distort or exaggerate. A person who stays close to home because he fears strangers does not learn how to test the validity of his fears or to discriminate between "safe" strangers and "dangerous" strangers. Through therapy he can learn to "reality-test" not only these fears but other fears as well.

The sense of mastery from solving one problem frequently inspires the patient to approach and solve other problems that he has long avoided. Thus, a bonus of successful therapy is not only freedom from the original problems,

but a thorough psychological change that prepares him to meet new challenges.

Aaron T. Beck

REFERENCES

Alexander, F. (1950). *Psychomatic medicine: Its principles and applications.* New York: W. W. Norton.

Bateson, G. (1942). Social planning and the concept of deutero-learning in relation to the democratic way of life. In: *Science, philosophy, and religion* (2nd Symposium). New York: Harper.

Ellis, A. (1962). *Reason and emotion in psythotherapy.* New York: Lyle Stuart.

Orne, M. T., & Wender, P. H. (1968). Anticipatory socialization for psychotheraphy: Method and rationale. *American Journal of Psychiatry, 124,* 1202–1212.

Rogers, C. R. (1951). *Client-centered therapy: Its current practice, implications, and theory.* Boston: Houghton Mifflin.

Truat, C. B. (1963). Effective ingredients in psychotherapy: an approach to unraveling the patient-therapist interaction. *Journal of Counseling Psychology, 10,* 256–263.

PART SEVEN

Social Processes

CHAPTER 15 Social Psychology

15.1 SOLOMON E. ASCH

Opinions and Social Pressure

People constantly influence one another, and one major type of social influence is conformity. Conformity occurs when an individual changes her or his behavior in order to fit social norms or expectations more closely. People tend to conform to be liked by others and to show appropriate behavior.

Social psychologist Solomon E. Asch (b. 1907) conducted research on conformity in the 1950s. He received his Ph.D. in psychology from Columbia University in 1932, then he taught at the New School for Social Research before going to Rutgers, the State University at New Brunswick, New Jersey. In addition to his research on conformity, Asch is known for his study of personality impression formation.

This selection, "Opinions and Social Pressure," was published in *Scientific American* in 1955. In it, Asch provides the background for his classic research on social conformity and then carefully describes the experiments. As you read the article, note how Asch goes from an idea to an experiment and finally to an explanation of the findings.

Key Concept: social conformity

T hat social influences shape every person's practices, judgments and beliefs is a truism to which anyone will readily assent. A child masters his "native" dialect down to the finest nuances; a member of a tribe of cannibals accepts cannibalism as altogether fitting and proper. All the social sciences take their departure from the observation of the profound effects that groups exert

325

on their members. For psychologists, group pressure upon the minds of individuals raises a host of questions they would like to investigate in detail.

How, and to what extent, do social forces constrain people's opinions and attitudes? This question is especially pertinent in our day. The same epoch that has witnessed the unprecedented technical extension of communication has also brought into existence the deliberate manipulation of opinion and the "engineering of consent." There are many good reasons why, as citizens and as scientists, we should be concerned with studying the ways in which human beings form their opinions and the role that social conditions play.

Studies of these questions began with the interest in hypnosis aroused by the French physician Jean Martin Charcot (a teacher of Sigmund Freud) toward the end of the 19th century. Charcot believed that only hysterical patients could be fully hypnotized, but this view was soon challenged by two other physicians, Hyppolyte Bernheim and A. A. Liébault, who demonstrated that they could put most people under the hypnotic spell. Bernheim proposed that hypnosis was but an extreme form of a normal psychological process which became known as "suggestibility." It was shown that monotonous reiteration of instructions could induce in normal persons in the waking state involuntary bodily changes such as swaying or rigidity of the arms, and sensations such as warmth and odor.

It was not long before social thinkers seized upon these discoveries as a basis for explaining numerous social phenomena, from the spread of opinion to the formation of crowds and the following of leaders. The sociologist Gabriel Tarde summed it all up in the aphorism: "Social man is a somnambulist."

When the new discipline of social psychology was born at the beginning of this century, its first experiments were essentially adaptations of the suggestion demonstration. The technique generally followed a simple plan. The subjects, usually college students, were asked to give their opinions or preferences concerning various matters; some time later they were again asked to state their choices, but now they were also informed of the opinions held by authorities or large groups of their peers on the same matters. (Often the alleged consensus was fictitious.) Most of these studies had substantially the same result: confronted with opinions contrary to their own, many subjects apparently shifted their judgments in the direction of the views of the majorities or the experts. The late psychologist Edward L. Thorndike reported that he had succeeded in modifying the esthetic preferences of adults by this procedure. Other psychologists reported that people's evaluations of the merit of a literary passage could be raised or lowered by ascribing the passage to different authors. Apparently the sheer weight of numbers or authority sufficed to change opinions, even when no arguments for the opinions themselves were provided.

Now the very ease of success in these experiments arouses suspicion. Did the subjects actually change their opinions, or were the experimental victories scored only on paper? On grounds of common sense, one must question whether opinions are generally as watery as these studies indicate. There is some reason to wonder whether it was not the investigators who, in their enthusiasm for a theory, were suggestible, and whether the ostensibly gullible subjects were not providing answers which they thought good subjects were expected to give.

The investigations were guided by certain underlying assumptions, which today are common currency and account for much that is thought and said about the operations of propaganda and public opinion. The assumptions are that people submit uncritically and painlessly to external manipulation by suggestion or prestige, and that any given idea or value can be "sold" or "unsold" without reference to its merits. We should be skeptical, however, of the supposition that the power of social pressure necessarily implies uncritical submission to it: independence and the capacity to rise above group passion are also open to human beings. Further, one may question on psychological grounds whether it is possible as a rule to change a person's judgment of a situation or an object without first changing his knowledge or assumptions about it.

In what follows I shall describe some experiments in an investigation of the effects of group pressure which was carried out recently with the help of a number of my associates. The tests not only demonstrate the operations of group pressure upon individuals but also illustrate a new kind of attack on the problem and some of the more subtle questions that it raises.

A group of seven to nine young men, all college students, are assembled in a classroom for a "psychological experiment" in visual judgment. The experimenter informs them that they will be comparing the lengths of lines. He shows two large white cards [see Figure 1]. On one is a single vertical black line—the standard whose length is to be matched. On the other card are three vertical lines of various lengths. The subjects are to choose the one that is of the same length as the line on the other card. One of the three actually is of the same length; the other two are substantially different, the difference ranging from three quarters of an inch to an inch and three quarters.

The experiment opens uneventfully. The subjects announce their answers in the order in which they have been seated in the room, and on the first round every person chooses the same matching line. Then a second set of cards is

FIGURE 1

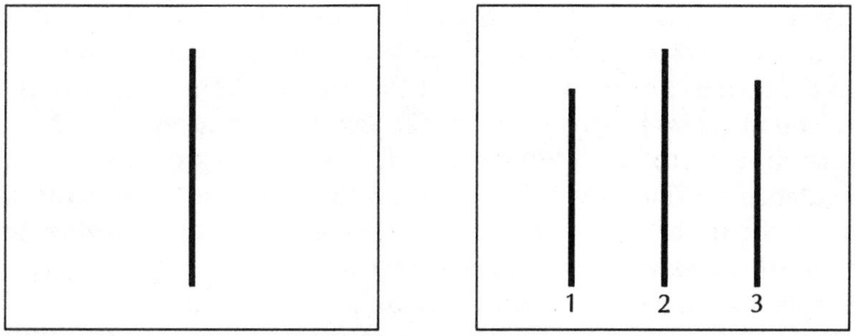

Subjects were shown two cards. One bore a standard line. The other bore three lines, one of which was the same length as the standard. The subjects were asked to choose this line.

exposed; again the group is unanimous. The members appear ready to endure politely another boring experiment. On the third trial there is an unexpected disturbance. One person near the end of the group disagrees with all the others in his selection of the matching line. He looks surprised, indeed incredulous, about the disagreement. On the following trial he disagrees again, while the others remain unanimous in their choice. The dissenter becomes more and more worried and hesitant as the disagreement continues in succeeding trials; he may pause before announcing his answer and speak in a low voice, or he may smile in an embarrassed way.

What the dissenter does not know is that all the other members of the group were instructed by the experimenter beforehand to give incorrect answers in unanimity at certain points. The single individual who is not a party to this prearrangement is the focal subject of our experiment. He is placed in a position in which, while he is actually giving the correct answers, he finds himself unexpectedly in a minority of one, opposed by a unanimous and arbitrary majority with respect to a clear and simple fact. Upon him we have brought to bear two opposed forces: the evidence of his senses and the unanimous opinion of a group of his peers. Also, he must declare his judgments in public, before a majority which has also stated its position publicly.

The instructed majority occasionally reports correctly in order to reduce the possibility that the naive subject will suspect collusion against him. (In only a few cases did the subject actually show suspicion; when this happened, the experiment was stopped and the results were not counted.) There are 18 trials in each series, and on 12 of these the majority responds erroneously.

How do people respond to group pressure in this situation? I shall report first the statistical results of a series in which a total of 123 subjects from three institutions of higher learning (not including my own Swarthmore College) were placed in the minority situation described above.

Two alternatives were open to the subject: he could act independently, repudiating the majority, or he could go along with the majority, repudiating the evidence of his senses. Of the 123 put to the test, a considerable percentage yielded to the majority. Whereas in ordinary circumstances individuals matching the lines will make mistakes less than 1 per cent of the time, under group pressure the minority subjects swung to acceptance of the misleading majority's wrong judgments in 36.8 per cent of the selections.

Of course individuals differed in response. At one extreme, about one quarter of the subjects were completely independent and never agreed with the erroneous judgments of the majority. At the other extreme, some individuals went with the majority nearly all the time. The performances of individuals in this experiment tend to be highly consistent. Those who strike out on the path of independence do not, as a rule, succumb to the majority even over an extended series of trials, while those who choose the path of compliance are unable to free themselves as the ordeal is prolonged.

The reasons for the startling individual differences have not yet been investigated in detail. At this point we can only report some tentative generalizations from talks with the subjects, each of whom was interviewed at the end of the experiment. Among the independent individuals were many who held fast because of staunch confidence in their own judgment. The most significant fact about them was not absence of responsiveness to the majority but a capacity to recover from doubt and to reestablish their equilibrium. Others who acted independently came to believe that the majority was correct in its answers, but they continued their dissent on the simple ground that it was their obligation to call the play as they saw it.

Among the extremely yielding persons we found a group who quickly reached the conclusion: "I am wrong, they are right." Others yielded in order "not to spoil your results." Many of the individuals who went along suspected that the majority were "sheep" following the first responder, or that the majority were victims of an optical illusion; nevertheless, these suspicions failed to free them at the moment of decision. More disquieting were the reactions of subjects who construed their difference from the majority as a sign of some general deficiency in themselves, which at all costs they must hide. On this basis they desperately tried to merge with the majority, not realizing the longer-range consequences to themselves. All the yielding subjects underestimated the frequency with which they conformed.

Which aspect of the influence of a majority is more important—the size of the majority or its unanimity? The experiment was modified to examine this question. In one series the size of the opposition was varied from one to 15 persons. The results showed a clear trend. When a subject was confronted with only a single individual who contradicted his answers, he was swayed little: he continued to answer independently and correctly in nearly all trials. When the opposition was increased to two, the pressure became substantial: minority subjects now accepted the wrong answer 13.6 per cent of the time. Under the pressure of a majority of three, the subjects' errors jumped to 31.8 per cent. But further increases in the size of the majority apparently did not increase the weight of the pressure substantially. Clearly the size of the opposition is important only up to a point.

Disturbance of the majority's unanimity had a striking effect. In this experiment the subject was given the support of a truthful partner—either another individual who did not know of the prearranged agreement among the rest of the group, or a person who was instructed to give correct answers throughout.

The presence of a supporting partner depleted the majority of much of its power. Its pressure on the dissenting individual was reduced to one fourth: that is, subjects answered incorrectly only one fourth as often as under the pressure of a unanimous majority. The weakest persons did not yield as readily. Most interesting were the reactions to the partner. Generally the feeling toward him was one of warmth and closeness; he was credited with inspiring confidence. However, the subjects repudiated the suggestion that the partner decided them to be independent.

Was the partner's effect a consequence of his dissent, or was it related to his accuracy? We now introduced into the experimental group a person who was instructed to dissent from the majority but also to disagree with the subject. In some experiments the majority was always to choose the worst of the comparison lines and the instructed dissenter to pick the line that was closer to

the length of the standard one; in others the majority was consistently intermediate and the dissenter most in error. In this manner we were able to study the
relative influence of "compromising" and "extremist" dissenters.

Again the results are clear. When a moderate dissenter is present the
effect of the majority on the subject decreases by approximately one third, and
extremes of yielding disappear. Moreover, most of the errors the subjects do
make are moderate, rather than flagrant. In short, the dissenter largely controls
the choice of errors. To this extent the subjects broke away from the majority
even while bending to it.

On the other hand, when the dissenter always chose the line that was
more flagrantly different from the standard, the results were of quite a different
kind. The extremist dissenter produced a remarkable freeing of the subjects;
their errors dropped to only 9 per cent. Furthermore, all the errors were of the
moderate variety. We were able to conclude that dissent *per se* increased independence and moderated the errors that occurred, and that the direction of
dissent exerted consistent effects.

In all the foregoing experiments each subject was observed only in a single
setting. We now turned to studying the effects upon a given individual of a
change in the situation to which he was exposed. The first experiment examined the consequences of losing or gaining a partner. The instructed partner
began by answering correctly on the first six trials. With his support the subject
usually resisted pressure from the majority: 18 of 27 subjects were completely
independent. But after six trials the partner joined the majority. As soon as he
did so, there was an abrupt rise in the subjects' errors. Their submission to the
majority was just about as frequent as when the minority subject was opposed
by a unanimous majority throughout.

It was surprising to find that the experience of having had a partner and
of having braved the majority opposition with him had failed to strengthen the
individuals' independence. Questioning at the conclusion of the experiment
suggested that we had overlooked an important circumstance; namely, the
strong specific effect of "desertion" by the partner to the other side. We therefore changed the conditions so that the partner would simply leave the group
at the proper point. (To allay suspicion it was announced in advance that he
had an appointment with the dean.) In this form of the experiment, the partner's effect outlasted his presence. The errors increased after his departure, but
less markedly than after a partner switched to the majority.

In a variant of this procedure the trials began with the majority unanimously giving correct answers. Then they gradually broke away until on the
sixth trial the naive subject was alone and the group unanimously against him.
As long as the subject had anyone on his side, he was almost invariably independent, but as soon as he found himself alone, the tendency to conform to the
majority rose abruptly.

As might be expected, an individual's resistance to group pressure in
these experiments depends to a considerable degree on how wrong the majority is. We varied the discrepancy between the standard line and the other lines
systematically, with the hope of reaching a point where the error of the major-

ity would be so glaring that every subject would repudiate it and choose independently. In this we regretfully did not succeed. Even when the difference between the lines was seven inches, there were still some who yielded to the error of the majority.

The study provides clear answers to a few relatively simple questions, and it raises many others that await investigation. We would like to know the degree of consistency of persons in situations which differ in content and structure. If consistency of independence or conformity in behavior is shown to be a fact, how is it functionally related to qualities of character and personality? In what ways is independence related to sociological or cultural conditions? Are leaders more independent than other people, or are they adept at following their followers? These and many other questions may perhaps be answerable by investigations of the type described here.

Life in society requires consensus as an indispensable condition. But consensus, to be productive, requires that each individual contribute independently out of his experience and insight. When consensus comes under the dominance of conformity, the social process is polluted and the individual at the same time surrenders the powers on which his functioning as a feeling and thinking being depends. That we have found the tendency to conformity in our society so strong that reasonably intelligent and well-meaning young people are willing to call white black is a matter of concern. It raises questions about our ways of education and about the values that guide our conduct.

Yet anyone inclined to draw too pessimistic conclusions from this report would do well to remind himself that the capacities for independence are not to be underestimated. He may also draw some consolation from a further observation: those who participated in this challenging experiment agreed nearly without exception that independence was preferable to conformity.

An Introduction to the Theory of Dissonance

Psychologists have studied attitude development and attitude change for many years. In the late 1950s, Leon Festinger proposed a somewhat radical view (at the time) of attitude change. According to his theory of cognitive dissonance, people experience tension when they hold two inconsistent ideas, and this state creates a drive to reduce the dissonance, or tension.

Festinger (1919–1989) obtained his Ph.D. in psychology from the State University of Iowa in 1942. He taught at several universities, including Stanford University, before going to the New School for Social Research in New York City in 1968. Although Festinger contributed numerous theories to social psychology, none has had greater impact than his theory of cognitive dissonance.

This selection is from chapter 1, "An Introduction to the Theory of Dissonance," of Festinger's *A Theory of Cognitive Dissonance* (Stanford University Press, 1957). As well as providing a readable introduction to the development of dissonance, Festinger offers some possible techniques for reducing dissonance in everyday situations. As you read this selection, think about what variables influence cognitive dissonance in your daily life.

Key Concept: cognitive dissonance

*I*t has frequently been implied, and sometimes even pointed out, that the individual strives toward consistency within himself. His opinions and attitudes, for example, tend to exist in clusters that are internally consistent. Certainly one may find exceptions. . . . [S]omeone may think little children should be quiet and unobtrusive and yet may be quite proud when his child aggressively captures the attention of his adult guests. When such inconsistencies are found to exist, they may be quite dramatic, but they capture our interest primarily because they stand out in sharp contrast against a background of consistency. It is still overwhelmingly true that related opinions or attitudes are consistent with one another. Study after study reports such consistency among one person's political attitudes, social attitudes, and many others.

There is the same kind of consistency between what a person knows or believes and what he does. A person who believes a college education is a good thing will very likely encourage his children to go to college; a child who knows he will be severely punished for some misdemeanor will not commit it or at least will try not to be caught doing it. This is not surprising, of course; it is so much the rule that we take it for granted. Again what captures our attention are the exceptions to otherwise consistent behavior. A person may know that smoking is bad for him and yet continue to smoke; many persons commit crimes even though they know the high probability of being caught and the punishment that awaits them.

Granting that consistency is the usual thing, perhaps overwhelmingly so, what about these exceptions which come to mind so readily? Only rarely, if ever, are they accepted psychologically *as inconsistencies* by the person involved. Usually more or less successful attempts are made to rationalize them. Thus, the person who continues to smoke, knowing that it is bad for his health, may also feel (*a*) he enjoys smoking so much it is worth it; (*b*) the chances of his health suffering are not as serious as some would make out; (*c*) he can't always avoid every possible dangerous contingency and still live; and (*d*) perhaps even if he stopped smoking he would put on weight which is equally bad for his health. So, continuing to smoke is, after all, consistent with his ideas about smoking.

But persons are not always successful in explaining away or in rationalizing inconsistencies to themselves. For one reason or another, attempts to achieve consistency may fail. The inconsistency then simply continues to exist. Under such circumstances—that is, in the presence of an inconsistency—there is psychological discomfort.

The basic hypotheses . . . can now be stated. First, I will replace the word "inconsistency" with a term which has less of a logical connotation, namely, *dissonance*. I will likewise replace the word "consistency" with a more neutral term, namely, *consonance*. A more formal definition of these terms will be given shortly; for the moment, let us try to get along with the implicit meaning they have acquired as a result of the preceding discussion.

The basic hypotheses I wish to state are as follows:

1. The existence of dissonance, being psychologically uncomfortable, will motivate the person to try to reduce the dissonance and achieve consonance.
2. When dissonance is present, in addition to trying to reduce it, the person will actively avoid situations and information which would likely increase the dissonance.

Before proceeding to develop this theory of dissonance and the pressures to reduce it, it would be well to clarify the nature of dissonance, what kind of a concept it is, and where the theory concerning it will lead. The two hypotheses stated above provide a good starting point for this clarification. While they refer here specifically to dissonance, they are in fact very general hypotheses. In place of "dissonance" one can substitute other notions similar in nature, such as "hunger," "frustration," or "disequilibrium," and the hypotheses would still make perfectly good sense.

In short, I am proposing that dissonance, that is, the existence of nonfitting relations among cognitions, is a motivating factor in its own right. By the term *cognition* . . . I mean any knowledge, opinion, or belief about the environment, about oneself, or about one's behavior. Cognitive dissonance can be seen as an antecedent condition which leads to activity oriented toward dissonance reduction just as hunger leads to activity oriented toward hunger reduction. It is a very different motivation from what psychologists are used to dealing with but, as we shall see, nonetheless powerful. . . .

THE OCCURRENCE AND PERSISTENCE OF DISSONANCE

Why and how does dissonance ever arise? How does it happen that persons sometimes find themselves doing things that do not fit with what they know, or having opinions that do not fit with other opinions they hold? An answer to this question may be found in discussing two of the more common situations in which dissonance may occur.

1. New events may happen or new information may become known to a person, creating at least a momentary dissonance with existing knowledge, opinion, or cognition concerning behavior. Since a person does not have complete and perfect control over the information that reaches him and over events that can happen in his environment, such dissonances may easily arise. Thus, for example, a person may plan to go on a picnic with complete confidence that the weather will be warm and sunny. Nevertheless, just before he is due to start, it may begin to rain. The knowledge that it is now raining is dissonant with his confidence in a sunny day and with his planning to go to a picnic. Or, as another example, a person who is quite certain in his knowledge that automatic transmissions on automobiles are inefficient may accidentally come across an article praising automatic transmissions. Again, at least a momentary dissonance is created.

2. Even in the absence of new, unforeseen events or information, the existence of dissonance is undoubtedly an everyday condition. Very few things are all black or all white; very few situations are clear-cut enough so that opinions or behaviors are not to some extent a mixture of contradictions. Thus, a midwestern farmer who is a Republican may be opposed to his party's position on farm price supports; a person buying a new car may prefer the economy of one model but the design of another; a person deciding on how to invest his money may know that the outcome of his investment depends upon economic conditions beyond his control. Where an opinion must be formed or a decision taken, some dissonance is almost unavoidably created between the cognition of the action taken and those opinions or knowledges which tend to point to a different action.

There is, then, a fairly wide variety of situations in which dissonance is nearly unavoidable. . . . If the hypotheses stated above are correct, then as soon as dissonance occurs there will be pressures to reduce it.

The presence of dissonance gives rise to pressures to reduce or eliminate the dissonance. The strength of the pressures to reduce the dissonance is a function of the magnitude of the dissonance. In other words, dissonance acts in the same way as a state of drive or need or tension. The presence of dissonance leads to action to reduce it just as, for example, the presence of hunger leads to action to reduce the hunger. Also, similar to the action of a drive, the greater the dissonance, the greater will be the intensity of the action to reduce the dissonance and the greater the avoidance of situations that would increase the dissonance.

In order to be specific about how the pressure to reduce dissonance would manifest itself, it is necessary to examine the possible ways in which existing dissonance can be reduced or eliminated. In general, if dissonance exists between two elements, this dissonance can be eliminated by changing one of those elements. The important thing is how these changes may be brought about. . . .

Changing a Behavioral Cognitive Element

When the dissonance under consideration is between an element corresponding to some knowledge concerning environment (environmental element) and a behavioral element, the dissonance can, of course, be eliminated by changing the behavioral cognitive element in such a way that it is consonant with the environmental element. . . . This method of reducing or eliminating dissonance is a very frequent occurrence. Our behavior and feelings are frequently modified in accordance with new information. If a person starts out on a picnic and notices that it has begun to rain, he may very well turn around and go home. There are many persons who do stop smoking if and when they discover it is bad for their health.

It may not always be possible, however, to eliminate dissonance or even to reduce it materially by changing one's action or feeling. The difficulty of changing the behavior may be too great, or the change, while eliminating some dissonances, may create a whole host of new ones.

Changing an Environmental Cognitive Element

Just as it is possible to change a behavioral cognitive element by changing the behavior which this element mirrors, it is sometimes possible to change an *environmental* cognitive element by changing the situation to which that element corresponds. This, of course, is much more difficult than changing one's behavior, for one must have a sufficient degree of control over one's environment—a relatively rare occurrence.

Changing the environment itself in order to reduce dissonance is more feasible when the social environment is in question than when the physical environment is involved. . . .

Whenever there is sufficient control over the environment, this method of reducing dissonance may be employed. For example, a person who is habitually very hostile toward other people may surround himself with persons who provoke hostility. His cognitions about the persons with whom he associates are then consonant with the cognitions corresponding to his hostile behavior. The possibilities of manipulating the environment are limited, however, and most endeavors to change a cognitive element will follow other lines. . . .

Adding New Cognitive Elements

It is clear that in order to eliminate a dissonance completely, some cognitive element must be changed. It is also clear that this is not always possible. But even if it is impossible to eliminate a dissonance, it is possible to reduce the total magnitude of dissonance by adding new cognitive elements. Thus, for example, if dissonance existed between some cognitive elements concerning the effects of smoking and cognition concerning the behavior of continuing to smoke, the total dissonance could be reduced by adding new cognitive elements that are consonant with the fact of smoking. In the presence of such dissonance, then, a person might be expected to actively seek new information that would reduce the total dissonance and, at the same time, to avoid new information that might increase the existing dissonance. Thus, to pursue the example, the person might seek out and avidly read any material critical of the research which purported to show that smoking was bad for one's health. At the same time he would avoid reading material that praised this research. (If he unavoidably came in contact with the latter type of material, his reading would be critical indeed.)

Actually, the possibilities for adding new elements which would reduce the existing dissonances are broad. Our smoker, for example, could find out all about accidents and death rates in automobiles. Having then added the cognition that the danger from smoking is negligible compared to the danger he runs driving a car, his dissonance would also have been somewhat reduced. Here the total dissonance is reduced by reducing the *importance* of the existing dissonance. . . .

Before moving on, it is worth while to emphasize again that the presence of pressures to reduce dissonance, or even activity directed toward such reduction, does not guarantee that the dissonance will be reduced. A person may not be able to find the social support needed to change a cognitive element, or he may not be able to find new elements which reduce the total dissonance. In fact, it is quite conceivable that in the process of trying to reduce dissonance, it might even be increased. This will depend upon what the person encounters while attempting to reduce the dissonance. The important point to be made so far is that in the presence of a dissonance, one will be able to observe the *attempts* to reduce it. If attempts to reduce dissonance fail, one should be able to observe symptoms of psychological discomfort, provided the dissonance is appreciable enough so that the discomfort is clearly and overtly manifested. . . .

The discussion thus far has focused on the tendencies to reduce or eliminate dissonance and the problems involved in achieving such reduction. Under certain circumstances there are also strong and important tendencies to avoid increases of dissonance or to avoid the occurrence of dissonance altogether. Let us now turn our attention to a consideration of these circumstances and the manifestations of the avoidance tendencies which we might expect to observe.

The avoidance of an increase in dissonance comes about, of course, as a result of the existence of dissonance. This avoidance is especially important where, in the process of attempting to reduce dissonance, support is sought for a new cognitive element to replace an existing one or where new cognitive elements are to be added. In both these circumstances, the seeking of support and the seeking of new information must be done in a highly selective manner. A person would initiate discussion with someone he thought would agree with the new cognitive element but would avoid discussion with someone who might agree with the element that he was trying to change. A person would expose himself to sources of information which he expected would add new elements which would increase consonance but would certainly avoid sources which would increase dissonance. . . .

The operation of a fear of dissonance may also lead to a reluctance to commit oneself behaviorally. There is a large class of actions that, once taken, are difficult to change. Hence, it is possible for dissonances to arise and to mount in intensity. A fear of dissonance would lead to a reluctance to take action—a reluctance to commit oneself. Where decision and action cannot be indefinitely delayed, the taking of action may be accompanied by a cognitive negation of the action. Thus, for example, a person who buys a new car and is very afraid of dissonance may, immediately following the purchase, announce his conviction that he did the wrong thing. Such strong fear of dissonance is probably relatively rare, but it does occur. Personality differences with respect to fear of dissonance and the effectiveness with which one is able to reduce dissonance are undoubtedly important in determining whether or not such avoidance of dissonance is likely to happen.

The Process of Obedience: Applying the Analysis to the Experiment

Obedience is a type of social influence in which an individual shows the behavior required by a command. One of the best-known studies on obedience was performed by Stanley Milgram at Yale University in 1963. In this series of experiments, Milgram told subjects that they were to be the teachers in a learning experiment and that they were to administer increasing levels of electric shocks to the "learner" (Milgram's accomplice) for each incorrect answer (which the learner deliberately gave the majority of the time). Surprisingly, Milgram discovered that 65 percent of the subjects, apparently responding to Milgram's authority, delivered what they believed to be the maximum level of electricity (marked "Danger—Severe Shock"), despite the learner's screaming protests and eventual death-like silence. This study has been a subject of controversy during the past three decades because of its ethical considerations as well as its social implications.

Milgram (1933–1984) studied under social psychologist Solomon E. Asch and earned his Ph.D. from Harvard University in 1960. He taught at Yale University and Harvard University before moving to the Graduate Center of the City University of New York in 1967. Milgram, a very creative social psychologist, has studied social communication, prejudice, interpersonal relationships, and, of course, obedience.

This selection is from chapter 11, "The Process of Obedience: Applying the Analysis to the Experiment," of Milgram's *Obedience to Authority: An Experimental View* (HarperCollins, 1974). In it, Milgram, who was dismayed by the results of his obedience study, attempts to explain the conditions that lead to such complete obedience in people. As you read this selection, consider the extent to which you obey in today's society.

Key Concept: obedience

First, we need to consider forces that acted on the person before he became our subject, forces that shaped his basic orientation to the social world and laid the groundwork for obedience.

Family

The subject has grown up in the midst of structures of authority. From his very first years, he was exposed to parental regulation, whereby a sense of respect for adult authority was inculcated. Parental injunctions are also the source of moral imperatives. However, when a parent instructs a child to follow a moral injunction, he is, in fact, doing two things. First, he presents a specific ethical content to be followed. Second, he trains the child to comply with authoritative injunctions per se. Thus, when a parent says, "Don't strike smaller children," he provides not one imperative but two. The first concerns the manner in which the recipient of the command is to treat smaller children (the prototype of those who are helpless and innocent); the second and implicit imperative is, "And obey me!" Thus, the very genesis of our moral ideals is inseparable from the inculcation of an obedient attitude. Moreover, the demand for obedience remains the only consistent element across a variety of specific commands, and thus tends to acquire a prepotent strength relative to any particular moral content.

Institutional Setting

As soon as the child emerges from the cocoon of the family, he is transferred to an *institutional system of authority*, the school. Here, the child learns not merely a specific curriculum but also how to function within an organizational framework. His actions are, to a significant degree, regulated by his teachers, but he can perceive that they in turn are subjected to the discipline and requirements of a headmaster. The student observes that arrogance is not passively accepted by authority but severely rebuked and that deference is the only appropriate and comfortable response to authority.

The first twenty years of the young person's life are spent functioning as a subordinate element in an authority system, and upon leaving school, the male usually moves into either a civilian job or military service. On the job, he learns that although some discreetly expressed dissent is allowable, an underlying posture of submission is required for harmonious functioning with superiors. However much freedom of detail is allowed the individual, the situation is defined as one in which he is to do a job prescribed by someone else.

While structures of authority are of necessity present in all societies, advanced or primitive, modern society has the added characteristic of teaching individuals to respond to *impersonal* authorities.... [T]he modern industrial world forces individuals to submit to impersonal authorities, so that responses are made to abstract rank, indicated by an insignia, uniform or title.

Rewards

Throughout this experience with authority, there is continual confrontation with a reward structure in which compliance with authority has been generally rewarded, while failure to comply has most frequently been punished. Although many forms of reward are meted out for dutiful compliance, the most ingenious is this: the individual is moved up a niche in the hierarchy, thus both motivating the person and perpetuating the structure simultaneously. This form of reward, "the promotion," carries with it profound emotional gratification for the individual but its special feature is the fact that it ensures the continuity of the hierarchical form.

The net result of this experience is the *internalization of the social order*— that is, internalizing the set of axioms by which social life is conducted. And the chief axiom is: do what the man in charge says. Just as we internalize grammatical rules, and can thus both understand and produce new sentences, so we internalize axiomatic rules of social life which enable us to fulfill social requirements in novel situations. In any hierarchy of rules, that which requires compliance to authority assumes a paramount position.

Among the antecedent conditions, therefore, are the individual's familial experience, the general societal setting built on impersonal systems of authority, and extended experience with a reward structure in which compliance with authority is rewarded, and failure to comply punished. While without doubt providing the background against which our subject's habits of conduct were formed, these conditions are beyond the control of experimentation and do not immediately trigger movement to the agentic state. Let us now turn to the more immediate factors, within a specific situation, that lead to the agentic state.*

Immediate Antecedent Conditions

Perception of Authority. The first condition needed for transformation to the agentic state is the perception of a legitimate authority. From a psychological standpoint, authority means the person who is perceived to be in a position of social control within a given situation. Authority is contextually perceived and does not necessarily transcend the situation in which it is encountered. For example, should the experimenter encounter the subject on the street, he would have no special influence on him. A pilot's authority over his passengers does not extend beyond the airplane. Authority is normatively supported: there is a shared expectation among people that certain situations do ordinarily have a socially controlling figure. Authority need not possess high status in the sense

*[i.e., the condition a person is in when he sees himself as an agent for carrying out another person's wishes.—Ed.]

of "prestige." For example, an usher at a theater is a source of social control to whom we ordinarily submit willingly. The power of an authority stems not from personal characteristics but from his perceived position in a social structure.

The question of how authority communicates itself seems, at first, not to require a special answer. We invariably seem to *know* who is in charge. We may, nonetheless, examine the behavior in the laboratory to try to dissect the process a little.

First, the subject enters the situation with the expectation that *someone* will be in charge. Thus, the experimenter, upon first presenting himself, fills a gap experienced by the subject. Accordingly, the experimenter need not assert his authority, but merely identify it. He does so through a few introductory remarks, and since this self-defining ritual fits perfectly with the subject's expectation of encountering a man in charge, it is not challenged. A supporting factor is the confidence and "air of authority" exhibited by the experimenter. Just as a servant possesses a deferential manner, so his master exudes a commanding presence that subtly communicates his dominant status within the situation at hand.

Second, external accouterments are often used to signify the authority in a given situation. Our experimenter was dressed in a gray technician's coat, which linked him to the laboratory. Police, military, and other service uniforms are the most conspicuous signs of authority within common experience. Third, the subject notes the absence of competing authorities. (No one else claims to be in charge, and this helps confirm the presumption that the experimenter is the right man.) Fourth, there is the absence of conspicuously anomalous factors (e.g., a child of five claiming to be the scientist).

It is the appearance of authority and not actual authority to which the subject responds. Unless contradictory information or anomalous facts appear, the self-designation of the authority almost always suffices.

Entry into the Authority System. A second condition triggering the shift to the agentic state is the act of defining the person as part of the authority system in question. It is not enough that we perceive an authority, he must be an authority relevant to us. Thus, if we watch a parade, and hear a Colonel shout, "Left face," we do not turn left, for we have not been defined as subordinate to his command. There is always a transition from that moment when we stand outside an authority system to that point when we are inside it. Authority systems are frequently limited by a physical context, and often we come under the influence of an authority when we cross the physical threshold into his domain. The fact that this experiment is carried out in a laboratory has a good deal to do with the degree of obedience exacted. There is a feeling that the experimenter "owns" the space and that the subject must conduct himself fittingly, as if a guest in someone's house. If the experiment were to be carried on outside the laboratory, obedience would drop sharply.

Even more important, for the present experiment, is the fact that entry into the experimenter's realm of authority is voluntary, undertaken through the free will of the participants. The psychological consequence of voluntary entry is that it creates a sense of commitment and obligation which will subsequently play a part in binding the subject to his role.

Were our subjects forcibly introduced to the experiment, they might well yield to authority, but the psychological mechanisms would be quite different from what we have observed. Generally, and wherever possible, society tries to create a sense of voluntary entry into its various institutions. Upon induction into the military, recruits take an oath of allegiance, and volunteers are preferred to inductees. While people will comply with a source of social control under coercion (as when a gun is aimed at them), the nature of obedience under such circumstances is limited to direct surveillance. When the gunman leaves, or when his capacity for sanctions is eliminated, obedience stops. In the case of voluntary obedience to a legitimate authority, the principal sanctions for disobedience come from within the person. They are not dependent upon coercion, but stem from the individual's sense of commitment to his role. In this sense, *there is an internalized basis for his obedience, not merely an external one.*

Coordination of Command with the Function of Authority. Authority is the perceived source of social control within a specific context. The context defines the range of commands considered appropriate to the authority in question. There must, in general, be some intelligible link between the function of the controlling person, and the nature of the commands he issues. The connection need not be very well worked out but need only make sense in the most general way. Thus, in a military situation, a captain may order a subordinate to perform a highly dangerous action, but he may not order the subordinate to embrace his girlfriend. In one case, the order is logically linked to the general function of the military, and in the other case it is not.

In the obedience experiment, the subject acts within the context of a learning experiment and sees the experimenter's commands as meaningfully coordinated to his role. In the context of the laboratory, such commands are felt to be appropriate in a general way, however much one may argue with certain specific developments that later occur.

Because the experimenter issues orders in a context he is presumed to know something about, his power is increased. Generally, authorities are felt to know more than the person they are commanding; whether they do or not, the occasion is defined as if they do. Even when a subordinate possesses a greater degree of technical knowledge than his superior, he must not presume to override the authority's right to command but must present this knowledge to the superior to dispose of as he wishes. A typical source of strain occurs in authority systems when the person in authority is incompetent to the point of endangering the subordinates.

The Overarching Ideology. The perception of a legitimate source of social control within a defined social occasion is a necessary prerequisite for a shift to the agentic state. But the legitimacy of the occasion itself depends on its articulation to a justifying ideology. When subjects enter the laboratory and are told to perform, they do not in a bewildered fashion cry out, "I never heard of science. What do you mean by this?" Within this situation, the idea of science and its acceptance as a legitimate social enterprise provide the overarching ideological justification for the experiment. Such institutions as business, the church, the government, and the educational establishment provide other legitimate realms of activity, each justified by the values and needs of society, and also, from the standpoint of the typical person, accepted because they exist as part of the world in which he is born and grows up. Obedience could be secured outside such institutions, but it would not be the form of willing obedience, in which the person complies with a strong sense of doing the right thing. Moreover, if the experiment were carried out in a culture very different from our own—say, among Trobrianders—it would be necessary to find the functional equivalent of science in order to obtain psychologically comparable results. The Trobriander may not believe in scientists, but he respects witch doctors. The fourteenth-century Spanish Jesuit might have eschewed science, but he embraced the ideology of his church, and in its name, and for its preservation, tightened the screw on the rack without any problem of conscience.

Ideological justification is vital in obtaining *willing* obedience, for it permits the person to see his behavior as serving a desirable end. Only when viewed in this light, is compliance easily exacted.

An authority system, then, consists of a minimum of two persons sharing the expectation that one of them has the right to prescribe behavior for the other. In the current study, the experimenter is the key element in a system that extends beyond his person. The system includes the setting of the experiment, the impressive laboratory equipment, the devices which inculcate a sense of obligation in the subject, the mystique of science of which the experiment is a part, and the broad institutional accords that permit such activities to go on— that is, the diffuse societal support that is implied by the very fact that the experiment is being run and tolerated in a civilized city.

The experimenter acquires his capacity to influence behavior not by virtue of the exercise of force or threat but by virtue of the position he occupies in a social structure. There is general agreement not only that he *can* influence behavior but that he *ought* to be able to. Thus, his power comes about in some degree through the consent of those over whom he presides. But once this consent is initially granted, its withdrawal does not proceed automatically or without great cost.

15.4 JOHN M. DARLEY AND BIBB LATANÉ

When Will People Help in a Crisis?

Social psychologists John M. Darley and Bibb Latané have been interested in discovering the conditions that influence helping behavior, in part because they see a distressingly low rate of helping in emergency situations. One problem they have found is that the larger a crowd of people is, the less likely one of them will help in an emergency. Darley and Latané explain this bystander effect with the concept of diffusion of responsibility, which holds that people feel less responsibility when they are in a large group than when they are in a relatively small group.

Darley (b. 1938) earned his Ph.D. from Harvard University in 1965. He is currently a professor of psychology at Princeton University. Latané (b. 1937) received his Ph.D. from the University of Minnesota in 1963. He taught at Columbia University and the Ohio State University before going to Florida Atlantic University. Darley and Latané wrote about their research on helping in their book *The Unresponsive Bystander: Why Doesn't He Help?* (Prentice Hall, 1970).

This selection, "When Will People Help in a Crisis?" was published in *Psychology Today* in 1968. In it, the authors examine the conditions necessary for someone to actually provide help in an emergency situation. They also discuss a number of studies and situations in which people's willingness to help was tested, generally with results that support their diffusion of responsibility theory. As you read this selection, notice how Darley and Latané designed their experiments to simulate real-life conditions. How do you think the incidence of helping behavior in our society could be increased?

Key Concept: helping behavior

Kitty Genovese is set upon by a maniac as she returns home from work at 3:00 A.M. Thirty-eight of her neighbors in Kew Gardens come to their windows when she cries out in terror; none come to her assistance even though her stalker takes over half an hour to murder her. No one even so much as calls the police. She dies.

Andrew Mormille is stabbed in the stomach as he rides the A train home to Manhattan. Eleven other riders watch the 17-year-old boy as he bleeds to death; none come to his assistance even though his attackers have left the car. He dies. . . .

Eleanor Bradley trips and breaks her leg while shopping on Fifth Avenue. Dazed and in shock, she calls for help, but the hurrying stream of executives and shoppers simply parts and flows past. After 40 minutes a taxi driver helps her to a doctor.

*John M. Darley
and Bibb Latané*

The shocking thing about these cases is that so many people failed to respond. If only one or two had ignored the victim, we might be able to understand their inaction. But when 38 people, or 11 people, or hundreds of people fail to help, we become disturbed. Actually, this fact that shocks us so much is itself the clue to understanding these cases. Although it seems obvious that the more people who watch a victim in distress, the more likely someone will help, what really happens is exactly the opposite. If each member of a group of bystanders is aware that other people are also present, he will be less likely to notice the emergency, less likely to decide that it is an emergency, and less likely to act even if he thinks there is an emergency.

This is a surprising assertion—what we are saying is that the victim may actually be less likely to get help, the more people who watch his distress and are available to help. We shall discuss in detail the process through which an individual bystander must go in order to intervene, and we shall present the results of some experiments designed to show the effects of the number of onlookers on the likelihood of intervention. . . .

Looking more closely at published descriptions of the behavior of witnesses to these incidents, the people involved begin to look a little less inhuman and a lot more like the rest of us. Although it is unquestionably true that the witnesses in the incidents above did nothing to save the victims, apathy, indifference and unconcern are not entirely accurate descriptions of their reactions. The 38 witnesses of Kitty Genovese's murder did not merely look at the scene once and then ignore it. They continued to stare out of their windows at what was going on. Caught, fascinated, distressed, unwilling to act but unable to turn away, their behavior was neither helpful nor heroic; but it was not indifferent or apathetic.

Actually, it was like crowd behavior in many other emergency situations. Car accidents, drownings, fires and attempted suicides all attract substantial numbers of people who watch the drama in helpless fascination without getting directly involved in the action. Are these people alienated and indifferent? Are the rest of us? Obviously not. Why, then, don't we act?

The bystander to an emergency has to make a series of decisions about what is happening and what he will do about it. The consequences of these decisions will determine his actions. There are three things he must do if he is to intervene: *notice* that something is happening, *interpret* that event as an emergency, and decide that he has *personal responsibility* for intervention. If he fails to notice the event, if he decides that it is not an emergency, or if he concludes that he is not personally responsible for acting, he will leave the victim unhelped. This state of affairs is shown graphically as a "decision tree." Only one path through this decision tree leads to intervention; all others lead to a failure to help. As we shall show, at each fork of the path in the decision trees, the presence of other bystanders may lead a person down the branch of not helping.

NOTICING: THE FIRST STEP

Suppose that an emergency is actually taking place; a middle-aged man has a heart attack. He stops short, clutches his chest, and staggers to the nearest building wall, where he slowly slumps to the sidewalk in a sitting position. What is the likelihood that a passerby will come to his assistance? First, the bystander has to *notice* that something is happening. The external event has to break into his thinking and intrude itself on his conscious mind. He must tear himself away from his private thoughts and pay attention to this unusual event.

But Americans consider it bad manners to look too closely at other people in public. We are taught to respect the privacy of others, and when among strangers, we do this by closing our ears and avoiding staring at others—we are embarrassed if caught doing otherwise. In a crowd, then, each person is less likely to notice the first sign of a potential emergency than when alone.

Experimental evidence corroborates this everyday observation. Darley and Latané asked college students to an interview about their reactions to urban living. As the students waited to see the interviewer, either by themselves or with two other students, they filled out a preliminary questionnaire. Solitary students often glanced idly about the room while filling out their questionnaires; those in groups, to avoid seeming rudely inquisitive, kept their eyes on their own papers.

As part of the study, we staged an emergency: smoke was released into the waiting room through a vent. Two-thirds of the subjects who were alone when the smoke appeared noticed it immediately, but only a quarter of the subjects waiting in groups saw it as quickly. Even after the room had completely filled with smoke one subject from a group of three finally looked up and exclaimed, "God! I must be smoking too much!" Although eventually all the subjects did become aware of the smoke, this study indicates that the more people present, the slower an individual may be to perceive that an emergency does exist and the more likely he is not to see it at all.

Once an event is noticed, an onlooker must decide whether or not it is truly an emergency. Emergencies are not always clearly labeled as such; smoke pouring from a building or into a waiting room may be caused by a fire, or it may merely indicate a leak in a steam pipe. Screams in the street may signal an assault or a family quarrel. A man lying in [a] doorway may be having a coronary or be suffering from diabetic coma—he may simply be sleeping off a drunk. . . .

A person trying to decide whether or not a given situation is an emergency often refers to the reactions of those around him; he looks at them to see

John M. Darley and Bibb Latané

how he should react himself. If everyone else is calm and indifferent, he will tend to remain calm and indifferent; if everyone else is reacting strongly, he will become aroused. This tendency is not merely slavish conformity; ordinarily we derive much valuable information about new situations from how others around us behave. It's a rare traveler who, in picking a roadside restaurant, chooses to stop at one with no other cars in the parking lot.

But occasionally the reactions of others provide false information. The studied nonchalance of patients in a dentist's waiting room is a poor indication of the pain awaiting them. In general, it is considered embarrassing to look overly concerned, to seem flustered, to "lose your cool" in public. When we are not alone, most of us try to seem less fearful and anxious than we really are.

In a potentially dangerous situation, then, everyone present will appear more unconcerned than they are in fact. Looking at the *apparent* impassivity and lack of reaction of the others, each person is led to believe that nothing really is wrong. Meanwhile the danger may be mounting, to the point where a single person, uninfluenced by the seeming calm of others, would react.

A crowd can thus force inaction on its members by implying, through its passivity and apparent indifference, that an event is not an emergency. Any individual in such a crowd is uncomfortably aware that he'll look like a fool if he behaves as though it were—and in these circumstances, until someone acts, no one acts.

In the smoke-filled-room study, the smoke trickling from the wall constituted an ambiguous but potentially dangerous situation. How did the presence of other people affect a person's response to the situation? Typically, those who were in the waiting room by themselves noticed the smoke at once, gave a slight startle reaction, hesitated again, and then left the room to find somebody to tell about the smoke. No one showed any signs of panic, but over three-quarters of these people were concerned enough to report the smoke.

Others went through an identical experience but in groups of three strangers. Their behavior was radically different. Typically, once someone noticed the smoke, he would look at the other people, see them doing nothing, shrug his shoulders, and then go back to his questionnaire, casting covert glances first at the smoke and then at the others. From these three-person groups, only three out of 24 people reported the smoke. The inhibiting effect of the group was so strong that the other 21 were willing to sit in a room filled with smoke rather than make themselves conspicuous by reacting with alarm and concern—this despite the fact that after three or four minutes the atmosphere in the waiting room grew most unpleasant. Even though they coughed, rubbed their eyes, tried to wave the smoke away, and opened the window, they apparently were unable to bring themselves to leave.

"A leak in the air conditioning," said one person when we asked him what he thought caused the smoke. "Must be chemistry labs in the building." "Steam pipes." "Truth gas to make us give true answers on the questionnaire," reported the more imaginative. There were many explanations for the smoke, but they all had one thing in common: they did not mention the word fire. In defining the situation as a nonemergency, people explained to themselves why the other observers did not leave the room; they also removed any reason for action themselves. The other members of the group acted as nonresponsive models for each person—and as an audience for any "inappropriate" action he might consider. In such a situation it is all too easy to do nothing.

The results of this study clearly and strongly support the predictions. But are they general? Would the same effect show up with other emergencies, or is it limited to situations like the smoke study involving danger to the self as well as to others—or to situations in which there's no clearly defined "victim"? It may be that our college-age male subjects played "chicken" with one another to see who would lose face by first fleeing the room. It may be that groups were less likely to respond because no particular person was in danger. To see how generalizable these results are, Latané and Judith Rodin set up a second experiment, in which the emergency would cause no danger for the bystander, and in which a specific person was in trouble.

Subjects were paid $2 to participate in a survey of game and puzzle preferences conducted at Columbia by the Consumer Testing Bureau (CTB). An attractive young woman, the market-research representative, met them at the door and took them to the testing room. On the way, they passed the CTB office and through its open door they could see filing cabinets and a desk and book-cases piled high with papers. They entered the adjacent testing room, which contained a table and chairs and a variety of games, where they were given a preliminary background information and game preference questionnaire to fill out. The representative told subjects that she would be working next door in her office for about 10 minutes while they completed the questionnaires, and left by opening the collapsible curtain which divided the two rooms. She made sure the subjects knew that the curtain was unlocked, easily opened and a means of entry to her office. The representative stayed in her office, shuffling papers, opening drawers, and making enough noise to remind the subjects of her presence. Four minutes after leaving the testing area, she turned on a high fidelity stereophonic tape recorder.

If the subject listened carefully, he heard the representative climb up on a chair to reach for a stack of papers on the bookcase. Even if he were not listening carefully, he heard a loud crash and a scream as the chair collapsed and she fell to the floor. "Oh, my god, my foot.... I ... I ... can't move it. Oh ... my ankle," the representative moaned. "I ... can't get this ... thing ... off me." She cried and moaned for about a minute longer, but the cries gradually got more subdued and controlled. Finally she muttered something about getting outside, knocked over the chair as she pulled herself up, and thumped to the door, closing it behind her as she left. This drama was of about two minutes' duration.

Some people were alone in the waiting room when the "accident" occurred. Seventy percent of them offered to help the victim before she left the room. Many came through the curtain to offer their assistance, others simply called out to offer their help. Others faced the emergency in pairs. Only 20 percent of this group—eight out of 40—offered to help the victim. The other 32 remained unresponsive to her cries of distress. Again, the presence of other bystanders inhibited action.

And again, the noninterveners seemed to have decided the event was not an emergency. They were unsure what had happened but whatever it was, it was not too serious. "A mild sprain," some said. "I didn't want to embarrass her." In a "real" emergency, they assured us, they would be among the first to help the victim. Perhaps they would be, but in this situation they didn't help, because for them the event was not defined as an emergency.

John M. Darley
and Bibb Latané

Again, solitary people exposed to a potential emergency reacted more frequently than those exposed in groups. We found that the action-inhibiting effects of other bystanders work in two different situations, one of which involves risking danger to oneself and the other of which involves helping an injured woman. The result seems sufficiently generally so that we may assume it operates to inhibit helping in real-life emergencies.

DIFFUSED RESPONSIBILITY

Even if a person has noticed an event and defined it as an emergency, the fact that he knows that other bystanders also witnessed it may still make him less likely to intervene. Others may inhibit intervention because they make a person feel that his responsibility is diffused and diluted. Each soldier in a firing squad feels less personally responsible for killing a man than he would if he alone pulled the trigger. Likewise, any person in a crowd of onlookers may feel less responsibility for saving a life than if he alone witnesses the emergency.

If your car breaks down on a busy highway, hundreds of drivers whiz by without anyone's stopping to help; if you are stuck on a nearly deserted country road, whoever passes you first is apt to stop. The personal responsibility that a passerby feels makes the difference. A driver on a lonely road knows that if he doesn't stop to help, the person will not get help; the same individual on the crowded highway feels he personally is no more responsible than any of a hundred other drivers. So even though an event clearly is an emergency, any person in a group who sees an emergency may feel less responsible, simply because any other bystander is equally responsible for helping.

This diffusion of responsibility might have occurred in the famous Kitty Genovese case, in which the observers were walled off from each other in separate apartments. From the silhouettes against windows, all that could be told was that others were also watching. . . .

The evidence is clear, then, that the presence of other bystanders and the various ways these other bystanders affect our decision processes, make a difference in how likely we are to give help in an emergency. The presence of strangers may keep us from noticing an emergency at all; group behavior may lead us to define the situation as one that does not require action; and when other people are there to share the burden of responsibility, we may feel less obligated to do something when action is required. Therefore, it will often be the case that the *more* people who witness his distress, the *less* likely it is that the victim of an emergency will get help.

Thus, the stereotype of the unconcerned, depersonalized *homo urbanis*, blandly watching the misfortunes of others, proves inaccurate. Instead, we find a bystander to an emergency is an anguished individual in genuine doubt, concerned to do the right thing but compelled to make complex decisions under pressure of stress and fear. His reactions are shaped by the actions of others—and all too frequently by their inaction.

And we are that bystander. Caught up by the apparent indifference of others, we may pass by an emergency without helping or even realizing that help is needed. Aware of the influence of those around us, however, we can resist it. We can choose to see distress and step forward to relieve it.

2.1 From "Hemisphere Deconnection and Unity in Conscious Awareness" by R. W. Sperry, 1968, *American Psychologist, 23*, pp. 723–733. Copyright © 1968 by The American Psychological Association. Reprinted by permission.

2.2 From "The Central Nervous System and the Reinforcement of Behavior" by J. Olds, 1969, *American Psychologist, 24*, pp. 723–733. Copyright © 1969 by The American Psychological Association. Reprinted by permission.

2.3 From "Mechanisms of Memory" by L. R. Squire, 1989. In K. L. Kelner and D. E. Koshland (Eds.), *Molecules to Models: Advances in Neuroscience* (pp. 235–250). Washington, DC: American Association for the Advancement of Science. (Updated and revised from *Science*, 1986, *232*, pp. 1612–1619.) Copyright © 1986, 1989 by The American Association for the Advancement of Science. Reprinted by permission.

2.4 From "Environment and Genes: Determinants of Behavior" by R. Plomin, 1989, *American Psychologist, 44*, pp. 105–108, 110–111. Copyright © 1989 by The American Psychological Association. Reprinted by permission.

3.1 From *The Psychology of the Child* (pp. 3–12) by J. Piaget and B. Inhelder, 1969 (H. Weaver, Trans.). New York: Basic Books. (Original work published 1966.) Copyright © 1969 by Basic Books, Inc. Reprinted by permission of Basic Books, a division of HarperCollins Publishers, Inc.

3.2 From "The Child as a Moral Philosopher" by L. Kohlberg, 1968, *Psychology Today, 214*, pp. 25–30. Copyright © 1968 by Sussex Publishers, Inc. Reprinted by permission of *Psychology Today*.

3.3 From "From Thought to Therapy: Lessons from a Primate Laboratory" by H. F. Harlow, M. K. Harlow, and S. J. Suomi, 1971, *American Scientist, 59*, pp. 539–549. Copyright © 1971 by *American Scientist*. Reprinted by permission.

3.4 From "Children's Understanding of Sexist Language" by J. S. Hyde, 1984, *Developmental Psychology, 20*, pp. 697–701, 703–706. Copyright © 1984 by The American Psychological Association. Reprinted by permission.

4.1 From "The 'Visual Cliff'" by E. J. Gibson and R. D. Walk, 1960, *Scientific American, 202*, pp. 67–71. Copyright © 1960 by Scientific American, Inc. All rights reserved. Reprinted by permission.

4.2 From "Pattern Vision in Newborn Infants" by R. L. Fantz, 1963, *Science, 140*, pp. 296–297. Copyright © 1963 by The American Association for the Advancement of Science. Reprinted by permission. Some notes omitted.

5.1 From *Some Must Watch While Some Must Sleep: Exploring the World of Sleep* (pp. 21–31) by W. C. Dement, 1978. New York: W. W. Norton. Copyright © 1972, 1974, 1976 by William C. Dement and The Stanford Alumni Association, Stanford, CA. Reprinted by permission.

5.2 From *The Interpretation of Dreams* (pp. 33–43) by S. Freud, 1950 (A. A. Brill, Trans.). New York: Random House. (Original work published 1900.) Copyright © 1950 by Random House, Inc.; copyright renewed 1978 by Random House, Inc. Reprinted by permission. Notes omitted.

6.1 From "Conditioned Emotional Reactions" by J. B. Watson and R. Rayner, 1920, *Journal of Experimental Psychology, 3*, pp. 1–7, 10, 13–14. Notes omitted.

6.2 From *Science and Human Behavior* (pp. 91–93, 98–104) by B. F. Skinner, 1953. New York: Free Press. Copyright © 1953 by Macmillan College Publishing Company. Reprinted by permission.

6.3 From "Imitation of Film-mediated Aggressive Models" by A. Bandura, D. Ross, and S. A. Ross, 1963, *Journal of Abnormal and Social Psychology, 66*, pp. 3–11. Copy-

352

right © 1963 by The American Psychological Association. Reprinted by permission.

Acknowledgments
6.4   From *King Solomon's Ring: New Light on Animal Ways* (pp. 41–50) by K. Z. Lorenz, 1952. New York: T. Y. Crowell. Copyright © 1952 by Thomas Y. Crowell Company, Inc. Reprinted by permission of HarperCollins Publishers, Inc.

7.1   From "Short-Term Retention of Individual Verbal Items" by L. R. Peterson and M. J. Peterson, 1959, *Journal of Experimental Psychology, 58*, pp. 193–196, 198.

7.2   From "How Many Memory Systems Are There?" by E. Tulving, 1985, *American Psychologist, 40*, pp. 385–388, 395–398. Copyright © 1985 by The American Psychological Association. Reprinted by permission.

7.3   From "Leading Questions and the Eyewitness Report" by E. F. Loftus, 1972, *Cognitive Psychology, 7*, pp. 560–567, 569, 572. Copyright © 1972 by Academic Press, Inc. Reprinted by permission.

8.1   From "Ability Tests, Measurements, and Markets" by R. J. Sternberg, 1992, *Journal of Educational Psychology, 84*, pp. 134–140. Copyright © 1992 by The American Psychological Association. Reprinted by permission.

8.2   From "The Minnesota Adoption Studies: Genetic Differences and Malleability" by S. Scarr and R. A. Weinberg, 1983, *Child Development, 54*, pp. 260–267. Copyright © 1983 by The Society for Research in Child Development, Inc. Reprinted by permission.

8.3   From "The Education of Sarah: A Chimp Learns the Language" by D. Premack, 1970, *Psychology Today, 5*, pp. 132–135. Copyright © 1970 by Sussex Publishers, Inc. Reprinted by permission of *Psychology Today*.

9.1   From "A Theory of Human Motivation" by A. H. Maslow, 1943, *Psychological Review, 50*, pp. 371–396. Notes omitted.

9.2   From "Current Status of the Internal–External Hypothesis for Obesity: What Went Wrong?" by J. Rodin, 1981, *American Psychologist, 36*, pp. 361–363, 366–372. Copyright © 1981 by The American Psychological Association. Reprinted by permission.

9.3   From "Work: Who Does Not Like It and Why" by E. L. Deci, 1972, *Psychology Today, 6*, pp. 57–58, 92. Copyright © 1972 by Sussex Publishers, Inc. Reprinted by permission of *Psychology Today*.

10.1   From "Cognitive, Social, and Physiological Determinants of Emotional State" by S. Schachter and J. E. Singer, 1962, *Psychological Review, 69*, pp. 379–399. Copyright © 1962 by The American Psychological Association. Reprinted by permission.

10.2   From "Facial Expressions of Emotion: New Findings, New Questions" by P. Ekman, 1992, *Psychological Science, 3*, pp. 34–38. Copyright © 1992 by The American Psychological Society. Reprinted by permission of Cambridge University Press. Some references omitted. A large section on smiling has been omitted for this volume.

10.3   From *The Triangle of Love: Intimacy, Passion, Commitment* (pp. 37–48, 51–61) by R. J. Sternberg, 1988. New York: Basic Books. Copyright © 1988 by Basic Books, Inc. Reprinted by permission of Basic Books, a division of HarperCollins Publishers, Inc.

11.1   From *An Outline of Psychoanalysis* (pp. 13–21) by S. Freud, 1969 (J. Strachey, Trans.). New York: W. W. Norton. (Original work published 1940.) Copyright © 1969 by W. W. Norton and Company. Reprinted by permission. Notes omitted.

11.2   From "External Control and Internal Control" by J. B. Rotter, 1971, *Psychology Today, 5*, pp. 37–38, 42, 58–59. Copyright © 1971 by Sussex Publishers, Inc. Reprinted by permission of *Psychology Today*.

11.3   From "Validation of the Five-Factor Model of Personality Across Instruments and Observers" by R. R. McCrae and P. T. Costa, Jr., 1987, *Journal of Personality and Social Psychology, 52*, pp. 81, 85–90.

12.1   From "The Evolution of the Stress Concept" by H. Selye, 1973, *American Scientist, 61*, pp. 692–699. Copyright © 1973 by *American Scientist.* Reprinted by permission.

12.2   From *Type A Behavior and Your Heart* (pp. 69–75, 83–96) by M. Friedman and R. H. Rosenman, 1974. New York: Fawcett Crest. Copyright © 1974 by Meyer Friedman. Reprinted by permission of Alfred A. Knopf, Inc.

13.1   From "On Being Sane in Insane Places" by D. L. Rosenhan, 1973, *Science, 179*, pp. 250–258. Copyright © 1973 by The American Association for the Advancement of Science. Reprinted by permission. Some notes omitted.

13.2   From *Helplessness: On Depression, Development, and Death* (pp. 93–95, 97–105) by M. E. P. Seligman, 1975. New York: W. H. Freeman. Copyright © 1975 by Martin E. P. Seligman; copyright renewed 1992 by Martin E. P. Seligman. Reprinted by permission of W. H. Freeman and Company. Notes omitted.

14.1   From "Intensive Treatment of Psychotic Behaviour by Stimulus Satiation and Food Reinforcement" by T. Ayllon, 1963, *Behaviour Research and Therapy, 1*, pp. 53–61. Copyright © 1963 by Pergamon Press, Ltd., Oxford, England. Reprinted by permission. Notes omitted.

14.2   From *A Way of Being* (pp. 114–135) by C. R. Rogers, 1980. New York: Houghton Mifflin. (Adapted from "The Foundations of a Person-Centered Approach" by C. R. Rogers, 1979, *Education, 100*, pp. 98–107.) Copyright © 1979 by Project Innovation, Chula Vista, CA. Reprinted by permission.

14.3   From *Cognitive Therapy and the Emotional Disorders* (pp. 213–227, 229–232) by A. T. Beck, 1976. Madison, CT: International Universities Press. Copyright © 1976 by Aaron T. Beck. Reprinted by permission. References omitted.

15.1   From "Opinions and Social Pressure" by S. E. Asch, 1955, *Scientific American, 193*, pp. 31–35. Copyright © 1955 by Scientific American, Inc. All rights reserved. Reprinted by permission.

15.2   From *A Theory of Cognitive Dissonance* (pp. 1–5, 18–24, 29–31) by L. Festinger, 1957. Stanford, CA: Stanford University Press. Copyright © 1957 by Leon Festinger. Reprinted by permission.

15.3   From *Obedience to Authority: An Experimental View* (pp. 135–143) by S. Milgram, 1974. New York: Harper & Row. Copyright © 1974 by Stanley Milgram. Reprinted by permission of HarperCollins Publishers, Inc. Notes omitted.

15.4   From "When Will People Help in a Crisis?" by J. M. Darley and B. Latané, 1968, *Psychology Today, 2*, pp. 54–57, 70–71. Copyright © 1968 by Sussex Publishers, Inc. Reprinted by permission of *Psychology Today.*

Index